Nuclear Illusion, Nuclear Reality

Nuclear Weapons and International Security since 1945

Series Editor: Professor John Simpson, Mountbatten Centre for International Studies, University of Southampton, UK

During the second half of the last century, the practical aspects of national nuclear weapon policies remained shrouded in state secrecy laws. This was an area where political and technical issues were intertwined, and understanding required knowledge and expertise of both. Archival material was sparse and most writings on the subject were based on information provided to well-placed journalists and confidential interviews with some of those involved. The result was that for the academic analyst, separating truth from fiction was a very difficult task, especially in the case of the United Kingdom. With the end of the Cold War, archival material became available from all of the five declared nuclear-weapon states on their activities and scholars were able to discuss the previous century's nuclear reality. A small community of scholars and former practitioners in the UK therefore started to rethink this history by producing a new series of volumes on the evolution of the United Kingdom's nuclear weapon policies from 1952 onwards, the date of the explosion of its first nuclear device.

Thanks to a grant from the UK Arts and Humanities Research Board to the Mountbatten Centre for International Studies at the University of Southampton, Professor John Simpson and his colleagues were able to start a systematic study of the post-1952 period, and to engage with those directly involved in its many aspects. What soon became clear was that in the period 1958–64 the course was set for UK nuclear policy in the next half-century. It is thus appropriate that Richard Moore's volume *Nuclear Illusion, Nuclear Reality: Britain, the United States and Nuclear Weapons, 1958–64* should be the first of the planned chronological volumes arising from this systematic process. This is reinforced by the current salience of debates over the future of the UK's nuclear deterrent force, and the role of the volume as the lead publication in Palgrave's wider series of studies on nuclear history.

Titles include:

Richard Moore
NUCLEAR ILLUSION, NUCLEAR REALITY
Britain, the United States and Nuclear Weapons, 1958–64

Nuclear Weapons and International Security since 1945
Series Standing Order ISBN: 978–0230–21775–1 hardback
(*outside North America only*)

You can receive future titles in this series as they are published by placing a standing order. Please contact your bookseller or, in case of difficulty, write to us at the address below with your name and address, the title of the series and the ISBN quoted above.

Customer Services Department, Macmillan Distribution Ltd, Houndmills, Basingstoke, Hampshire RG21 6XS, England

Nuclear Illusion, Nuclear Reality

Britain, the United States and Nuclear Weapons, 1958–64

Richard Moore
Visiting Research Fellow, Mountbatten Centre for International Studies, University of Southampton

© Richard Moore 2010

All rights reserved. No reproduction, copy or transmission of this publication may be made without written permission.

No portion of this publication may be reproduced, copied or transmitted save with written permission or in accordance with the provisions of the Copyright, Designs and Patents Act 1988, or under the terms of any licence permitting limited copying issued by the Copyright Licensing Agency, Saffron House, 6–10 Kirby Street, London EC1N 8TS.

Any person who does any unauthorized act in relation to this publication may be liable to criminal prosecution and civil claims for damages.

The author has asserted his right to be identified as the author of this work in accordance with the Copyright, Designs and Patents Act 1988.

First published 2010 by
PALGRAVE MACMILLAN

Palgrave Macmillan in the UK is an imprint of Macmillan Publishers Limited, registered in England, company number 785998, of Houndmills, Basingstoke, Hampshire RG21 6XS.

Palgrave Macmillan in the US is a division of St Martin's Press LLC, 175 Fifth Avenue, New York, NY 10010.

Palgrave Macmillan is the global academic imprint of the above companies and has companies and representatives throughout the world.

Palgrave® and Macmillan® are registered trademarks in the United States, the United Kingdom, Europe and other countries.

ISBN-13: 978-0-230-23067-5   hardback

This book is printed on paper suitable for recycling and made from fully managed and sustained forest sources. Logging, pulping and manufacturing processes are expected to conform to the environmental regulations of the country of origin.

A catalogue record for this book is available from the British Library.

A catalogue record for this book is available from the Library of Congress.

10 9 8 7 6 5 4 3 2 1
19 18 17 16 15 14 13 12 11 10

Printed and bound in Great Britain by
CPI Antony Rowe, Chippenham and Eastbourne

Contents

List of Illustrations	viii
Acknowledgements	ix
List of Abbreviations	xi
Introduction	1
Historiography	5
Macmillan and his ministers	8
Decision-making structures	12
Part I Nuclear Illusion	**23**
Chapter 1 Policy-making 1958–61	25
Government policy	26
Macmillan, Eisenhower and bilateral defence collaboration	32
Arms control	36
Bombers and ballistic missiles	40
Politics and force levels	46
Political opposition to nuclear weapons	50
NATO strategy	53
Nuclear sufficiency	57
Global war studies	59
NATO and ballistic missiles	62
Holy Loch, Skybolt and Polaris	64
The multi-lateral force and the Kennedy administration	69
Circumstances short of global war	71
Worries about Skybolt	73
Chapter 2 Policy Execution 1958–61	78
Military requirements	79
Fissile material	83
Aldermaston and warheads	85
Using American warhead information	87
Australia	91
Nuclear forces	95
Controlling nuclear operations	101
Megaton bombs	104

Blue Steel	105
Blue Streak	108
Kiloton bombs	112
Skybolt	116
Skybolt warhead	118
Red Beard replacement	122
Defensive weapons	125
Battlefield nuclear weapons	129
The future	133

Part II Nuclear Reality — 143

Chapter 3 Policy-making 1961–64	145
Change at the top	147
Nuclear testing	150
NATO and the central front	155
France, West Germany and Europe	157
Defence policy east of Suez	160
Deterrent systems	164
Skybolt	166
Explaining the Skybolt crisis	170
Cuba	173
The Nassau meeting	175
The multi-lateral force	182
Buying Polaris	186
Party politics	189
Chapter 4 Policy Execution 1961–64	194
Military requirements and fissile material	195
Warheads	199
V-bombers	203
Megaton weapons	210
Other nuclear forces	214
WE177	217
Other tactical nuclear weapons	220
Alternative weapons	224
Choice of Polaris missile	227
Polaris system and facilities	231
Polaris warheads and Aldermaston	236
Conclusions	240
Britain and the United States	243
Other nuclear motivations	247

Technology, strategy and politics 250
Wartime experience and nuclear culture 253

Appendices 256
　Appendix 1　Estimated deliverable nuclear weapons stockpile 256
　Appendix 2　Estimated fissile materials stockpile 257

Notes 258

Bibliography 301

Index 315

List of Illustrations

Red Beard bomb undergoing vibration trials.
Blue Water missile awaiting test firing.
Blue Streak missile with re-entry vehicle.
Blue Steel missile and Vulcan bomber.
Harold Watkinson.
Peter Thorneycroft.
Sir Dermot Boyle.
Sir Thomas Pike.
Lord Mountbatten at Seacat missile launch.
Early sketch of a Skybolt missile.
Missile compartment of a Polaris submarine.
Mountbatten and Sir Solly Zuckerman.
Weapons development timeline.
Map 1 Nuclear weapons production.
Map 2 British nuclear forces, end 1962.

Acknowledgements

I should like to thank staff at Cambridge University Library, the Mountbatten Archive at the Hartley Library in Southampton, the RAF Museum at Hendon, the Archives Department at the UEA Library in Norwich, the Library of Congress in Washington and in particular the Public Record Office in Kew. Whoever has masterminded the changes made at the PRO in recent years – new opening hours, the online catalogue and the enlightened policy on digital photography – deserves special thanks for making it possible for me to work much more happily and effectively. The late John Slater collected a wealth of documentary material on British nuclear history, focusing in particular on the period 1958–64, and I have had the benefit of access to his extensive papers, now at the Mountbatten Centre in Southampton. This book would have been much harder to write without Slater's painstaking and scholarly work. Ian Clark and Eric Grove taught me to love nuclear history. Lorna Arnold is an inspiration to everybody in the field, and I feel privileged to have heard her speak, for example on the Windscale accident of 1957. Kate Pyne and the incomparable Roy Dommett have given freely and patiently of their time and expertise, and my mistakes are many times fewer as a result. Nick Hill and Dave and Lesley Wright have brought the British rocketry community together every year at Charterhouse, and their vision and hard work has allowed a most enjoyable and stimulating exchange of views there and in the pages of *Prospero*. Some of the material here on Skybolt and Polaris has previously been presented at Charterhouse, and I have learned a great deal from the resultant discussion. I am grateful to everyone at the Mountbatten Centre, and especially John Simpson and Angela Murphy, for their extensive support. As an (occasional) visiting research fellow, I have been made to feel very welcome indeed by John and his team; John has also offered much useful comment and encouragement for this book in particular. Iain Goode, Steve Roper and Ray Nolan in MoD helped with the declassification of documents, especially on WE177. In the course of my research, I have spoken with or emailed Brian Burnell, Tony Buttler, Steve Clifton, John Coker, Mike Fazackerley, Dave Forster, Jock Gardner, Chris Gibson, Brian Jamison, David Mackenzie, Chris Maddock, Richard Maguire, Frank Panton, Michael Price, Mark Smith, Kristan Stoddart, Jerry Stocker, Richard Vernon, John Walker and Robin Woolven, and I am very grateful for their kindness, insights and information. Chris in particular has been enormously helpful, but Brian Burnell must head the list: he has worked indefatigably in the PRO, his knowledge is encyclopaedic and he has been exceptionally generous with facts, opinions, advice and copies of documents, always at his own expense. Massive thanks meanwhile to my father and Ed Wynn, whose extensive comments on the text led to huge improvements to its readability. Ann Barradell-Black insisted on a happy ending. I owe the biggest debt of all to my wife Alison, who has been more supportive – in this book, and in everything I do – than I shall ever deserve. I love her completely. But the book is dedicated to Joseph and Lilia. My generation has, so far, managed to live with nuclear weapons without using them, and I pray theirs can too. If understanding the past can ever help in this regard, then perhaps it will have been worth writing.

List of Abbreviations

1L	First Lord (of the Admiralty)
1SL	First Sea Lord
A/	Assistant to
ABM	Anti-ballistic missile
ACAS(Ops)	Assistant Chief of the Air Staff for Operations
ACAS(OR)	Assistant Chief of the Air Staff for Operational Requirements
ACdre	Air Commodore
AD/AArm3	Assistant Director Air Armaments 3 (MoA)
ADM	Atomic demolition munition
AFB	(US) Air Force Base
AGPS	Australian Government Printing Service
AM	Air Marshal
AOC-in-C	Air Officer Commanding-in-Chief
ASW	Anti-submarine warfare
AVM	Air Vice-Marshal
AWE	Atomic Weapons Establishment (present-day name of AWRE)
AWRE	Atomic Weapons Research Establishment
BAC	British Aircraft Corporation
BAOR	British Army of the Rhine
BJSM	British Joint Staff Mission (at the embassy in Washington)
BMEWS	Ballistic Missile Early Warning System
BNDSG	British Nuclear Deterrent Study Group
CA	Controller Aircraft
CAS	Chief of the Air Staff
Cdr	Commander
CDS	Chief of the Defence Staff
CENTO	Central Treaty Organisation
CGWL	Controller Guided Weapons and Electronics
CIA	Central Intelligence Agency
CIGS	Chief of the Imperial General Staff
CINCSAC	Commander-in-Chief, (USAF) Strategic Air Command
CINCUSNAVEUR	Commander-in-Chief, US Naval Forces Europe

xii *List of Abbreviations*

Cmnd.	Command paper (i.e., UK government white paper)
CND	Campaign for Nuclear Disarmament
CO	Commanding Officer
D Ops(B&R)	(Air Ministry) Director Operations (Bomber & Reconnaissance)
DAArm	Director Air Armaments (MoA)
DAWD	Director Atomic Weapons Development (MoA)
DAWDP	Director Atomic Weapons Development & Production (MoA)
DCAS	Deputy Chief of the Air Staff
DDOR1	(Air Ministry) Deputy Director Operational Requirements 1
DDOR2	(Air Ministry) Deputy Director Operational Requirements 2
Debs.	Debates
Dept	Department
DGAW	Director-General Atomic Weapons (MoA)
DGD	(Admiralty) Director Gunnery Division
DNOR	(Admiralty) Director of Naval Operational Research
DOR(A)	(Air Ministry) Director Operational Requirements (A)
DOR(C)	(Air Ministry) Director Operational Requirements (C)
DRPC	Defence Research Policy Committee
ECM	Electronic counter-measures
ed. dir.	Editorial director
ed.	Editor
edn	Edition
EEC	European Economic Community
ENI	External neutron initiation
FBM	Fleet Ballistic Missile
FO	Foreign Office
FPC	Future Policy Committee
FRUS	Foreign Relations of the United States
ft	Feet
GCapt	Group Captain
Gen	General
GPS	Global Positioning System
GW	Guided weapons

H of M	(Admiralty) Head of Military Branch
HE	High explosive
HMG	Her Majesty's Government
HMS	Her Majesty's Ship
HMSO	Her Majesty's Stationery Office
HoC	House of Commons
HoL	House of Lords
HTP	High-test peroxide
IANF	Inter-Allied Nuclear Force
ICBM	Inter-continental ballistic missile
IMD	Increased Military Demand
in	Inches
IRBM	Intermediate-range ballistic missile
JCS	(US) Joint Chiefs of Staff
JFK	(US President) John F Kennedy
JIGSAW	Joint Inter-service Group for the Study of All-out War
JOWOG	Joint Working Group
JPS	Joint Planning Staff
JRSWG	Joint Re-entry Systems Working Group
kg	Kilogrammes
kt	Kilotons (thousands of tons of TNT equivalent)
LABS	Low-altitude bombing system
lb	Pounds (weight)
LOX	Liquid oxygen
LtCdr	Lieutenant-Commander
LtGen	Lieutenant-General
MC	(NATO) Military Committee (document)
MC	Medium capacity (ratio of HE to overall weight of a bomb)
MCIS	Mountbatten Centre for International Studies, Southampton University
MGen	Major-General
MIRV	Multiple independently-targeted re-entry vehicles
MIT	Massachusetts Institute of Technology
Mk.	Mark
MLF	(NATO) Multi-lateral force
MoA	Ministry of Aviation
MoD	Ministry of Defence
MoS	Ministry of Supply
MP	Member of Parliament

MRAF	Marshal of the Royal Air Force
MRBM	Medium-range ballistic missile
Mt	Megaton (millions of tons of TNT equivalent)
mtg	Meeting
NAC	North Atlantic Council
NASA	(US) National Aeronautics and Space Administration
NATO	North Atlantic Treaty Organisation
nm	Nautical miles
NRDC	Nuclear Requirements for Defence Committee
OAW	Operational Use of Atomic Weapons (Working Party)
OR	Operational requirement
ORP	Operational readiness platform
pers. comm.	Personal communication
PRO	Public Record Office
PS/	Private Secretary to
PSAC	(US) Presidential Scientific Advisory Committee
Pu	Plutonium
QRA	Quick-reaction alert
R&D	Research and development
RAE	Royal Aircraft Establishment
RAF	Royal Air Force
RIIA	Royal Institute of International Affairs
RN	Royal Navy
ROF	Royal Ordnance Factory
RUSI	Royal United Service Institution
RV	Re-entry vehicle
SA/AC	Scientific Advisor to the Army Council
SAC	(USAF) Strategic Air Command
SACEUR	(NATO) Supreme Allied Commander Europe
SACLANT	(NATO) Supreme Allied Commander Atlantic
SAGW	Surface-to-air guided weapon
SAM	Surface-to-air missile
SEATO	South East Asia Treaty Organisation
sec	Seconds
SHAPE	(NATO) Supreme Headquarters Allied Powers Europe
SHAPEX	An annual staff exercise at SHAPE
SINS	Ship's Inertial Navigation System
SIOP	Single Integrated Operational Plan

SIPRI	Stockholm International Peace Research Institute
SofSAir	Secretary of State for Air
SPO	(US Navy) Special Projects Office
SSGW	Surface-to-surface guided weapon
SSN	Nuclear-powered (usually hunter-killer) submarine
TNT	Trinitrotoluene
TSR	Tactical Strike and Reconnaissance (aircraft)
TTCP	Tripartite Technical Cooperation Programme
U235	Uranium-235 (highly-enriched uranium)
UE	Units effective (no. of front-line aircraft in an RAF squadron)
UEA	University of East Anglia
UK	United Kingdom
UKAEA	United Kingdom Atomic Energy Authority
UKDEL	UK Delegation
UN	United Nations
UP	University Press
US	United States
USAEC	United States Atomic Energy Commission
USAF	United States Air Force
USN	United States Navy
USS	United States Ship
USSR	Union of Soviet Socialist Republics
V-bombers	Vickers Valiant, Avro Vulcan, Handley Page Victor (aircraft)
V-force	RAF V-bomber force
VAdm	Vice-Admiral
VCAS	Vice-Chief of the Air Staff
VCNS	Vice-Chief of the Naval Staff
VLF	Very low frequency
WS	(USAF) Weapons System

Introduction

This is a study of the technological development of Britain's nuclear weapons in the context of domestic, United States and NATO policy. It is the second in a four-volume set produced under the auspices of the Mountbatten Centre for International Studies at the University of Southampton. It begins in the summer of 1958, with the signing of the UK-US Agreement for Cooperation on the Uses of Atomic Energy for Mutual Defence Purposes; and it ends in October 1964, with the election of Harold Wilson's Labour government.

Britain's whole nuclear defence policy did not begin afresh in 1958. On the contrary, it is hard to understand without reference to wartime and even prewar politics and practical experience. Nor did it end in 1964. There is, however, some justification in focusing on the years between 1958 and 1964, for this was a crucial period in determining Britain's nuclear posture for many years to come. Before 1958, Britain's pursuit of a nuclear-weapons capability had been a lonely one: barred from specific atomic cooperation with the United States, Britain built its own atomic bombs and then tested its own designs for a thermonuclear warhead. After 1958, Britain's nuclear weapons were more closely linked to America's. A period of rapid change and development followed. By 1964, when 13 years of Conservative rule came to an end in the UK, political crises had come and gone – Blue Streak, Holy Loch, Skybolt – but a mature nuclear capability had been created, and plans were in place for its further development into the force recognisable nearly 30 years later at the end of the cold war.

The main body of the book is in two parts. Part I, *Nuclear Illusion*, covers the period roughly up to the autumn of 1961, and Part II, *Nuclear Reality*, the rest of the story. I am not trying to suggest that Britain's nuclear-weapons capability was a sham until 1961, and a reality thereafter, or that I have identified a particular turning-point. Nor do I support the idea that a 'thermonuclear bluff' was behind Britain's achievement of an atomic relationship with the United States.[1] Nevertheless, it does seem

1

that a period in which a nuclear defence policy was mostly politicians' talk gave way, gradually, to a period in which more and more real operational nuclear capabilities became available. Britain's independent nuclear forces were confidently described in the 1958 white paper on defence as 'significant' and 'substantial',[2] at a time when a stockpile of perhaps 50 hand-built atomic bombs was available, command and control arrangements were rudimentary and just one fully successful British two-stage megaton thermonuclear device had been tested. In 1964, Prime Minister Douglas-Home was master of a stockpile of over 250 well engineered, British-made nuclear weapons, including 120 or more megaton H-bombs, free-fall and powered; of a well exercised bomber force, including a number of aircraft constantly at 15 minutes' readiness to strike; and of scientists and engineers at Aldermaston and elsewhere working on a programme of new British warheads and weapons. Curiously, as Britain's forces grew significantly, an opposite trend was apparent in most national and international perceptions of Britain's nuclear strength. Home was beset publicly by criticism of the 'so-called independent, so-called British, so-called deterrent'.[3] Which of these realities was real: the military, or the political?

Following Margaret Gowing's official history of Britain and atomic energy between 1945 and 1952,[4] I have divided my attention between 'policy-making' and 'policy execution'. Nearly half of these pages are devoted to an often familiar account of Britain's political struggle for a credible nuclear defence posture and the international diplomacy, especially in the United States and NATO, necessary to support this endeavour. The rest are devoted to an attempt to establish, as neutrally and factually as possible, the story of British progress in the development and production of fissile material, nuclear warheads, weapons and delivery systems; and of their modes of operation by the armed forces. Neither can be viewed in isolation, but they are not as closely or simplistically related as the reader might assume. Rather, it sometimes appears that there were two distinct British nuclear weapons programmes underway at the same time: one in the cloisters of Whitehall and Westminster, focusing almost exclusively on future spending plans and their justification; and one in research establishments, factories and military bases across the United Kingdom and overseas, focusing on the creation of a real nuclear capability in the here and now. Again a gap between illusion and reality, this time between the making and execution of policy, is apparent. The British armed forces were not necessarily equipped or trained in practice to do what politicians and strategists were talking about.

This is certainly not another history of British decline – of deluded British policy-makers clinging to a belief that only nuclear weapons would make them interesting and important in the post-imperial age. I believe the story is more complex than this. Indeed, it seems to me that politicians and officials also struggled with the opposite illusion: acutely conscious of their technical and economic difficulties and loss of international independence of action, they nevertheless supervised, from a distance, a huge and costly national nuclear enterprise. Perceptions of Britain's reliance or otherwise on the United States for its nuclear capability were also subtly at variance with reality. The first substantial growth in nuclear weapons available to British forces, for example, came from the US under 'dual-key' custody arrangements – indicating, at least in theory, an American veto over their use. There were as many as 100 US nuclear bombs earmarked for use by the RAF in this way in late 1958, and 60 US warheads for Thor missiles by April 1960. Only later, however, with the cancellation of the Blue Streak and later Skybolt missile systems, did Britain's nuclear deterrent come to be *seen* to rely on the United States. By early 1963, dual-key American nuclear weapons were no longer used by the RAF's V-bombers, and British-made, independently controlled forces had replaced them; and yet Britain was assumed by many to have been forced into a much more subordinate nuclear role.

Finally, the theme of *Nuclear Illusion and Reality* is also a respectful tribute to Sir Solly, later Lord Zuckerman, whose thoughts on nuclear weapons and nuclear strategy appeared under this title in 1982. For Zuckerman, Chief Scientific Adviser in the Ministry of Defence for much of the period under study, the illusion was that nuclear weapons were a rational response to the defence needs of the United Kingdom: 'There is, in fact, no realistic and no theoretical justification for the belief that nuclear weapons could ever be used as a rational extension of conventional armaments'.[5] Prepared somewhat grudgingly to concede that the existence of large stockpiles of nuclear weapons in the hands of the superpowers – and perhaps even the United Kingdom – acted as a deterrent to major war, Zuckerman was supremely dismissive of the need for elaborate strategies and doctrines for their use. He was particularly strongly opposed to NATO plans for the use of tactical nuclear weapons on the central front in Europe. The period between 1958 and 1964 saw, partly under the influence of Zuckerman and his close friend Lord Mountbatten, a gradual move away from the massive-retaliation strategy of the 1957 defence white paper, which based Britain's defence policy explicitly on the early use of nuclear weapons, and towards a debate focused more on conventional defence. Defence minister Duncan Sandys was the figure most closely associated with the nuclear emphasis of 1957. He had been charged with achieving significant financial savings, and did so by reducing markedly the size of Britain's conventional forces. It became clear in succeeding years, however, that the intellectual case for the massive-retaliation strategy was weak; and also that, far from guaranteeing savings, it required new and expensive technical capabilities to make it a credible reality. By 1961 a 'retreat from Sandys' was recognised by contemporaries. Later defence white papers were far less stark, and in 1962 Britain's nuclear-weapons programme was severely scaled back, with individual weapons projects cancelled and major reductions in fissile material production agreed. Even the reduced programme of 1962, however, left Britain much stronger than before in nuclear terms. It would be wrong to see the Sandys policy as a nuclear illusion and the more moderate policy of succeeding years as a conventional reality; rather, the pendulum had ceased to swing violently and the new reality in Britain's worldwide defence was a balanced nuclear and conventional posture.

I have aimed in this study at some measure of detachment, for the cold war is over and we can look back at the events of the 1950s and 1960s from a distance. Nevertheless, Britain's nuclear weapons are once again a matter of some political controversy and some of the choices made in the period under study remain relevant to policy-makers today. I would suggest therefore that, although in one sense now is a good time to write a history of British nuclear weapons, in another sense it has become a little harder in the past two years to maintain the necessary objectivity. I shall make no recommendation whatsoever relating to twenty-first-century policy, and indeed I do not believe in the power of 'didactic' history to generate specific 'lessons' for the present day. Readers may still feel that I have written a somewhat admiring history. I am fascinated by the technology of the cold war, by the alarming political atmosphere in which it was developed, and by the attitudes of participants in the official debates about nuclear weapons. This fascination extends equally to arch-cold warriors like US Air Force General Curtis LeMay and more ambiguous figures like Zuckerman. This is certainly not therefore an 'anti-history' of nuclear weapons, seeking to demonstrate that strategies for their use were ill-conceived or wrong. Neither, however, does it glory in the atomic age, for nuclear weapons are the most terrible engines of destruction ever devised, and their use, at any point during our period, would have brought European civilisation to an end, damning tens of millions of people to the grimmest possible struggle for survival in a new dark age. Bases in my home county of Lincolnshire would have been on the front line. That Britain's nuclear weapons were *not* used, between 1958 and 1964, at least means this is a story with a happy ending. The makers of the films *Dr Strangelove* (1964) and *The War Game* (1965) foresaw an altogether grimmer conclusion. But what did humanity think it was *doing* during the cold war? Specifically, what did British ministers, officials and senior military officers think they were doing? These are surely legitimate and useful questions to try to answer.

Aspects of the story are undeniably missing from these pages, not particularly because they remain shrouded in secrecy, but because nuclear history is a gemstone with too many facets to polish. Constrained by time, space and the limits of my own expertise and research, I have not covered civil defence policy, atomic intelligence, academic strategic debates, Britain's nuclear power and propulsion programmes, or the politics of the European NATO countries. Each of these nevertheless had implications for the weapons programme. Nuclear power and propulsion, for example, certainly affected atomic diplomacy between Britain and the United States, at a time when access to reactor technology was thought to be an important source of national commercial advantage. The attitude to nuclear weapons of France and West Germany also complicated Anglo-American relations, in particular during the Skybolt, Polaris and NATO multi-lateral force (MLF) controversies – although questions of French and German politics had little practical bearing on the implementation of British policy. I have been unable to make much use of the copious archives now open in the US and NATO; this too may be counted a weakness in a book that aspires to tell an international story. But a line has to be drawn somewhere. I am confident enough to suggest, with suitable humility, that future scholars, better placed to widen the enquiry, will be able to expand and add colour to, but not to re-write wholesale, the story of Britain's nuclear weapons programme in these years.

Historiography

A comprehensive literature survey on British nuclear weapons in our period would be quite an undertaking, for a great deal was written at the time and has been written since. Readers will find some pointers to further reading in the footnotes and bibliography. I should like, however, to dwell for a moment on the historiography of the British nuclear weapons programme, partly in order to introduce and set in context the present volume.

Postwar British defence policy has typically been studied either as a microcosm of British economic and political decline or as an aspect of Britain's relationship with the United States. These lines of enquiry, the documentary evidence available from interviews and Whitehall documents – and occasionally the political outlook of the writer – have often conspired to create a gloomy account of retreat and subservience.[6] The study of Britain's postwar military campaigns and the associated policy-making has tended to reinforce this view.[7] Within this context, specific documentary histories of British nuclear weapons policy have been appearing since the late 1980s, when, under the then 30-year rule, archive material covering the early years of the British programme first began to be declassified. Since then, a great wealth of material has become available, and although researchers have had to mine the archives painstakingly by hand, various seams and galleries have been opened and explored. Several earlier accounts of British nuclear policy, based on interviews and contemporary published writings, have stood the test of time, demonstrating at least in broad outline that there has been no grand political deception at work – no wizard behind the curtain, waiting to be revealed many years later by patient documentary research.[8]

The search for the strategic ideas behind British nuclear policy has been one important focus for historians. This work has tended to highlight 'bureaucratic politics' explanations for nuclear policy, partly because the evidence it uses is in the form of briefings and submissions, setting out the position of one party against another in the eternal struggle for resources to procure equipment.[9] The Chiefs of Staff, the Admiralty and the Air Ministry, forever at loggerheads in Whitehall, come out especially badly in such histories, their views always self-serving and their tactics cynical. The motivations of nuclear-weapons designers at Aldermaston have also come under scrutiny.[10] Policy is shown, correctly, to emerge by compromise between powerful individuals and interest groups; its implementation, however, is seldom followed in detail by these historians.

Other writers have been fascinated by the Anglo-American relationship and especially the establishment (or perhaps more correctly re-establishment) of atomic cooperation in 1958.[11] A still more productive area of research, with an important nuclear angle, has been the diplomatic history of summit meetings and correspondence between heads of state and government: Eisenhower and Macmillan; Kennedy and

Macmillan; Kennedy and de Gaulle; Kennedy, Macmillan, de Gaulle and Adenauer.[12] Diplomatic history of this kind has a long tradition in Britain's universities, and personal warmth (or otherwise) between leaders certainly appears important to international relations. But this literature too strays only occasionally into the reality of implementing the nuclear policies discussed at the commanding heights. At times the result seems to be little more than a deconstruction of diplomatic letters and telegrams – a modern equivalent of 'kings and battles' history. The very evidence used by diplomatic historians also tends to over-emphasise foreign-policy drivers or at times abstract notions of geopolitics, of the kind airily discussed on occasion by presidents and prime ministers. Domestic factors are sometimes neglected. Why did Macmillan press Eisenhower and especially Kennedy towards nuclear test limitation? Not because he saw himself as a latter-day Castlereagh or Lloyd George, sealing the fate of nations at the conference table, but because he and a clear majority of the British electorate were worried about the public health implications of atmospheric testing in particular, and thought it was right to end it. Why did Macmillan press Kennedy for independent control at Nassau in 1962? Partly because the Conservative party was baying for it – a rather grubby domestic concern which the Prime Minister was not anxious to raise in front of the President, and which does not therefore leap out of the printed record of the meeting.

In the United States, there is a respectable tradition of academic study of defence procurement, perhaps especially in the years of the Kennedy administration covered by this study.[13] In Britain, however, there has been a great deal less academic work on the hardware aspects of defence policy, and what has appeared is of variable quality. British university departments teaching history, international relations and strategic studies live generally in arts and social-science faculties, where the detailed study of military technology lacks a certain respectability. Writers with an understanding of technical issues tend to concentrate on specific – often cancelled – aircraft projects, seeing these almost invariably as lost opportunities, and lack subtlety in their political analysis; some archive-based work meanwhile lacks a coherent understanding of technical issues, or is frankly confused.[14] Only a minority of writers has successfully linked technical, policy and sometimes also operational issues, and it is this tradition I seek to follow.[15]

The second part of this introduction presents some of the main characters, institutions and decision-making structures that will appear in the rest of the story. The rest of the book is divided into four chapters.

Chapter 1 looks at the political and strategic background to nuclear policy-making between 1958 and 1961; Chapter 2 covers policy execution in the same period. Chapters 3 and 4 mirror this structure for the period between 1961 and 1964. A short conclusion offers comments on the roots of British nuclear policy and the nature of the Anglo-American relationship, which conditioned it so heavily. I have included appendices with outline information on stockpiles of weapons and fissile materials. A glossary of nuclear projects is available elsewhere.[16] Weights and measures are given in the usage of the time: British imperial, except for fissile materials which, for obscure reasons, were already, even in the 1950s, quoted in kilogrammes. It is tiresome always to quote equivalents, and if necessary readers will easily find conversion tables in reference books and on the internet.

Macmillan and his ministers

Harold Macmillan, Prime Minister between 1957 and 1963, looms large in these pages. A great deal has been written about Macmillan and his foreign and security policies.[17] Nevertheless, a further brief effort must be made to describe and understand the Prime Minister's views, as the most senior and influential figure in determining Britain's nuclear defence policies, and indeed the final arbiter of the use of British nuclear weapons.

Patrician and aloof, playing a part, sometimes a man of paradoxical views – Macmillan was a mystery to many contemporaries. Most at home in high society and London's clubland, his politics were profoundly affected by his experience of the trenches, then of mass unemployment on Teesside in the 1930s. He was, partly as a result, an unashamed populist, forever linked in the public imagination with the end of austerity and 'most of our people have never had it so good'.[18] Being all things to all people was an important part of his political success. Coming to power after Suez, and faced from time to time with acute political and financial problems, he was also forced more than once to reconsider Britain's position in the world.

It is possible nevertheless to see consistency in Macmillan's views on defence, notably in three broad areas: Anglo-American relations, cost and centralised control. He was committed from the beginning of his premiership to improve relations with the US after the low point of Suez, an aspect of his foreign policy which has attracted much attention, and will be covered here too. At least as important to the Prime Minister was the search for financial savings in Britain's defence commitments: as one of his ministers recalled, 'the economic background was what dominated us ... Macmillan was primarily interested in reducing expenditure on defence'.[19] Hence his appointment of Duncan Sandys as Minister of Defence in January 1957, with strict instructions to reduce the defence budget and in particular to bring peacetime conscription to an end. The logic of these instructions led Sandys to reduce expenditure on conventional forces, especially those intended for fighting a major war, and to place instead greater reliance on preventing war through nuclear deterrence. This policy was enshrined in Sandys's first and most controversial defence white paper: 'The time has come to revise not merely the size, but the whole character of the defence plan'. As the minister explained in parliament, 'we believe that the British people will agree that the available resources of the nation should be concentrated not upon preparations to wage war so much as upon trying to prevent that catastrophe from ever happening'.[20] Finally Macmillan also embarked, more than once, on attempts to reform the central organisation of defence and strengthen control over the rival strategies and spending plans of the armed forces.

Macmillan's interest in nuclear issues did not, however, arise simply as a by-product of his diplomatic or economic policies and his attempts at organisational reform. At a fundamental level, 'he was driven by a sense that he was destined to be Churchill's true heir and believed his place in history would be determined by his performance on the world stage'.[21] Like Churchill before him, Macmillan saw clearly that the H-bomb was one of the central issues of the age, and was from time to time plunged into gloom by questions of peace, war and the future of humanity. For all his aristocratic hauteur, he was also a moderniser who saw the civil application of nuclear energy, for example, as important to Britain's economic prospects. Macmillan saw personal political advantage in cutting a dash on the international stage and becoming closely involved, in particular, in efforts to limit nuclear testing – an issue of some importance to the British electorate. As Nigel Ashton points out, however, it is difficult to see pure political calculation behind his words to President Kennedy, at the start of 1962, on nuclear weapons and humanity's 'setting out on a path at once so fantastic and so retrograde, so sophisticated and so barbarous, as to be almost incredible'.[22] Macmillan was secure in the knowledge that Britain had successfully tested thermonuclear weapons during 1957, subsequently achieving an unprecedented level of cooperation with the US in the atomic field, but he was no war-monger and his commitment to arms control was real. For all these reasons he was driven to involve himself closely in nuclear weapons issues over a period of many years.

In all sensitive matters, Macmillan relied on the advice of those civil servants closest to him, in particular the Cabinet Secretary since 1947, Sir Norman Brook. A grammar-school boy from Wolverhampton who rose to the heights of the civil service after a good war dealing with the home front, Brook was a devotee of good order, of all that was proper in government organisation and indeed in dress. As Macmillan put it, revealing something of his own snobbery as well as his respect, 'Norman has most wonderful judgement. He is always right. Pure inborn judgement, because, as I expect you know, he had no background'.[23] Having created this impression, Brook became 'influential beyond a point that traditionalists would think proper'.[24] His elegant drafting can be seen in many of the papers on nuclear matters signed by Macmillan. So, it seems clear, can his opinions.

Peppered with earls and viscounts, and indeed a large number of relatives of the Prime Minister, the Conservative administration was a socially exclusive group. Peter Thorneycroft, Macmillan's first chancellor of the exchequer, was one of a large number of ministers educated, like Macmillan himself, at Eton, whereafter 'his reputation in the county, especially in field sports' helped him to his first parliamentary seat in Stafford.[25] George Ward, Secretary of State for Air, was the youngest son of an earl. Home, the Foreign Secretary, and Selkirk and Jellicoe – at various times First Lords of the Admiralty – *were* earls. Sandys was Churchill's son-in-law and Julian Amery, a junior minister in the War Office and wartime associate of King Zog of Albania, was Macmillan's. It would be a mistake, however, to caricature the small number of ministers who enjoyed real influence over nuclear policy as a group of braying toffs. On the contrary, they were talented and intelligent politicians with their own perspectives on defence policy. The ambitious Thorneycroft resigned in 1958 over monetary policy, citing amongst other things the expense of Britain's nuclear policies:

> For 12 years we have been attempting to do more than our resources could manage, and in the process we have been gravely weakening ourselves ... First, we have sought to be a nuclear power, matching missile with missile and anti-missile with anti-missile ... At the same time, we have sought to maintain a welfare state ... We have been trying to do those things against the background of having to repay debt abroad during the next eight years of a total equivalent to the whole of our existing reserves; against the background of having to meet maturing debt in this country ... against the background of seeking to conduct a great international banking business and against a background of sustaining our positions of one of the

world's major overseas investors. In those circumstances, it is small wonder that we find some difficulties.[26]

Macmillan was careful thereafter to choose more pliant chancellors, first Derick Heathcoat-Amory and later Selwyn Lloyd.

Sandys, meanwhile, was far from pliant. Employed by Macmillan 'in a succession of demanding posts where an abrasive and forceful hatchet man was seen as being necessary',[27] he achieved success despite inspiring widespread dislike. His first major contribution to defence policy, in line with his instructions, was to abolish conscription and rely more heavily on the threat of nuclear weapons as a deterrent to war. In addition, however, and in line with his own wartime and postwar experience – on the Crossbow committee dealing with German V-weapons, and then as Churchill's Minister of Supply – Sandys pursued the replacement of old-fashioned conventional weapons with ballistic and guided missiles. Sandys came into sharp confrontation with the service chiefs. The *Sunday Express* painted a lively scene in 1958:

> Picture the drama that swirls about this rugged, red-haired, remarkable figure. Every morning at 9.30 sharp he walks hatless up the steps into the Ministry of Defence building overlooking St James's Park. Every morning he sits himself firmly behind his desk and gazes with his cool, unblinking eyes at the procession of service chiefs and other officials who come to see him. Most of them gaze back with equal coolness. For in their minds is but a single thought. *How on earth can we get rid of this fellow?*[28]

Sandys is said at one point literally to have come to blows with Field Marshal Sir Gerald Templer.[29] The Prime Minister, with affected world-weariness, found such behaviour tiresome and described both Sandys and Thorneycroft as *cassant*.[30] Mountbatten, the First Sea Lord, alone among the chiefs, made it his business to get along with the minister. In October 1959 Sandys was moved sideways, but only as far as the new Ministry of Aviation, where he remained in a perfect position to champion Britain's aerospace industry and especially, as before, guided weapons. Selkirk was another enthusiast for missiles, his voice often raised in support of the American Polaris submarine-launched ballistic-missile system, although, as we shall see, his professional advice on the subject from within the navy was cautious.

Aubrey Jones, Minister of Supply until 1959, conformed rather less to the aristocratic stereotype. Born in Merthyr Tydfil, the son of a coal-miner, he was 'more comfortable as a technocrat than as a politician' and brought experience of the iron and steel industry.[31] Sandys's replacement as Defence Minister, Harold Watkinson, was another with business experience, and had trained as an engineer. Watkinson, like Sandys, was charged above all with achieving defence economies: 'It is clearly in our interest to continue to contribute to the nuclear deterrent if we can. Only by so doing can we stay in close relations with the USA in this vital field ... But we can only afford to pay the minimum subscription to stay in the club'.[32]

Decision-making structures

The Prime Minister sits, with the cabinet, at the top of the British system of government. Power ebbs and flows between the two, but in theory, cabinet is a collective executive and the Prime Minister merely a first among equals, 'who leads, coordinates and maintains a series of ministers'.[33] To this general prime-ministerial responsibility are added others more specific, including for example the appointment of the Chiefs of Staff of the armed forces. Potentially most burdensome of all, the Prime Minister is also responsible for authorising explicitly any use of British nuclear weapons.

In constitutional theory, all British ministers are answerable to parliament, which also formally votes money for defence. As we shall see, discussion in parliament was hampered by divisions within the Labour opposition, which at times avoided the subject because it was seldom able to create as much trouble for the government as for itself. Reasonably frequent questions were asked of ministers – five times in a month, for example, in November and December 1957, when MPs were concerned about the safety of American bombers flying from UK bases.[34] Perfunctory announcements were made to parliament regarding the government's policy on nuclear testing and various deterrent delivery systems, and there were occasional moments of theatre – for example when the Blue Streak ballistic missile was cancelled and Labour members poked fun at the absent Minister of Aviation, Duncan Sandys.[35] Full-scale debates on defence were just an annual ritual, however, and only the most problematic nuclear issues – Blue Streak was one – merited an unscheduled debate. For government ministers, such unscheduled debates were occasionally embarrassing and to be avoided where possible, but debates in the legislature tended to have little direct impact on nuclear-weapons policy in this period. Defence decisions were made by ministers and officials – not in parliament, where discussion of defence was neither frequent nor especially well informed.[36]

Macmillan was happier than some of his predecessors to involve his cabinet in discussion of nuclear matters, taking the test-ban issue, for example, to the full cabinet at least 26 times.[37] Detailed questions of nuclear defence policy, however, tended to be dealt with elsewhere. The Ministers of Defence and Supply were members of the cabinet, but the three single-service ministers – the First Lord of the Admiralty, Secretary of State for War and Secretary of State for Air – were not. They might be present at cabinet meetings for some discussions of defence matters, and occasionally speak when spoken to, but they were described in the minutes as merely 'in attendance'. The Defence Committee of the cabinet, usually chaired by the Prime Minister, did include the service ministers as well as those of their more senior colleagues with a direct interest in defence matters, including the Chancellor of the Exchequer and Foreign Secretary. During the second half of 1958, this committee discussed nuclear matters – testing, the nuclear weapons programme, fissile material, strategic nuclear delivery systems and atomic cooperation with the United States – at least eight times.[38] Not all questions could be referred to so august a body, however, and various *ad hoc* meetings of ministers and officials had inevitably to be convened, as for example on the last day of 1959 when Macmillan, Heathcoat-Amory and Sandys met with various officials to consider the nuclear-weapons production programme.[39]

In addition to their collective cabinet responsibility, most ministers were responsible for the direction and operation of a department of state. Those departments directly involved in the direction of nuclear policy were the Ministry of Defence (MoD), Admiralty, War Office, Air Ministry and Ministry of Supply (later of Aviation). Several of these no longer exist and require some introduction. The MoD, for example, in Storey's Gate, was not the huge organisation it has become today; on the contrary, its powers were limited and its staff numbered in the hundreds rather than thousands. Until 1958, the minister's authority derived chiefly from his responsibility to allocate resources between the three single-service ministries; he 'had no powers of initiative either in the field of strategic planning or of weapons procurement'.[40] In that year the Minister of Defence was given, for the first time, responsibility for 'the formal and general application of a unified policy relating to the Armed Forces of the crown'.[41] Hitherto no such unified policy had been attempted. The post of Chief of the Defence Staff (CDS) was created; also a Defence Board, chaired by the minister and including the service ministers, Minister of Supply, chiefs, MoD Permanent Secretary and Chief Scientific Adviser, usually known as the chief scientist.

This Board sat below the Defence Committee and dealt with 'major matters of defence policy affecting the size, shape, organisation and disposition of the armed forces and their weapons and war-like equipment and supply (including defence research and development)'.[42] The MoD also acted as a channel for most dealings with NATO and, through the person of the chief scientist, controlled the Defence Research Policy Committee (DRPC), which reviewed and prioritised research and development projects. Although the DRPC was unable formally to reject the requirements submitted to it by the single-service ministries, it did provide a way of coordinating, and if necessary questioning the feasibility of, the projects initiated in response. The DRPC's sub-committee on the Strategic Uses of Atomic Energy (DRP(AES)), again chaired by the chief scientist but under a further blanket of security, discussed nuclear-weapons requirements in more detail.

Alongside the chief scientist, the Permanent Secretary, the MoD's most senior non-scientific civil servant, also exercised an increasing influence during our period. The Permanent Secretary, for example, chaired a British Nuclear Deterrent Study Group (BNDSG), looking from 1959 onwards at future nuclear delivery systems, and also an inter-departmental Nuclear Test Policy Committee. In 1960 the responsibilities of the latter group were transferred to a new inter-departmental Nuclear Requirements for Defence Committee (NRDC), still chaired by the MoD Permanent Secretary, and under instruction 'to consider major issues of policy concerned with the nuclear requirements of the services and the testing of nuclear weapons'.[43] This body came to assert greater 'civilian' administrative control over the detailed nuclear-weapons agenda, hitherto dominated by military and scientific advisers, and it channeled advice thereon to ministers.

Successive MoD chief scientists and Permanent Secretaries came to be very influential in setting the British nuclear policy agenda in these years. Sir Frederick Brundrett, chief scientist until the end of 1959, was a career defence researcher with a keen interest in guided weapons and all nuclear matters: 'This was a new scientific field', he observed, 'which gave plenty of room for the exploitation of our national scientific genius'.[44] The son of a company secretary in Ebbw Vale, Brundrett studied maths at Cambridge and then worked his way up through the scientific ranks, starting in the Royal Navy's signals school, playing hockey and cricket for the civil service and acting as deputy for his two predecessors before taking the top job.[45] Brundrett was the complete insider, and a very keen proponent of the British ballistic missile Blue Streak, but not, generally, a man of the limelight. His successor, Sir Solly

Zuckerman, was very different.[46] Originally an anatomist, pursuing an academic career and a long association with the London zoo, Zuckerman at the same time followed a parallel career in government service, offering outspoken and controversial views on strategic bombing policy during the Second World War and on nuclear weapons in the 1960s and beyond. Zuckerman was a consummate networker, with a large number of friends in senior positions in the American defence-research hierarchy. He was also a close associate of the equally controversial Lord Mountbatten, and later of Prime Minister Harold Wilson, becoming the government's Chief Scientific Adviser on leaving the MoD. Zuckerman's relations with senior figures in the RAF were not so good. The personal views of the MoD's Permanent Secretaries in this period, Sir Richard Powell (to the end of 1959), Sir Edward Playfair (to 1961) and Sir Robert Scott, were seldom put forward as trenchantly as Zuckerman's, but none of them was slow to engage in politics behind the scenes to arrive at workable defence-policy decisions. Watkinson assessed that 'Rob Scott had more direct influence on defence policy than his predecessors'.[47]

Formally a part of the Ministry of Defence, but in practice owing no particular loyalty to the minister, was the Chiefs of Staff Committee. The fiercely independent chiefs – the First Sea Lord, Chief of the Imperial General Staff and Chief of the Air Staff – were the professional heads of their services and met frequently as a body where they were 'collectively responsible to the government for professional advice on strategy and military operations and on the military implications of defence policy'.[48] The chiefs also enjoyed a right of access, *in extremis*, to the Prime Minister. Their chairman, the CDS – between 1957 and 1959 Marshal of the RAF Sir William Dickson – had few powers of his own, and the effectiveness of the chiefs varied according to the personalities and policies of the individuals involved. Too often, the atmosphere between them was tense and jealous. Mountbatten, who succeeded Dickson as CDS, dominated the chiefs during our period with his political skill and the force of his personality. But he was disliked and distrusted by his colleagues, and often found it both necessary and desirable to work around, rather than through them. Nevertheless, when the chiefs did agree, as for example in early 1960 over the military inutility of Blue Streak, ministers found them difficult to ignore. Reporting to the chiefs was a Joint Planning Staff (JPS), comprising the Directors of Plans from the three services and charged, as the name suggests, with drawing up and commenting on plans for the employment of the services. The chiefs also controlled a working party on the operational use of atomic weapons, known by the initials OAW and including the deputy chiefs of the three service staffs. Few of the OAW working party's papers have been declassified, but this was evidently the source of authoritative military advice on the types and numbers of nuclear weapons required, and on planning for their actual employment. As discussed above, requirements had still to be passed to the Ministry of Supply and the DRPC's atomic sub-committee for approval.

The Admiralty, at the north end of Whitehall, was the department responsible for building, maintaining and administering the Royal Navy. It enjoyed a wider remit than the War Office or Air Ministry, retaining responsibility for most of its own research and procurement and acting, in addition, as an operational headquarters. The Royal Navy's minister, the First Lord, and its professional head, the First Sea Lord, were supported in reaching their decisions by a Board referred to – usually affectionately – as 'their lordships'. Like their army and RAF counterparts, naval officers generally dreaded service in Whitehall and preferred to be more active; for most, command of a major warship at sea was the height of ambition. Despite receiving a good technical education in one of the sea-going specialisms, often gunnery, naval officers were generally dismissive of academic cleverness and therefore of most strategic discussions. Admiralty officials and naval officers aimed above all to preserve a general-purpose surface navy centred on the aircraft carrier. Although they sought to equip carrier aircraft with tactical nuclear weapons for use against naval targets, they did not in general aspire to a share of the strategic nuclear deterrent role. I have argued elsewhere, at considerable length, that as far as nuclear weapons were concerned the Admiralty, and the Royal Navy, were generally unenthusiastic.[49] They feared in particular the expense involved and the strategic doctrine of Duncan Sandys, and the impact of both on general-purpose conventional naval forces. For some time, as we shall see, they pressed hard the argument that mutual deterrence between east and west begot the need to invest in conventional forces for limited war, especially outside Europe. Some historians, however, persist in arguing otherwise: that the Admiralty plotted from an early date to seize the nuclear deterrent role from the RAF and thereafter took every opportunity to press the merits of Polaris.[50]

Admiral of the Fleet Earl Mountbatten of Burma, First Sea Lord to July 1959 and CDS thereafter, was the dominant figure in the Royal Navy of the time. Ex-viceroy and supreme allied commander – uncle to the Duke of Edinburgh, brother to the queens of Greece and Sweden – Mountbatten moved effortlessly in the highest social circles. He was an exceptionally experienced, devious and well connected political manipulator. His father had been First Sea Lord before him, and he was dark blue through and through, but a moderniser rather than a traditionalist. Although as CDS he tried, he could not hide his partiality from his contemporaries, and his letters to Zuckerman for example – encouraging him to speak up against the RAF's TSR.2 aircraft and in favour of the naval Buccaneer, then to 'burn this' – perfectly capture him at work.[51] I firmly believe that Mountbatten was far keener on aircraft carriers and nuclear hunter-killer submarines than on Polaris, and I shall continue to maintain, as we go along, that the Admiralty and navy were forced only reluctantly to accept responsibility for Britain's strategic nuclear force. Certainly Mountbatten's successors as First Sea Lord, Sir Charles Lambe and then, after the latter's illness in 1960, Sir Caspar John, were very measured in their response to Polaris and very much more concerned with other matters. It cannot be denied, however, that from time to time Mountbatten spoke enthusiastically about Polaris, including in correspondence with his American counterpart, Arleigh Burke. We shall see too that he took pleasure in using nuclear issues – Polaris and indeed the Buccaneer – to make trouble for the RAF.

The War Office, responsible for the direction and administration of the army and situated on the east side of Whitehall opposite the Admiralty, was less central to the debates on nuclear weapons in these years. Army officers tended to have even less inclination than their naval counterparts to engage in strategic debate, and it is no coincidence that today far less material on nuclear policy has survived in War Office than in Admiralty or Air Ministry archive files. Field Marshal Sir Gerald Templer, hero of Malaya and professional head of the army as Chief of the Imperial General Staff (CIGS), found his 'whole period as CIGS … an unhappy one, including as it did the fiasco of Suez and the reductions in the size of the army resulting from the decision … to work towards the end of conscription'.[52] Sir Francis Festing, his successor, had won his reputation in Burma and 'did not like being confined to an office dealing with politics and politicians'.[53] When it did debate strategy, the War Office anyway found some difficulty in deciding its priorities during the postwar period. The continental commitment – deprecated by Liddell-Hart, the doyen of military strategists – remained controversial, and most army officers were inclined to worry more about the possibility of warlike operations outside Europe, either in the middle east or south-east Asia. The army's tradition, one writer said, 'is one of victory, but of victory by muddling through, of success won mainly by toughness, of not knowing when you are beaten and of applying horse sense'.[54] Festing nevertheless took some trouble to read up on the problems of 'nuclear sufficiency' on his arrival in September 1958, pronouncing himself in complete agreement with Templer and therefore Mountbatten. Also, as we shall see, doctrinal changes had been made in preparation for the nuclear battlefield of the future, and the War Office found itself arguing strongly for the possession of short-range battlefield nuclear weapons of various kinds. Sir Richard Hull, a cavalry officer who took over from Festing as CIGS in 1961, took a keener interest than his predecessors in these ideas, and clashed repeatedly with Zuckerman over concepts of their use. At one war-game presentation, organised by Hull, Zuckerman was shown 'scores and scores of nuclear explosions, and then victory for our side … "Well", [he recalled saying], "I don't see our fellows stopping in the middle of all that for a brew-up".' He could never quite believe that the undemonstrative Hull really believed in such scenarios.[55]

Perhaps the best summary of attitudes to nuclear weapons among the two senior services was that of Vice-Admiral Sir Peter Gretton in 1965: 'I am anxious for many reasons not to get involved in a discussion of the British contribution to the deterrent and whether it is independent or not. This I believe is mainly a political question dependent on estimates of statesmen's characters and reactions in crises … it does not affect … the main issues'.[56]

No such sentiment could possibly have been expressed in the Air Ministry or RAF. For the Air Council – 'their airships', in counterpoint to the Board of Admiralty – nuclear deterrence and the manned bomber were the overriding concerns of the postwar era.[57] The RAF's founder, Lord Trenchard, bequeathed a doctrine and self-image based on strategic bombing, i.e., direct air attack upon the war-making capacity of an enemy. Drawing on Britain's supposedly traditional 'maritime' strategy of building and funding alliances and controlling the world beyond Europe, but not fighting on the continent, the development of the strategic-bombing doctrine was motivated in addition by the appalling experience of the trenches in the First World War.[58] Strategic bombing remains the most controversial subject in British military history.[59] The prophets of air warfare looked to a short-cut to future victory, believing that an enemy's will to fight would collapse in the face of bomber attack and that the bomber war – focusing on the attack and defence of bomber bases – would determine future conflict. Whether this prophecy really came true or not in the Second World War is not strictly relevant to the present argument, but there is no doubt that senior RAF officers in the 1950s and 1960s thought that it had. They also remembered the very serious Anglo-American differences over the conduct of the bomber war. In both senses, wartime experience of strategic bombing was enormously important to the postwar Air Ministry and RAF. The RAF was not, however, so dominated by 'bomber generals' as the postwar US Air Force. As Mike Worden has highlighted, Strategic Air Command (SAC) was the route to greatness in the USAF until the 70s. Hence for example in 1960 the Chairman of the Joint Chiefs of Staff, Nathan Twining, the air force chief Thomas White, his vice-chief Curtis LeMay and three of his five deputy chiefs were all bomber generals.[60] Successive Chiefs of the Air Staff in Britain on the other hand – Sir Dermot Boyle (to the end of 1959) and Sir Thomas Pike (1960–64) – came to the job from Fighter Command, although Boyle had some earlier bomber experience and both were staunch defenders of the strategic deterrent role. Nor was Dickson, the first CDS, a bomber man; he had started his career in the naval air service, and his wartime and postwar experience had been in Fighter Command and the middle east.

Boyle, Pike and Dickson were experienced and knowledgeable senior officers, but they were not quite the giants of the RAF's recent past – wartime leaders like Tedder, Dowding and Harris. Boyle, in the assessment of one study, 'was no match for Mountbatten's wiles'.[61] Partly for this reason, the Air Ministry, located at the southern end of what is now the MoD main building, was considered by outsiders to be less effective than the Admiralty.[62] It is important also to note a nuance to the air lobby's strong support for nuclear deterrence. Their belief in its efficacy was visceral: 'The strategic deterrent is the keystone of our defence policy, and we believe that without it all the rest of our defence effort is meaningless. Moreover we have seen that it works'.[63] Lurking not far beneath the surface of such a statement, however, was a concern that, if the ballistic missile were to be adopted in future as the main deterrent delivery system, manned bomber aircraft were doomed. Duncan Sandys had said as much at the time of his 1957 white paper, cancelling the planned Avro 730 supersonic bomber. The intense political battles over deterrent systems between 1958 and 1962 were fraught with risk for the air marshals, who always had at the back of their minds the desire to reverse Sandys's decision to replace the current generation of bombers with missiles. As Guy Finch has argued, for many airmen in these years, the nuclear role was a means to a more viscerally important end: more aeroplanes, and in particular the marvellous TSR.2, intended to replace the RAF's Canberra light bombers.[64]

A final weakness was the Air Ministry's lack of control over research and procurement activities. Not that these were neglected – indeed, as David Edgerton has argued so persuasively, Britain had a love-affair with the aeroplane, and the aeroplane manufacturing industry, going back many years.[65] Direct relations with industry were, however, the preserve of the Ministry of Supply (MoS), based at Shell-Mex House on the Strand and Castlewood House on Oxford Street. The MoS furnished supplies and carried out research, design, development and procurement for the army, the RAF and also – as far as aircraft, guided weapons and ammunition were concerned – for the navy. It even had certain responsibilities for the procurement of common stores for civil government. In October 1959 the ministry was made larger and more powerful still, when it shed responsibility for munitions for the army but gained civil aviation. Now renamed the Ministry of Aviation (MoA), it controlled a vast hinterland of military research establishments including, most importantly for our purposes, the Royal Aircraft Establishment (RAE) at Farnborough, which was very heavily involved in research and development on nuclear delivery systems, dealing extensively for example with missiles, guidance, ballistics and aerodynamics.[66] The MoA's most senior officials included the powerful Controllers of Aircraft (CA) and of Guided Weapons and Electronics (CGWL), and a chief scientist. Successive occupants of these posts, including Sir George Gardiner (CA 1959–63), Sir Robert Cockburn (CGWL 1956–59, then chief scientist 1959–69), Sir Steuart Mitchell (CGWL 1951–6 and 1959–62) and Sir Morien Morgan (CA 1963–6 and CGWL thereafter), were career defence scientists with key roles in the implementation of nuclear policy. Their advice on the feasibility of nuclear policies was often most important, and CA was responsible, amongst other things, for the formal safety 'release' to the services of aircraft and air-launched weapons. Equal in rank to these scientists was the civilian Permanent Secretary – between 1959 and 1961 Sir William Strath, famous for his 1955 report on the effects of a thermonuclear attack on the UK.

There was also a Director-General of Atomic Weapons in the MoA, but direct involvement in managing the nuclear research establishments had been taken away from the MoS in 1954 when, by act of parliament, the United Kingdom Atomic Energy Authority (UKAEA) was created as a separate government agency outside departmental control, initially reporting to the Lord President of the Council, then in 1957 to the Prime Minister himself and later still, from 1959, to the Minister for Science, Lord Hailsham. The atomic weapons research establishment (AWRE) at Aldermaston was a division of the UKAEA, and was authorised to develop nuclear weapons against the requirements of the MoS (and later MoA). The Authority's chairmen, Lord Plowden (1954–59) and then Sir Roger Makins (1960–64) were exceptionally powerful figures. Plowden had been an industrialist; Makins, a more conventional mandarin, moved effortlessly from a prize fellowship at All Souls to the Foreign Office, then became ambassador in Washington in the late 1940s. They both gained important Treasury experience before taking over the Authority. Sir William Penney, Director of AWRE until 1959, his deputy Sir William Cook, who was especially involved in the H-bomb programme, and to a slightly lesser extent Penney's successor Dr Nyman Levin (1959–65), also enjoyed considerable prestige within the defence establishment. All of the nuclear barons engaged frequently in Anglo-American diplomacy, and their fiefdoms came to be thought of as important to the British economy.

Accounts of bureaucratic politics tend to emphasise the differences between ministers, officials and military officers. Even bitter personal and professional rivals, however, were in many ways similar in outlook, and it is worth pausing to consider for a moment the significance of these similarities. Levels of strict technical understanding varied, but in most respects these men, whether scientists or classicists, had a rather similar world-view. Public and grammar schools alike, for example, taught the history and geography of empire in a way that reinforced assumptions of British greatness. Prewar British experience of disarmament and appeasement had been unhappy, and this tended further to reinforce certain views about the maintenance and exercise of British power. The wartime experience of the policy-making elite, on the other hand, had been of personal, organisational and national success; everybody had had a good war. These men were now at the peak of their professions, often with little to prove to themselves or others; their American counterparts, by contrast, were often younger. After the intrusion of a number of 'wartime irregulars', Whitehall was reasserting a closed, clubbish, deliberative and rather superior atmosphere in the 1950s and 1960s. To be 'sound' – to share the values and assumptions of the establishment – was a virtue. Policy-makers were disinclined to listen to academics, pressure groups or other outsiders. This made Zuckerman's life, for example, harder; again there was a contrast with the situation in the United States. Some have seen great advantages in the British system of government – certainly Britain was more politically stable than almost any other European country in this period. Others have bemoaned the institutional stasis in British policy: 'It would be difficult to think of a system more designed to perpetuate the basic policies carried on to date and to inhibit their questioning'.[67] This, however, is a key element of the background to policy-making that historians need to understand.

Part I
Nuclear Illusion

1
Policy-making 1958–61

Between 1958 and 1961, Macmillan's government saw considerable success in aligning itself internationally with the United States, in a deepening bilateral defence relationship with a strong nuclear focus. Britain's official defence policy depended very heavily on the threat of using nuclear weapons. American ballistic missiles were transferred to the RAF and based in eastern England. Joint targeting arrangements were implemented, command and control policies and new early-warning facilities agreed. The new bilateral agreement to share some of the most sensitive design information on nuclear weapons, and to transfer a US nuclear reactor for submarine propulsion, was first implemented and then revised to allow further areas of cooperation. Macmillan felt stronger as a result, and better able to influence his most powerful ally in pursuit of a number of foreign-policy aims, including the limitation or abolition of nuclear testing and the revision of NATO defence strategy. He even felt able to talk of 'interdependence' in some senses between the leading countries of the west – in an age when all would stand or fall together. Although, as we shall see, Macmillan came to play down, at least privately, the strict need for British independence in the nuclear field – and repeatedly questioned the value of a significant nuclear capability in the future – the answer was always that the British nuclear deterrent was too important to let go.

Inside the Whitehall village, a series of heated debates was underway on the future means of delivering the strategic nuclear deterrent. The merits of bombers, land-based missiles and submarines were argued tirelessly. The Admiralty and War Office, led by Mountbatten, also mounted a long campaign under the banner of 'nuclear sufficiency' to limit expenditure on nuclear forces and find more money for Britain's conventional defence. In April 1960, Macmillan was forced publicly to change course, dropping the British ballistic missile Blue Streak as a military weapon. For the first time, in the wake of this cancellation, public opposition to nuclear weapons became politically significant. Macmillan's American alliance came to the rescue, however, and another nuclear agreement was reached with President Eisenhower: the life of Britain's V-bombers would be extended using the American air-launched ballistic missile Skybolt. The Air Ministry was delighted. Compared to completing the development of Blue Streak, buying Skybolt would even be cheap. In return, the US Navy was given access to a base in Scotland for its Polaris nuclear-missile submarine force. For now, the offer of Skybolt was as far as the US was prepared to go; a British Polaris was not on the agenda, although some political efforts were made to pursue the idea. No progress was possible at this stage in nuclear arms control or – once President Kennedy took office – in the revision of NATO strategy in line with British policy. There were clearly limits to Macmillan's influence therefore, and his recent policy successes began to look fragile. As 1961 went on, British concerns about the future of Skybolt began to grow.

In this chapter, I shall begin by reviewing official government policy on nuclear weapons, both as it was described in successive defence white papers, and as it was elaborated privately by ministers. I shall go on to cover the international diplomacy and politics around a number of issues: nuclear testing and Anglo-American defence cooperation; strategic nuclear delivery-systems debates, leading up to the Blue Streak cancellation; political opposition to nuclear weapons and the nuclear travails of the Labour party; debates over military strategy, especially in NATO but also relating to limited war outside Europe; the Skybolt deal and the difficulties created by the Holy Loch base and the related question of a NATO ballistic-missile force; and finally, opposition to Skybolt and the resumption of the bitter delivery-systems debate in late 1960 and 1961.

Government policy

General statements of the government's nuclear defence policy were given annually in this period in white papers on defence, generally presented to parliament in February. The policy tone had been set by Sandys in 1957:

> [It is] more than ever clear that the overriding consideration in all military planning must be to prevent war rather than to prepare for it ... The free world is today mainly dependent for its protection

upon the nuclear capability of the United States. While Britain cannot by comparison make more than a modest contribution, there is a wide measure of agreement that she must possess an appreciable element of nuclear deterrent power of her own. British atomic bombs are already in steady production and the Royal Air Force holds a substantial number of them. A British megaton weapon has now been developed. This will shortly be tested and thereafter a stock will be manufactured.[1]

The following year Sandys was clearer still:

> The west ... relies for its defence primarily upon the deterrent effect of its vast stockpile of nuclear weapons and its capacity to deliver them ... the strategy of NATO is based on the frank recognition that a full-scale Soviet attack could not be repelled without resort to a massive nuclear bombardment on the sources of power in Russia. In that event, the role of the allied defence forces in Europe would be to hold the front for the time needed to allow the effects of the nuclear counter-offensive to make themselves felt ... The strategic nuclear deterrent is the decisive factor in preventing major war.[2]

So the defence of the western alliance depended on nuclear weapons, and Britain was building up a contribution on that basis. Conventional forces were certainly also required:

> [The deterrent] does not obviate the need for maintaining a substantial shield of land forces, with air and naval support, to defend the frontiers of the free world. Nor could it, of course, be used in localised emergencies, still less for preserving order and stability. For these tasks, which represent a large part of the present responsibilities of all three services, conventional forces equipped with non-nuclear weapons are required.[3]

In the 1960 white paper, however, conventional forces were described rather dismissively as 'a necessary complement to nuclear armaments'.[4]

Conveniently for historians, the Prime Minister presented the thinking behind this nuclear defence policy in rather more detail for the benefit of the Defence Committee in July 1958. Britain's nuclear force – more and more commonly described over time as its 'deterrent' – was intended:

(a) To retain our special relation with the United States, and, through it, our influence in world affairs, and, especially, our right to have a voice in the final issue of peace or war.

(b) To make a definite, though limited, contribution to the total nuclear strength of the West – while recognising that the United States must continue to play the major part in maintaining the balance of nuclear power.

(c) To enable us, by threatening to use our independent nuclear power, to secure United States co-operation in a situation in which their interests were less immediately threatened than our own.

(d) To make sure that, in a nuclear war, sufficient attention is given to certain Soviet targets which are of greater importance to us than to the United States.[5]

Macmillan's ordering of these points is significant, as is the omission of any direct intention to frighten the Soviets; as points (a) and (c) make clear, the *political* target of Britain's nuclear force was not the Soviet Union at all, but the United States. Point (b) was primarily about resources: Macmillan was not prepared to make an unlimited commitment to the deployment of large numbers of nuclear weapons. The use of the word 'independent' in point (c) was especially significant. Although as we shall see Macmillan himself strove to achieve a greater measure of 'interdependence' with the United States, in the general sense of making common cause internationally and in specific matters of defence procurement, independence (or lack of it) became an issue for Macmillan's back-benchers, and increasingly for the Labour opposition. Indeed, it continues to bedevil discussion of Britain's nuclear history and policy. Finally, although nuclear weapons were primarily intended as a *deterrent* to global war, point (d) made clear that there was still some official interest in nuclear war-fighting. In particular, the need was recognised, in the event of nuclear war, to blunt an attack on the UK by destroying quickly certain Soviet medium-range bomber and missile bases.

Policy was not, however, necessarily static. Towards the end of 1958, Macmillan was in philosophical mood at a meeting of the Defence Committee:

> The Prime Minister said that before the committee examined the proposals set out in the papers on their agenda it would be useful to have a more general discussion of defence policy and its impact on public expenditure ... It was for consideration whether the fundamental assumptions on which our present defence policy rested were still tenable, or whether a reappraisal of the situation should now be made. The decision to produce a nuclear deterrent independently of

the United States had been taken at a time when the Americans had possessed an overwhelming superiority in that field over the Soviet Union. It had been taken partly on account of the influence and prestige which we should gain in our relations not only with the United States, but also within the Commonwealth and with the other countries of western Europe; a second reason had been the military value of having an independent deterrent. This policy had paid good dividends and been fully justified by events, especially the development of our relationship with the Americans during recent months. The basic situation had recently changed, however, in that the Soviet Union was now a major nuclear power and that the two strongest nations in the world would shortly reach a state of 'nuclear sufficiency', in which each could destroy the other. In this situation it was for consideration whether we still needed to take into account the possibility of having to use the nuclear deterrent independently of the United States, or to bring pressure to bear on them when our interests were threatened.[6]

Heathcoat-Amory agreed, citing the £1500 millions spent annually on defence. Sandys announced that 'after long and careful discussions with the service ministers and the Chiefs of Staff and in the United States, he had found it difficult to come to a firm conclusion on the policy we should adopt in the position of stalemate resulting from "nuclear sufficiency"; his considered view, however, was that we should continue to pursue the policy of having an independent nuclear deterrent'. After a seemingly inconclusive discussion, during which 'concern was expressed', probably by Selkirk, 'lest the concentration of our effort on the deterrent and its defence would leave insufficient resources available for conventional forces', Macmillan summed up: 'There was a general agreement that conventional forces should not be reduced below the levels already agreed [in the 1957 white paper] ... The two main possibilities of making significant economies were in relation to the deterrent, and its defence'.[7] In his hour of atomic triumph, was Macmillan contemplating turning his back on nuclear weapons, or at least reversing the Sandys emphasis on deterrence? As we shall see, Mountbatten and Templer had been making this argument inside Whitehall for some time. The Defence Committee minutes seem to record an essentially practical discussion following these deeper points. Perhaps ministers were perplexed by Macmillan's questioning, or assumed his monologue was no more than a tactic to increase pressure for savings.

In June 1959 at Chequers, however, at a meeting of officials to mark the start of an exceptionally wide-ranging study of future UK policy, Macmillan again posed similar questions:

> In the state of nuclear parity, which we had virtually reached already, both sides were equally deterred ... was this balance to our advantage, and if so, could it be maintained? Would it ... permit or even encourage a whole range of minor hostile actions and encroachments? ... In terms of foreign policy the British contribution to the Western deterrent had paid a handsome dividend up to now, but we should have to consider whether it would continue to do so.[8]

The audience's first response was to restate existing policy assumptions:

> Under conditions of nuclear parity, limited war in Europe would be most unlikely, provided that the west maintained an effective strategic retaliatory capability and the shield forces were strong enough to convince the Russians that even a minor aggression would carry the risk of global war ... It was suggested that we should still need to have an independent nuclear capability in 1970 since otherwise we could not count on American support in all circumstances and would be less able to stand up to Soviet threats against the United Kingdom or British interests overseas. Though our retaliatory power would be small, it would not be negligible and we could still inflict sufficient damage to deter the Russians ... having paid the entrance fee to the nuclear club, we could not easily withdraw, more particularly when others, e.g. the French, were likely to join it ... Assuming, however, that we should maintain a British contribution to the deterrent, we must decide what its future size and shape should be. Should we invest in land-based rockets, missile submarines or manned vehicles delivering guided bombs? A separate technical study of this question would be required at an early date.[9]

As we shall see later, a great deal of energy was spent in the next five years, in Whitehall and beyond, arguing the merits of different delivery systems, but the basic assumptions stated at Chequers – specifically by Boyle, the Chief of the Air Staff – held good. Although, as Brook indicated in summarising the conclusions of the future policy study, 'no real purpose would be served by adding to the striking power of the opposing forces', neither did any of Macmillan's advisers feel on this occasion – despite their having been given ample opportunity to express the view – that any purpose would be served by abandoning Britain's nuclear weapons.[10] On the contrary, the future policy study concluded in February 1960 that:

> We need to maintain a strategic nuclear force which is accepted by the Americans, and by the Alliance as a whole, as a significant contribution to the western deterrent. Without this our standing in the Alliance would suffer and we should lose a valuable means of influencing American policy in the event of a serious disagreement with them over the importance of a particular Communist threat. In practice, a contribution significant in American eyes must also have significance for the Russians.
>
> Certain principles emerge which should govern the decisions to be taken about the United Kingdom strategic nuclear deterrent during the next ten years. These are as follows:
>
> (a) to retain our status in the Alliance, we must make a significant effort in the field of the strategic nuclear deterrent;
>
> (b) to retain this status, it will not be enough simply to make a scientific contribution, however outstanding. We must maintain a viable force in being, under our ultimate control, which is sufficiently large to accomplish our political purpose;
>
> (c) we should therefore maintain, at the least, the ability to provide British warheads for whatever weapons systems may be adopted; but
>
> (d) we shall have to accept that there will be periods in which our deterrent cannot be maintained at the strength which we are now about to achieve if it would mean introducing costly new weapons systems which would be effective only over a limited period.[11]

This was not quite a blank cheque, but it was certainly a strong restatement of the need for a British nuclear force. The Soviet Union, once again, was almost an afterthought. It is interesting that Macmillan turned for such a far-reaching study to unelected advisers, and not to his ministers. Perhaps, for example at the Defence Committee in November 1958, he had despaired of interesting the latter in such long-term questions, or perhaps he was simply familiar enough with their views, and confident enough of their loyalty, to need no reassurance. But the fact that Macmillan repeatedly questioned his own nuclear policy so fundamentally, in whatever forum, is surely significant. He may have been more concerned than commentators have so far assumed by the opposition that Sandys had encountered over 'nuclear sufficiency' within the defence establishment, and the criticism the 'massive retaliation' policy had received, including from some in his own party. Backbench unease at government policy, though muted, was consistent in its focus on the impact nuclear expenditure was having on Britain's defence commitments overseas.[12] A few Conservative back-benchers were vocal in criticising government policy; they included former Defence Minister Anthony Head, who had refused the instruction to cut conventional forces taken up so enthusiastically by Sandys.[13] Others, however, could still wax lyrical in favour of the independent deterrent: 'It is not being jingoistic to say that we often tend to underestimate our potential influence ... How would America react now if we renounced the deterrent? Would we not hear again the charge: "Britain stinks of defeat"?'[14]

Macmillan, Eisenhower and bilateral defence collaboration

A great many books have been written about the close personal relationship between Macmillan and successive American Presidents, and it is undeniable that the Prime Minister took great pains to cultivate Eisenhower and later Kennedy – as well he might, for Britain's relationship with its most powerful ally was, at the political level, in rather poor shape when he first came to power in the aftermath of Suez. Most commentators would agree that 'the fact that Dwight D Eisenhower and Harold Macmillan had known each other since the early days of World War II made a difference in the way that they and their advisors conducted foreign policy'; that 'the Eisenhower-Macmillan partnership was largely successful'; and indeed that 'although Britain remained a junior partner of the United States during the late 1950s, it was a functioning and highly respected partner'.[15] It is important to remember, however, that Eisenhower was not the undisputed master of his country's foreign policy. In alliance, defence and especially nuclear matters he had to defer not only to his powerful Secretaries of State, John Foster Dulles (who died in May 1959) and then Christian Herter; but also to his Secretaries of Defense, successively Charles Wilson (to October 1957), Neil McElroy (to December 1959) and Thomas Gates; and to the powerful chairmen of the US Atomic Energy Commission, Lewis Strauss (to June 1958) and John McCone. The Secretaries of Defense were heavily influenced in turn by the Joint Chiefs of Staff, and so forth. Not all of these individuals could remotely be described as anglophile.

Macmillan's most famous contribution to the long history of analysis of Anglo-American relations was his analogy of the Greeks and the Romans, with himself in the role of a cultured and knowledgeable Greek advising the vigorous and occasionally disagreeable Romans.[16]

Perhaps a more appropriate prime-ministerial analogy, however, was that of the dinosaur and the bee: 'The dinosaur was [once] the largest beast but it was inefficient and therefore disappeared. The bee is efficient, but it is too small to have much influence. Britain's most useful role is somewhere between the bee and the dinosaur'.[17] Already, in the early 1950s, Britain had found a useful niche of this kind. A number of areas of defence collaboration flourished within NATO and bilaterally. In particular, numerous US bases in Britain had been established, and the US funded a number of British defence programmes, including for example the procurement of some Valiant atomic bombers, under mutual defence assistance arrangements. Agreement had also been reached to supply British troops and aircraft with American nuclear warheads in wartime. Although much is made of Macmillan's contribution to improving Anglo-American defence relations, we should remember that he was building on solid foundations.

During 1957, Macmillan's patient work secured a further improvement in Anglo-American relations. Outline agreement was reached in March on the deployment of Thor intermediate-range ballistic missiles to the UK, and a 'declaration of common purpose' was issued by the President and Prime Minister after their meetings in Washington in October. This announced 'an enlarged Atlantic effort in scientific research and development' and Eisenhower's intention 'to request the Congress to amend the Atomic Energy Act' which prevented US-UK collaboration in the nuclear field, both civil and military. More discursively, the two leaders noted that 'the countries of the free world are interdependent and only in genuine partnership, by combining their resources and sharing tasks in many fields, can progress and safety be found'.[18] Some commentators have found the notion of interdependence between Britain and the US laughable.[19] Eisenhower's use of the word in the joint declaration needs to be understood, however, in the context of the launch on 4 October, just days before his meetings with Macmillan, of the first Sputnik. American military and scientific superiority over the Soviet Union suddenly looked illusory. James Killian, the President's science adviser, wrote that 'as it beeped in the sky, Sputnik created a crisis of confidence that swept the country', and senator Henry Jackson demanded a 'national week of shame and danger'.[20] Khrushchev was not slow to exploit such sentiments, claiming a huge propaganda victory. Widely criticised for complacency, Eisenhower needed his friends about him, and the British ambassador in Washington, Sir Harold Caccia, spotted an opportunity: 'with luck and judgement, we should be able to turn this in some way to our special advantage'.[21]

Besides its emotional appeal, the word interdependence came also to have a technical meaning relating to Eisenhower's and Macmillan's commitment to greater cooperation in defence research and development. At a December 1957 meeting, to which Canadian representatives were also invited, a structure of tripartite sub-committees was recommended to foster cooperation in missile delivery systems, chemical and biological defence, ballistic missile defence, undersea warfare, aircraft and aero engines, infra-red research and electronics. Brundrett took a close interest in the setting up and operation of these groups. The more active groups continued to meet within a structure known as the Tripartite Technical Cooperation Programme (TTCP), which still exists in the twenty-first century. The Skybolt missile first came to British notice, for example, in the context of TTCP sub-group D on delivery systems,[22] and sub-group F on missile defence made some of the early running on plans for the BMEWS early-warning radar, later installed at Fylingdales.[23]

Although a good deal of fruitful discussion emerged from the interdependence groups, they failed to meet any aspiration there may have been for an agreed division of defence research effort between the allied nations. As an April 1959 sub-group G paper noted, 'there is some reluctance to take into service items which have been developed in other countries when this means abandoning national development which has already started'. Important commercial interests were in play on both sides of the Atlantic: 'firms of all countries are reluctant to release detailed information to firms in other countries unless some commercial agreement is arranged. How patent and proprietary rights are to be protected in the context of full collaboration is a serious problem'.[24] American firms, put simply, were far more interested in making sales to the UK than in mounting genuinely collaborative development efforts, and were certainly not prepared to surrender responsibility for promising avenues of research.

Exchanges on nuclear weapons were initially encumbered in a quite different way. The US Atomic Energy Act of 1946 had forbidden almost all discussions in the area, bringing to an end a period of wartime collaboration during which British scientists had been integrated into the atomic bomb project in the US.[25] Britain mounted a diplomatic campaign over many years thereafter to reverse this setback, and the story of the Act's revision in 1958, and the subsequent achievement of a fruitful Anglo-American collaboration in the nuclear-weapons field, has been told several times.[26] Admiral Strauss's reluctance had to be overcome with a direct instruction from Eisenhower to cooperate 'in the spirit as well as the letter' of what he had agreed with Macmillan in

October 1957.[27] Talks progressed in the spring, with US interest stimulated by the prospect of reciprocal information on Britain's Calder Hall power reactors – especially desired by the head of the US submarine nuclear propulsion programme, Admiral Rickover. On 3 July an Anglo-American agreement for cooperation on the uses of atomic energy for mutual defence purposes was finally signed in Washington, coming into force a month later. The agreement provided for the exchange of sensitive information by the parties for the purposes of defence planning, research and development, training, intelligence and 'to improve the recipient's atomic weapon design, development and fabrication capability'. The agreement also contained a number of provisions around the transfer of a nuclear-propulsion reactor and associated fissile material for the submarine HMS *Dreadnought*. Although the agreement was not as commercially difficult as some of the activities already mentioned under the interdependence banner, Westinghouse and Rolls-Royce were involved in the reactor transfer and the agreement included a lengthy article on the management of intellectual property.[28] Care had been taken on the US side to word the relaxation of the act so as to permit such agreements to be made with countries that had made 'substantial progress' in the nuclear weapons field – a formula designed purposely to include Britain but not France. We shall see later what use British scientists were able to make of the agreement.

The issue of fissile material supply to the UK, part of the atomic negotiating agenda since at least 1957, was initially shelved because of the atomic energy commission's difficulty in agreeing financial arrangements, and because of concerns on the US side on end-use of the materials. Again the US attempted to use the negotiations to gain access to civil reactor technology.[29] Eventually, in March 1959, UKAEA Chairman Lord Plowden led a delegation to the US which removed the remaining difficulties, and agreement was reached on a barter arrangement. British plutonium, produced in civil reactors, would be exchanged for American materials. An amendment to the 1958 bilateral agreement was therefore signed in May, coming into force in July and agreeing to transfers of fissile material for 'military applications'.[30] The opportunity was taken to make a number of minor revisions to the 1958 agreement, in particular allowing the transfer of non-nuclear components of nuclear weapons – the decision had meanwhile been made in the UK to produce 'anglicised' versions of US designs.

Related indirectly to progress on sharing design information and nuclear materials were Anglo-American discussions on command and control and joint targeting. Here too, considerable progress was made during 1958. The so-called Murphy-Dean agreement, clarifying the arrangements for consultation between the US and UK in the event of serious consideration of the use of nuclear weapons, was an important step forward. Macmillan suggested talks in April, mindful of recent parliamentary questions on US bases and the possibility, in particular, of the use of these bases to mount a nuclear attack without the British government's consent. Robert Murphy, a senior State Department official, and Sir Patrick Dean met to codify an existing set of informal agreements that the use of these bases would be 'a matter for joint decision by the two governments in the light of the circumstances at the time', and to set out consultation and communication procedures. The agreement covered SAC aircraft based in the UK, Thor missiles and those British bombers using US weapons under dual-key arrangements; it was later extended to UK and US tactical aircraft based in the UK and committed to SACEUR.[31] In October 1958, as we shall see, formal joint targeting arrangements for SAC and Bomber Command were also adopted.

Arms control

International efforts to secure a measure of nuclear arms control had been gathering momentum since a series of controversial US H-bomb tests early in 1954, at which time India's President Nehru first proposed the idea of a test moratorium. During 1956 and 1957, the British and American governments repeatedly discussed the testing issue. At a meeting in London of the five-nation UN disarmament commission sub-committee, US ambassador Harold Stassen, Eisenhower's special representative for disarmament, submitted proposals to end both testing and the production of fissile material. Macmillan, having agreed with Eisenhower to align the British and American positions, was somewhat wrong-footed by the fissile-material proposal, and as prospects for agreement improved over the summer of 1957, with Soviet acceptance of the principle of inspection and verification of a test ban, Britain's thermonuclear test series in the Pacific became a race against the clock. Would Aldermaston manage to demonstrate a satisfactory thermonuclear design before testing became impossible?

Pressure on Macmillan was relieved slightly by the successful test of a British two-stage thermonuclear device yielding 1.8Mt on 8 November. At the start of 1958, Macmillan was able to take advantage of continuing improvements in Anglo-American defence relations to suggest to Eisenhower a linkage: 'I must be quite frank and say that from my own government's point of view, we could not accept the abolition or suspension of tests in the present state of our knowledge. But ... if you were prepared, after a revision of the Atomic Energy Act, to make your knowledge available to us, our position would be different'.[32] At this stage, there was no strong flavour of counter-proliferation in the political debate over testing. Macmillan, and indeed the British public, were mainly concerned about the health implications of fall-out. French and later Chinese atomic tests came as no particular surprise, and only in the specific case of West Germany did British policy aim clearly to prevent the spread of nuclear weapons. The Prime Minister nevertheless also made a point to Eisenhower about proliferation: in reaching agreement to suspend tests, 'we would at least improve the chances of stopping the nightmare of all the other countries coming along with their tests, and therefore, in fact, prevent them from becoming nuclear powers'.[33]

By the time Eisenhower secured congressional agreement to the necessary changes to the Atomic Energy Act, paving the way for the US-UK bilateral agreement on nuclear sharing, the Soviet Union was in the middle of a unilateral test suspension. A conference of experts was also making progress in Geneva on the possibility of detecting test-ban violations. The perceived importance of these talks was such that, on the British side, both Sir William Penney and his counterpart Sir John Cockcroft from the civilian Atomic Energy Research Establishment at Harwell were present, although Penney did break to attend high-level meetings in the US on weapons collaboration. The experts' conference ended in agreement that an international system to detect tests was possible. Despite this progress and the Soviet moratorium, Britain conducted a further, larger thermonuclear test on 28 April and ministers agreed to stage another test series in the autumn. Duncan Sandys, asked by the cabinet what conditions he might set for the end of testing by the UK, mentioned the supply of nuclear-weapons information *and* additional fissile material from the US. The chiefs were, at the same time, pressing him for British tests to reduce reliance on American information.[34] Support for testing was muted in Britain, however, compared to the US, where the joint chiefs and the US Atomic Energy Commission were in the middle of a long and bitter campaign to frustrate a test-ban agreement. When Eisenhower on 22 August proposed a moratorium and talks, starting in the autumn, General Nathan Twining, chairman of the joint chiefs, told him, 'this is the worst mistake you've ever made, Mr President. You'll regret it'.[35]

As Ian Clark has argued, the US-UK bilateral agreement of July 1958 was a turning-point in UK policy on testing. Hitherto, Britain had been 'more recalcitrant' than the US on testing; afterwards, it was more enthusiastic. 'As soon as the British government was assured of information from the United States which would serve as a substitute for tests, it could afford to pursue the internationalist objective of a test ban in the comfortable knowledge that such a virtuous policy would also suit British interests'.[36] It would naturally also make the Conservative government more popular at a time of considerable public concern over testing. This was more than just political cynicism, however; it seems clear that Macmillan's commitment to nuclear arms control was strong, and his description of nuclear-weapons collaboration with the US as 'the great prize' needs to be seen in the context of the progress it allowed, not just in building Britain's nuclear arsenal, but in arms control. Britain's test series Grapple-Z finally came to an end on 23 September, and on 31 October, with high hopes, talks began in Geneva. The UK's objectives in Geneva were to ban all tests, immediately and indefinitely, through a comprehensive multi-lateral treaty incorporating detailed control provisions and a verification system – as agreed in the experts' meeting, with control posts worldwide and onsite inspections.[37] It soon became clear that progress was going to be slow.[38] During the Christmas recess of the test-ban talks, objections began to be raised in the US that the Soviet Union could cheat the verification system by conducting small tests in extremely large underground caverns, 'decoupling' the explosion from its surroundings and significantly reducing its seismic signature. Edward Teller, head of the Livermore nuclear-weapons laboratory and one of the test ban's leading opponents, argued that 'in the competition between prohibition and bootlegging, the bootlegger will win'. The 'wild schemes' for Soviet cheating devised in Teller's laboratory perhaps doomed the talks.[39]

By March 1959, Macmillan was coming to realise that a comprehensive test ban might be out of reach, and ministers and officials were discussing instead the possibility of an agreement to end atmospheric testing.[40] At a meeting at Camp David later in the month, the Prime Minister tried to encourage Eisenhower. Macmillan described his recent trip to Moscow – unsanctioned by, and a considerable annoyance to, the President – and pressed for a three-nation summit meeting to resolve outstanding issues with Khrushchev, especially Berlin and the test ban.[41] More than one of Eisenhower's close associates attested to Macmillan's influence over the President in the matter of testing, for example in his 'scepticism about these far-fetched schemes for concealing tests',[42] and it seems the British and American leaders were able to make common cause against some of their more hawkish advisers. In April, when the Geneva talks resumed after an Easter break, the UK and US stated their continuing interest in a comprehensive agreement but also proposed, as an alternative, an atmospheric ban with a commitment to continued joint research on seismology. During June and July, a further experts' meeting convened on the question of detecting high-altitude tests. In London, the cabinet decided there would be no further British tests for as long as worthwhile talks were underway in Geneva, and Home Secretary Rab Butler made an announcement to this effect in parliament.[43]

Towards the end of the year, the joint chiefs in Washington fell in line grudgingly with a new proposal for a comprehensive test ban above a certain threshold, expressed not in nuclear yield but in the Richter scale: 4.75 equated to about 20kt, and was thought to be the limit below which a test could not reliably be detected.[44] This idea was launched in Geneva in February 1960 and caused a renewed bout of optimism. The Soviets suggested that, in addition, an unsupervised moratorium should continue even below the threshold, a proposal that Macmillan found appealing. As the Prime Minister's cherished summit meeting approached during the spring, an agreement seemed within reach, notwithstanding the continuing 'internecine warfare' within the US administration.[45] Unfortunately, as Macmillan, Eisenhower and Khrushchev gathered in Paris in May, the controversy over a downed U-2 spy plane in the Soviet Union doomed both the summit and the short-term prospects for nuclear arms control. At the meeting, western leaders were treated to 'a profane, obscene series of insults directed at Eisenhower, and delivered in Khrushchev's earthy, peasant idiom'. Only those present with a good knowledge of Russian fully appreciated this moment of theatre, for the Soviet leader's interpreters bowdlerised his remarks in translation.[46]

Historians have become critical of Eisenhower's ability to corral the warring factions in Washington during this period, and indeed his commitment to end testing has been questioned.[47] This seems unfair. The President bashed his head against the brick wall of testing for much longer than form alone would have dictated, and 'if [he] had followed JCS advice, there certainly would have been no testing moratorium'.[48] Clark's assessment appears closer to the mark: 'Eisenhower himself was hostage to various bureaucratic interests which felt threatened by the test cessation proposals'.[49] Moreover, 'with scarcely half a term left, [Eisenhower] held little terror for anyone, least of all the national security bureaucracy which could easily resist change for that much longer'.[50] The U-2 incident was just the icing on the cake. The President's distress at the failure of the summit, however, was palpable. As he told his science adviser, George Kistiakowsky, 'very sadly ... he saw nothing worthwhile left for him to do now until the end of his presidency'.[51] Macmillan was no less upset, as his private secretary Philip de Zulueta observed: 'I never saw him more depressed. He was really cast down and glum ... Apart from all the effort he had personally put into it, this was the moment he suddenly realised that Britain counted for nothing; he couldn't move Ike to make a gesture towards Khrushchev ... I think this represented a real watershed in his life'.[52]

During the summer, the test-ban talks continued after a fashion in Geneva, and a rather bizarre suggestion arose of 'calibration tests' of a known yield, to resolve once and for all the various disputes over verification. As a result, for a time in June and July, British officials and scientists became involved in the search for an uncomplicated nuclear weapon of a known yield that could be given to – or at least shown to – the Soviets for testing purposes. The obvious candidate was the first-generation atomic bomb Blue Danube, although it would be difficult to reduce its yield below a certain point. There could be no question of using any more advanced weapon of the kind Aldermaston was now working on.[53] In August 1960, discussion was suspended as the talks in Geneva entered a recess; they were not to resume until the new American administration took office.

Bombers and ballistic missiles

In the early 1950s, on both sides of the Atlantic, delivering nuclear weapons was primarily the business of the manned bomber. Defence policy in the United States in particular was dominated – not too strong a word – by General Curtis E LeMay USAF, Commander-in-Chief of SAC until 1957, then Vice-Chief and finally Chief of the US Air Staff (1961–5). The legendarily taciturn LeMay, was, in the understated words of one academic study, 'not a sophisticated strategist'.[54] He ruthlessly fashioned SAC into a colossal heavy-bomber force with just a single purpose: to destroy the war-making capacity of the Soviet Union, if necessary, in the shortest possible time.

A few visionaries could see that change was coming. Ballistic-missile research in the US dated to before the war, but only began to gather speed and political backing after John von Neumann's USAF Strategic Missiles Evaluation Committee, and a group of influential scientists led by James Killian of the Massachusetts Institute of Technology, both recommended accelerating ballistic missile research. By the time Killian had raised the possibility of an 'atomic Pearl Harbor', the US Navy was ready – with some reservations – to move forward swiftly with the fleet ballistic missile programme, later known as Polaris. The USAF was investigating inter-continental ballistic missiles (ICBMs) including the huge, liquid-fuelled, heavy-payload Atlas and Titan and the smaller solid-fuelled Minuteman. The launch of Sputnik in October 1957 added tremendous urgency to all these developments.

The USAF, however, was in two minds over ballistic missiles. LeMay, for example, was deeply sceptical: missiles were unreliable and inaccurate, and until proven they were only 'political and psychological weapons' or 'penetration aids' for manned bombers.[55] His successor at SAC, Thomas Power, agreed: 'regardless of the missile programme, it is the opinion of this headquarters that the continued advance in the art of manned flight to high altitudes and long ranges should be at all times a priority objective of the air force's development programmes'.[56] The USAF put most of its political capital not into missiles but into faster, longer-range, higher-flying bombers. This was understandable; air officers of LeMay's and Power's generation had seen uninterrupted technological advance in manned bombers since the 1920s. Who was to say this progress was nearing its end?[57] LeMay's feelings on the subject of manned bombers and bomber aircrew were nicely illustrated by his response to a reporter's question on whether his opposition to missiles extended to another new technology, the computer. LeMay recalled telling him: 'I had nothing against computers – we employed a lot of them in the air force. "But", I said, "I never yet found one who was willing to die for his country".'[58] The Air Force poured money into aircraft programmes like the monstrous B-70 Valkyrie, designed to fly at Mach 3 and 75,000ft, and the still more exotic atomic-powered bomber, described colourfully but somewhat obscurely by Secretary of Defense Charles Wilson as 'a shitepoke'.[59]

In Britain, it is fair to say there had been uncertainty about the future of both bombers and ballistic missiles. Three 'V-bombers' – the Vickers Valiant, Avro Vulcan and Handley-Page Victor – were being designed against a 1946 requirement for a jet-powered medium bomber, but in the early 1950s a debate was already raging within the Air Ministry on the likely future vulnerability of these aircraft to Soviet guided-missile defences. Powered bombs were suggested, to increase the stand-off range of the aircraft, and a new requirement was discussed for a low-flying bomber to penetrate beneath radar defences.[60] At this stage, the Air Ministry could not quite make itself believe that fast, high-flying bombers were not still the better bet, and a requirement was issued instead for a supersonic equivalent to the B-70. This was cancelled, however, by Sandys. Meanwhile another requirement had been issued in August 1955 for a medium-range ballistic missile with around 2000nm range, 'complementary to the bomber force'. As Humphrey Wynn has argued, 'the idea of missiles entirely replacing bombers never became accepted doctrine'[61] – at least, not as far as the Air Ministry was concerned – but as the development of the missile proceeded, it became more and more clear that the question could not be ducked. The technical history of the British Blue Streak medium-range ballistic missile will be told in Chapter 2; here, I intend only to give an account of its political history, although the two are inevitably inter-connected. Blue Streak was to face two crises – surviving the first, in autumn 1958, but not the second, in the winter of 1959–60.

By September 1958, when our story opens properly, risk-reduction measures had been cut from the Blue Streak programme for cost reasons, and the in-service date of the missile had been put back from 1963 to 1965. But the date by which the V-bombers were supposed to become vulnerable to Soviet defences stood at 1962; a 'deterrent gap' was looming. Sandys presented options to the Defence Committee: accelerating Blue Streak, which seemed difficult; or halting it in favour of a new collaborative project with the US. Perhaps, in the years before this could bear fruit, an interim system might be procured – either Blue Steel Mk.2, a long-range British powered bomb; or Thor, a US 1500nm-range ballistic missile, already planned for the RAF with warheads under American peacetime custody but now proposed 'without strings' – i.e., with no American in the firing chain.[62] The committee agreed that, pending further investigation, work on Blue Streak should be 'unobtrusively retarded'.[63] Sandys then travelled to Washington, where he secured from Defense Secretary McElroy a clear agreement that Thor could be purchased by the UK for 'no-strings' deployment with a British warhead.[64] He was also told that the Americans might cooperate in developing new and improved versions of the missile, but was concerned by their anxiety to pursue this idea in a NATO, rather than a bilateral Anglo-American context.[65]

Brundrett, accompanying the minister, seemed to have heard a different story: the Americans would definitely be abandoning further development of intermediate-range ballistic missiles (IRBMs), including Thor, and so Blue Streak was the only suitable missile available to the UK.[66] Brundrett's account, differing subtly from the formal record of Sandys's talks, was clearly intended to further the cause of the favoured British missile. Neither Brundrett nor Sandys was remotely interested in the idea of a NATO or European collaborative missile development. At the Defence Board on 16 October, Brundrett argued that 'the best way of ensuring the indefinite continuance of an effective independent deterrent would be to continue with Blue Streak'.[67] Selkirk, the First Lord, dissented from this conclusion, regretting later that there had been insufficient time to express 'the broader Admiralty arguments against the present nuclear deterrent programme'.[68]

In November, Sandys twice went back to the Defence Committee, now strongly advocating Blue Streak. He put forward various technical arguments, for example on warheads. Thor was no better in itself than Blue Streak, but the particulars of its warhead were now available to the UK, under the new bilateral atomic sharing arrangements, and so this warhead could be fitted to the British missile, allowing a range extension or penetration improvements. Blue Streak might also be improved with new storeable liquid propellants. Although Selkirk outlined the merits of Polaris as an alternative,[69] Sandys pointed out that, in the current state of knowledge, any such solid-fuelled missile as Polaris would inevitably have shorter range and a smaller payload than the liquid-fuelled Blue Streak. The cost, and indeed the feasibility, of Polaris were still unclear. The Polaris warhead, meanwhile, was very extravagant in fissile material. Finally, Blue Streak was more than just a missile – it was 'an investment in the facilities and acquisition of knowledge for long-range rockets generally'. Macmillan, as we have seen, made a rather long philosophical digression about independent deterrence at this point, but neither Sandys nor Brundrett could bear to think of Britain's giving up in the missile and space race.[70]

Blue Streak survived this first cancellation crisis, but the next round of politicking over deterrent systems started almost immediately. At the first Chiefs of Staff meeting of 1959, Mountbatten suggested a new study of delivery systems, to be chaired by Sir Richard Powell. Boyle and his vice-chief, Sir Edmund Hudleston, naturally preferred the DRPC – chaired by Brundrett – to conduct such a study, but Mountbatten's proposal won the day.[71] With Sandys making valiant efforts to shelve the Powell study, Macmillan had to insist on its going ahead.[72] In July, therefore, the British Nuclear Deterrent Study Group (BNDSG or, to at least one wag, 'benders'[73]) was finally set up, charged 'to consider how the British controlled contribution to the deterrent can most effectively be maintained in the future, and to make recommendations'.[74] The BNDSG assumed a deterrent criterion of 50 per cent damage to each of 40 Soviet cities, based explicitly on the then planned capability of the V-bombers with Blue Steel Mk.1 powered bombs.[75]

Not every twist and turn of the BNDSG's deliberations can be analysed here in detail, but its 'interim' report, delivered at the end of 1959, was an important document and deserves close attention. The technical vulnerability of the different delivery systems on offer – on the ground, before firing; and in the air after launch – had been central to the BNDSG's work. The central, unspoken assumption was that a vulnerable deterrent system would not be credible and would not deter. By 1965, the report concluded, V-bombers armed with Blue Steel Mk.1 would, in the event of war, suffer 50 per cent casualties from Soviet missile defences, and the 40-city damage criterion could no longer be met. Three options for deterrence beyond this point were studied: V-bombers with Blue Steel Mk.2; V-bombers with the US air-launched ballistic missile WS 138A; and Blue Streak. None would be entirely satisfactory. Blue Streak in particular would be vulnerable to pre-emptive attack on its bases in the UK, unless the missiles were held at 30 seconds' readiness to fire – a posture that could not be sustained for long. It might take 300 or more Soviet megaton weapons directed at the UK to neutralise Blue Streak, but the missile 'would therefore be effective only if it were fired first, for example, in reply to a Soviet attack with conventional weapons'. Arguably, the V-bomber force was almost equally vulnerable to a pre-emptive strike, but if there were *just* enough time to get the bombers off the ground then they could be held in the air while a political decision was made to retaliate. Blue Streak, conversely, could not be recalled once launched, and there was no suggestion that a British government would feel comfortable with an irrevocable launch-on-warning posture – not when the alarm might be false.

The BNDSG went on to list the options available after about 1970, including Polaris and a new long-endurance aircraft using WS 138A, 'but the adoption of either course would depend on the present United States authorities agreeing to cooperate with us, on their successors honouring the agreements made, and on the weapons, when fully developed, matching up to the present theoretical designs. It would also mean that our deterrent capability would be known to be completely dependent on United States weapons'. Concerns about independence and 'fire-first' were crucial to the report's recommendations:

(c) If a 'fire first' weapon is acceptable the development of the Blue Streak missile should continue ...
(d) ... ministers should decide whether further work to enable Blue Streak to be fired from underground sites should proceed.
(e) Ministers should consider whether it would be acceptable for this country to be seen to be wholly dependent between 1965 and 1970 upon the United States for the weapons (apart from the warheads) used by the British contribution to the nuclear deterrent.

(f) If the answer to (e) is 'yes', an approach should be made to the United States government with a view –
  (i) to securing that the V-bombers should be armed with WS 138A by 1966; or
  (ii) to obtaining a number of Polaris-firing submarines by a comparable date
(g) If the answer to (e) is 'yes' and when satisfactory arrangements as to dates and quantities on either of the lines proposed in (f) have been negotiated, Blue Streak should be cancelled.
(h) If the answer to (e) is 'no' or if satisfactory arrangements on either of the lines proposed in (f) cannot be negotiated, a thin period for some time after 1965 will be inevitable and the choice will lie between –
  (i) accepting the limitations of Blue Streak and proceeding with its development and deployment; and
  (ii) cancelling it and accepting whatever gap there may be in the continuity of the British-controlled contribution to the nuclear deterrent.[76]

The BNDSG rightly concluded that such decisions were political, but its attempts to exclude political assessment from its deliberations had led it to ignore some significant points. Three in particular seem worthy of attention. First, an Air Ministry official had pointed out at one stage that 'Mr K[hrushchev] is more likely to be impressed by a ballistic rocket or at least by a mixed deterrent force that by a V-[bomber] force'.[77] This valid and interesting point about the missile-obsessed Soviet leader seems to have been set aside altogether. A second point about the BNDSG's conclusions was made more often and more widely. The report noted that 'before embarking on a pre-emptive attack on the United Kingdom alone, the Soviet leaders would need to be satisfied that they could discount the possibility of retaliation from the United States, whose bases the Soviet forces could not neutralise by pre-emptive attack'.[78] But the BNDSG was talking about a Soviet pre-emptive attack on the UK with 300 or 400 three-megaton nuclear weapons. In what possible political context did the group imagine such an attack? The US response would be at best unpredictable, and in practical terms the fall-out would devastate eastern Europe and the Soviet Union.[79] Third, the 'independent' UK-only deterrent scenario – however far-fetched – underlay many of the report's weaker assumptions. As the Scientific Adviser to the Army Council pointed out at one point, if the V-bombers were attacking peripheral military targets in a joint Anglo-American atomic offensive, they would not be so vulnerable as in an independent attack on cities, and there would be no need to spend vast amounts on their replacement at all.[80] Zuckerman complained to Watkinson, now Minister of Defence, that such Clausewitzian thinking about political scenarios had been 'set aside as something that falls into some field of "religious" discussion'.[81] Richard Chilver, a senior MoD official, also noted some aspects of unreality in commenting on the report for Watkinson, concluding that Blue Streak would probably be acceptable in the real world. Tellingly, however, he also offered the opinion that 'obviously an invulnerable deterrent would be better'.[82] We shall see that the rather abstract pursuit of 'betterness' was a characteristic of the British nuclear weapons programme.

While the BNDSG had been meeting, the Air Ministry had formed an internal Strategic Scientific Policy Committee to look at the same issues. Zuckerman became chairman of this group, and thereby re-entered the strategic-bombing debate, after a break of several years. The group's conclusions were similar to the BNDSG's: a new and highly mobile and survivable missile, either air-launched or submarine-launched, would have to succeed land-based missiles and/or the V-bombers by 1970. After a brief flirtation with the submarine, the committee turned to look in detail at the requirement for a successor aircraft to the V-bombers.[83] This would need long endurance but only moderate performance to mount a constant air patrol, or use 'temporary and random stops on overseas bases so as to present such a multiplicity of possible targets that their destruction would pose an insuperable military problem'.[84] Like the USAF, the Air Ministry had a visceral preference for new bombers over missiles.

Politics and force levels

Two other important political issues for Blue Streak emerged during 1959. The first was basing. The Air Ministry had been assuming from an early date that Blue Streak would use hardened underground launch facilities, and as time wore on it became necessary to look for sites and approach the Treasury for funding. Approval was not, however, forthcoming, and a sharp series of exchanges followed between Sandys, now Minister of Aviation, and Heathcoat-Amory. As the chancellor primly noted, 'the whole situation is the reverse of satisfactory'.[85] The cost of underground basing was simply being used by the Treasury as a delaying tactic; officials there were hoping for an early report from the BNDSG recommending cancellation. It became clear, however, that there were also civil-defence implications of underground basing. On grounds of geology and suitability for underground works, the Air Ministry were looking at sites in the west country. However, because of the prevailing westerly winds over the British Isles, any nuclear attack on these sites would create a serious fall-out problem over densely populated southern England. This concern was new, for it did not apply so obviously to the existing V-bomber bases in Lincolnshire and East Anglia.[86] No final decision was ever made on Blue Streak deployment, and early in 1960 a wide range of sites was still being considered. One was at Upavon in Wiltshire, 'a beautiful village set in the middle of Salisbury plain, with picturesque cottages and gorgeous scenery'.[87] Politicians had little appetite for despoiling chocolate-box rural England with Blue Streak silos; not when the whole tenor of Whitehall discussion was the missile's vulnerability to overwhelming Soviet nuclear attack. Rather more prosaically, they were also concerned about the vulnerability of 60 widely scattered Blue Streak silos to incursions from anti-nuclear protesters.[88]

The other new factor in 1959 was WS 138A, later and better known as Skybolt. The technical history of this ambitious solid-fuelled air-launched ballistic missile will be covered in more detail in Chapter 2. Its political importance was in providing an alternative to Blue Streak; and one of increasing interest to the RAF. British scientists had been briefed in Washington in November 1958 on a USAF requirement for a 1000nm-range air-to-surface missile.[89] The Air Ministry continued to monitor progress as work continued, thinking that this missile might be relevant to its own requirements for long-range powered bombs. When the BNDSG reported at the end of 1959, the weapon system was described as unproven, and it was not clear that it would meet its stated range and accuracy requirements.[90] Britain's interest (or not) in the system was sensitive to these two requirements in particular, partly because of the state of British warhead design. Heavy missile warheads would reduce range, but light warheads would do less damage and require greater accuracy. On 14 January 1960, British embassy observers attended one of a series of committee hearings in Washington on WS 138A. They reported that a 900nm range had already been achieved in tests of a simple air-launched ballistic missile, and that service entry might now be possible in 1964 or even 1963, rather than 1966 as previously suspected.[91] George Ward, the Secretary of State for Air, visited the US later in January, discovering a new enthusiasm:

> I am convinced that we must have it or something like it to ensure that the V-bomber force, in which we have invested so many millions of pounds, remains a worthwhile and effective contribution to the

deterrent in the years after 1965. During my visit ... I had the opportunity of discussing WS 138A with the Secretary of the Air Force, with Strategic Air Command ... and also with the manufacturers. It is quite clear now that the Americans are continuing with the project, and also that it will be compatible with carriage on the V-bombers.[92]

This was the kind of evidence the Air Ministry needed for a sudden change of horses in the delivery-systems handicap. Discussing the BNDSG's paper on 2 February 1960, the Chiefs of Staff now agreed a paper for Watkinson, damning Blue Streak as a 'fire-first' weapon and recommending its cancellation: 'we attach no military value to Blue Streak as a weapon'. They also noted there was now 'much more reassuring information about WS 138A than was available to the study group', and they recommended that 'our initial approach should be designed to secure this weapon'.[93] On 24 February, the Defence Committee confirmed the decision to cancel Blue Streak, subject to satisfactory discussions with the US.[94] On 13 April – with Eisenhower's agreement to offer Skybolt in the bag – Watkinson announced the cancellation to a stormy House of Commons.[95]

Why was Blue Streak cancelled? In his book *Politics and force levels*, Desmond Ball addresses some of the nuclear-weapons procurement decisions of the Kennedy administration. He argues convincingly that, despite an image of rational analysis projected by Secretary McNamara and his 'whiz-kids' in the Pentagon, Kennedy's decisions were best explained in political, not logical terms. Despite the many careful strategic arguments presented in declassified British documents, Ball's is also a useful frame of reference for the Blue Streak cancellation. It is notable that the political cast of characters had changed significantly since the end of 1958, when the missile had last been in danger. Sandys had been moved. Brundrett left office on 31 December 1959, the day the BNDSG's report was finalised. Zuckerman, the new chief scientist, was no friend of Blue Streak. Brundrett took the stand at the Royal United Service Institution (RUSI), in a widely reported lecture: 'I have not the slightest doubt that if Russia really concentrated her efforts on the destruction of our deterrent forces, she could do so. But does anyone think such a suggestion makes any sense? ... my last word on the subject of rockets, satellites and military thinking is that we in this country cannot possibly afford to stop the development of Blue Streak'.[96] But despite these fine words, the missile's arch-protector of the year before was now powerless.

Of the missile's likely enemies, one – the Royal Navy – was equivocal. An Admiralty official wrote in April 1960 that 'our prime objective must be to ensure that Blue Streak is removed from the programme'.[97] But naval officers were nervous about Polaris as an alternative, partly because they had no strong belief in the deterrent and partly because, if it were adopted in place of Blue Streak, they would have to pay for it. In October 1958, Mountbatten had hesitated because 'to bid for Polaris would unbalance our arguments concerning nuclear sufficiency'.[98] Over the winter of 1959–60, he maintained a studious silence. His own files on the Blue Streak cancellation survive, but his personal views – at a time when he had a golden opportunity to rubbish Skybolt and push for Polaris – are not to be found in them. Curiously, as we shall see, only later – around June 1960 – did he and Watkinson become more active in putting Polaris back on the political agenda.[99] Selkirk remained an enthusiast for Polaris, but the new First Sea Lord, Lambe, advised caution: 'I am far from certain that it is wise for us at this moment to give this subject another stir-up'.[100] Selkirk left office in October 1959 and his successor, Lord Carrington, made less running in the deterrent debate. In early 1960, Lambe fell ill and his stand-in, Sir Walter Couchman, drafted a note to the Washington embassy which is worth quoting at some length – especially as it includes personal opinions (here in italics) which were removed from the final version of the letter:

> After Dermot Boyle left as [Chief of the Air Staff], the Chiefs of Staff agreed unanimously that Blue Streak was militarily a nonsense ... The Admiralty line (very successful too under Charles Lambe) is to be completely objective ... in contrast to the incessant and often foolish Air Ministry intrigue and false presentation of facts which I'm ashamed to say still goes on ... *my own feelings are frankly of some doubt whether Polaris (or any British native deterrent) will follow the V-bomber force. It seems curious to me to expect the Pentagon to supply us with weapons for an independent British deterrent whose purpose, quite frankly, is more to influence State Department policy than to frighten the Russians ... Their reasons, however, are their business. Naturally there are variations on the Polaris theme, including building them ourselves. But the more we go into this, the greater are the problems we must face, including a serious disruption of our capacity (design staff wise) to rebuild the conventional navy.*[101]

Small wonder then that, as Clark has shown, the Admiralty mounted no strong bid for Polaris in 1960.[102] The problem could be shelved, and naval officers acquiesced in the deal to swap Blue Streak for Skybolt. Adverse Admiralty views on Skybolt were muted, certainly compared to those coming from the MoA – where Strath, the Permanent Secretary, lamented that: 'If we stop the development of Blue Streak there is no way of avoiding a situation that in terms of industry is little short of disastrous'.[103]

Couchman's reference to Boyle is especially interesting. Boyle, in the words of one observer, 'represented that "cavalry school" of air officer most attached to the traditional appearance of an air force'; in the words of another, 'by repeatedly proclaiming his own belief in the future of the manned aircraft he made a major personal contribution to the national debate ... a timely demonstration of inspired leadership'.[104] Boyle's memoirs make no specific mention of Blue Streak, although they highlight his attachment to manned aircraft and his quarrel with Sandys.[105] Pike, the incoming air chief at the start of 1960, was meanwhile described by Wynn as 'single-mindedly enthusiastic about Skybolt', and by Maurice Dean, the Air Ministry Permanent Secretary of the time, as an opponent of Blue Streak.[106] In February, Pike made a revealing comment: 'I think the time has come for us to tell the Ministry of Aviation that we have serious ideas of introducing the VC-10 as a follow-on to the Comet and also as a carrier for Skybolt'.[107]

The cancellation of Blue Streak is usually explained by reference to the BNDSG's strategic arguments about independence, vulnerability and fire-first.[108] As we have seen, these were based on assumptions that many, even at the time, knew to be far-fetched. The *political* explanation for the cancellation, on the other hand, seems to be a simple one. With Brundrett gone, Sandys was isolated in his support for the ballistic missile. Once they discovered there was a viable alternative to Blue Streak – perhaps even using a brand-new manned aircraft – the RAF and Air Ministry, led by Boyle and Pike, turned against it. This political reality was reflected in a note from Watkinson to Sandys: 'I am afraid Dermot sold the pass here to begin with'.[109] Watkinson and Macmillan could secure Sandys's agreement to cancellation by offering the sop of potential uses in space, whilst saving the political and financial cost of underground deployment. This was a momentous decision. For a short time after the cancellation, the political future of the British deterrent appeared seriously to be in question.

Political opposition to nuclear weapons

Public concern over the development, possession and above all the testing of nuclear weapons had been seen in Britain, rather surprisingly, as early as 1943 – well before their existence was widely known.[110] It only began to grow strongly in the years after 1954, largely on the back of controversy over H-bomb testing. On 15 January 1958, the Campaign for Nuclear Disarmament (CND) was established, holding its first public meeting a month later at Central Hall in Westminster, attended by as many as 5000 people.[111] The leadership of CND was scarcely less socially exclusive than Macmillan's cabinet: of its president and 19 executive members in its first year, 14 featured in *Who's Who* and three were peers of the realm. The campaign had no formal membership, and there are few statistics to analyse, but all commentators agree that its appeal was overwhelmingly to the politically active middle classes. David Marquand dismissed some CND sympathisers as 'the slightly faded political driftwood left behind by the storms of the last 30 years ... former subscribers to the left book club, former ardent supporters of the Spanish republic, former opponents of the foreign policy of Ernest Bevin and of the rearmament of Western Germany'.[112] But CND's annual Easter marches to or from Aldermaston still attracted many thousands of people – perhaps 100,000 in the peak year of 1960. CND might not have been on the scale of, say, chartism or suffragism, but it still qualified as a genuine mass movement and it aroused considerable passion. One clergyman was heard to shout to passing marchers, from the safety of his vicarage: 'Where do you think you're going? – your policy will take us to Siberia'.[113]

Like many single-issue campaigns, CND was not especially coherent, and its chairman, Canon John Collins of St Paul's Cathedral in London, struggled to control its more radical adherents, such as the Direct Action Committee who fought with Irish workmen and RAF personnel at North Pickenham in Norfolk at the end of 1958, and the Committee of 100 who staged sit-down protests, most famously in Trafalgar Square in London on 17 September 1961. Nor did CND offer a single alternative political or military strategy for Britain, its adherents veering between neutralism and a vague commitment to a non-nuclear NATO.

Popular opposition to Britain's nuclear weapons appears to have peaked in the spring of 1960, after the cancellation of Blue Streak, when for the first and only time a full third of those polled by Gallup advocated giving them up (51 per cent meanwhile thought Britain should keep them or pool them with NATO). Popular *concern* peaked a little later, in September 1961, when the superpowers ended their nuclear test moratorium and Gallup asked: 'Does all this talk about H-bombs, rockets, satellites and guided missiles worry you a lot, a little, or not at all?' Just 27 per cent replied 'a lot', although a more phlegmatic 35 per cent said 'not at all'.[114] The full measure of the threat posed by CND to the nuclear establishment is nicely captured in a story from February 1961, when Lord Russell made to nail a list of demands to the door of the Ministry of Defence. A helpful civil servant appeared from within to offer him, instead, a roll of sticky tape.[115] Even an internal CND assessment found after the Trafalgar Square protest that 'we have become a public spectacle ... a rowdy show ... for the interest and amusement of a majority who are not with us'.[116]

Britain's opposition Labour party, however, did not have the luxury of such detachment. CND's core support, although middle-class, were natural Labour voters and the question of what to do about nuclear disarmament therefore found its way, in time, onto the party's agenda. Labour's official policy going into the 1959 general election advocated multi-lateral disarmament and deplored nuclear testing, but included a strong commitment to NATO and (implicitly) supported Britain's ownership of its own nuclear weapons.[117] Not for nothing did Sandys describe Labour as '99.5 per cent sound' on defence.[118] Labour politicians repeatedly and specifically claimed that the Blue Streak cancellation was an important turning-point.[119] Labour policy was now revised, partly to appeal to party left-wingers but partly too because an opportunity to question Britain's ability to sustain a credible nuclear force had now arisen: 'For the Labour party the end of Blue Streak served as a potent catalyst'.[120] Labour's new policy favoured a non-nuclear Britain within a nuclear NATO. Dramatically, and most damagingly for Labour leader Hugh Gaitskell, this policy was rejected by the party's annual conference at Scarborough in October 1960, in favour of no-strings unilateral nuclear disarmament and (implicitly) abandonment of the NATO alliance.[121] Trouble had been brewing for several months as trades unions large and small made clear their voting intentions. Gaitskell, in the assessment of one of his recent biographers, privately 'gave only tentative support to the British bomb and had misgivings about it on financial and technical grounds'.[122] He felt unable, however, to press these points publicly, not wishing to create an impression of Labour weakness in the eyes of the electorate. He also believed strongly that to undermine NATO would simply be wrong, and rightly perceived, finally, a serious challenge to his leadership over this and other issues. He 'thought he was arguing to try to save his country from pacifism, the Western Alliance from neutralism and the Labour Party from permanent electoral oblivion as well as his career from ending'.[123]

Gaitskell made a justifiably famous speech in Scarborough, lost the subsequent votes,[124] but salvaged his career. A Campaign for Democratic Socialism was set up soon after by Labour right-wingers including Tony Crosland and Roy Jenkins. Following a great deal of behind-the-scenes work, the conference's decision – anyway not binding on the party leadership – was overturned the following year at Blackpool. Again the block votes of the trades unions determined the outcome, and whereas such hot-heads as the shale miners and the packing-case makers remained true to unilateralism, their more influential brothers the railwaymen, shop-workers and most importantly Bill Carron's amalgamated engineering union had switched allegiance.[125]

In truth, middle-class CND's attempt to hijack the Labour party was doomed at the grass roots because of the conservatism, on defence and foreign policy issues, of working-class voters. It is interesting meanwhile that CND's followership was exceeded in these years by the number of volunteers for civil defence duty – as many as 600,000 citizens.[126] CND also, more generally, failed to lobby successfully in the sense of connecting with policy-makers: 'private consultation with decision-makers, discreet and persistent, must be the ideal of those seeking to change or maintain particular policies'.[127] Nevertheless Labour's 'policy for peace', endorsed in Blackpool, had shifted materially since 1958. The opposition now committed Britain to 'cease the attempt to remain an independent nuclear power, since this neither strengthened the alliance nor is it now a sensible use of our limited resources'.[128] Cabinet ministers no longer described Labour as '99.5 per cent sound', and were able instead to make political capital over the opposition's divisions.

NATO strategy

Except for the rather special case of the possible independent use of Britain's V-bomber force against 'national' targets, which in strategic terms had little clear foundation, British nuclear strategy in the late 1950s was alliance strategy. As a member of the North Atlantic Treaty Organisation (NATO), Baghdad Pact (after 1959 the Central Treaty Organisation or CENTO) and the South-East Asian Treaty Organisation (SEATO), Britain was committed to support alliance military plans, including with nuclear weapons.

NATO in 1958 was a politically mature alliance facing contradictory military planning pressures. Every allied government wished to signal its determination to resist a Soviet attack in Europe. But how were they to plan this resistance? On the one hand, Britain and other alliance countries wished to minimise the financial cost of their commitments to NATO. In the Sandys white paper of 1957, this wish was translated into a reduction in conventional forces and a correspondingly increased reliance on the threat of 'massive retaliation' with strategic nuclear forces. On the other hand, many in the alliance saw the weakness, in strategic terms, of a doctrine of overwhelming force in response to the least provocation. By extension, they felt that an unrealistic strategy undermined the political credibility of the alliance. Surely, subversive or paramilitary moves, or minor harrassment by Soviet forces, for example in Berlin, would not merit the full weight of atomic attack in response? On the other hand, where exactly should the line be drawn? Perhaps a full and ruinously expensive spectrum of appropriate responses would be necessary? At no point in the cold war did NATO truly resolve this basic dilemma, and the story of NATO strategy is one of debate over time, veering sometimes towards one or other of the extremes.

NATO's overall strategic concept for the defence of Europe and the North Atlantic was set down in the alliance military council's planning document MC 14/2, agreed in May 1957.[129] This concept gave expression to a political directive agreed by NATO foreign ministers in December 1956, and in particular formally recognised, for the first time, the possibility of limited forms of aggression, against which a non-nuclear response would be conceivable. MC 14/2 was thus, to some extent, a retreat from the 'massive retaliation' doctrine:

> The Soviets might ... conclude that the only way in which they could profitably further their aim would be to initiate operations with limited objectives, such as infiltrations, incursions or hostile local actions in the NATO area, covertly or overtly supported by themselves, trusting that the Allies in their collective desire to prevent a general conflict would either limit their reactions accordingly or not react at all. Under these circumstances NATO must be prepared to deal immediately with such situations without necessarily having recourse to nuclear weapons.

The document made it clear, however, that 'in no case is there a NATO concept of limited war with the Soviets'. It retained a strong focus on likely operations in general war, in which, it said:

> NATO defence depends upon an immediate exploitation of our nuclear capability, whether or not the Soviets employ nuclear weapons. The Allies, in the initial and critical phase, would need to conduct a series of mutually dependent land, sea and air campaigns of maximum intensity. The objectives of these campaigns which include the nuclear strategic campaign would be to defend the populations, territories, vital sea areas and offensive striking power of NATO, and to destroy the ability and the will of the enemy to pursue

general war … Following the advantage gained by NATO in this initial onslaught, there would be a period of reorganization, rehabilitation and the assembly of residual resources to accomplish the remaining necessary military tasks leading to a termination of hostilities.

NATO strategy envisaged therefore a short and intense nuclear phase, lasting perhaps 30 days, followed by an uncertain period of 'broken-backed warfare', especially at sea 'where anti-submarine operations are likely to continue for an indefinite period'. I have argued elsewhere that the idea of broken-backed warfare had a good deal more practical and intellectual foundation than many have given it credit for.[130] Nevertheless the concept was somewhat controversial, and many in the UK, especially among the air lobby, found the notion of even 30 days of conflict against the Soviet Union unrealistic.

Shield forces on the central front would officially play a containing role during the 30-day offensive, 'until the will and ability of the enemy to pursue general war has been destroyed by our nuclear counter-offensive', and would themselves be provided with 'an integrated nuclear capability' for 'operations … generating appropriate targets for Allied nuclear weapons'. MC 14/2 went on to list objectives for other theatres of operations, including the British Isles – which would, first and foremost, 'provide an effective base for, and effective protection of, the strategic nuclear counter-offensive capability'.[131]

The nuclear focus of MC 14/2 is undeniable, although commentators have been quick to see, in the document's references to minor incursions, the origins of the later flexible-response doctrine. General Lauris S Norstad USAF, NATO Supreme Allied Commander in Europe (SACEUR) between 1956 and early 1963, was uncomfortable with the MC 14/2 strategy for a number of reasons, and was to mount a campaign over several years both to increase conventional shield forces and to organise a NATO nuclear force to support and channel the nuclear ambitions in particular of the British, French and Germans.[132] In contemplating the provision of adequate shield forces, Norstad faced two obstacles in particular: the cost of providing new conventional capabilities, and the growing nuclearisation, in practice, of those forces he already had at his disposal. NATO had announced, as early as 1954, the need for tactical nuclear weapons to halt a Soviet conventional advance, and US forces had taken delivery of substantial numbers by 1958. In addition, specifically to fight a tactical nuclear battle, the US Army was talking about infantry divisions in Europe on 'pentomic' lines, with five small dispersed battle-groups in place of three infantry regiments, and integrated nuclear artillery, both guns and missiles. Similarly, the British Army of the Rhine (BAOR) revised its doctrine for the corps-level tactical battle on nuclear lines: 'the time has now arrived when the quantity and quality of nuclear weapons becoming available on the battlefield impose a necessity for completely new tactical methods. These are weapons of a new order, and minor adjustments in outlook are no longer sufficient'. Mobility, dispersal, deception, independence of operation and firepower were key to tactical units. 'Nuclear artillery will become the predominant arm on the battlefield with armour and infantry in support of it ... planning will tend to be centred around the positioning of the nuclear missiles to achieve the aim'. Defensive operations, intended to destroy the enemy's ability to cross natural obstacles, would be followed by a nuclear counterstroke. The army recognised that 'the standard of leadership at all levels will need to be of the very highest order. Wide dispersion and isolation, lack of information and fear of the unknown will in the future greatly increase the tension on all ranks in battle; and these will be in addition to the awe inspiring effects of enemy nuclear explosions which will occur throughout the battle area'. This new nuclear doctrine, circulated in what was known colloquially as the army's 'purple pamphlet', was described by one ex-general turned peace campaigner as 'a brilliant attempt to make sense of an impossible situation'.[133] Zuckerman, for one, would have disagreed strongly with this assessment.

NATO plans now began to be made to defend the lines of the Weser and Lech, and no longer simply to fall back on the Rhine.[134] Air forces, meanwhile, would tend to be involved in deep nuclear strike operations, and not in direct support of land fighting. This assumption reflected a dismal lack of air-land cooperation in British doctrine and operations, dating back to the Second World War and before. Norstad too found that all US tactical aircraft in Europe were now nuclear-capable, and that plans assumed most would be withheld, on the outbreak of war, pending the start of nuclear operations against 'interdiction' targets behind enemy lines.[135] Again, planning for air operations harked back to the war when the effectiveness of interdiction attacks had been demonstrated (to the satisfaction of US planners) in the run-up to the Normandy landings.[136] Although Norstad 'constantly reiterated his expansive view of the role of the shield forces in NATO strategy',[137] he therefore faced a number of problems in weaning allied planners away from a strongly nuclear focus. Duncan Sandys, at the NATO council meeting in December 1958, restated forcefully the British policy of relying on nuclear deterrence: 'the safety of the west continues to depend on our ability to convince the Russians that a major attack upon any member of NATO will provoke a massive nuclear retaliation'.[138] Such views were not inconsistent with NATO's official strategy, but Norstad would undoubtedly have put greater emphasis on shield forces.

At sea, too, Britain was now challenging NATO orthodoxy. Admiral Jerauld Wright USN, Supreme Allied Commander Atlantic (SACLANT), included in his emergency defence plan throughout this period offensive action for sea control and anti-submarine warfare, 'nuclear strikes against naval targets', and then in the broken-backed phase 'tasks required for reorganisation, re-supply and ... necessary military tasks leading to the conclusion of war'.[139] Although in the mid-1950s the Royal Navy had placed much faith in the broken-backed war concept, such preparations were now seen as an unnecessary expense. Interestingly, however, as Mountbatten pointed out to Watkinson late in 1960, the US Navy was now interested in shifting its doctrinal position away from a nuclear 'phase I' and post-nuclear 'phase II', and towards 'what might be called "phase minus one"'.[140] Naval interest in *pre*-nuclear operations, and shield forces, was growing.

Nuclear sufficiency

In highlighting the possibility of conventional operations, Mountbatten was building on a long series of debates within Whitehall on the implications of 'nuclear sufficiency' – a future condition in which both east and west would possess enough nuclear weapons to destroy the other, and in which global war would become a more and more appalling prospect. The Joint Intelligence Committee was predicting, in 1958, that a state of nuclear sufficiency might exist as early as 1962.[141] Reactions to this state of affairs depended upon one's original point of view. Naval thinkers, inevitably, tended to line up in opposition to their RAF counterparts. As early as 1957, Mountbatten was prepared to argue semi-publicly that in future 'the concept of "nuclear stalemate" may be so firmly embedded in our way of thought that the deterrents themselves may have begun to rust in our hands, and a new concept of conventional warfare may be arising'.[142] During 1958, Mountbatten and Templer began to attack the prevailing orthodoxy that nuclear forces to prevent global war demanded first priority in the Whitehall battle for resources. James Mackay, a senior Admiralty official, summarised the arguments:

> It is only a matter of time before the United States and Russia move into a state of nuclear parity or sufficiency ... In this state it is hardly conceivable that either side will ever use the nuclear weapon

... [the Soviet Union] will continue to back up even more effectively her successes in the cold war and to use more confidently and openly her forces in limited wars, without believing that her activity will provoke nuclear attack upon her. If this is so, the west must look to her conventional defences.[143]

At the Defence Board, Selkirk pursued the line further: 'a reappraisal of the emphasis given to nuclear retaliation within Britain's defence programme was essential'. The Secretary of State for Air was naturally 'unable to accept this thesis'.[144] Dickson, the CDS, reported sadly to Sandys that 'there is a complete difference of opinion between the First Sea Lord and the CIGS on the one side, and the Chief of the Air Staff (CAS) on the other. Recent discussions have tended to increase the divergence and I see no likelihood of agreement'.[145] Sandys summoned the service chiefs for a discussion which lasted for nearly three hours. Stratton, the Vice-Chief of the Imperial General Staff, substituted for his new boss, 'Frankie' Festing, and reported that 'the whole thing ended up as far as I was concerned in a scene of intense confusion ... it will be interesting to see what the minutes contain'.[146] Mountbatten wanted no less than a re-ordering of Britain's strategic priorities, promoting preparations for conventional war above the contribution to the western deterrent, with surviving a global war now a distant third. Complex strategic arguments were aired: whether the United States, or indeed Britain, would defend Europe if cities at home were at risk of Soviet nuclear attack. Sandys evidently felt the need to defend the whole concept of Britain's nuclear deterrent,[147] and indeed Mountbatten and Templer were close to expressing outright opposition to Britain's stated defence policy: 'While we accept a political contribution to the western deterrent, we absolutely oppose the concept of an independent UK nuclear deterrent if this means a strategic nuclear stockpile complete with delivery systems entirely under the control of HMG, and fully adequate by itself to inflict unacceptable devastation on Russia'.[148] The rebel chiefs were more concerned by the prospect of limited war outside Europe than conventional war on the central front.

During 1959, such unorthodox discussions of the deterrent within the defence establishment were moderated. Mackay wrote a new Admiralty paper, counselling caution.[149] In discussing this paper, Sir Charles Lambe, the new First Sea Lord, asked, 'should we come out into the open at once and say that the Admiralty could no longer support an independent United Kingdom contribution to the deterrent, or should we play for time?'[150] Their lordships were unable to agree a definite position. The nuclear sufficiency argument continued, however, outside Whitehall.

Sir John Cowley, a serving lieutenant-general and, as Controller of Munitions, one of the most senior officials in the MoA, broke cover in November 1959 to criticise the official independent-deterrent line in a lecture at RUSI. First outlining his practical opposition to the notion of fighting a limited war with nuclear weapons, Cowley turned next to the strategic deterrent. In a state of nuclear sufficiency, he argued:

> The objectives which can be seized by either side short of provoking mutual annihilation have grown more substantial. The range of conditions with which the deterrent can deal has narrowed until all sorts of unpleasant things can happen without the deterrent being used, or even being threatened with conviction.

As to whether possession of an independent British deterrent was advisable, he went on to note that:

> Our deterrent now costs something like 20 per cent of the total defence budget ... It is therefore necessary to assess the minimum credible size of the deterrent necessary to maintain an unacceptable threat, and to resist the temptation to increase it above this minimum. If, having done this exercise, there should still be a direct conflict within the total defence vote between, on the one hand, the minimum credible deterrent and, on the other, the minimum necessary forces to give timely military aid to friendly countries who ask for military help, then my choice would be the latter ... Nobody in the army, nor indeed either of the other two services, has any ambition to play a prominent part in the battle of Armageddon. Our job is to keep peace in the world.[151]

Cowley's views were widely reported, and his indiscretion, in expressing them so publicly and so strongly, came to the notice of the Prime Minister.[152] Arguments within the defence establishment on nuclear sufficiency passed in this way into the public domain and, as we have seen, provided some of the background to Macmillan's future policy study of 1959-60. Nuclear sufficiency also provided a stimulus for later studies of British 'limited war' strategy outside the NATO area.

Global war studies

Thinking on nuclear strategy was also now developing beyond 'massive retaliation' at more junior levels in the British defence machinery. A Joint Global War Committee, chaired by the MoD chief scientist and reporting to the chiefs, had been meeting since 1956.[153] Its studies employed operational-research methods to investigate the likely nature of a future strategic nuclear war. This committee, although rather curiously dismissed at one stage by Boyle as too scientific,[154] had its attention directed during 1958 towards more specific defence-policy problems, and was given the support of a full-time study group, later known as the Joint Inter-service Group for the Study of All-out War, or JIGSAW. During 1959, this group looked at the merits of different strategic nuclear delivery systems, generally highlighting the advantages of the submarine.[155] It also began to consider the concept of 'breakdown' in countries under nuclear attack, initially concluding that between 35 and 50 per cent damage in 300 Soviet cities would be necessary, but also considering the effect of smaller attacks in line with existing British targeting plans. One of the global-war committee's reports in 1960, on the implications of mutual deterrence, was considered politically controversial and had to be withdrawn. It discussed the unreliability of US support in an age of mutual deterrence and the need for collective or individual national deterrents in Europe 'if NATO is abandoned or weakened'. It also discussed a nuclear West Germany, suggesting that, by about 1970 'the Federal German Republic will be actively considering ways and means of recovering part of the territory lost to Poland'. It was poor form to express such fears aloud in Whitehall, and the committee had rather exceeded its terms of reference.[156]

Perhaps the JIGSAW group's most significant contribution was to the study of battlefield nuclear warfare on the NATO central front. Zuckerman had become convinced, early in his tenure as chief scientist, that such a concept was entirely without value, a view reinforced by discussions in the US.[157] During 1961, under Zuckerman's direction, the group applied itself to a number of specific studies of the effects of nuclear weapons. On 16 November 1961, in the Admiralty cinema, these studies were presented to a large audience, including Watkinson, Thorneycroft, the single-service ministers, Sir Norman Brook, Macmillan's private secretary de Zulueta, Mountbatten, Zuckerman, the Chiefs or Vice-Chiefs of Staff and other members of the Defence Board.[158] John Kendrew, the global-war committee's chairman, gave a short introduction. Presentations followed on the effects of a one-megaton attack on Birmingham; of nine one-megaton attacks on the Leningrad region of north-western Russia; of a strategic exchange between west and east; of a 20kt attack on Carlisle; and finally of a tactical nuclear battle in Germany. Birmingham had been chosen as a representative city, and because Zuckerman was associated with the university there and knew it well.[159] Carlisle was chosen as a major railway junction and therefore a typical 'interdiction' target. The conclusions were close to home, and sobering. In Birmingham, for example,

> there would be one third of a million dead ... As an organised unit capable of contributing to a war effort Birmingham would have ceased to exist. The survivors in different parts of the city would be wandering about trying to find some place better than the one where they happened to be when the bomb went off – searching for food, for better shelter, for relatives, for help of any kind ... The problems confronting the communities would be on a scale vaster than any experience of World War II, and this, in a context where other cities would also be attacked, so that there could be no question of any help from outside.[160]

Slides were shown of a model city, the buildings carefully destroyed in varying degrees according to their closeness to ground zero.[161] In Carlisle, 'the situation would be very similar to that prevailing in Birmingham after a megaton attack ... communications through the city would be utterly disrupted and ... short of re-building, there would be no chance of re-establishing even a modicum of through traffic; it would be simpler to by-pass the city'.[162]

The Leningrad study showed the inter-related effects of a number of attacks in creating overall breakdown: 'the percentage of population killed is a hopelessly inadequate measure of the effects of a nuclear attack and ... the best estimate must include allowance for the interaction of effects'.[163] A similar and important conclusion arose from the study of tactical nuclear warfare in Germany. Capitalising on war-gaming by the army's own operational-research group, JIGSAW reported that well dispersed troops in small units – a company of infantry, a squadron of armour or a battery of guns – presented hard targets. On a corps front, with certain advances in mobility and command and control, there might be 200 such targets, meaning that to reduce a Soviet force below the three-to-one margin of superiority usually assumed necessary to prosecute a successful attack, literally hundreds of kiloton-range nuclear weapons would have to be used. Even 100 such explosions would, over the corps tactical battle area of around 5000 square miles, 'devastate' 400 square miles, severely damage another 1200, and affect 500,000 people. 'If these people were to stay where they were, with the sort of protection they have now they would be at serious risk of death or injury; if they moved out they would present military forces in the area with a very serious refugee problem'. Given this level of damage, asked the study rhetorically, 'which is the factor which determines the course of the battle? Is it the number of enemy casualties? Or is the very chaos of the battlefield sufficient by itself to bring operations to a halt?'[164]

It is hard to see the November 1961 Defence Board presentation as a turning point in Britain's cold war defence policy. Zuckerman himself was unclear how well it had been received.[165] Nevertheless, he was able to take advantage of the conclusions on the tactical nuclear battle, both at the time and later, claiming eventually that he had won the argument on NATO strategy and brought an end to plans to wage tactical nuclear war.[166] This was an exaggeration, but the seeds of the later renewal of NATO strategy under 'flexible response' were now being sown by Zuckerman and others in the UK, as well as by officials of the Kennedy administration.

NATO and ballistic missiles

Norstad's ambitions for NATO in the late 1950s, and his disagreements with the UK, went beyond improvements to conventional shield forces. From as early as 1957, he was also interested in modernising his nuclear forces, and addressing the political problem of alliance control of nuclear weapons. In addition to existing tactical nuclear weapons, he wished to deploy IRBMs of around 1500nm range under some form of NATO – i.e., in operational terms, his own – control. Norstad suggested short-term deployments of Thor and Jupiter, then a new second-generation solid-fuelled missile of similar range.[167] US defence officials, in the wake of Sputnik and spurred on by the conclusions of the Gaither committee,[168] were desperate to begin deployment of ballistic missiles with the range to attack targets in the Soviet Union – a major driver behind the bilateral Thor agreement with the UK. Initial British reactions were to explore the possibility of selling Blue Streak to NATO, perhaps in a solid-fuelled version. As late as February 1959, the NATO requirement was seen as an opportunity to further the Blue Streak programme.[169] Norstad preferred instead a land-based version of the US Navy's Polaris missile. Towards the end of 1958 – thanks to progress with ICBMs, which could be fired from the continental US – American military interest in missile deployments to Europe, beyond the agreed deployment of Thor to the UK and now Jupiter to Italy and Turkey, was waning.[170] Norstad, however, remained interested, eventually convincing the joint chiefs in April 1959 to endorse a military requirement for NATO medium-range ballistic missiles (MRBMs), of around 300–1500nm range, rather than IRBMs.[171] He remained keen on Polaris, the only missile meeting this range requirement and likely to be available by 1963. Polaris also had considerable appeal in Washington, partly because it seemed the French would be unable to produce a warhead for it.[172] A NATO defence ministers' meeting in spring 1960 was therefore presented with a proposal for a force of 300 land-based Polaris missiles.[173] As we shall see, grudging British support for this plan had been secured as part of the deal on Skybolt and Holy Loch, reached a few days previously. Already, however, thinking was moving on in the US, where a proposal for a multi-lateral NATO force of submarines, rather than land-based missiles, was developed during the summer.

By this time, British ministers and officials were becoming less and less happy with NATO's new strategic concepts, both because of the expense potentially involved in Norstad's plans for ballistic missiles and increased conventional forces, and because of growing suspicions that a dangerous nuclear war-fighting mindset was developing in NATO. In July 1960, Norstad had talks with Watkinson, but there was no meeting of minds; Watkinson considered Polaris a most unsuitable weapon for theatre use because of its long range and high yield, and soon afterwards described the general's plans for a NATO multi-lateral nuclear force as 'a piece of eyewash'.[174] In September 1960 a major chiefs' assessment was produced on NATO strategy,[175] and Richard Chilver, a senior MoD official, prepared a similar paper for Watkinson. Chilver agreed with the chiefs that the risks of global war were now so great that the release of tactical nuclear weapons to SACEUR might in practice be politically difficult, even if war came; but also that a large enough conventional defence in Europe was impractical on cost grounds. As Chilver put it, 'the only tolerable course is discriminate nuclear reaction'[176] – the trick was to understand what nuclear reaction might count as discriminate. The concept of 'graduated deterrence', now advocated in public by retired Rear-Admiral Sir Anthony Buzzard and others, was rejected by the defence establishment as too expensive and, if announced in advance, too easy to defeat. The chiefs, though uncomfortable with the concept of nuclear war-fighting, could hardly recommend that *all* plans to fight on in the face of an all-out Soviet assault should be abandoned. Neither paper drew any definite conclusions, and so – at the Prime Minister's suggestion – a study was begun in October under Frank Mottershead, another senior defence official, initially addressing the NATO MRBM issue and later broadening into consideration of wider NATO strategy.

Mottershead was dismissive of the military justification for the MRBM force – a costly over-reaction to the problems of using manned aircraft over eastern Europe in the face of improved air defences – but not of its political aim to strengthen the alliance.[177] Watkinson wished to be more constructive and forward-leaning, and by February 1961 he had available a set of questions and answers from Mottershead, which provided an illuminating insight into the central problem. 'In this era of nuclear equipoise the aim must be, without wasting resources, to provide a general Western deterrent to all forms of Soviet aggression without suggesting any weakness of the manifest resolve of the west to use its strategic nuclear forces in the last resort'.[178] Mottershead's paper envisaged a situation in which SACEUR was faced with a Soviet attack that had proved impossible to halt without the use of nuclear weapons. A nuclear response by SACEUR, he argued, *might* not inevitably lead to global war, but 'it would be unwise to plan to fight a nuclear war in Europe on the assumption that escalation can be avoided'. The first use of nuclear weapons would have to be extremely carefully limited: to the battlefield, and – however politically unpalatable this conclusion might be – to NATO territory. No 'shot across the bows' or pre-announced threshold would be useful. Days, not weeks, might then pass before operations either ceased or escalated to the strategic nuclear level. During this time, only operations to resist and delay a Soviet advance, using short-range, accurate and low-yield weapons would be possible. Indeed, as far as forces on the central front were concerned, targets and objectives would be no different during a subsequent strategic nuclear exchange. There was no point in SACEUR's using large, long-range nuclear weapons like MRBMs, or indeed trying to contribute to favourable war-termination or post-nuclear operations, given the huge resources available to SAC.[179] Watkinson began to press these views on his US and NATO counterparts.

Holy Loch, Skybolt and Polaris

Many historians see the 1958 atomic bilateral agreement as a turning-point or culmination in British nuclear history. Its importance to Britain's weapon designers, and its scope and character in such a sensitive area of national endeavour, were exceptional. It was also, however, as we have seen, just one in a series of moves to establish closer Anglo-American defence relations during the period. These moves continued. Towards the end of 1959, for example, the US Navy began to express interest in forward-basing Polaris missile submarines in the UK, where they would have no need of a lengthy transit before commencing a patrol within range of targets in the Soviet Union.[180] In February 1960, Harold Caccia, the British ambassador in Washington, was told in outline of a possible deal to offer a Polaris base in return for the supply of Skybolt missiles – now required, as we have seen, because of the Blue Streak cancellation.[181] This deal was eventually struck, although it was severely complicated along the way – wilfully or not – by diplomatic misunderstandings and by British, US and NATO politics.[182]

Ministers had agreed, in cancelling Blue Streak, to approach the Americans about Skybolt as a first-choice alternative. Polaris might be discussed later, if – and only if – Skybolt could not be secured. This agreement began to unravel, however, as Watkinson, Mountbatten, Arleigh Burke and others spotted an opportunity to suggest a different deal, or deals. So, for example, in preparation for the Camp David summit meeting between Eisenhower and Macmillan in March 1960, both the State Department and the joint chiefs prepared briefings for the President on the possibility of an agreement to supply Skybolt *or Polaris*. They suggested tying any such agreement to British support for the NATO MRBM proposals, However, because it was Polaris which had hitherto been closely and publicly associated with the NATO initiative, they did concede that it was marginally less important to attach this condition to a Skybolt than to a Polaris deal.[183] This suited Macmillan, who travelled to Camp David basically in search of Skybolt without strings, but it is interesting that Eisenhower had been briefed to expect an approach for either missile or both. The details of the two leaders' discussions at the summit remain obscure; some of them took place in private. Macmillan seems, however, to have picked up on the possibility of Polaris, for he mentioned it explicitly in his draft summary of the discussions, thanking the President for his willingness to provide 'whatever appears to be the better alternative system, either Skybolt or Polaris or a combination of these'.[184] Polaris was discounted explicitly, however, in the parallel American draft: 'it does not appear appropriate to consider a bilateral understanding on Polaris until the problem of SACEUR's MRBM requirements had been satisfactorily disposed of in NATO'. It was therefore removed from Macmillan's final summary.[185] Macmillan had therefore secured a straight agreement to acquire Skybolt (only), in return for a US Polaris base in Scotland. Unfortunately, this direct linkage – clearly understood by the majority of American participants – was not so clearly recalled in later discussions by the British.

Burke also appears, at this point, to have misunderstood the distinction between the British decision to pursue Skybolt now, in the short term, and the BNDSG's conclusions about the long-term need for an airborne or submarine-launched successor system in around 1970. He wrote to Lambe to suggest that Polaris should immediately replace Skybolt at the centre of the discussion – receiving a lukewarm reply from Couchman.[186] The Air Ministry, which was naturally pressing ahead with detailed arrangements to procure Skybolt, became fearful that decisions were being reopened. Perhaps Skybolt would be delayed beyond 1965, or perhaps Polaris could be made available earlier than 1970? If so, the Defence Committee's short-term/long-term distinction might be invalidated. At the start of May, Watkinson wrote to Mountbatten, noting a 'new flexibility in missile policy' and asking 'could we not do a really good Anglo-US [Polaris] venture based on the Gareloch ... we could also perhaps go so far as to consider purchasing, say, Polaris submarines on, I hope, fairly easy terms'. It is hard to believe Mountbatten was entirely innocent of soliciting this letter, to which he replied fairly positively – pointing out, however, that an outright purchase of US submarines might be the most sensible procurement option, to 'avoid having to lock up large numbers of our skilled design staff to the detriment of our own SSN building programme'.[187]

Armed with this and other briefings, Watkinson travelled to the US at the start of June, accompanied by Mountbatten. Here he appears to have sown confusion by attempting to tease apart the agreement on Skybolt and a base for the US Navy. Signing a memorandum of understanding on Skybolt on 6 June – which indeed made no mention of the US base – he now saw this part of the deal as complete. Britain would acquire around 100 of the missiles, on a straight procurement basis with no contribution to remaining US research and development costs.[188] Meanwhile Watkinson claimed the Scottish base was still for negotiation, and he asked specifically for two Polaris submarines for the Royal Navy under 'a sort of lend-lease arrangement' as a *quid pro quo*. In so doing, he clearly surprised his hosts. Indeed, he appears to have exceeded his authority. In turn, and in line with earlier US thinking, he was pressed by Gates to commit to a NATO MRBM solution. By agreeing to this condition, he once again exceeded his authority, although he managed to secure a positive response.[189] On his return, he announced to Macmillan that 'we ought to be in both the air-launched and undersea-launched missile business if we are going to be able to exert a continuing influence on the Americans'.[190]

This expensive brainwave, and its tie-in to NATO, can hardly have been welcome to the Prime Minister, but Watkinson persisted. In a draft paper for the Defence Committee, he revealed some of his thinking: the Americans were so keen on the NATO MRBM scheme that without it, 'in their present state of tension, they might take very strong action, such as a bilateral agreement to supply missiles to the Germans'.[191] To head off this possibility, some kind of British involvement was preferable. Ministers gathered to list a new set of conditions for the US Navy's base deal. The base would have to be a 'partnership project' involving the transfer of one or two submarines, and be moved to Loch Linnhe, further from any large centres of population. Glibly ignoring his recent discussions with Gates and their very explicit linkage between Polaris and NATO, Watkinson now explained that 'the United States need of a Polaris submarine base might enable us to reach some advantageous bargain for the procurement of Polaris submarines ourselves, and at the same time to avoid any additional commitment in respect of the NATO MRBM project'.[192] Sensing considerable annoyance in the US at this turn of events, Sir Caspar John, the new First Sea Lord, meanwhile felt the need to apologise to Burke, disavowing any Admiralty interest behind these new proposals.[193]

On 20 June, most unusually, the full cabinet – not just the Defence Committee – took two papers from Watkinson on Skybolt and Polaris. The Skybolt paper was a factual and uncomplicated account of the memorandum of understanding, and Watkinson was given the approval he sought to pursue a detailed technical and financial agreement. The cost of Skybolt was given as between £76.5 and £115.5 millions, depending on the number of missiles.[194] The Polaris paper was more controversial. Watkinson described Polaris in glowing terms: the submarines would be 'virtually invulnerable, and the United States authorities regarded them as a very important part of the diversified deterrent force which they planned to build up ... The United States government would welcome our close association with the US Navy in this development and they hoped that the United Kingdom government would feel able to participate, if only on a limited scale, in their Polaris submarine plans'. This was, at best, a misunderstanding of the US position. Watkinson went on to say that 'he had explained to Mr Gates that the project raised important political and defence considerations. In order to justify it to public opinion in this country it would have to be presented as a joint project. This could be achieved if the United States government were to give us an option to purchase or build our own Polaris submarines ... it would be necessary to consider carefully the relationship of any United Kingdom Polaris missiles to the medium-range ballistic missile scheme under which the Americans envisaged that Polaris would be deployed in Europe'.[195] Watkinson was right, finally, to point out that the deal on a Polaris base was proving domestically unpopular in the UK, especially in Scotland.

Macmillan wrote to Eisenhower a few days later outlining his conditions, now including the option to buy Polaris submarines, access to information to allow them to be built if necessary in the UK, and an extension of the Murphy-Dean agreement on command and control to cover any Scottish-based US submarines, not just in territorial waters, but up to 100 miles offshore.[196] As Geelhoed and Edmonds explain, 'Macmillan's letter created serious problems in Washington, at both the State Department and the Pentagon'. The President rejected the deal, noting with rather British understatement that joint operation and control of the base 'would present difficulties', and in particular that 'a bilateral agreement with the UK on Polaris missiles outside the NATO framework could jeopardise favourable consideration of the NATO MRBM programme. For this reason, I heartily support the initial discussions of our respective defence ministers along the lines that the acquisition of Polaris submarine missile systems by the UK should constitute a British contribution to the NATO MRBM programme'.[197] Perhaps Macmillan realised only now that Watkinson had effectively deceived him over this linkage; he anyway chose, at this point, not to push matters further. By August he had given way on all points, including the suggested move to Loch Linnhe, confirming to Eisenhower that a base at Holy Loch would be acceptable.[198] A detailed technical and financial agreement on Skybolt (27 September 1960) and a memorandum of understanding on Holy Loch (31 October 1960) were later signed.

I have taken some trouble to detail the problems Macmillan created for Eisenhower over Holy Loch and Skybolt, and Watkinson's simultaneous attempt at personal atomic diplomacy to secure Polaris for the UK, partly because they are not fully covered in the standard nuclear histories. It is surely significant, however, that the associated issues were debated in the full cabinet. It must be remembered that the months following the Blue Streak cancellation were the high-water mark for CND and for the unilateralist tendency within the Labour party. Macmillan's concern over siting the American base near Glasgow was real – and perhaps justified, at least politically, by the demonstrations and protests that later greeted the arrival of the submarine tender USS *Proteus* in Holy Loch. There was a brief storm of protest in parliament when the deal was announced, and even a full-scale debate, although government ministers were not present in numbers.[199] The Prime Minister risked a sharp exchange of letters with the President, after which the series of deepening Anglo-American defence and nuclear agreements dried up. Holy Loch should perhaps take its place, alongside Blue Streak and Skybolt, in the list of British nuclear political crises.

The multi-lateral force and the Kennedy administration

The spring 1960 US proposal for a NATO land-based Polaris force had been received coolly in Europe. Norstad, Gates and officials in the State Department nevertheless remained keen to press for NATO nuclear modernisation. During the summer, Secretary Herter commissioned a report on NATO tasks for the 1960s from a State Department group under Robert Bowie. Bowie explained to Eisenhower that he saw 'an urgent need for a new look at the strategy of NATO' because of mutual deterrence and the fact that the 'Europeans want to have some nuclear weapons under their own control'. He dismissed earlier proposals for nuclear sharing, and the bilateral deals favoured by the joint chiefs with key allies, such as the UK, suggesting instead 'indigenous strike forces of a multinational, multilateral character (even including mixed crews in all probability)'. Such forces would constitute a contribution to strategic deterrence, not a tactical nuclear war-fighting capability, and Bowie recommended a seaborne Polaris force, rather than any more growth in medium-range land-based nuclear systems. He also specifically offered Eisenhower his opinion that 'separate national deterrents do not make political, economic or military sense'.[200] Neither Norstad nor the joint chiefs were keen on the new and essentially political concept of a joint NATO deterrent force but, at the December 1960 NATO council meeting, this is what Herter proposed.[201] Five US Polaris submarines would be committed to a NATO MLF, and the allies would later contribute jointly manned and controlled forces of their own. Again the European NATO allies demurred, no doubt wondering what the incoming Kennedy administration would make of the proposal a month later.

Kennedy's reaction, on taking office, was to ask former Secretary of State Dean Acheson to report to him on NATO policy. The MLF idea gained further currency as a result. Acheson's report began grandly: 'The political nexus between North America and Western Europe ... is and must continue to be the foundation of US foreign policy. The purpose of that policy is to maintain an environment in which free societies may flourish'. His recommendations led to a new official statement of US policy, approved by Kennedy in April. The new policy was Europeanist, in line with State Department views: 'The US should make clear its support for the movement toward European integration. The UK should not be encouraged to oppose or stay apart from that movement by doubts as to the US attitude or by hopes of a "special" relation with the US'. Acheson liked the direction in which NATO strategy was moving: 'First priority [should] be given, in NATO programs for the European area, to preparing for the more likely contingencies, i.e., those short of nuclear or massive non-nuclear attack ... the objective of improving NATO's non-nuclear forces should be to create a capability for halting Soviet forces ... for a sufficient period to allow the Soviets to appreciate the wider risks of the course on which they are embarked'. On nuclear forces, more specifically:

> The President should state that an effective nuclear capability will be maintained in the European area and that nuclear weapons will not be withdrawn without adequate replacement ... The US should announce its intention to commit, say, five Polaris submarines to NATO ... [and] urge the UK to commit its strategic forces to NATO, in the same manner ... Over the long run, it would be desirable if the British decided to phase out of the nuclear deterrent business. If the development of Skybolt is not warranted for US purposes alone, the US should not prolong the life of the V-bomber force by this or other means.[202]

Thus the incoming administration supported the developing State Department line on NATO nuclear weapons, incidentally adopting a very clear policy of opposition to Britain's independent deterrent force. Most writers have assumed, with the benefit of hindsight, that Kennedy was disinclined to take this policy seriously when discussing nuclear matters with Macmillan, but its significance should not be underestimated. Kennedy's views on nuclear weapons, and those of McNamara, were coloured on taking office by horrifying briefings on SAC nuclear war plans, then still based on a single overwhelming offensive against the war-making potential of the Soviet Union and its allies.[203] Both men became determined to assert greater political control over the planning and possible execution of nuclear war, and to create more options than a single, all-out nuclear strike; McNamara, at least, would have preferred to have a policy of 'no first use' of nuclear weapons, although he was unable to adopt this principle officially.[204] A NATO deterrent force – over which the US could exercise a veto, either directly or through SACEUR, who was always a US general – was in this context vastly preferable to a British independent deterrent, especially as commentators were more or less openly discussing the utility of the latter in a situation of US 'abandonment' of Britain or NATO.

At least initially, the Prime Minister found Kennedy harder to deal with than Eisenhower. Worried by Kennedy's Irish-American background, and his father's dreadful reputation as ambassador in London at the start of the Second World War, Macmillan had a curious and somewhat unsatisfactory first meeting with the new President at Key West.[205] Mottershead's rather well founded analysis of NATO strategy was used in the following months as a basis for discussion, both at the Defence Committee and bilaterally in an attempt to influence the new administration, but there remained crucial areas of disagreement. In particular, the British suggested that the 'pause' that might be forced in a global war was far shorter than that envisaged by Acheson: something like 48 hours against 20 days, or indeed 30 days as stated in MC 14/2.[206] The MLF was meanwhile of no interest to politicians or strategists in the UK. The idea of a mixed-manned submarine force in particular was the butt of occasionally humorous but always dismissive remarks: 'the conning towers of Babel'.[207] Although for now 'berthed at the planning level in the State Department',[208] the MLF was to put to sea again in the storm of the Skybolt cancellation.

Circumstances short of global war

British nuclear defence planning for the world outside Europe was not generally so politically fraught as in NATO, tending to be discussed not openly with a large number of allies but in private, by British military planners consulting at most with their regional American counterparts. Britain was already quietly committed to putting in place nuclear forces as a contribution to CENTO and SEATO; these plans had been agreed in the mid-1950s. In the event of global war, CENTO planners envisaged using British nuclear weapons against tactical military and 'retardation' targets in the southern USSR and perhaps beyond, for example in the mountain passes of the Zagros. In SEATO planning, similar retardation attacks were envisaged against advancing Chinese forces.[209]

Partly in response to specific ministerial questions, and partly as an outgrowth of vague references to 'limited' war in the earlier nuclear-sufficiency debates, wider studies began in 1959 into British strategy outside Europe. The JPS initially struggled to devise meaningful force requirements for a variety of situations, especially in the absence of agreed guidance on whether large fixed military bases such as Aden and Singapore would continue to be available for British use in future.[210] At the start of 1960, Charles Lambe proposed a wider study.[211] This would build on the conclusions of Macmillan's future-policy study and propose 'a coordinated United Kingdom strategy for limited war, the tasks of all three services and the consequent force requirements'.[212] The inter-service politics behind this report were bitter, and the question of whether or not Aden, Singapore and other bases would continue to be available was never properly answered. Festing was deeply unhappy about any assumption that the bases would go, believing that without them it was wholly unrealistic to plan for British military interventions overseas. Mountbatten, Lambe and Caspar John were very anxious to put forward the contrary view – that a small, mobile and flexible force could usefully underpin British foreign-policy objectives in the middle and far east, and restore stability when necessary. Their anxiety related primarily to the need to justify expenditure on a new generation of large aircraft carriers. The Air Ministry, totally opposed to carriers, either lined up behind the War Office or tried to push its own competing concept of island bases – not big facilities like Aden and Singapore, but small footholds where aircraft and air-mobile forces would cling, posing a deterrent threat or if necessary using minimum force to restore order. This concept harked back to the inter-war period, when the RAF, rather than large and expensive ground forces, had been responsible for imperial defence in Iraq.

Nuclear weapons were not the main focus of work on military strategy for circumstances short of global war, which led eventually to a blockbuster report endorsed by the chiefs in July. The report nevertheless provides useful evidence for the nuclear historian. At an early stage, the assumption had been made, in line with existing SEATO planning, that nuclear weapons could be useful in the case of limited war against China – too formidable an opponent to defeat by conventional means. On the other hand, in these years before the Sino-Soviet split, there was concern that even here the use of any nuclear weapon carried considerable risk of escalation.[213] When the chiefs reviewed the paper in June, and in the light of comments from Zuckerman, a wider discourse on nuclear weapons was added. 'Views on the need for nuclear weapons and their possible uses are widely divergent', the chiefs noted: 'Further, the complete lack of any precedent for their tactical employment ... and the vast number of associated political, psychological and ethical factors make it difficult to formulate even a strictly military policy'. Various types of tactical nuclear weapons were considered in turn: nuclear weapons on land, nuclear depth-bombs, or nuclear surface-to-air missiles for use against high-flying aircraft. Their collateral effects on the battlefield and surrounding population would vary, and for this reason the use of depth-bombs, in particular, might – the chiefs did not venture a definite opinion – be considered more acceptable. Whether any tactical nuclear weapons had to be independently British made and owned was not clear.[214] When the chiefs' views reached the Defence Committee,

Macmillan 'saw no need for nuclear units in any of these regions' – not even the far east – although, as James notes, he was later to moderate this view.[215] At a further meeting at Chequers in October 1960, a nuclear commitment to SEATO in line with existing plans was agreed,[216] but there were no useful conclusions on the wider issues of carriers and fixed bases, or indeed British overstretch and financial weakness more generally.

During 1961 Watkinson, clearly under the influence of Mountbatten, began to offer his own policy prescription to the Prime Minister. In September, he wrote advocating further centralisation of defence organisation, a submarine-based successor to Skybolt, less emphasis on conventional weapons in NATO, fewer overseas bases and more mobility. These ideas found no favour with Macmillan, and came under sustained attack during 'one of [the] more argumentative meetings' of the chiefs.[217] In one sense, those advocating a reduced reliance on fixed bases were moving with the times: Aden and Singapore would certainly not be available for ever. However, it certainly was unrealistic to expect to mount sustained military operations far from the United Kingdom without local political and logistic support. Although withdrawal from overseas bases might save money in the short term, it might also affect export opportunities, and even if governments remained friendly they would still expect some kind of compensating military aid. In June 1961, a successful rapid-reinforcement operation was mounted in Kuwait, but this did nothing to resolve the longer-term political issues of overseas strategy. Macmillan submitted a paper to the Defence Committee in October, describing the Kuwait operation as atypical and suggesting a series of potential economies, for example in Cyprus, Africa, Hong Kong and post-independence Malaya. He noted further that he saw the need for a replacement deterrent system – whether Polaris, or VC-10 with Skybolt – as 'questionable'.[218] Although Britain's defence policy was shifting subtly towards an east-of-Suez emphasis that would become stronger in subsequent years, the Prime Minister's questioning attitude is again significant. Despite considerable effort, there was no accepted military strategy to back up any kind of choice or prioritisation between the deterrent, NATO conventional forces and commitments east of Suez.

Worries about Skybolt

Although it was more or less enthusiastically adopted in place of Blue Streak in early 1960, Skybolt was never without its political problems. Commentators have often asked whether the British were somehow blind to the warning signs over Skybolt – the conclusion generally being that they were well aware of the programme's difficulties, but found it politically convenient to give the contrary impression.²¹⁹

The Pentagon's Weapons Systems Evaluation Group commented adversely on technical problems with Skybolt as early as April 1959, and again in the autumn.²²⁰ This internal criticism was to be a continuing theme of Skybolt's history. In July 1959, an *ad hoc* group on air-to-surface missiles was appointed under the chairmanship of Dr James Fletcher – later, as head of NASA, instrumental in starting the Space Shuttle programme. Fletcher's committee reported to Pentagon research and development chief Herbert York in January 1960, assessing that the missile was feasible but that cost and timescale had been underestimated and that 'development of the guidance system is considered to be the most difficult problem'. Fletcher's group concluded that, 'unless considerable effort is applied on detailed design and specification and on testing, the overall reliability will be so low as to make the system of questionable value as an operational weapon'.²²¹ When Gates subsequently approved the project's continuation, his approval was hedged about with requirements for tight control of funding and project change, and regular reporting to the Pentagon.²²² Meanwhile the missiles panel of the Presidential Science Advisory Committee (PSAC), in a May 1960 report to chairman George Kistiakowsky, concluded that 'we are not yet persuaded that the Skybolt has great merit'. In December, as the administration worked on its budget proposals for US fiscal year 1962, the PSAC pressed for Skybolt's cancellation. Interestingly Zuckerman was shown a version of the May 1960 report later in the year, and quoted from it almost verbatim in a note to his minister. Recognising that 'from a rational point of view the right thing to do was to drop the whole programme', Gates nevertheless shied away from cancellation at the end of 1960. Instead he markedly reduced Skybolt funding.²²³

The incoming Kennedy administration therefore inherited a tightly managed, lightly funded and still controversial research programme in January 1961. New Defense Secretary Robert McNamara was at first favourably disposed towards Skybolt, partly because his confidence in rival systems was limited; Polaris was just about at sea, but there were only a dozen Atlas ICBMs and Minuteman had yet to be tested successfully. Kennedy had been elected on a strong defence ticket, making much of the non-existent 'missile gap', which he 'undoubtedly exaggerated ... for electoral reasons'.²²⁴ McNamara accelerated Polaris and Minuteman in response, also putting more money into Skybolt in March 1961. As York recorded, 'domestic political factors, as well as relations with our British ally', made cancellation impossible at this point.²²⁵ James Schlesinger recalled that Skybolt survived in 1961 because McNamara 'had enough fights on his hands with the Air Force already'²²⁶ – first and foremost over the B-70, which he first turned into a strategic reconnaissance aircraft and later succeeded in cancelling. Meanwhile Congress was solidly pro-USAF and pro-Skybolt: the Senate and House Armed Services and Appropriations Committees were headed by 'elderly, conservative southerners … all "super-hawks"'.²²⁷ Arch-conservative Georgia senator Richard B Russell, for example, chaired the Senate Armed Services Committee, and was much admired by LeMay.

In the UK, too, there was opposition to Skybolt. The RAF, through its Skybolt liaison officer in Washington, Group Captain Geoffrey Fryer, circulated a series of glowing progress accounts. There is no denying, however, that Zuckerman played a more important part in shaping British political opinions of Skybolt, or that, through his unrivalled Washington contacts, he was more often briefed against Skybolt than for it. With nice understatement, Zuckerman noted in August 1962 that 'as a rule, my assessments of the progress of Skybolt have been somewhat less rosy than the information sent us by Fryer'.²²⁸ For his opposition, Zuckerman was branded a 'traitor' by the Air Ministry.²²⁹ But when he reported, for example, that 'a number of major technical difficulties still appear to be unresolved for the Skybolt guidance system', and that 'there is widespread lack of faith in Skybolt as a system',²³⁰ he was doing no more than relaying honestly what his contacts – more senior and influential in Washington than the RAF's – were telling him. It is only fair to point out, in addition, that Zuckerman was from time to time impressed with what he saw in the US on Skybolt, and relayed this message to his masters in the UK. In June 1960, for example, he met Dr William Ballhaus, the Skybolt guidance chief at Nortronics, and reported to Watkinson that 'it was all extremely interesting, and made me realise that Skybolt is probably as near to a homing pigeon as we are likely to achieve … Dr Ballhaus is absolutely confident that Skybolt will materialise'.²³¹

Nevertheless, partly because of the ongoing level of concern over Skybolt, and partly because there remained constituencies favouring either Polaris or a home-grown system, Skybolt was never quite secure as Britain's first-choice deterrent system. As early as March 1960, Ronald Kent, a senior Air Ministry official, was concerned by a chiefs' paper on Polaris, by a favourable mention of Polaris made by Watkinson in parliament, and by the forthcoming resumption of BNDSG discussions, which would notionally focus on a 1970s successor system to the V-bombers with Skybolt.²³² The chiefs' paper was just a response to a query from

Watkinson on the number of submarines that might constitute an adequate deterrent force but, coming in the middle of the decision-making on Blue Streak and Skybolt, it was naturally seen as a threat. Pike was briefed that the paper contained 'assumptions and conclusions from which you will wish to dissociate yourself'.[233] When Sir Edward Playfair, the new MoD Permanent Secretary and BNDSG chairman, set out a programme of work for his group, five of the six future scenarios he listed involved Polaris in one form or another.[234] As we have seen, Watkinson made a strong play for Polaris during the Holy Loch negotiations in the early summer of 1960. As a long-term successor to the V-bombers and alternative to Skybolt, the Air Ministry was now desperate instead to push the Vickers VC-10, a planned transport aircraft and civil airliner, as a 'multi-role' Skybolt carrier.

By September 1960, the BNDSG was considering not just a 1970s successor but also short-term 'insurance' against the failure of Skybolt. The Air Ministry preferred to consider money spent on TSR.2 as their premium in this regard. The Ministry of Aviation, on the other hand, betrayed its preference for a British-made missile as a solution, for example in papers for the BNDSG on possible Blue Steel improvement projects and new deterrent weapons for the TSR.2.[235] Towards the end of 1960, Air Ministry operational requirement OR.1182 was drafted, calling explicitly for a British alternative to Skybolt. The 'not-invented-here' opposition to Skybolt never quite went away. The Admiralty, meanwhile, was bitterly opposed to TSR.2, and therefore preferred to see Polaris as the insurance, if any, for Skybolt. The Deputy Chief of the Naval Staff, Admiral Sir Laurence Durlacher, felt it necessary to dissent from one BNDSG paper on these grounds.[236] By October, faced with these fundamental disagreements, Zuckerman was proposing the creation of an 'independent' group of scientists to advise on long-term deterrent systems, whilst Playfair was toying with the idea there should be *no* successor system to Skybolt: 'I think that we are all agreed that the idea of continuing to buy components of an American system is not very helpful. There is no reason to expect that the Americans will sell them to us for independent use'. Soundings taken by the Foreign Office were suggesting that 'political strings on American weapons were likely to be drawn tighter under Kennedy than under Eisenhower'.[237]

Zuckerman's technical sub-group met a number of times during 1961 and the ill-tempered observations of Hayne Constant, the Air Ministry's scientific adviser, provide a fascinating insight into its proceedings. For his supposed advocacy of Polaris, the Air Ministry now considered Zuckerman a lost soul: 'I am afraid that he had no compunction in resorting to verbal sniping and clever dialectics whenever convenient', Constant reported.[238] James Lighthill, the young Director of RAE, was equally unhappy, writing to Zuckerman that 'the distinction between carefully sifted UK technical judgement on the one hand and hunches based on slanted US tittle-tattle on the other is being blurred in MoD ... I regard some of your remarks about the status of Skybolt as ... unfounded, or founded on information deliberately slanted for propagandist purposes. Only an impartial assessment of information from all available US sources by those in the scientific civil service whose job it is to make such assessments can obtain trustworthy results'.[239] In an effort to demonstrate the vulnerability of Polaris, the more air-minded members of Zuckerman's group had considered a number of extremely far-fetched scenarios, including peacetime attrition of Polaris submarines – which they suggested might covertly be sunk by the Soviets in 'accidents' – and also 'pin-down' attacks on submarine patrolling areas, using large numbers of nuclear weapons to prevent launch. Their strong reaction to Zuckerman's own tactics forced him to compromise, and the technical group was unable to reach a firm conclusion:

> The only ballistic missile weapon systems which promise a reasonable assurance of maintaining a real threat against enemy targets, and which both allow time for decision and remain flexible in use [are] mobile platforms of long endurance, continuously maintained on station. These platforms could be either submarines, preferably nuclear-powered, or aircraft on continuous air patrol ... both have a good chance of providing a credible and viable deterrent during the period 1970–80, as far as can be foreseen.[240]

This at least meant that systems designed to meet OR.1182 could be disregarded, but readers of Zuckerman's report were no closer to a judgement between the aircraft and the submarine. Before taking the BNDSG's deliberations any further, Sir Robert Scott, who now took over from Playfair, was inclined to wait until Skybolt was in more definite trouble.

2
Policy Execution 1958–61

The British nuclear-weapons programme grew in maturity in the period between 1958 and 1961. At the end of 1958, there were probably only 58 deliverable first-generation Blue Danube bombs available to the RAF, and five of the interim megaton bomb Violet Club. Three years later, there were nearly 200 weapons of British manufacture in the stockpile, including much more operationally flexible designs: the light-weight kiloton weapon Red Beard and the megaton H-bomb Yellow Sun Mk.2. The acute constraints of fissile material shortage, engineering capacity and the testing moratorium were eased by the growing atomic relationship with the United States. Great strides appear to have been made at Aldermaston – not just in copying, or more strictly speaking anglicising, US nuclear warhead designs, but in original and joint US/UK work on new requirements. Collaboration with the US appears not to have led to a feeling of subordination, but to have increased confidence at Aldermaston. The RAF certainly also gained in confidence, exercising its growing number of V-bomber squadrons to forge a real nuclear bombing capability, with real targets in real war plans, and improving in particular its state of operational readiness. British nuclear weapons were deployed overseas, to equip RAF Canberras in Cyprus and naval strike aircraft worldwide. British guided weapons of all types were tested, and some deployed; Aldermaston worked on associated nuclear warheads.

There were also setbacks. The cancellation of Blue Streak, in particular, deprived British industry and the research establishments of a substantial foothold in ballistic-missile work. But in many technology areas, British scientists and private companies remained active. Work on inertial guidance survived, a little behind the Americans in precision engineering of gyroscopes and accelerometers, and found a later focus in the low-level navigation and attack system of TSR.2. British work on re-entry science, decoys and penetration aids remained healthy, and British contributions were also made to anti-ballistic missile research – despite the Blue Streak cancellation, and the resulting loss of focus for both offensive and defensive ballistic-missile work.

In this chapter I shall look in detail at this flowering of work to underpin and implement British nuclear-weapons policy, beginning with military requirements and the basic work necessary on fissile materials and warhead technology, before moving on to the operations, control and targeting of the V-bombers and other nuclear forces, and finally the many projects to build bombs and missiles – some in service, some in testing and some no more than twinkles in the eye. I have tried to give some weight and prominence to tactical as well as strategic weapons, for although the main deterrent force and its possible future weapons – especially Blue Streak, Skybolt and Polaris – received most attention in Whitehall, much time and energy was spent on other activities.

Detailed knowledge of the status and progress of a variety of individual weapons projects and operational forces is an important foundation for any real understanding of Britain's nuclear posture in these years. My purpose, however, is not simply to pile detail upon detail, but to create an overall impression of Britain's nuclear-weapons programme as a considerable national and indeed international enterprise with many different aspects, from the precision-engineered diffusion cascades of Capenhurst to the cyclone-proof housing of Talgarno and the concrete hardstandings of East Anglia. A nuclear-weapons capability is not something to be conjured at a cabinet meeting or an international summit, but a long, difficult and expensive undertaking.

Military requirements

Thus far we have examined the political requirement for nuclear weapons and certain specific political decisions about delivery systems. To translate these broad political needs into project action to create a nuclear weapons capability, each of the service ministries maintained a staff to formulate and issue more or less detailed requirements. The Air Ministry's operational-requirements staff, headed by an Assistant Chief of the Air Staff (ACAS(OR)), tended initially to issue a vague 'air staff target' and later a firmer 'air staff requirement' incorporating more detail. Requirements were considered and prioritised by the DRPC, and then issued to the MoS (later MoA) for project action. The project – not the requirement – would then be allocated a codename, and the MoS would turn to the research establishments and/or industry teams to begin work. Sometimes confusingly, requirements and projects did not always correspond one-to-one, and so a requirement might match more than one codename. The OR.1159 requirement for a long-range powered guided bomb, for example, was originally to be met by the Blue Steel Mk.2 project, and later by Skybolt. For many years the MoS issued picturesque 'rainbow' codenames with a colour followed by a supposedly randomly selected noun, but upon its creation in late 1959 the MoA decided to use more modern-sounding 'reference numbers' with two letters followed by three numbers. There was nothing unique about the basic procedures and codename systems for nuclear weapons; these rules applied to all weapons projects.

Although the system appeared to be one in which service requirements nicely drove all project and procurement activity, the reality was rather less clear-cut. As anybody who has worked in project management will know, requirements do not always simply describe a desirable capability in general terms, but are sometimes written with specific technical solutions in mind. Sometimes, therefore, the technical tail was wagging the service dog. Acceptance criteria such as yield, range, speed, accuracy and environmental limitations might be laid out in great detail in a requirement; sometimes more latitude was necessarily allowed, and sometimes the service staffs asked explicitly for the art of the possible. As we shall see, as we turn to some of the individual weapons projects, some dissatisfaction was from time to time apparent as a result of arms-length relationships and lack of communication between the customers and suppliers of nuclear weapons. The services had little insight into the process of designing nuclear warheads and the complex trade-offs involved for example between safety, reliability, yield and economy in the use of fissile material. In turn they commonly failed to convey to scientists and engineers at Aldermaston the operational imperatives of readiness, dispersal, storage and command and control.

The RAF's requirements for nuclear weapons were more varied and numerous than those of the other services, and it was conscious of its predominance. As the Deputy Chief of the Air Staff put it early in 1958, 'compared with the other two services our needs ... are very much greater because we are already involved, from a nuclear point of view, with the Americans in Project E, Genie and Thor as well as in coordinating planning and targeting and the detailed problems of storage. Whereas the army's only interest at the moment is Corporal and the navy's nothing lethal'.[1] Until the mid-1950s, nuclear-weapons requirements had been constrained heavily by the scarcity of fissile material, and at times by lack of knowledge and experience at Aldermaston. The total number of weapons, in particular, had been dictated by the amount of fissile material available – and not, for example, by the number of targets strategists wished to threaten with destruction. By 1959, this situation was changing, and the Air Ministry realised that no formal statement of its overall needs had ever been put together. A paper was prepared for submission to the Air Council in the summer, which handily summarised the considerable extent of the RAF's nuclear ambitions. The Air Ministry's first priority was to ensure as soon as possible that each of 144 front-line V-bombers had a nuclear weapon to match – preferably either a megaton Blue Steel or free-fall bomb, or if necessary a Red Beard or Project E kiloton weapon. An early draft of the paper listed a total of 294 megaton weapons needed for the V-bombers and later Blue Streak and anti-ballistic missiles; also 624 kiloton weapons for the V-bombers, for NATO, CENTO and SEATO commitments, for defensive surface-to-air guided weapons (SAGW) and for anti-submarine warfare.[2] By the time the paper reached the Air Council, it had been moderated somewhat, but 164 megaton and 534 kiloton weapons of British manufacture were still listed, with more needed from the Americans under dual-key arrangements.[3] These totals did not include the requirements of the army and Royal Navy.

As to variety, the table below summarises those nuclear weapons requirements current between summer 1958 and autumn 1961. Many of these will be described in more detail later in this chapter. Those listed with a date issued were accepted by the MoS (MoA) and serious project action initiated; the others had not progressed (or did not progress) beyond an earlier stage of discussion.

Reqt. No.	Issued	Service	Description
OR.1001	1946	RAF	Atomic bomb (Blue Danube) (service deliveries complete by 1958)
OR.1127	1953	RN/RAF	Small kiloton bomb (Red Beard)
OR.1132	1954	RAF	100nm-range powered guided bomb (Blue Steel Mk.1) – megaton warhead OR.1141
OR.1136	1955	RAF	Megaton free-fall bomb (Violet Club/Yellow Sun Mk.1/Mk.2)
OR.1139	1955	RAF	Medium-range ballistic missile (Blue Streak) – megaton warhead OR.1142
	c.1955	RN	Seaslug SAGW – kiloton warhead Indigo Hammer, later RO106/Tony
	c.1957	Army	8-inch artillery shell (Yellow Anvil)
	c.1957	Army	Surface-to-surface guided weapon (Blue Water) – low-yield kiloton warhead Indigo Hammer, later RO106/Tony; high-yield kiloton warhead under discussion
	1957	Army	Atomic demolition munition (Violet Mist)

Reqt. No.	Issued	Service	Description
OR.1153		RAF	Multi-megaton warhead for free-fall or powered bomb or ballistic missile (under discussion 1957)
OR.1155		RAF	Anti-ballistic missile – megaton warhead OR.1157 (under discussion c.1958)
OR.1156		(RN)/RAF	Nuclear depth-bomb (under discussion 1958)
		RN	Megaton weapon for naval aircraft (under discussion 1958)
OR.1159	1958	RAF	600nm-range powered guided bomb (Blue Steel Mk.2 or Skybolt) – replaced earlier OR.1149 for a 1000nm-range weapon – megaton warhead OR.1160 under discussion
OR.1161		RN/RAF	Light-weight (500lb) megaton warhead for ballistic missile, powered bomb or defensive missile after 1965 (under discussion 1958–59)
OR.1166	1958	RAF	Command-guidance Bloodhound SAGW – kiloton warhead (Indigo Hammer, later RO106/Tony) OR.1167
OR.1171	1959	RAF	Common megaton warhead capsule for free-fall or powered bomb or ballistic missile (Red Snow)
OR.1172	1959	RN/RAF	Common kiloton warhead capsule for Bloodhound, Seaslug, Blue Water (RO106/Tony)
OR.1177	1960	RN/RAF	Improved kiloton bomb or Red Beard replacement, air- or ground-burst or depth-bomb (WE177) – variable-yield kiloton warhead OR.1176
		Army	Sub-kiloton warhead for Davy Crockett atomic mortar (BQ267) (under discussion 1959–61)
OR.1178		RAF	Nuclear depth-bomb (under discussion 1959)
OR.1179	1960	RAF	Megaton warhead for Skybolt (formalisation of requirement previously covered by OR.1160/1161 and/or Red Snow)
OR.1182	1960	RAF	Long-range air-to-surface missile (alternative to Skybolt)
OR.1187	1961	RAF	Skybolt weapons system (formalisation of interest in Skybolt previously covered by OR.1159)

Not included: (a) RAF requirements for US warheads for Genie and Thor; army requirements for US warheads for Corporal, Honest John etc. – all to be provided under dual-key arrangements; (b) political requirements for 'calibration' warhead for nuclear test verification and NATO MRBM warhead – neither formally issued.

Did Britain need *all* of these nuclear weapons? Thorneycroft – returning to the cabinet in July 1960 after his self-imposed exile, replacing Sandys as Minister of Aviation, and keen again to economise – thought not. Zuckerman, Mountbatten and others, probably including Macmillan himself, agreed. At the October 1960 Chequers meeting of the Defence Committee, at which bases and carriers were discussed inconclusively, Thorneycroft volunteered a detailed review of the nuclear warhead programme. This proceeded, well out of the political limelight, in two phases. The first concerned strategic warheads, together with the fairly urgent question of continued production of the Red Beard tactical bomb, which as we shall see had now begun in earnest, and the development programme for the tactical missile warhead RO106/Tony. The chiefs noted the review's conclusions, but for whatever reason ministerial meetings – the first scheduled for February 1961 – did not take place, although the Prime Minister was briefed on the review in March.[4] This phase of the review seems not to have resulted in any major reduction in warhead requirements, and such questions as the number of Skybolt and RO106/Tony warheads were deferred until 1962.

Fissile material

One of the first necessities for a nuclear weapons programme is sufficient fissile material. The extraction of highly enriched uranium and weapons-grade plutonium is a complex and extremely expensive business, and the capital facilities necessary for Britain's nuclear programme were built up over many years, during which the stories of nuclear weapons and nuclear power generation were interwoven. The operation of nuclear reactors for plutonium production and power generation, for example, posed different problems.[5] Ten nuclear reactors in the UK, eight of which were at commercial power stations, were used to produce plutonium for nuclear weapons in these years, and a major reprocessing plant at Windscale in Cumberland was constructed for plutonium recovery. The first two plutonium-production reactors, also at Windscale, were closed permanently in 1957 after a fire broke out at the facility, but four more were coming on line at the adjacent Calder Hall site, a further four were under construction at Chapelcross in southern Scotland, and these eight were to continue operation on a military fuel cycle until 1964. A large gaseous-diffusion plant at Capenhurst in Cheshire was built to enrich uranium, starting operation in 1956 and running until 1963. In addition, as we have seen, 'special nuclear materials' were available from the United States under barter arrangements after 1959.

To determine the amount of weapons-grade plutonium produced in these reactors is not a trivial exercise. In the past, writers including John Simpson and David Albright *et al.* have attempted to calculate a theoretical throughput of plutonium from the sites, arriving at figures of around 2700kg for gross production to 1964. Allowing for material consumed in nuclear tests and losses during the reprocessing process, this gives a net figure available for weapons production and stockpiling of between 2150kg and 2400kg.[6] In 2000, the Ministry of Defence released documents listing the transfers over many years of weapons-grade plutonium to and from Aldermaston. Although somewhat confusing, these documents appear to confirm very closely the estimates made by Simpson and Albright: by the end of financial year 1964/5, 2690kg of reprocessed plutonium had arrived at Aldermaston from Windscale, and after transfers to and from various research reactors 2473.3kg remained at Aldermaston, presumably mostly available for use in weapons.[7]

Figures for highly enriched uranium production at Capenhurst are harder to come by. Simpson quotes one estimate of 4536kg, and Albright gives a range of 3800–4900kg.[8] Figures in declassified documents relating to the run-down of Capenhurst after 1962, on the other hand, indicate a significantly higher total of around 7600kg.[9] Not all of this will have been available for weapons use, however; 30 per cent of production was allocated to civil reactor research and development, and Britain's nuclear submarine propulsion reactors also required highly enriched uranium.

What is certain is that fissile material was in extremely short supply in the years up to 1959. Again and again, documents referred to this shortage, and described weapons or proposed weapons as 'extravagant' in fissile material.[10] Brundrett for example, discussing Skybolt and its warhead with Herbert York at the Pentagon, repeatedly stressed the acute shortage of fissile material in the UK, but reported that York – who had worked until recently at the Livermore weapons laboratory in the US – could not conceive of such a problem and 'merely thinks I am being silly on this issue'.[11] Moreover, tritium, a gas with a short half-life required for advanced boosted-fission designs, was available only in minute quantities; and the British were having difficulty setting up processes to separate lithium-6 and fabricate lithium deuteride, a brittle and highly reactive material required as a fusion fuel in thermonuclear secondaries. A lithium-6 plant was apparently constructed at the Royal Ordnance Factory (ROF) at Chorley in Lancashire, but never used in anger.[12]

The terms of the fissile-material barter agreement set up after the 1959 amendment to the atomic bilateral agreement were as follows: 7500kg of highly enriched uranium was to be supplied by the United States – 500kg in 1964, 1500kg in each of the succeeding four years, and a final 1000kg in 1969. In return, the UK was to supply 4261.4kg of reactor-grade plutonium, in a ratio of 1:1.7. In addition, 4.5kg of tritium was to be supplied by the US between 1959 and 1965 in return for a further 360kg of plutonium, in a ratio of 1:80.[13] An option to buy outright a further 5000kg of highly enriched uranium from the US was not exercised, but 6000kg of lithium-6 was purchased between 1959 and 1962, and later 2450kg of an option for a further 8000kg.[14] Britain's immediate problems in nuclear materials supply were over although, as we shall see, further concerns were to emerge as demand for fissile material became difficult to predict in later years.

Aldermaston and warheads

Research into nuclear warhead and weapons design was centred at the Atomic Weapons Research Establishment (AWRE) at Aldermaston, a sprawling former airfield near Reading in Berkshire with a scientific and industrial workforce of several thousands. In organisational terms, AWRE formed the weapons group of the UKAEA. Two other groups were responsible for research, at Harwell in Oxfordshire, and fissile and special materials production, in the north of England – as outlined briefly above. In addition to research and development activities, AWRE conducted a certain amount of materials and component production and storage at the Aldermaston site. This activity tended to reduce over time, as production activities, including final assembly of weapons, were transferred to the MoS-controlled Royal Ordnance Factory (ROF) at nearby Burghfield.[15] Other ROFs, at Cardiff, Chorley and Patricroft, near Manchester, were involved in producing various materials and warhead and weapons components, as were private companies up and down the country. Hudswell Clarke, for example, the locomotive builder at Hunslet in Leeds, built bomb carcasses. Hunting Engineering, at Ampthill in Buckinghamshire, was heavily involved in the weapons programme for many years, assembling the centre sections for weapons; later, Hunting was prime contractor for the multi-purpose nuclear bomb WE177 and indeed took a share in the privatised AWE management company of the 1990s. Denis Ferranti, at Bangor in north Wales, produced electronic firing units. Kelvin and Hughes in Glasgow produced barometric switches for bomb fuzes. Map 1 gives some indication of the reach of nuclear weapons and delivery-systems manufacturing across Britain: truly a national enterprise for the 'warfare state'.

Sir William Penney, the Director of AWRE, was the son of an army sergeant-major from Kent, and during the war he put aside a promising career as a mathematician to begin a long history of involvement in nuclear-weapons research, working initially at Los Alamos. He was an inspiring figure at Aldermaston: 'at heart, an academic, a young professor caught up into government service with all the "wartime irregulars" ... he had a gift for communication and for building trust and confidence'. He was widely respected in America, in Australia and indeed by Macmillan personally.[16] Handing over his leadership of AWRE in 1959 to Dr Nyman Levin, Penney nevertheless remained close at hand, continuing to advise Macmillan on atomic and arms-control issues. In 1964 he was to become UKAEA chairman. William Cook, Penney's deputy, also from a modest background, and by training an applied rather than pure mathematician, was a defence scientist and a protege of Brundrett's before being brought in to head the H-bomb programme in 1954. 'Cook was a superb organiser, and a decisive project manager, with a powerful grasp of detail and an infallible eye for essentials ... a scientific civil servant from 1928 until he retired in 1970, he was the complete professional and, in Penney's words, "at heart a defence man" ... at Aldermaston his first concern was to "mind the shop" while Penney dealt with the wider world'.[17]

Penney and Cook worked well together, and transformed AWRE during the mid-1950s. In 1954, they had been asked by Churchill's government to build a megaton H-bomb. The terms 'megaton' and 'H-bomb' are not synonymous, although at first this was poorly understood. A megaton bomb explodes with a power equivalent to a million tons of TNT; a hydrogen bomb derives at least some of its explosive power from the fusion of light elements. The government ideally wanted a 'two-stage' thermonuclear fusion weapon, like those already tested the Americans, to give multi-megaton yields. At first, this two-stage technique was unknown in Britain, and the most promising avenues to a megaton yield were thought to involve the fission of large assemblies of plutonium and/or highly enriched uranium, with or without 'boosting' using light elements within or around the assembly. Gradually, sufficient knowledge was developed to test, not just large fission warheads, but also two-stage devices, starting near Christmas Island in the Pacific in May 1957. Importantly, Aldermaston also made advances in fission weapons design. In the US, the goal of warhead designers tended to be an improved yield-to-weight ratio, or greater explosive power within a certain overall warhead weight. This was driven by the range and accuracy requirements of aircraft and missiles. Both could be relaxed if yield-to-weight could be improved: bombers could fly further, and missiles need not be so accurate. As Carey Sublette puts it, 'except for safety, the weight of a weapon required to provide a given yield is the most important design criterion ... Since the cost of the delivery vehicle is much greater than the cost of the warhead, making the warhead as light as possible for the intended yield quickly came to dominate the weapon design process'. Yield-to-weight improved in the late 1950s in the US to about 2.2kt/kg in the Mk.47 warhead for Polaris, or 4kt/kg and more in some test devices.[18] One way to improve yield-to-weight was to use boosting, a technology finally mastered by the UK in autumn 1958 with the testing, during the Grapple-Z series, of a tritium gas-boosted device known as Burgee. Another was to use more fissile material, but this was impossible for Aldermaston designers, partly for safety reasons but mostly because of the acute scarcity of plutonium and, in particular, highly enriched uranium. In the UK, warhead improvements therefore came in particular from advanced implosion systems, using conventional high-explosive in innovative ways to achieve the maximum possible compression and therefore efficiency in a relatively small fissile core. This appears to be one reason why British designs were generally somewhat larger and heavier than the equivalent American designs, for the additional high-explosive used by the British outweighed the reduction achieved in fissile material. This focus on implosion technology also seems to explain why the minor trials in Australia, in particular the Rats and Tims implosion experiments, described later in this chapter, were considered so important by British designers.[19] It is interesting that, as we shall see, British improvements in implosion techniques appear to have been of some interest to US designers once exchanges began under the bilateral agreement. When the bilateral atomic agreement was concluded in July 1958, British scientists were able to win the admiration and indeed support of their US counterparts by demonstrating a physical and practical knowledge of advanced fission weapons design and the two-stage megaton H-bomb.[20]

Using American warhead information

The question immediately arose: what next? AWRE representatives, led by Penney and Brundrett, discussed possible avenues of cooperation at a series of meetings in the US in August and September 1958.[21] It soon became clear that it would be possible to produce warheads of American design in the UK, and that this would solve many practical engineering problems. Britain's two-stage H-bomb designs of the so-called Granite type were, at best, at an early stage of engineering development. Further nuclear tests were planned to perfect the designs: Grapple-Z in September 1958, Grapple-M in March 1959, Lighthouse in Australia in autumn 1959, and Grapple-N in January 1960.[22] Grapple-Z aimed at perfecting the basic design for a warhead with a megaton yield, weighing a ton or less overall and 'immune' to countermeasures – a reference to the so-called R-1 effect, which will be discussed below. This requirement was driven primarily by the need to produce a warhead for Blue Streak, the payload of which would be considerably less than that of the V-bombers. To these ends, Grapple-Z also demonstrated, as mentioned above, tritium gas-boosting of the fission primary for an H-bomb. At Lighthouse, Aldermaston might then try to apply boosting to kiloton weapons to increase yield or reduce fissile material requirements, and/or to test a warhead for an artillery shell. At Grapple-M, two- and three-stage megaton designs might be refined.[23] The difficulty, of course, was the impending test moratorium. None of these tests was likely to be possible. Although Britain's designs were perfectly satisfactory in scientific principle, the moratorium was a major obstacle to their further development for use in real operational weapons. The Americans, however, were prepared to offer sufficient design information to allow the British to produce copies of their warheads. Three in particular were of interest in this regard: Mk.28, a fully engineered two-stage H-bomb warhead of less than a ton in weight; Mk.44, a fully engineered boosted fission warhead; and Mk.47, the unusual light-weight megaton warhead for the Polaris missile.

A specific decision to produce British warheads of American design – or not – is difficult to find in the documentary record. At the DRPC atomic sub-committee on 11 November 1958, a series of detailed points was made and then 'the committee agreed:- (1) that a UK version of the Mk.28 warhead should be developed for production at the highest priority as a Mt warhead ... (4) that a UK version of the XW44 warhead should be produced to meet the in-service date of the Stage $1^1/_2$ SAGW system ...'.[24] (The Mk.47 warhead was not mentioned). However, the minutes of the meeting also refer to recommendations from earlier discussions between Brundrett and the chiefs, suggesting that the committee was merely elaborating an earlier in-principle decision to manufacture American warhead designs. It is hard to determine, from the terms of reference of the various officials and committees involved, who constitutionally had the right to make such a decision. The Defence Committee met on 29 October, and may have discussed the matter, but the minutes have not all been declassified. Or there may have been no 'decision' as such, for the conclusion must have been staring everybody in the face:

without testing, building to American drawings was the quickest available route to well engineered operational weapons.

Thus AWRE was instructed to apply itself to the problem of 'anglicising' American warhead designs, and to set aside further work on various of its own investigations, including the Granite type warheads, the large fission warhead Green Grass, and the kiloton warheads Indigo Hammer, Pixie and Yellow Anvil. By December, AWRE was said to be 'fully committed to the analysis of technical data provided by the United States' and any plans to test were being put back as a result.[25] The Prime Minister was briefed in January that there was no need for testing until 1960, when a Grapple-O series might be staged to prove the first British weapons of American design; by June 1959 he was informed that 'the weapons being produced for delivery to the services are ... virtual copies of tested United States designs. Sir William Penney considers that the risks arising from our inability to carry out normal proving trials are acceptable'.[26] The following month, the Defence Committee approved, on this basis, the indefinite suspension of British plans to conduct nuclear tests, allowing Macmillan and the British delegation in Geneva more leeway to pursue a comprehensive test ban.[27]

As I have argued elsewhere, the term 'virtual copies' was simplistic.[28] Certainly British scientists and engineers received documentation on US warheads by the crate-load, and were able to visit US production facilities. However 'it was by no means the case ... that, once given the American engineering drawings and specifications, it was a simple and relatively unskilled matter to produce "Chinese copies"'.[29] In nuclear-weapons engineering, even following an engineering drawing is an ambitious and indeed hazardous undertaking. It was soon realised that some materials were unavailable in the UK to the same specifications as in the US, and at least until 1959 could not be procured directly. With the 1959 revision of the bilateral agreement, component procurement in the US became possible, but for Mk.28 at least – or Red Snow, to give it its British name – this was not a complete answer. It seems that only a few components were procured directly, including certain polyurethanes which could not be made in the UK.[30] Meanwhile differences in manufacturing methods, tooling and techniques still meant that *exact* copies were impossible.[31] A significant problem soon arose over the high-explosive used in the proposed American warheads, which was more sensitive than British equivalents and had caused more than one fatal industrial accident in the US. Its use could not be contemplated in the UK, especially in the aftermath of a fatal accident at Aldermaston itself, where on 26 February 1959 two workers were killed by a piece of (British) high-explosive assembly that fell from a lorry, rolling out of its protective casing and detonating on a concrete surface. The report on the accident was critical of high-explosive handling procedures and management inattention to this aspect of safety.[32] The British high-explosive used in anglicised warheads was not only less sensitive but more bulky than the American, and so the British warheads were slightly larger than the originals. This in turn affected casing design, and as we shall see it contributed to problems over the selection of a warhead and re-entry vehicle for Skybolt. Peter Jones, a later Director of AWRE, has also written of the problems of anglicisation and the requirement for implosion and safety calculations to be laboriously repeated in the UK.[33]

In the end, anglicisation proved far more difficult than expected, and some came to regret the decision to adopt US designs. Original work had not altogether been stopped in November 1958, however: the DRPC atomic sub-committee had also decided 'that work should continue, in cooperation with the US on the development of lighter and smaller megaton weapons and practical yield kiloton weapons'.[34] Early in 1959, work began in joint working groups (JOWOGs) on Anglo-American investigations into at least two new warheads: a megaton design of 500–600lb weight, in line with an earlier draft UK Air Ministry requirement OR.1161; and a warhead of unknown (presumably high kiloton) yield and 100–200lb weight.[35] At least 15 JOWOG groups were set up during 1959, and exchanges were soon underway between British and American scientists investigating such varied subjects as:

> one-point safety, computer codes, metallurgy and fabrication technology for beryllium, uranium and plutonium, corrosion of uranium in the presence of water and water vapour, underground effects tests, outer-space testing, clandestine testing, the technology of lithium compounds, high-explosives, deuterium monitors, extinguishing plutonium fires, high-speed cameras, mechanical safeing, liquid and solid explosive shock initiation, environmental sensing switches, neutron sources, tritium reservoirs, telemetry, hydrodynamic and shock relations for problems with spherical and cylindrical symmetry, cross sections, radiochemistry, atomic demolition munitions, warhead hardening, asymmetric detonations, terrorist nuclear threat response, nuclear weapons accidents and waste management.[36]

One is struck, not simply by the depth of collaboration in such a sensitive area of hitherto national endeavour, but by the very complexity of the nuclear-weapons business. Regular 'stocktake' meetings began, at which the operation of the bilateral agreement would be reviewed and new JOWOGs created as necessary. The Prime Minister was told in March 1961 that British nuclear-weapons development was now 'confined almost entirely to copying US designs',[37] but in the light of the above evidence, this appears to have been a considerable oversimplification.

Australia

The Commonwealth of Australia was and remains a proud, sovereign country, and the reader may be forgiven for wondering why it does not feature more prominently in the discussions of international politics in Chapter 1. In truth, Australia was a good deal more important to the implementation of British nuclear policy than to its formation. The Australian Prime Minister, Robert Menzies, occasionally discussed arms control issues with Macmillan but was more often cast in the role of loyal ally – in his own words, 'British to the boot heels' – agreeing readily to a series of requests for assistance with Britain's missile and nuclear-weapons programmes. Historians have debated the underpinnings of this loyalty: Anglophile sentiment, a genuine belief that Australia's best interests were served by 'imperial defence' in the interwar sense of the term – and the off-and-on pursuit of the idea of an Australian nuclear weapons capability, to be supplied by the UK – all appear to have had their place.[38] Whatever the reasons, the result of this policy was that Australia made available extensive facilities for full-scale nuclear testing and 'minor' atomic trials, latterly at Maralinga in South Australia; and for guided-weapons testing at the huge Woomera range, whose facilities stretched across the continent.

Although, as we have seen, the British cabinet Defence Committee decided in 1959 to postpone indefinitely any plans for full-scale nuclear tests, and although the last of these on Australian soil had taken place in 1957, the minor trials remained very significant to the British weapons programme. In 1958, as the suspension of tests approached, there was a flurry of concern to ensure that these trials were not in any way covered by the moratorium.[39] To avoid reinforcing any (false) impression that they were very small nuclear explosions, their name was changed, first to 'assessment tests' and later to the still more neutral 'Maralinga experimental programme'.[40] Four types of experiment were involved, each in their own way important to nuclear weapons design: Kittens, Rats, Tims and Vixens.[41] The Australian Royal Commission on nuclear testing was later to complain that 'the most secretive aspects of the entire UK weapons testing programme were the minor trials' – even that this constituted 'a drama characterised by persistent deception and paranoid secrecy'.[42] Unfortunately the Vixen experiments also caused more environmental damage than any of the full-scale tests in Australia.

Kittens were tests of the internal neutron initiators used in Blue Danube and Red Beard; there had been five at Emu Field in 1953, and there were 94 between 1955 and 1961 at Maralinga. A source of neutrons, to begin the nuclear chain reaction at precisely the right moment in a fission weapon, is important for efficiency and reliability. British internal initiators were initially troublesome, and improvements to extend their life were most important to the deployability of Red Beard weapons, for example on aircraft carriers and on V-bombers at high states of readiness. Kittens ended in 1961 after the successful introduction of a long-life initiator in Red Beard Mk.2 (see below), and external neutron initiation (ENI) was used in all later British weapons.

Tims were tests of high-explosive implosion assemblies; there were 321 of these experiments at Maralinga between 1955 and 1963. The conventional high-explosive in a weapon assembly was fired, with a natural uranium core to simulate the fissile material in a real weapon, and the resultant movement of materials and shockwaves was measured externally with telemetry, high-speed photography and radiography. The implosion system and the compression it generates are fundamental to the efficiency and miniaturisation of fission weapons and thermonuclear primaries. Implosion was therefore most important to weapon design, and successive generations of British warheads had smaller and more advanced assemblies. Rats were very similar to Tims, but measured by gamma-ray output from small sources embedded within the assemblies. There were 125 Rats experiments at Maralinga between 1956 and 1960. Tims and Rats in late 1958 were conducted on Indigo Hammer, Red Beard and Green Grass assemblies, but by May 1959 experiments were also being made on Red Snow assemblies.[43]

Vixens were safety tests, coming in two flavours: Vixen-A, in which warheads or components were destroyed in petrol fires, of which there were 31 at Maralinga between 1959 and 1961; and Vixen-B, which were one-point explosive safety tests in which a single lens or firing point in the explosive assembly of a complete warhead was detonated – to ensure that, if this should ever happen accidentally, no nuclear yield would result. A total of 13 Vixen-B tests were conducted between 1960 and 1963. The need for the Vixen tests, especially the Vixen-Bs, appears to have been in part a result of the new Anglo-American nuclear relationship; US scientists had expressed surprise in 1958 that the current generation of in-service British nuclear warhead designs had not been made inherently one-point safe.[44] The US could not guarantee the one-point safety of its designs if British components were used; therefore, as the safety authorities in the UK refused to use US high-explosive, such trials were needed.

Meanwhile at Woomera another huge enterprise was underway. Although Australian access to nuclear secrets was limited to what was strictly necessary to understand the safety risks of nuclear testing, the Woomera range was a joint project to which Australia made a more extensive contribution and from which it gained more know-how. Peter Morton has written a splendid history of Woomera, and the joint project cannot be described here in anything but impressionistic detail.[45] Flight testing of many guided weapons and test vehicles with a nuclear connection took place at Woomera: Blue Water, Blue Steel, Bloodhound, Seaslug, Ikara. Blue Streak was the biggest undertaking of all: 'trials on the colossal scale required for Blue Streak went far beyond any purpose to which Woomera had yet been put'.[46] Firings of the Black Knight research rocket began in 1958. Two huge concrete launch emplacements were built for Blue Streak itself at the top of a rocky escarpment overlooking a salt pan, where exhaust gases would escape relatively harmlessly. 'Each had a servicing tower, 500 tonnes in weight and eight storeys high, running on rails along a causeway out to the apron ... Built into and around each emplacement was a mass of equipment: fire-fighting gear, storage and filling systems for fuel and oxidant, a tall umbilical mast and all the communications, control and monitoring networks'.[47] A still more impressive requirement was for a fully instrumented impact zone at Talgarno, in the Great Sandy Desert on the north-west coast of Western Australia. Here, a prohibited area 'bigger than France' was declared at the end of 1958. There would be a primary impact zone 60 miles across, where cameras would

> chart the path of the incoming dummy warhead and special telemetry would record signals from the fuzes as they triggered on impact ... further plans for Talgarno included elaborate experiments into anti-ballistic missile decoy discrimination radar ... a hemispherical receiving aerial made of a thousand tonnes of foamed polystyrene was only one component ... in this dismal place cyclone-proof housing for a thousand workers was put up or planned, and it had already seen a grand opening dinner with caviar, thrown for

the surrounding pastoralists by the [Australian] Minister [of Supply, Alan Hulme] himself.[48]

One cannot fail to be impressed by the dedication and hard work of the Australian hosts, or to feel some sympathy for their disappointment when cancellation came – without consultation. The first Blue Streak intended for firing at Woomera had got as far as the port of Los Angeles.

It is less easy to sympathise with, or at this stage fully to understand, Australia's ambition to possess nuclear weapons. That British and Australian ministers and officials discussed the subject, and occasionally made the assumption that weapons would be transferred, is now well documented.[49] During 1956, the Defence Committee of the Australian cabinet had noted that 'the effectiveness of all three Australian services would be considerably increased if they were equipped with low yield [kiloton] nuclear weapons' and recommended that 'an initial approach be made to the United Kingdom for agreement to obtain such weapons to be held by Australia'.[50] Menzies noted to Macmillan, during the latter's visit to Australia in early 1958, that he personally 'held considerable doubts about the wisdom of any such action', although the subject continued to be discussed in air-force channels, and it seems that Sir Dermot Boyle persuaded his fellow chiefs to support the idea.[51] The Australian air force was also interested in procuring V-bombers, the TSR.2, and even at one stage the Mk.3 nuclear-tipped Bloodhound surface-to-air guided weapon. Between 1958 and 1960, the Australians held similar discussions on nuclear weapons with the US, apparently winning air chief Thomas Power's support.[52] In 1961, Menzies made an attempt, in correspondence with Macmillan, to tie his endorsement of a nuclear test ban to a British agreement to supply weapons.[53]

In Jim Walsh's assessment, 'the only thing more surprising than Australia's interest in nuclear weapons was Britain's willingness to provide them'[54] – or at least to consider providing them. The prospect of arms sales provides one explanation: TSR.2 and Bloodhound both competed with rival American nuclear-capable systems, the F-111 and Nike Hercules, and British companies and officials will certainly not have wanted to lose out just for want of a nuclear option. Both countries were also conscious of SEATO plans for the nuclear defence of south-east Asia. Britain had made plans for Canberras and V-bombers to be able to use Red Beards, including from the Australian forward airbase at Butterworth in Malaya; what was wrong with the

Australian air force doing the same, perhaps under similar dual-key arrangements as had been introduced in NATO? Britain was hampered however, after the 1958 bilateral agreement, by the fact that its nuclear secrets were no longer necessarily all its own to give away.

Nuclear forces

For Bomber Command, the mainstay of Britain's nuclear force in these years, 'readiness was all'.[55] This obsession reflected that of SAC in the US, and especially LeMay, who had discovered to his horror in 1948 that:

> The Air Force had gone to utter hell. This was in the days when, if you went into flight equipment supply and needed to draw some equipment along about Saturday morning, you found some raunchy civilian in charge, sleeping on the counter. And, when you waked him up, he said that it would be impossible for you to draw any equipment before Monday: the sergeant had gone into town for the weekend with the keys to the lockers in his pocket ... I should go on record and say this flatly: we didn't have one crew, *not one crew* in the entire command who could do a professional job. Not one of the outfits was up to strength – neither in airplanes nor in people nor anything else.[56]

But, as LeMay reflected, 'the atomic bomb was with us, and the atomic bomb was here to stay; it had replaced the horse and buggy'.[57] Slacking therefore had no place in SAC, which in LeMay's estimate had to be ready instantly to mount a full-strength strategic strike against the Soviet Union. SAC was drilled and drilled and drilled again to perfection; the RAF followed suit. The influence of Air Marshals Sir Harry Broadhurst and Sir Kenneth Cross, successive chiefs of Bomber Command between 1956 and 1963, was important in this regard. Both came from Fighter Command, and Broadhurst, on his arrival, was as disappointed as LeMay by the prevailing culture. A bomber crew in the mid-1950s could take up to six hours to get briefed and airborne, whereas 'in the quick-reaction fighter world, a pilot often had to take off with no briefing time at all because fighter men realised that the nuclear jet age made leisurely responses a thing of the past ... Sir Harry's first priority therefore was to change the whole mental approach of his command to bring it in line with the jet age and the atomic bomb'.[58]

96 Nuclear Illusion, Nuclear Reality

One air marshal summarised the years between 1958 and 1962 in Bomber Command thus:

> Much more comprehensive and detailed alert and readiness plans were devised and progressively implemented ... The V-force had to be able to generate and disperse at any time of the day or night, including weekends and holidays. So additional specialist ground equipment, dispersals and ORPs [operational readiness platforms at the runway end, to reduce taxying], manpower for two shifts, and improved communications, were essential requirements. The 'bomber controller' arrangement, whereby changes in readiness states and the scramble instructions could be passed by landline direct to every crew at cockpit readiness (emulating Fighter Command's telescramble arrangements), was introduced.[59]

The reality of the very earliest dispersal exercises was a little less smooth than this calm precis suggests:

> 'There was a great deal of inane running about', says one captain. 'Chaps would slither around in mud or on ice, or jump from moving lorries encumbered with heavy bags and twist ankles, all in the cause of trying to get airborne five minutes ago'. More haste and less speed led six aircrew to get into one aircraft and four in the other, resulting in the unedifying sight of two co-pilots fighting over one seat. Then, with the older men still croaking and gasping for breath, garbled messages would come through so that aircraft scrambled when they should have taxied or crews got out when they should have carried on.[60]

Such performances were soon improved. In 1958, Bomber Command set a requirement for 20 per cent of V-bombers to be armed and dispersed within two hours of the order to go, and 75 per cent within 24 hours. Aircraft were to be sustainable at 15 minutes' readiness for take-off for a week, or 40 minutes' readiness for a month. In June 1959, only one V-bomber squadron was able to meet this requirement – the main problem being shortages of maintenance personnel – but in February 1960, Cross was able to report that all 12 of his squadrons met the target.[61] There were 16 dispersal airfields ready for use, so that bombers would be less likely to be caught on the ground by a pre-emptive Soviet attack. In April 1960, a new four-engine start drill enabled a Vulcan B.1 at Waddington to scramble within 57 seconds.[62]

This was just as well, for the Air Ministry now feared – partly because of its knowledge of BMEWS – that *in extremis* only three minutes' warning of an incoming Soviet missile attack might now be available. This was no mere academic point, for the Blue Streak cancellation had been justified publicly by the argument that the missiles were vulnerable to pre-emptive attack, and it was becoming hard to argue convincingly that the V-force was any less exposed. Bomber Command's very existence was therefore at stake. At the end of 1961, the Air Council decided to put the whole V-bomber force on quick-reaction alert (QRA), with one aircraft of each squadron permanently at 15 minutes' readiness.[63] The first of the Micky Finn series of no-notice dispersal exercises was also held in December 1961.

Britain's three types of V-bomber were built in response to a 1946 requirement for medium bombers able to penetrate Soviet airspace at high altitude (55,000ft) and high subsonic speed. The Vickers Valiant, appearing first, was something of an interim design but provided, for some years, the mainstay of RAF Bomber Command's nuclear capability, in addition dropping test devices over Maralinga and near Christmas Island. The Avro Vulcan and Handley Page Victor were more advanced aircraft, and themselves progressively updated over time until the final B.2 versions entered service, with much improved performance.[64] Already, by the end of 1958, there were 82 V-bombers operational – exceeding the number of British nuclear weapons available. There were Valiants at Marham in Norfolk, Honington in Suffolk and Wittering in Leicestershire; Vulcans at Waddington and Scampton in Lincolnshire, and Finningley in Yorkshire; and a few Victors working up at Cottesmore, in Rutland. Finally several more Valiants were operational in the auxiliary roles of photo-reconnaissance and electronic counter-measures (ECM), and there was a training unit for Valiants and Victors at Gaydon in Warwickshire.[65] Delivery of Valiants was complete, but Vulcans and Victors continued in production. A final target force of 144 front-line bombers had been agreed by the Defence Committee in 1957, including 104 of the advanced B.2s (72 Vulcans and 32 Victors) and 40 of the original B.1s. During 1959 and 1960, more Victors arrived at Honington; by the summer of 1960, there were around 100 B.1 aircraft in service.[66] At around this time, the final target force total was revised downwards by one Victor squadron to 96 front-line aircraft. Although the V-force was now therefore numerically complete, its aircraft continued to be updated. In October 1960, the first Vulcan B.2s entered service at Scampton, where two more squadrons received the same aircraft during 1961. During 1960 and 1961, Valiants began to be retired from the front-line bomber force, three squadrons at Marham being resubordinated to SACEUR for tactical targets in Europe, and others becoming air-refuelling tankers.

In view of the growth of Soviet surface-to-air missile (SAM) defences and continuing delays with the introduction of the stand-off weapon Blue Steel, new plans were now drawn up to penetrate to V-bomber targets. As Julian Amery noted in September 1961, Bomber Command now proposed 'to reduce the effectiveness of SAM defence by the following methods: (i) the use of ECM. By the end of the year the bulk of the force should have an ECM capability. (ii) Tactical routeing to avoid known SAM sites … (iii) Increasing the number of aircraft allocated to the more important and heavily defended targets … There is the further consideration that the Russian SAM crews are only now receiving their operational equipment, and that it will be some time before they can work up to peak efficiency'.[67]

As well as the V-bombers, RAF Canberra light bombers were given a nuclear role in the late 1950s. Some Canberras were based in the UK; others were in Germany, at Akrotiri in Cyprus, and at Tengah in Singapore. Training for nuclear delivery using a low-altitude bombing system (LABS) manoeuvre, in which the aircraft approached at low level before tossing the bomb towards the target in a sudden climb, began in earnest in 1958–59. LABS bombing was not as accurate as high-altitude bombing, and it was intended for use against fairly large but heavily defended tactical targets such as vehicle parks and railway yards in eastern European towns and cities.[68] Four squadrons of Canberras, based in Germany, were assigned to SACEUR in the nuclear role, starting in 1958. They were equipped initially with US Mk.7 tactical bombs stored under Project E arrangements (see below) at Wildenrath, Bruggen, Laarbruch and Geilenkirchen.[69]

For a time, there were also nuclear-armed Canberras based at Bomber Command stations in the UK, although there are few references to them in the secondary literature. The UK Canberra force was run down fairly quickly after the Sandys defence review, and only four squadrons (64 aircraft UE) survived into 1960: two at Coningsby in Lincolnshire, and two at Upwood in Huntingdonshire. Coningsby aircraft certainly exercised in the LABS role in 1959, and three of the Canberra squadrons were inspected by SACEUR, to whom they were assigned, in October 1960.[70] It is not entirely clear whether and how many Red Beard or US Mk.7 weapons, or both, were available for these aircraft.[71] The Air Council had decided, even before the UK-based Canberras were given a nuclear capability, to replace them with a smaller number of more capable Valiants once the build-up of the main V-force allowed. As noted above, one Valiant squadron at Marham was therefore assigned to SACEUR from 1 January 1960, and two more from July 1961; the Canberra squadrons were disbanded. Agreement was reached in April 1960 that each of the 24 Valiants would carry two US Mk.28 bombs.[72] Meanwhile, however, Canberras at Akrotiri were given an interim nuclear capability in March 1960, 16 aircraft having access to weapons normally stored in the UK but capable of being moved to Cyprus for up to 90 days in an emergency. A permanent storage site for 32 Red Beards was opened in November 1961.[73]

Under the formal Thor agreement, published in February 1958, 60 of the American missiles were deployed at 20 RAF bases in eastern England. Thor was a single-stage 1500nm-range IRBM, similar in conception to, but smaller than, Blue Streak. Weighing 110,000lb at launch, Thor was 64ft 10in long and eight feet in diameter.[74] Douglas was prime contractor for the missile; the Rocketdyne division of North American Aviation made the liquid-oxygen (LOX)/kerosene-fuelled motors; the AC Spark Plug division of General Motors the inertial guidance system; and General Electric the blunt cone-shaped heat-sink type re-entry vehicle (RV). The Mk.49 warhead, based on the same Mk.28 design as Britain's Red Snow but using a thinner case, had a design yield of 1.44Mt. Thor was designed to fire in 15 minutes from guidance system start, through missile erection and fuelling and target checking, to the launch order.

Thor bases were manned by the RAF, but each had a US authorisation officer, responsible for warhead custody and holding one of the two keys necessary to launch the missile. By the time the first RAF-standard Thor was test-flown in the United States in November 1958, 15 pre-production missiles were already available in the UK. The first RAF-crewed launch took place at Vandenberg Air Force Base in California in April 1959, and in June the first Thor squadron was ready for operation at RAF Feltwell in Norfolk. Curiously, the official story for some time was that Thor was only a 'training' weapon, and an operational capability was only avowed by the government in December 1959.[75] By April 1960, the Thor force was complete, and additional measures were taken to improve its readiness over the succeeding months, for example routinely mating warheads to the missiles and conducting 'double propellant flow' or 'wet' countdowns, in which the missile fuelling procedure was tested realistically. By mid-1961, the RAF had gained a great deal of experience in missile operations, although with the cancellation of Blue Streak – just months after Thor's introduction – it was already unclear that this experience would be of any practical future benefit. In September, the Air Council discussed the continuation of the Thor force; Maurice Dean, the Permanent Secretary and one of the leading proponents of Blue Streak in the past, was now disinclined to support the argument that a liquid-fuelled missile, deployed on the surface, could add any useful element of deterrence.[76] Thor was second best to the V-force in the eyes of the RAF, its bases quiet and its personnel some way out of the career mainstream. Still, Thor was a real nuclear capability at a time when the rest of the RAF was struggling to catch up.

The Royal Navy's aircraft carriers constituted a further nuclear-capable force after 1960. In contrast to the RAF's V-bombers and Thor missiles, the navy thought of itself primarily as a sub-strategic force, and its strategy and doctrine for the 1960s tended to focus on operations outside Europe, in particular east of Suez. As I have argued elsewhere, experience during the Second World War had left naval officers and Admiralty officials with the feeling that a flexible, balanced surface navy, centred upon the carrier, was required to deal with the broad spectrum of military operations.[77] Nobody was more assiduous than Mountbatten in furthering this concept. Tactical nuclear weapons had their place, as a reliable means of destroying various targets of particular naval interest: *Sverdlov*-class cruisers, perhaps, or later the fast deep-diving nuclear-powered submarine (SSN). In war, the carriers would have added their nuclear strength to the carrier 'striking fleet' of the US Navy, but although the US Navy certainly aspired to a strategic strike role, the Royal Navy's carriers were conceived as the centrepiece of a balanced all-purpose navy, not as a force for use against strategic targets on land. The navy had five operational carriers in this period – HMS *Ark Royal*, *Eagle*, *Victorious*, *Hermes* and *Centaur* – and with seafaring practicality the Admiralty appears to have based its nuclear weapons requirements on the storage capacity of their magazines, rather than – as the RAF now did – the number of targets it planned to attack. The carriers were deployed worldwide as required, but the navy took special care to have one carrier on station east of Suez at all times. Naval jet aircraft – the Scimitar, Sea Vixen and the projected NA.39, later the Buccaneer – were all expected to be able to deliver Red Beard. The Admiralty at one time contemplated using US nuclear weapons, in an arrangement akin to the RAF's Project E and referred to occasionally as Project N. Although a requirement existed by December 1959 to use the US Mk.28 weapon on the Buccaneer, the practical difficulties of US storage and custody on ships at sea, and the troublesome measures necessary to modify and clear the combination of weapon and aircraft, meant the idea was not in the end pursued.[78]

Controlling nuclear operations

As Zuckerman liked to point out from time to time, deterrence was a political construct, and war-fighting plans as such were less important than the simple fact of the possession of nuclear weapons. For any nuclear-capable force, however, it was necessary to train in delivery techniques and to become familiar with operational plans. A V-bomber crew could hardly find its way to a target in the Soviet Union as part of a major coordinated attack, if this became necessary, without detailed preparatory work. For military officers in particular, the *political* credibility of the nuclear deterrent – the will to use it in a believable scenario – therefore became inextricably linked to its *technical* or *operational* credibility – having a plan that might just work.

There were two targeting plans for British strategic nuclear forces in this period: national, and Anglo-American. The national 'Bomber Command emergency war plan', adopted on 1 October 1958, involved attacks on 44 targets in major Soviet cities.[79] It seems possible that the 44 targets were in 40 cities, with two in Leningrad and four in Moscow. The national plan somewhat arbitrarily aimed to wipe out a third of the urban population of the Soviet Union – surely enough to constitute unacceptable damage, and therefore to deter the warlike pursuit of any significant Soviet political objective *vis-à-vis* the United Kingdom.[80] However far-fetched this might have seemed politically, the national plan was predicated on going into action without American support.

The Anglo-American plan, agreed between Bomber Command and SAC and also effective from 1 October 1958, had the V-bombers attacking 69 cities, 17 air bases and 20 air-defence installations. The Thor force, being under dual-key control, also later worked to the joint targeting plan (only). Thor was apparently targeted against cities because of its large warheads and relative inaccuracy.[81] The discrepancy in numbers between the national and joint plans can be explained by the practice of doubling up attacks on some targets; and by the shortage of British weapons for the purely national plan. The military targets in the joint plan may have been of particular interest to the UK – for example medium-range bomber bases, which had the potential to threaten the UK but were of less immediate concern to the US. There had been a number of discussions during the early and mid-1950s on the need to eliminate such targets early in the event of war. The joint targets perhaps also reflected Bomber Command's ability to act in the first wave of an attack, blasting a path for the larger SAC force to follow; this had been another theme of earlier discussions. Although it was now embarrassing for senior RAF officers effectively to accept instructions from the much larger USAF, the adoption of the joint plan in 1958 did reflect a restoration of something approaching arrangements during the Second World War, when Bomber Command and the then US Army Air Force had been able to debate, and indeed violently disagree over, targeting plans on much more equal terms.

For RAF Canberras, and later the Valiants assigned to NATO, suitable tactical targets in eastern Europe were chosen by SACEUR. Coordination between SACEUR and SAC was limited in the days before the creation of an American single integrated operational plan (SIOP), and in theory there could have been duplication between the SACEUR and joint Bomber Command/SAC targeting plans. If so, I have found no declassified British comment on the peculiarity of the situation. Targets for army regiments armed with Corporal, and later Honest John and nuclear artillery, would have been determined by suitably authorised corps and divisional commanders according to their wartime needs.

As to when and how a nuclear attack might be launched by the UK, policy was laid down in 1958: 'The final decision to commit Britain's nuclear forces would not be taken "until there is confirmation that an attack has been launched by the Soviet Union".'[82] On receipt of information that an attack was likely, first, ministers, the chiefs and US intelligence authorities would be informed; second, the Chief of the Air Staff would immediately order all possible *unobtrusive* measures to bring the RAF to readiness, and the Air Ministry would inform SAC; third, the cabinet and chiefs would meet; fourth, the cabinet would decide on any further preparatory measures to be taken; and finally the Prime Minister would try at least to speak personally to the American President. Once launched, the V-force would either proceed directly to attack, if the Prime Minister had authorised this, or else remain airborne for a time to await instructions. The Chief of the Air Staff had authority, *in extremis*, to order the V-force into the air if he believed it would otherwise be destroyed on the ground; but not to order it to proceed to attack. This practical but somewhat cumbersome set of arrangements was subject to review during 1961 because of concerns about warning times, and an *ad hoc* committee of ministers was formed for the purpose. The chiefs also set up a Nuclear Strike Coordinating Committee during 1961, which for the first time involved the Royal Navy and which spawned working parties on targeting, the USSR and the far east.[83]

To underpin these arrangements for the political control of Britain's nuclear forces, a Bomber Command alert and readiness plan was adopted in 1959, listing a series of alert states from five ('normal') up to one ('when an imminent risk of attack exists').[84] Alert levels up to three were at the discretion of the RAF chain of command, and included all of the unobtrusive measures referred to in the 1958 political directive. The very visible movement of the V-force to its dispersal airfields would come at alert level two. Practical problems remained: the maintenance of communications in an emergency; the chain of command in the event of the Prime Minister's death or incapacity; and safeguards in the event of his 'going bananas' and randomly trying to launch a strike. It is also clear that, in the absence of permissive action links or an equivalent technology, there was nothing *physically* to stop the launch of British nuclear weapons by the forces, although there is evidence of efforts to ensure a 'two-person' rule was in operation at all levels of command.[85] Even in the case of the Thor force, subject to dual-key arrangements, stories have surfaced of hair-raising ways around the command and control system: a screwdriver substituting for the US authentication officer's key, or a weapon armed accidentally by leaning against the control panel, or even 'shooting the American officers concerned'.[86] Some of these theoretical and practical issues were addressed later.

A final important aspect of the control of nuclear weapons was safety, and here too arrangements were revised in the late 1950s. The Ordnance Board, an independent inter-service technical trials and advisory organisation administered by the MoS and involving the Third Sea Lord, the Controller of Munitions at the War Office, and Controller Aircraft (CA), was responsible for advising on the (conventional) explosive, electrical and mechanical aspects of nuclear warhead safety. CA remained responsible for the overall safety release of free-fall bombs and missiles carried by aircraft, being advised on various aspects by the Ordnance Board, AWRE and the Aeroplane and Armament Experimental Establishment at Boscombe Down.[87] An inter-departmental Nuclear Weapons Safety Committee, chaired by Brundrett and including independent members, was set up in 1959 to advise the Minister of Defence on the safety aspects of transport, storage, handling, operational training and use of nuclear weapons.[88] Some writers have described safety 'problems' with British nuclear weapons, especially Violet Club and Yellow Sun Mk.1 with their large fission warheads, but it seems clear that the safety authorities erred on the side of caution and that operational flexibility was in all cases sacrificed for safety. One of the major contributions made by the safety authorities was the Ordnance Board's insistence on the use of British rather than American high-explosive in British warheads – a somewhat curious position to take, given that CA released several US Project E weapons using the same US high-explosive for carriage in British aircraft.

Megaton bombs

The requirement for a megaton free-falling bomb for the V-bombers had been issued in 1955, and by 1957 two lines of development were being followed in response: Yellow Sun, a 7000lb weapon, 21ft long and four feet in diameter, which was expected to enter service in 1959; and the larger 'interim megaton bomb' Violet Club, 9000lb in weight and mounted in a Blue Danube casing, 24ft long and five feet two inches in diameter. Both weapons used the large fission warhead Green Grass, the operational limitations of which were a considerable inconvenience to the RAF, and there were hopes by 1958 that a 'stage 2' Yellow Sun could be introduced at a later date to take advantage of progress in testing and incorporate instead a Granite-type thermonuclear warhead. Green Grass included a large amount of highly enriched uranium – probably many tens of kilogrammes – and the danger existed of super-criticality in the event of an accidental deformation of the warhead. Road transport of the complete warhead would be dangerous.[89] An elaborate safety mechanism was devised, consisting eventually of around 120,000 small steel balls in a cavity inside the warhead, adding over 1000lb to the safe warhead weight but keeping the fissile components apart. Final arming involved removal of the steel balls, but this lengthy and delicate process affected dispersal and readiness plans for the V-force. On at least one occasion, the ball-bearings were lost accidentally on the floor of an aircraft hangar, to general consternation.[90] Deliveries of Violet Club to the RAF nevertheless began in February 1958, and at around the same time Yellow Sun ballistic shapes were being drop-tested.[91] The Yellow Sun casing had an extremely blunt nose, to make its air-burst barometric fuze more reliable, to slow the weapon's fall so that the delivering aircraft could reliably escape, and to avoid aircraft release problems with Blue Danube (tests had shown that, in certain conditions, Blue Danube would fly in company with the launching aircraft after being 'dropped'). The new Yellow Sun shape did not eliminate release disturbance problems entirely, however. Although the weapon did nose down rapidly, as required, on at least one occasion this happened so quickly that the tail hit and damaged the trials aircraft. Various modifications were suggested in response.[92]

The availability of US warhead designs under the bilateral agreement of July 1958 made a big difference to plans for megaton bombs, and the DRPC's atomic sub-committee decided in November to bring an early halt to further development of Green Grass and substitute the Red Snow warhead in later Yellow Suns. Thus there would be a Mk.1 Yellow Sun with Green Grass, and a Mk.2 Yellow Sun with Red Snow.[93] The US warhead was superior in several ways; in particular, its more economical use of fissile material would mean a unit cost of only £500,000 for Yellow Sun Mk.2, against £1.2 millions for the Mk.1.[94] As the Red Snow warhead was also considerably lighter than Green Grass, it was clear that the ballistic behaviour of Yellow Sun Mk.2 would differ from the earlier version, but rather than repeat all manner of wind-tunnel and drop tests, the Mk.2 was ballasted up to the weight of the Mk.1. Still, new fuzing and internal structural changes meant for example that ground handling equipment had to be modified and 'what seemed a fairly trivial change gave rise to a large development programme running almost in parallel with the original [Mk.1] although of course slightly behind in timescale'.[95] Yellow Sun could have been used in air- or ground-burst mode, using barometric or impact fuzes.

In November 1958, an Air Ministry official noted that 'Bomber Command wish to get rid of Violet Clubs as soon as possible'.[96] Production of the interim megaton bomb was therefore curtailed at five, and the weapons were withdrawn from service as soon as possible. The warheads were removed and reworked into Mk.1 Yellow Suns in the spring and summer of 1959.[97] Initially it was envisaged that only 22 Mk.1 Yellow Suns would be procured, including the five conversions from Violet Club, but this number was increased later to 26 and finally, at the end of 1959, to 37, largely because the Air Ministry wanted the quickest possible build-up of megaton weapons for the V-bombers. The first order for 24 Red Snow warheads was also placed in 1959, and the Air Ministry requirements for Yellow Sun, Blue Streak, Blue Steel and its longer-range successor OR.1159 were revised to incorporate the new warhead.[98] At this stage, the Air Ministry envisaged a final total of 104 megaton weapons for the front-line V-bombers, and later 120 warheads for Blue Streak.[99] Yellow Sun Mk.2 weapons began to enter service in January 1961. By May, emergency clearance had been given for Vulcan B.1/1A aircraft to carry the bomb, and by the end of the year a respectable stockpile of 43 Yellow Sun Mk.2s had been delivered, as well as all 37 Mk.1s.[100]

Blue Steel

The powered bomb Blue Steel, a guided 'stand-off' weapon to obviate the need for the V-bombers to penetrate short-range air defences in the immediate vicinity of their targets, had meanwhile been in development for a number of years. The original requirement, issued in 1954, called for a weapon for the V-bombers with a 100-mile range, a speed of Mach 2, inertial guidance, a megaton warhead and a service entry date of 1960.[101] The development and production of Blue Steel was many times more challenging than a simple free-fall bomb. 'Blue Steel, both in size and in the number and complication of its control systems, was virtually an aeroplane – in fact the company regarded it as such'.[102] Avro, at Woodford in Cheshire, was chosen – despite having little experience with guided weapons – as lead contractor; Elliott Bros in London worked on inertial guidance under RAE Farnborough as design authority; Armstrong Siddeley provided rocket motors; and de Havillands were involved in internal missile power supply. Like Yellow Sun, Blue Steel was designed around the Green Grass warhead – to the annoyance of the Air Ministry, who would have preferred a more operationally flexible warhead, perhaps of the Granite type – until in November 1958 the decision was made to fit Red Snow.

The final weapon was a little over 35ft long and weighed around 13,000lb. It had a cigar-shaped fuselage with a maximum diameter of just over four feet; delta wings aft with a span of 13ft, turned downwards at the tips to fit under the Victor; vertical stabiliser fins, also aft; and canard foreplanes. Blue Steel was powered by high-test peroxide (HTP) and kerosene. Modifications to the launch aircraft were required in order to exchange accurate navigational information with the missile; the aircraft navigation and missile guidance systems were closely coupled up to the point of launch. After launch, from about 40,000ft, the missile was designed to fall a short distance before engine start, climb to over 70,000ft and accelerate to Mach 2.5, then dive to the target. Air- or ground-burst mode could be used, with barometric or impact fuzing.[103]

By 1958, Blue Steel was running some six months behind schedule, but Humphrey Wynn, for one, is inclined to be forgiving of the missile's problems: 'With so many exacting [trials] authorities, with the problems of new technology (a supersonic flying bomb had never before been produced in Great Britain) and with the elaborate planning necessary for every trials weapon ... it is no wonder that the Blue Steel programme got behind schedule – making the air staff hopes of an introduction into service in 1960 ever less realisable'.[104] By the end of the year, flight trials with two-fifths scale models at Aberporth in Wales had been completed, confirming Avro's estimates of aerodynamics and providing useful experience in managing and instrumenting air-launched missile trials. Scale-model trials were also conducted at Woomera during 1958–59. Full-scale trials were now required with stainless-steel missile structures approximating closely to the operational weapon, in order to obtain information on supersonic flight over a realistic trajectory, to check environmental conditions within the missile, and to examine the release and interfaces between the aircraft and missile. Delays in producing stainless-steel pressings for the double-curved fuselage meant the first full-scale trials had to use aluminium-alloy structures. The inertial navigation system meanwhile was huge and complex, based on thermionic valves and not transistors, and required refrigeration. American gyroscopes had eventually to be incorporated. By the middle of 1961, it was clear that Blue Steel service entry could not come before 1962, and friction was developing between the Air Ministry and the prime contractor, Avro. Indeed, Wynn assesses that 'there can be few major British defence contracts which caused such bitter feelings'. In October 1960, the Secretary of State for Air was told of 'grave shortcomings in the project management' of Blue Steel, and of an escalation in research and development costs from £35 millions to £60 millions.[105]

Part of the friction arose because of Avro's continuing interest in touting for future work on longer-range missiles, and the Air Ministry's contrary focus on getting the basic Blue Steel Mk.1 in service as soon as possible. At the end of 1959, Blue Steel Mk.2 – not in fact a variant of Blue Steel but effectively a whole new missile, intended to meet the OR.1159 requirement – was cancelled on the advice of the BNDSG. The missile's range and speed were impressive, but its accuracy was not; and it had become clear that Avro's work on it was interfering with the Mk.1 Blue Steel and even the stable platform for the TSR.2 aircraft's navigation system.[106] In September 1960, as the BNDSG began again to meet to discuss future deterrent systems and insurance against the failure of Skybolt, Avro and the MoA nevertheless presented a new menu of possible Blue Steel developments: Mk.1A with external fuel tanks for a 250nm range, but reduced accuracy; Mk.1* (pronounced one-star) with HTP/hydrazine fuel and a new wing shape for a 400nm range, but still less accuracy; Mk.1*D with the new wing and tanks but not the new fuel; Mk.1*E with the new wing, fuel *and* tanks for a range of 440nm; and Mk.1*KG with a whole new engine.[107] Later, these potential variants were joined by Mk.1S, essentially the Mk.1A weapon with a different internal arrangement, using the lighter Skybolt warhead in place of Red Snow to make way for more fuel.[108] None of these variants was adopted, and the Air Ministry felt work on them was distracting Avro from its rightful concentration on the basic missile. Avro, on the other hand, will have viewed with concern the Air Ministry's interest in Skybolt and its own likely future exclusion from the long-range missile business.

By February 1961, Blue Steel was in a 'crisis', with correspondence between ministers on delays to the first test launch of a fully navigated missile round. The question, as Sandys admitted, was 'whether we will know that Blue Steel will work by January 1962. The answer appears to be "No" ... on any realistic assessment of the development firing programme, we cannot expect to have proved Blue Steel even to the very minimum standard by January 1962'.[109] This gloomy assessment was informed by further firings: 'Complete Blue Steels started to fly [at Woomera] in 1961 with poor results at first ... because of a new problem with the auxiliary power unit, a small HTP-driven turbine which supplied hydraulic power to the alternators and control surfaces'. In June, a navigated round was fired in Australia, but after a series of unscheduled climbs and dives it had to be destroyed by range safety.[110] There were 57 missiles on order to equip 48 front-line aircraft, and 57 Red Snow warhead 'pods' had been ordered to match, but by the end of 1961 none of the warheads was available.[111]

Blue Streak

The OR.1139 requirement for a medium-range ballistic missile, which led to the Blue Streak project, was issued by the Air Ministry in 1955. Research work into ballistic missiles had been underway on a small scale for several years already, and once on a formal project footing it became clear that Blue Streak was an extremely complex undertaking. De Havilland Propellers acted as prime contractor, responsible for overall coordination, missile assembly, the conduct of trials and also the missile's control systems; de Havilland Aircraft took responsibility for the airframe; Rolls-Royce for propulsion; Sperry and English Electric for inertial guidance; and Marconi for ground-based radar and communications. Saunders-Roe were to build a test vehicle, Black Knight, designed to study re-entry phenomena for Blue Streak. RAE Farnborough also played a major part in the programme.[112]

Blue Streak was a single-stage, LOX/kerosene-fuelled, twin-motored missile with a design range of 2000nm.[113] Ten feet in diameter, 60 or more feet long – an exact figure is difficult to quote, as the final RV design had not been agreed at cancellation – Blue Streak weighed around 200,000lb at launch. The missile's characteristic corrugated appearance was the result of vertical 'stringers' for structural strength around unpressurised parts of the missile body. The warhead, required to yield a megaton and weigh a ton (2240lb), had already caused design problems for the missile. Whereas in the US the Polaris missile, for example, was designed around the assumption that a light warhead of around 600–700lb would be available by the time the missile was ready for service, in the UK the designers of Blue Streak had been less optimistic; hence the 1955 decision to use twin-motor propulsion.

By 1958, the Orange Herald warhead for Blue Streak – a large fission design akin to Green Grass, but considerably smaller – had been tested. English Electric and Marconi had been eliminated from the guidance programme, and only Sperry remained. Marconi's proposed beam-riding radio guidance system, potentially vulnerable to electronic countermeasures, had been an unnecessary complication, but some regretted the removal of risk-reduction or 'insurance' elements from the programme. Sperrys had eventually to buy in American gyroscope designs from Kearfott, manufactured under licence in Edinburgh by Ferranti. The stable platform, accelerometers and other components of the guidance system were home-produced. Rolls-Royce had been given access to North American Aviation's rocket motor design, used in the US Atlas missile, and this – with modifications in particular to ignition and shut-down arrangements – formed the basis for Blue Streak's engine, the RZ-2. De Havilland also had access to know-how from Convair in the US on the construction of the thin pressurised stainless-steel missile body.

Blue Streak was designed with retaliatory underground launch in mind. Morton describes the operation of the weapon in dramatic terms: 'Even if the landscape was desolated and most of the population dead, the great portals protecting the missile shafts would still yawn open, their great bulk and powerful water jets sweeping aside the shattered ruins on the surface. Each cover weighed 750 tonnes and was strong enough to withstand the steel-melting heat of a nuclear fireball nearby. Just 17 seconds later Blue Streak … would emerge on its … journey of vengeance'.[114] The seven-storey underground structure and its protection against external blast, heat and the hazards of highly combustible liquid fuel, vibration and noise were a huge undertaking.[115] The pumping of fuel into the missile before launch, for example – necessarily in a very short period of time and under very high pressure – was quite a feat.

A deployment of 60 missiles was envisaged by 1959, although smaller numbers were considered around the time of cancellation. Following launch, control systems would tilt Blue Streak towards its target; the engines would burn for three to four minutes. An Anglo-American conference was told in 1957 that 'the missile at [engine] cut-off would be climbing with an attitude of some 36° to the launch horizontal and would be required therefore to turn through approximately 90° to achieve the re-entry angle ... This would be effected by the firing of two cartridge "bonkers", carried in the head, after separation, thereby generating the required angular movement. When the correct re-entry orientation was attained, the head would be spun'.[116] Air-burst or impact, at 2000nm range, would be around 20 minutes after launch.

The stop-go political attitude to Blue Streak during 1958 made the missile's progress somewhat difficult. The decision in September that work should be 'unobtrusively retarded' was a particular nuisance, especially as previous instructions had been to find ways of accelerating service entry from the expected date of 1965 to 1963 or even earlier. Although no insuperable problem stood in the way of the Blue Streak programme at this time, there was concern in particular over slippage to the ambitious schedule of static firings at the Spadeadam range in Cumberland and test flights at Woomera. Test firings were very much on the programme's critical path, and as most capital expenditure was currently on these facilities it would be equally hard to accelerate or delay Blue Streak without taking very dramatic measures. During 1958 Sandys set up a working party under Richard Chilver to advise him on these issues. Chilver reported that the 1965 date could not be advanced 'unless all control of expenditure is abandoned', and although missile rounds of an 'uncertain standard of reliability and accuracy' might be available in 1963, he did not recommend putting such missiles into service.[117] Here was another difference of approach between Blue Streak and the US Polaris programme – the US Navy was quite happy to accept a Polaris missile into service with short range and an 'emergency capability' warhead in 1960, for the sake of the programme schedule. To British engineers, quality, and (when pressed) cost, appear to have been more precious than time. Nevertheless Chilver reported that the first guided flight in Australia was still expected in mid-1961, in line with expectations a year previously.[118]

At the end of 1958, in line with other megaton weapons, Blue Streak's projected warhead was replaced with Red Snow, and the separate warhead requirement OR.1142 was revised thus: 'The warhead package (comprising the warhead installation less fuzing system and power supplies) is to be Red Snow. The same warhead package ... will be used in the bomb OR.1136 (Yellow Sun Mk.2) and its successor and the warhead installations OR.1141 (Blue Steel) and OR.1159. Any mountings, lugs or attachments which are required must allow ready interchangeability'.[119] The following year, the separate warhead requirement OR.1142 was cancelled in favour of a 'standard megaton warhead capsule' requirement OR.1171, written specifically with Red Snow in mind.[120] The new warhead meant re-work in the RV design. As Roy Dommett recalls, 'RV design evolved rapidly ... It started from a simple sphere just as did the Soviet man[ned] space vehicles, through the rather blunted high semi-angle cones as used on the US air force Atlas and Thor ballistic missiles, and then to fine single and finally faired triconic shapes'[121] ... 'For low radar cross section, with a pointed nose, well rounded corners and a shaped rear, [the RV] looked like a child's whipping top'.[122] Launches of the Black Knight research rocket, beginning in September 1958, helped understand the complex physical phenomena associated with re-entry.[123] Zuckerman was later told that work on Black Knight to reduce the radar cross-section of the RV almost left the British with the embarrassing problem of having no radar at the Woomera range able to track it successfully.[124]

Alongside work on the RV and warhead came work on decoys and penetration aids to help defeat the then-suspected Soviet anti-ballistic missile (ABM) defence. Correspondence on the subject dated back to at least April 1957.[125] Blue Streak decoys 'were going to weigh about 20lb and provision was to be made to carry up to 30 or 40 of them'.[126] A typical decoy would consist of 'a ten-inch diameter sphere at the wide end of a three feet long cone',[127] but other shapes were possible: 'it is hoped to carry some 20 of these decoys and as a bonus a number of extra spheres might also be inserted. Measurements are continuing on hollow cylinders and jacks'.[128] Each decoy was designed to have the same drag-to-mass ratio as the RV, and efforts were made to make them approximate to the RV in hot-body radiation properties and coatings, so that behaviour on re-entry would be similar to that of the RV. Light-weight balloon decoys and the dispersal pattern of parts of the boost rocket were also considered effective elements of counter-ABM penetration. Finally noise jammers were included to stop an ABM tracking radar finding its range. A separating mechanism had to be devised in order that a cloud of about ten miles radius around the real RV could be created, with the warhead's position variable within the cloud.[129] In the words of one scientist, this Blue Streak penetration suite was 'more than enough to flatten the opposition at the time'.[130] Although work on the RV and decoys was never finally completed, it was advanced enough to influence later thinking on Skybolt and Polaris. Sir Steuart Mitchell looked back on it with pride: 'The design of the re-entry head which we finally ended up with for Blue Streak is: (a) of British origin; (b) it is now joint UK/US information; (c) it is agreed by the US to be much better than their designs as regards invulnerability and US has now copied it; (d) as regards invulnerability it is so advanced that neither the US nor ourselves can conceive a counter to it'. And on decoys: 'This is a top secret field in which we are well ahead of the USA'.[131]

Kiloton bombs

Britain's first atomic bomb design, known by its MoS project codename Blue Danube or its service designation 'Bomb, HE, 10,000lb MC', was old technology by 1958 and the available evidence suggests that production had ceased, with a stockpile of about 58 weapons available.[132] Blue Danube was large: 24ft long, 62 inches in diameter and weighing nearly four and a half tons. V-bombers were the only possible carrier aircraft. Blue Danubes were hand-assembled at Burghfield on what could hardly be described as a production-line basis. An RAF ground-crew instructor of the time recently described the weapon as 'a mass of chattering relays'.[133] Modifications and changing production techniques over time meant that individual weapons differed, and the complexity of the design, for example its multiple fuzing arrangements, meant that it had serviceability problems. The DRPC atomic sub-committee was told that:

> For political reasons, Blue Danube was introduced into the service at a fairly early development stage, which would normally be regarded as premature. The service has thereby witnessed at close hand, a considerable number of development faults, which normally would have been cleared before entry into the service, and this has had a tendency to bias service opinion against the weapon ... in extreme cases, such as the firing installation and the time fuze, the supply [of components] has failed even to match the number of weapon cores ... a total number of 222 defect reports has been raised by the services in a period of approximately two years ... to date, 150 modifications have been incorporated.

Of less importance than the firing installation and time fuze, problems also included 'a failure of the nose junction box which would have resulted in the inability to produce an air-burst ... splitting of the polythene sleeves of firing cable connectors, and excessive loss of pressure in airbags ... [and] inefficient travel of the [tail] flip-out mechanism'.[134] As a result of these and other problems, full CA release was not achieved until July 1957, almost four years after the first Blue Danube had been delivered to RAF Wittering.[135] Blue Danube was not a *crude* nuclear weapon;

if anything, its engineering was too elaborate. It existed in at least two versions: the Mk.1 weapon had to be armed on the ground by insertion of the fissile core in its 'gauntlet' through the side of the bomb casing; Mk.2 had 'in-flight insertion' of the core for extra safety on take-off. There is a suggestion that the Mk.2 modification proved too troublesome and was later abandoned. As stocks of Red Beard weapons were built up during 1961 and 1962, Blue Danubes were taken out of service and the fissile material in their cores reworked into the newer weapons.[136]

Red Beard was the second British nuclear weapon to be conceived, after Blue Danube, but the fourth to enter service, having been overtaken by Violet Club and Yellow Sun Mk.1. It was intended as a tactical atomic bomb for carriage on a number of different Royal Navy and RAF aircraft. The bomb weighed a nominal 2000lb – in fact nearer to 1650lb[137] – and measured 12ft ten inches long by 28 inches in diameter. Red Beard had its origins in studies of tactical nuclear weapons in the early months of 1951. The discussions soon came to revolve around 'small' bombs – smaller, that is, than the 10,000lb Blue Danube. By July 1953, a working party of the chiefs had recommended a weapon recognisable as Red Beard: 30 inches in diameter, yielding ten kilotons and for carriage on the RAF's Javelin and the navy's N113 (later Scimitar). A joint operational requirement was issued to the MoS on 5 November 1953. The navy was interested in attacking enemy warships, especially the new *Sverdlov*-class Soviet cruisers, either in harbour or at sea, where they might be operating in a commerce-raiding role in the North Atlantic. The RAF was interested in attacking targets in eastern Europe, such as troop concentrations and airfields.[138] AWRE was confident, because of advances in implosion techniques, that it could achieve a similar yield to Blue Danube in a much smaller bomb. Red Beard used a technology described as 'air lenses' in an implosion system known to AWRE as Tortoise.[139]

Red Beard bombs had originally been required for service in 1957, but in the autumn of 1958 the in-service date was still slipping. It is possible that Aldermaston's attention had been diverted towards higher-yield variants of the Red Beard warhead using mixed or composite plutonium/uranium cores; these were certainly developed for use as primaries in some of the Granite-type weapons tested in the Pacific, and one was fired separately in Australia at the end of the Antler test series in 1957. The latest version of the operational requirement for Red Beard now called for a weapon in two versions: 'ballistic' for free-fall delivery by V-bombers, and 'loft' for delivery by naval aircraft and RAF Canberras using LABS. The weapons differed in their fuzing arrangements, the ballistic version using radar and the loft version a barometric fuze. Earlier hopes for a 'retarded' version, allowing low-level delivery without the risk of climbing into enemy radar coverage near the target, were on hold. Yield was specified as 20 kilotons, although more was hoped for in later versions of the weapon, which would hopefully also have in-flight safety and be fuzed for 'universal' loft or ballistic use.[140]

Project E, an arrangement whereby US nuclear weapons, under US peacetime custody, were made available for some RAF aircraft, has been mentioned several times already. It should be seen as a stop-gap arrangement in the context of slower-than-expected deliveries of Red Beard and serviceability problems with Blue Danube. A memorandum of understanding on Project E had been signed with the United States in May 1957.[141] With effect from 1 October 1958, 72 US Mk.5 atomic bombs with a yield of up to 100kt were supplied for V-bombers based at Honington, Marham and Waddington. The special nuclear storage areas at these bases were given over to the US. A problem with dispersal of aircraft carrying US weapons was already apparent, but seems never to have been resolved: how could the RAF independently disperse the V-force, when the weapons had to be released by the US? In particular, how could the UK national strike plan be executed when some V-bomber stations had no British weapons stored locally? Much road movement of weapons would be required, making a rapid dispersal impossible. During 1959, the Air Council decided not to pursue US offers of more modern Project E weapons, and when it later discovered that the Mk.5 weapons already assigned had only a 50-kiloton yield, the decision was made instead to bring the arrangement to a close. Project E weapons were replaced by British weapons at Honington on 1 July 1961 and at Waddington on 30 March 1962.[142] Canberras, and the SACEUR-assigned Valiants, continued to use Project E weapons.

Meanwhile deliveries of warhead components for Red Beard were slower than planned. Environmental trials at Farnborough were taking longer than expected, and the Admiralty was especially unhappy with the news that the warhead's internal neutron initiator would have just a six-month life before having to be returned to Aldermaston for replacement.[143] This would not fit the navy's schedule of carrier deployments, and so although HMS *Victorious* made a number of preparations to embark Red Beard in 1958–59, she eventually sailed without.[144] In January 1959, during a ten-hour vibration trial, it was discovered that cold was causing shrinkage and loosening of the Red Beard warhead structure, and warhead deliveries were again delayed: 'AWRE had not been able to physically show that the warhead was safe and were not prepared to sign a safety certificate'. In March, a submission for limited approval of the operational Red Beard was rejected; amongst other things there were problems with 'rubber bags, polythene liners and styrofoil discs' in the warhead. Only inert drill weapons for ground training had yet been delivered to the services.[145] Voluminous correspondence between the MoS and RAE Farnborough shows that, in the wake of the Anglo-American bilateral agreement, various alternatives to Red Beard were now being canvassed.[146] But the American Mk.28 weapon, now of great interest to the UK and potentially available in a low-yield tactical version, was too long for internal carriage in some of the aircraft listed in the OR.1127 requirement, and the Air Ministry was arguing strenuously for priority to be given to the ballistic Red Beard, needed urgently in sufficient numbers to match V-bomber deliveries. Red Beard was therefore saved from cancellation, but improvements to the design were now to be limited to a smaller loading tube (for in-flight safety), a new long-life initiator and perhaps increased yield.[147]

During 1959, deliveries of operational Red Beard to the services remained tantalisingly close, and the Air Ministry detailed its aspiration to acquire 136 of the weapons: 32 for Canberras based on Cyprus, 48 for V-bombers in the far east, 16 for Valiants with a dual bombing/photo-reconnaissance role and 40 for Mk. 1 V-bombers in the UK.[148] 'In September, AWRE stated that the natural creep of [high-explosive] when subject to heat and then cooling made it necessary to increase the supercharge dimensions by a small amount and that this would further limit the storage temperature range' to between 18 and 23°C.[149] This kind of limitation presented serious operational disadvantages: the RAF wanted to disperse bombers at readiness to locations all around the UK, including in winter; and the navy wanted to use Red Beard on carriers deployed worldwide, potentially from the tropics to the Barents Sea. Planning for a Red Beard Mk. 2 weapon was 'abandoned pending clarification of requirements', and studies of alternatives to Red Beard continued. The Air Council was told there had been no deliveries to date because of design weaknesses revealed during environmental tests which would impose, at least initially, severe restrictions on service use.[150]

In February 1960, at last, there was better news. Although Red Beard had yet to be accepted for service use, a small number was now available and the Admiralty and Air Ministry met to discuss the delivery schedule.[151] The Air Ministry, having now acquired Project E weapons for its V-bombers in the UK, had reversed its earlier priorities and was keener to achieve clearance to use the loft Red Beard weapon on Canberras, which might now deploy to the far east as well as Cyprus. The number of RAF weapons required had been reduced to 110: still 32 for Cyprus and 48 for the far east, but now just 30 for the UK. The Royal

Navy meanwhile seems to have set a requirement for 28.[152] During the summer, emergency service approvals were issued for Red Beard, and in October the First Sea Lord announced to his fellow chiefs the deployment of the weapon aboard HMS *Hermes*, soon heading for the far east.[153] By the end of the year, 49 Red Beards had been delivered to the RAF and three to the navy, the design was frozen and plans to convert Mk. 1 to Mk. 2 weapons were back on.[154] In November 1961, these Mk. 2 weapons, a more robustly engineered version with in-flight safety and fewer environmental limitations, were approved for service use.[155]

Skybolt

As we have already seen, British involvement in Skybolt dated to the very earliest days of the missile's development in the United States. In early 1959, for example, companies bidding for work on the USAF's general operational requirement for a long-range hypersonic stand-off bomb were given data on the RAF's V-bombers, so that compatibility with British as well as US aircraft could be factored in. Two British observers were at Dayton, Ohio in March 1959 when 15 companies made presentations on the requirement to the USAF Air Research and Development Command.[156] In May 1959, one of these companies, Douglas, was awarded an initial development contract for what was now referred to as USAF weapons system (WS) 138A. At this stage, the missile was officially just the subject of a development contract for the USAF and under consideration as a possible Blue Steel successor for licensed manufacture in the UK.[157] At 18ft long, it was fairly short and fat, and proposed for external carriage on – in priority order – the USAF's B-58, B-52 and B-70 bombers; and also for *internal* carriage on RAF Vulcans and Victors. Range was supposed to be 1000nm, with an accuracy of 3000ft circular error probable – the distance within which 50 per cent of weapons fired would land. The precise form of guidance system and (one-megaton) warhead had yet to be determined, and major sub-contractors had yet to be identified.[158]

WS 138A was later also referred to by its US service designation, GAM-87 (for guided air-launched missile), but today it is best known by the name Skybolt, adopted at the start of 1960, perhaps at the specific suggestion of USAF Chief of Staff General White.[159] Drawings from summer 1959 show the missile six feet longer, its afterbody control surfaces reduced in size because the earlier version looked too difficult to accommodate on the B-58.[160] There were also now small canard control surfaces forward, and the whole missile was to be mounted further forward under the carrying aircraft's wing to allow visibility for a star-tracker window.[161] Nortronics, a division of Northrop with earlier experience in stellar-inertial systems, were selected as the missile guidance contractors in October 1959.[162] For this reason, it now became impossible to consider internal carriage in the V-bombers: the missile would need to be able to see the stars. Indeed, because the Victor lacked ground clearance, only the Vulcan could now carry Skybolt for the RAF. The missile had also become heavier, in order to accommodate a larger warhead.

USAF Air Research and Development Command now asserted greater management control over the project. Towards the end of 1959 a further aerodynamic design for the missile was produced by the air force's own team at Dayton. The missile was now even longer, the afterbody control surfaces even smaller, and the canard controls on the missile forebody had been replaced with steerable exhaust nozzles for the second stage motor. In this configuration, Skybolt was approved by the Pentagon for further development, but still not production, in February 1960.[163] At this point – purely coincidentally, as far as the US programme team was concerned – Blue Streak was cancelled, and the RAF became not simply interested in, but *dependent upon* the US missile for the future credibility of its strategic nuclear deterrent force.

The missile design was further refined during 1960 to include four fixed strakes between the afterbody control surfaces, and a single steerable second stage nozzle, and this was the missile design inherited by the new US administration in January 1961. Launch was intended to be from fairly high altitude: 40,000ft and Mach 0.8 for the B-52, or slightly higher and faster for the Vulcan. Launch from as low as 10,000ft was also possible in theory, but true low-level capability for the carrying aircraft was unnecessary given the range of the missile: it would not be necessary for the B-52 or Vulcan to approach within range of Soviet air-defence radars. The missile would fall freely for a couple of seconds before first-stage ignition and a 30–40° pull-up.[164] The second stage would fire shortly after separation then accelerate to final velocity of 95,000ft/sec and separation of the gently spinning RV.

Guidance was widely regarded as the most challenging problem to be solved by the programme. As one British technical commentary noted, 'daylight star-trackers of themselves are extremely refined examples of the instrumental art', and it was feared that 'over-refinement [was] being built in to the detriment of overall system reliability'.[165] The launch computer contained an estimated 17,000 electronic components and its mean time between failure was variously estimated at between 13 and 46 hours. The star-tracker sub-system in the missile would receive azimuth and elevation data from the parent aircraft's navigation systems, ideally accurate to within five minutes of arc, and its telescope would then be directed in turn to the predicted position of two stars with an appropriate angular separation, selected from around 260 stored in the launch computer's memory. Through a programmed expanding rectangular spiral search pattern, the tracker would acquire (or lock on to) the two stars in turn for final guidance alignment and trajectory calculations, continuously thereafter swapping between the stars to update calculations until the moment of missile release. If either of the stars could not be found, perhaps because of the position of the sun or occultation by the aircraft, alternatives would be selected from memory. Precise sidereal time was also needed in order to select appropriate stars, and one account suggested the USAF was planning 'to rush the clock on board just before take-off [because] they consider it necessary to continually correct it on the ground with reference to an astronomically correct time signal' – an interesting cold-war version of the longitude problem.[166] Calculations would be shared between the missile's own on-board computer and another, larger computer on the aircraft. The guidance system was split in this way for two reasons: the star-tracker could not be mounted in the aircraft, because the transfer of data between aircraft and missile, both non-rigid, would have introduced too much inaccuracy; and the launch computer could not be mounted entirely in the missile for reasons of weight and cost. After release from the aircraft, the guidance system would revert to a purely inertial mode and track speed and position throughout the flight, until final thrust termination and RV separation. Impact would be about 12 minutes from launch, and the weapon could have been fuzed for air- or ground-burst.

Vulcan flights with dummy Skybolt shapes, four of which were delivered to the UK in February 1961, began at West Freugh in Scotland and also by September at Eglin Air Force Base in Florida, where two Vulcans were detached.[167] The potentially troublesome guidance system was also trialled during 1961, first at Mount Palomar observatory in California, then aboard a C-131 test aircraft and later a B-52.[168]

Skybolt warhead

The choice of a warhead and RV for Skybolt was an extremely long and at times a vexed process, and even came to complicate government-to-government negotiations on the system. As we have seen, the choice had to be made during a nuclear testing moratorium, which limited the creativity American or British designers could apply to the problem; and the UK was hampered by its continuing need to conserve fissile material. Although many details remain classified, a remarkably full account of the development of ideas on Skybolt warheads on both sides of the Atlantic can nevertheless now be constructed.

When serious discussion of Skybolt warheads began, the US assumption was that the Mk.47 warhead, developed for the earliest Polaris missiles, would be used on the new weapon. Lightness – and therefore missile range – was the key consideration: Mk.47 was a very innovative thermonuclear design from Edward Teller's new Livermore laboratory. Published accounts from the US suggest it was designed to be integral to the missile RV for weight saving, used an ovoid primary and spherical secondary and a novel mechanical safeing device.[169] The British, on the other hand, were anxious to use the heavier but better known and better engineered Red Snow warhead. Brundrett was insistent: 'if there is to be a successor to Blue Steel at all, it must use the Red Snow warhead'.[170] This was partly for safety reasons – dislike of the safeing device and the sensitive high-explosive used by the US in Mk.47[171] – and partly because it was unclear at first that Mk.47 would be available 'without strings' under the embryonic US/UK atomic collaboration arrangements.[172] Mostly, however, it was because Mk.47 used so much fissile material: four times the highly enriched uranium and nearly twice the plutonium of Red Snow.[173]

Red Snow, meanwhile, was well and good, but 1000lb heavier overall than Mk.47. It therefore carried a considerable range penalty. Specifically, at 600 miles range with Red Snow, compared to 1000 miles with Mk.47, Skybolt could not be used to attack Moscow – or other important targets – without the Vulcan's having to penetrate Soviet airspace.[174] Despite an initial decision to the contrary, in December 1959 the DRPC atomic sub-committee therefore decided to commit to producing a UK version of Mk.47, later codenamed Steven,[175] although by the time the sub-committee next met in July 1960, this decision was again in question.[176] Whether this was because thinking had moved on, or because of the known difficulties and problems with Mk.47, is unclear. The idea of a British Mk.47 warhead was anyway short-lived.

Paradoxically, the USAF had meanwhile become keen on a heavy warhead option, partly because of the sub-megaton yield of Mk.47 and partly simply because of its association with the US Navy. It now considered using the Mk.49 warhead which, like Red Snow, was derived from the earlier US Mk.28 and would yield a satisfying whole megaton. Mk.49 was, however, very slightly smaller and lighter than the UK warhead, indeed described as 'Red Snow in a thinner case'.[177] Annoyingly therefore, even configured for Mk.49, Skybolt would still be unable *quite* to carry Red Snow unless the Americans themselves accepted a further 25-mile range penalty.[178] At this point it became clear that two versions of Skybolt might in fact be produced, one with a heavy warhead and RV, and one with a light warhead and RV. The RAF briefly envisaged fitting a quarter of its 100 or so Skybolts with Red Snow and the remainder with a more expensive light warhead, allowing greater range.[179]

During 1959 and 1960, a great many more warhead ideas were canvassed, including some that were evidently based on original work in the UK. This contradicts the widely held view that, after 1958, Aldermaston ceased to work on its own indigenous warhead designs and confined its activities to copying US designs.[180] A British warhead called Acorn, similar in weight to Mk.47 at 700lb but evidently using the small kiloton warhead Tony as a primary, was discussed for a time in spring 1960.[181] In October, so were various flavours of another warhead, Filbert.[182] These designs no doubt addressed some of the perceived shortcomings of Mk.47. New American possibilities were also in play, including Livermore's Mk.56 or Fife design,[183] and a Los Alamos competitor, originally called J-21 and later Mk.59. Like Acorn, these designs were at the time untested because of the moratorium; instead documents describe them as 'extrapolations' from existing tested designs. In other words safety and performance calculations were extrapolated from similar or related tested designs.[184] Progress with – and confidence in the safety of – these light warheads was so good by September 1960 that plans for heavy warheads and RVs were dropped, on both sides of the Atlantic. A firm Air Ministry warhead requirement, OR.1179, now existed, specifying (only) a 700lb weight, megaton-range warhead for a 1000nm-range range missile to enter service in 1964. A heavy warhead, the requirement noted, would mean Skybolt would be able to cover only half of the necessary targets in the Soviet Union.[185]

This delay on both sides of the Atlantic in selecting a single warhead and RV had a significant impact on the negotiations for the Skybolt technical and financial agreement, finally signed on 27 September 1960. Both sides were anxious to avoid liability for any incompatibility between the RV and warhead, and the agreement eventually specified that:

> In order to avoid the need to design a special British re-entry vehicle, a British warhead, compatible with a US re-entry vehicle, will be selected and provided by the appropriate authorities of the United Kingdom after consultation with the United States Air Force. Thereafter, the

parties will collaborate at all stages of development of the system and make every reasonable effort to ensure that the design of the chosen British warhead and the re-entry vehicle and the missile remain compatible; specifically, if the United States Air Force wishes to introduce changes to the design of the re-entry vehicle and its related supplies and components, or the United Kingdom authorities wish to introduce changes in the warhead, the parties shall consult together and make every reasonable effort to ensure that such changes do not affect compatibility of the two items.[186]

In January 1961, after almost a year during which a final decision on the warhead had appeared to be imminent, the US finally chose the Los Alamos light warhead, Mk.59, for Skybolt.[187] The design used, as its fission primary, the kiloton warhead Tsetse, which the British already planned to anglicise and manufacture in the UK as Tony. A visiting British team was able to report from the US that 'we have a good knowledge of [the Skybolt warhead's] design … [and it] is comparable with the general ideas we have in mind for our own development'.[188] This wording suggests again that Aldermaston contemplated a design of its own for the Skybolt warhead, and not simply an anglicised copy of an American warhead.[189]

The advantages of a narrow tapering sphere/cone RV over the previous cone/cylinder/flare design were recognised in around March 1961, and led to the final major design change to Skybolt, ending with a sleeker and again somewhat longer missile. The advantages included a 20 or 30-mile range extension, an end to a problem with differential erosion of ablative material on the RV flare section, and an end to problems with air-flow distortion over the star-tracker window, affecting accuracy. British documents also indicate that the radar cross-section of the new Mk.7 RV will have been markedly lower, improving ABM penetration, and that its internal dimensions relaxed any concerns over fitting a British warhead.[190] Mk.7A or Mk.8 RV ideas, the former certainly incorporating some simple decoys, were considered in the US, but rejected.[191] For the Americans, who still envisaged using Skybolt for defence-suppression attacks on SAMs and radars, ABM penetration was never really an issue; and it is not clear that there was really enough weight margin available for a meaningful payload of penetration aids. For the British, however, who envisaged targeting cities where ABM might one day be deployed, penetration was more of an issue: in November 1961, a MoD official noted with concern that Skybolt remained 'a "simple" warhead to any defensive system'.[192]

Red Beard replacement

A further stimulus to new British work on warhead design was the requirement, discussed as early as December 1958,[193] for a Red Beard replacement. Red Beard had been designed in the early 1950s and its various problems have been described above. New avenues of collaboration with the US, after the 1958 bilateral agreement, meant that consideration could be given to a more modern and operationally flexible alternative weapon. For a time, studies at Farnborough focused on the possibility of using the American Mk.28 bomb and/or warhead. The length of the Mk.28 bomb casing, and the nuisance of repeating ballistic and aerodynamic tests and modifying aircraft interface arrangements, reduced enthusiasm for a new bomb. Attempts were made instead to fit the Mk.28 warhead or its primary, known in the US as Python but to Aldermaston as Peter, into Red Beard. Alternatively, a brand new 'tailored bomb' case could still be produced.[194]

These studies of kiloton bombs based on the US Mk.28 were ultimately a dead end, but Air Ministry and Admiralty interest had been stimulated. In June 1959, the Air Ministry believed Red Beard would be obsolete by 1965 and was looking at a number of possible warheads for a replacement: Una, a warhead with a variable yield of 50–200kt, was described as the 'likely RAF standard' for future tactical bombs, surface-to-air guided weapons and depth bombs.[195] The Director of the Admiralty's Gunnery Division, having seen some kind of 'shopping list' of warheads, also now believed 'that a weapon built around the Una warhead will give us the best possible value in terms of time-scale, cost, weight, safety and ease of ship stowage', as well as offering a useful extension of aircraft range.[196] The nature of the Una warhead is a mystery. There was some disagreement during the summer of 1959 over whether it would require testing; Levin, the AWRE Director, thought not.[197] This suggests that it varied hardly at all from an existing tested design. Other documents, however, suggest that work was not due to start on Una before 1962, and that it would not become available before 1965.[198] It may have been a proposed American design for the future, or perhaps one of the proposed Anglo-American joint warhead projects. It was later said to use the Tony warhead as a primary.[199]

In August 1959, first drafts of the Air Ministry requirement for an improved kiloton bomb OR.1177, and its warhead OR.1176, were circulated.[200] The ministry's overriding concern was to acquire a bomb suitable for use on the OR.343 aircraft (TSR.2), and able in particular to be used against hard targets from low level at supersonic speed. The Admiralty's interest was, by comparison, lukewarm, and related chiefly to the need to operate in wartime alongside the US Navy's strike carriers:

> The Royal Navy's primary role is limited war, and to fulfil this the preponderance of effort must be directed towards conventional weapons and their associated means of delivery. The secondary role, in which units of our carrier force are allocated to NATO at the outset of global war, calls for a considerable nuclear strike potential; without this, our carriers would constitute more of a liability than an aid to the existing powerful USN nuclear-armed carrier forces.

In addition, there was some interest, as we shall see later, in nuclear anti-submarine weapons:

> it is possible that the fleet might be counter-attacked by modern high-speed submarines, against which present detection gear and homing torpedoes are likely to be only marginally successful ... defence against such submarines by nuclear depth charges may easily become essential. Although there is no naval staff requirement for such a depth charge at present, DGD foresees that an underwater capability for the bomb will be ... a most desirable emergency feature in the future. For this reason, and for attacks against dockyards, canals, surface warships, etc., it is necessary that a future nuclear bomb shall be capable of ... being dropped into water, even if it is not provided with full NDC features.[201]

Despite these rather different interests, OR.1177 was issued formally as a joint naval and air staff requirement at the end of May 1960,[202] and was discussed by the DRPC atomic sub-committee in July. A brief for this meeting noted that: 'OR.1176 defines a warhead suitable for use in a tactical bomb, anti-submarine bomb and possibly guided weapons ... OR.1177 details requirements for the tactical bomb', to be carried by V-bombers, Canberras, TSR.2 and other aircraft. The bomb was wanted in service by 1964 or 1965.[203] A bomb weight of 900lb and diameter of 20 inches were by now envisaged, and the warhead would need to be capable of a number of different yields between ten and 300kt.[204] These new requirements seem to have been contending for priority with the Mk.47 warhead for Skybolt (see above) and the sub-kiloton warhead for Davy Crockett (see below).[205] The sub-committee appears to have discussed all of these requirements inconclusively at its July 1960 meeting, raising the possibility – no more – that a family of multi-purpose warheads might be desirable, capable of incorporation in weapons ranging from Skybolt, through the Red Beard replacement, to Blue Water and Seaslug (see also below).[206] This idea may now have been preferred to the Una warhead, but, in the absence of a clear policy line in Whitehall on tactical nuclear weapons, the OR.1177 requirement had not yet been approved and real work was delayed.[207]

A retarded or lay-down mode, to allow accurate delivery from low level without the need to 'pop up' into enemy radar cover for free-fall or LABS delivery, was an important part of the OR.1177 requirement. A party led by the MoA visited the US during October and November 1960 to look at possibilities. Parachute retardation of the falling bomb was required, to reduce its speed to 40ft/sec in the case of a 'fragile' warhead, or 250ft/sec in the case of a specially ruggedised warhead. Considerations of warhead design, as well as bomb design, would therefore affect the feasibility of a lay-down weapon. Red Snow, for example, was a 'fragile' warhead. In the context of the search for insurance against the cancellation of Skybolt – and the Air Ministry's fight against Polaris – interest was now growing in a lay-down weapon for TSR.2, not just with a kiloton yield for tactical use, but in a megaton strategic version.[208] This was the first hint of a proposal that would eventually materialise after the Skybolt cancellation.

In early 1961, the DRPC added the OR.1176 requirement to its 'list of major items' and a reference number PT176 was assigned by the MoA.[209] Eventually, in the summer, MoD approval was forthcoming for real project work on the bomb to OR.1177, and a one-year feasibility study began.[210] By December 1961, the MoA reference number WE177 had been allocated to the project.[211] Contracts began to be placed: with Hunting Engineering for general system design, J Langham Thompson for fuzing, Elliott Bros for radar, and others.[212] The likely size of the bomb was reducing.[213] Ministerial decisions on Thorneycroft's review of nuclear warheads were still awaited, however, and the Red Beard replacement was not therefore approved for production. OR.1176 was now associated with a warhead known as Ulysses; whether and how Ulysses related to Una, which seems to have disappeared from the record in mid-1960, is not clear.[214] As we shall see, the War Office was now showing considerable interest in a common warhead for the Red Beard replacement and the high-yield version of its own Blue Water.

In July and August 1961, the DRPC atomic sub-committee twice more discussed the subject. A brief for one of the meetings recorded that the OR.1176/7 requirements had been set aside the previous year, in anticipation of a project for multi-purpose warheads. There had now been some progress with this latter possibility, and a paper was submitted on using the Skybolt warhead (RE179) as the 'basic design for a multipurpose warhead'. The Admiralty, however, now broke ranks, submitting a separate paper on the Red Beard successor. A further brief explained that 'the Admiralty have never really been happy about their entanglement in ... OR.1177. They have seized on CA's remarks, at the last meeting, about the complexity of OR.1177 to pursue their reasonable preference for a lighter-weight lower-yield Red Beard replacement than would flow from OR.1176/1177'.[215] The future of what later became the long-lived WE177 family of tactical bombs was therefore still, at this stage, in the balance.

Defensive weapons

The story of the various plans and projects for the postwar air defence of the UK and the armed forces is a long and complicated one, and I have attempted to disentangle the threads elsewhere.[216] The possibility of nuclear-tipped SAGW was mentioned as early as 1951, only to be dismissed on the grounds of scarcity of fissile material. During 1955 and 1956, however, more concrete plans began to be made along these lines, stimulated for a time by the discovery at Aldermaston of the so-called R-1 effect, also described as 'neutron poisoning' or 'delayed neutron production in the core' of a nuclear weapon. R-1 raised the possibility that the proper functioning of a nuclear weapon, carried for example by an attacking bomber, could be affected for a time by a nearby defensive nuclear explosion. It was soon realised that R-1 would wear off quickly – indeed within the time a bomb would take to fall – and that blast, heat and fragmentation effects would dominate.[217] Nevertheless a defensive nuclear explosion would clearly be more damaging to an attacking bomber or formation of bombers than a conventional one, in several different ways. By 1958, formal requirements had been stated for nuclear warheads for an SAGW for the RAF, known as command-guidance Red Duster, and for another for the Royal Navy, Seaslug. Command-guidance Red Duster was a proposed new version of a semi-active radar-homing weapon, already at a late stage of development by Bristol and Ferranti against the Air Ministry's requirement for 'Stage 1' and 'Stage 1½' air defence. Red Duster entered service at the experimental station RAF North Coates, near Grimsby in Lincolnshire, towards the end of the year, and became better known by the manufacturer's trade name, Bloodhound. It was hoped that, with command guidance and a nuclear warhead, the missile would be simpler and safer to operate and could be used at longer ranges with a less stringent accuracy requirement. The command-guidance version was also seen as a possible stepping-stone to an ABM. Seaslug, meanwhile, was the centrepiece of the navy's new guided-missile destroyer project, eventually to emerge in the early 1960s as the County class.

Aldermaston tested two warheads in Australia in 1957, Indigo Hammer and the smaller Pixie, intended to address or at least explore the Red Duster and Seaslug requirements. Because of their small size, both warheads were expensive in fissile material – Pixie was said to require twice the plutonium of Red Beard, for one-sixteenth the yield.[218] Once US warhead designs became available in late 1958, both Indigo Hammer and Pixie were described as 'out of date',[219] and the US Mk.44 was adopted in their place. This design, also known in the US as Tsetse, would be suitable for both Red Duster and Seaslug – and indeed, as we have seen, in the Red Beard replacement and as a primary in various possible thermonuclear weapons. In its anglicised version, it became known as Tony, and the interchangeable warhead capsule in which it would be fitted to Red Duster, Seaslug and the army's weapon Blue Water (see below), was given the MoA reference number RO106. Tony was a well understood and well engineered warhead weighing as little as 175lb, measuring 14.5 inches in diameter and offering a yield of between one and ten kilotons. It also used less fissile material than Indigo Hammer.[220]

In 1958, the USAF suggested that Fighter Command might equip its new Mach 2 manned fighter aircraft, the English Electric Lightning, with an American nuclear-tipped air-to-air unguided rocket known as Genie, using warheads on Project E terms. Genie in some sense competed with a British air-to-air missile, Red Top, but by the end of 1959 George Ward, the Secretary of State for Air, was enthusiastic. In the following spring, the JPS added their support – conditional, however, on the removal of 'strings'. In an echo of the debate on arming V-bombers at dispersal with Project E weapons, it was felt impractical to use cumbersome custody arrangements for an aircraft that would have to scramble quickly in an operational emergency. Genie would have been used to extend the reach of the Lightning, whose operational concept involved a very quick-reaction climb to intercept a Soviet high-altitude bomber attack.[221]

During 1959 and 1960, air defence became a rather more politically charged subject than previously. It had been recognised several years earlier that the air defence of the *whole* of the UK, or even of certain smaller 'vulnerable areas', was impractical. Expenditure was now officially justified on the grounds of defence only of the deterrent, i.e., of Britain's bomber and missile bases. Even so, air defence was also becoming very expensive, with the Lightning, new radars and control systems, and two broadly similar types of SAGW entering service – Bloodhound, and the army's mobile weapon Thunderbird, produced by a rival team at English Electric. Assessments of the threat to the UK were now changing. For some time, the Air Ministry had clung to the view that high-altitude aircraft, equivalent to Britain's own V-bombers, posed the greatest threat to the UK. Belatedly, it was now realised that Soviet medium-range ballistic missiles were deployed in greater numbers than bombers, which might anyway attack at low level. Bearing in mind the need to justify the TSR.2, low-level operations were now of considerably greater interest to the RAF and its Whitehall supporters. Was the SAGW programme, unable to counter low-flying enemy aircraft, a waste of money? Ominously, Sandys noted in May 1959 that 'the defence of the deterrent is one of the few remaining sectors of our defence programme where we still have room for manoeuvre'.[222] By manoeuvre, he was naturally referring to cuts. For a time, Whitehall vultures circled over the Bloodhound and Thunderbird projects in turn; Ward complained that it seemed impossible 'to follow a policy of adopting deployed versions of Bloodhound and Thunderbird alternately in alternate years, in view of the waste of time, scientific and industrial effort and money'.[223] In March 1960, the Defence Committee discussed command-guidance Red Duster – now referred to as Bloodhound Mk.3 – and although the discussion was not quite conclusive, in practice work now ceased on this version of the weapon and the MoA was left to pursue such research into command guidance as it might later see fit.[224]

In July and October, Watkinson and Ward recommended a package deal on air defence to two further meetings of the Defence Committee. The Lightning was at this point very politically vulnerable, the case for its procurement resting on non-nuclear operations, either outside Europe or investigating intrusions into UK airspace in peacetime or in times of tension. The two ministers agreed 'that we should abandon plans to introduce the American nuclear headed rocket Genie, since: (a) it is not suitable for the prevention of intrusion and jamming; (b) although we have yet to decide whether there should be nuclear air defence overseas, it seems evident that any agreement with the Americans on Genie would preclude its use overseas'. They also agreed Bloodhound Mk.3 would not be revived; the Lightning, on the other hand, survived.[225] As they had been over the Blue Streak cancellation, Air Ministry and industrial interests were now working in opposition. The military case for nuclear SAGW and Genie was weak, in the face of a threat mainly from ballistic missiles. Once Bloodhound came to be seen as a clear competitor to a particular manned aircraft, the Lightning, it also ceased to have the Air Ministry's political support. The MoA and the industrial firms concerned were desperate, on the other hand, to stay in the missile game, and in fact Bloodhound, in its various non-nuclear versions, was to win a number of export orders and survive in operation for many years afterwards.

For the Admiralty, Seaslug was not a competitor to, but an integral and important part of, a desired weapons platform – the guided-missile destroyer. This ensured its political survival. For the time being, a nuclear version of Seaslug Mk.2 remained a part of the Admiralty's plans, offering a package of performance improvements for use against bomber formations, supersonic aircraft or, in a secondary surface-to-surface role, against other ships. The magazines and internal handling arrangements of the County-class destroyers were designed to accommodate nuclear warheads for a proportion of the missiles, at some cost to other capabilities. A total procurement of 48 warheads was envisaged.[226] In 1959 the case for Mk.2 Seaslug was said 'primarily' to rest on the nuclear warhead but, as with any nuclear-weapons requirement, their lordships remained somewhat sceptical, feeling 'it was doubtful whether the use of such a weapon would ever be allowed in limited war; and even if this doubt were set aside, the nuclear-headed Seaslug would be prohibitively expensive for use against many of the surface targets which a cruiser would normally be expected to engage, and would normally be useless in the army support role'.[227]

British scientists were also, in this period, looking at the possibilities of ABM defence. As early as 1954, contract studies had been placed with English Electric and Marconi to look at the problem of defence against ballistic missiles, and in 1955 a draft operational requirement was circulated in the Air Ministry. It was clear that a nuclear warhead would be required for an ABM because of likely accuracy problems.[228] By 1957, the use of 20 or 30 decoys to accompany an attacking ballistic missile RV was being studied, and 'RAE Farnborough was examining a range of proposals submitted by the Bristol Aircraft company and English Electric, code-name Violet Friend'.[229] A new operational requirement was issued, and another for the necessary warhead which, it was now thought, would need to have a megaton yield. The studies involved: a missile; various radars for early-warning and tracking, impact prediction, target acquisition and interception; and associated data processing. It was clear that ABM defence was a complex and costly problem, but it was hoped some limited operational capability might be possible within a decade.[230] In early 1959, an eventual requirement for 104 megaton warheads for ABMs was envisaged, although following internal discussion within the Air Ministry this ambitious total was revised down to 36 warheads in the high kiloton range.[231] The DRPC had recently approved work on a prototype decoy discrimination radar. The subject had also been discussed actively in one of the tripartite interdependence sub-groups, where the siting of the BMEWS radar at Fylingdales provided a major focus for discussion. Early warning, a necessary preliminary for any active defence system to be alerted, was one aspect of the ABM problem that proved tractable.[232]

By January 1961, the BNDSG's technical sub-committee was able to state confidently that 'no defence system which has been proposed against ballistic missile attack has, as yet, been proved on examination to be technically and economically worthwhile. This is true even when limiting the nature of the threat to those ballistic missiles which would be operational by 1965, and when considering the defence of small areas only'. Defence against a *simple* ballistic missile with no decoys might be possible; 'the present day studies on active defence have, however, foundered on the problem of providing an economic system in the presence of artificial decoys accompanying the warhead'. Discrimination inside the atmosphere was easier than at extremely high altitudes, because decoys and warheads would usually differ markedly in mass and therefore behave differently on re-entry, the heavier objects generating greater heat and ionisation effects. Even here, discrimination imposed extreme problems of tracking and computation on hundreds of incoming objects. Some arcane technology was involved; British scientists had even looked at American work on 'death rays'.[233]

This work was significant, not because a deployed UK ABM system was seriously in prospect, but because the designers of offensive missiles – in particular Blue Streak, Skybolt and later Polaris – had to bear in mind the conclusion that *simple* ballistic missiles, without decoys, might be vulnerable. As Roy Dommett recalls, 'the projects were interactive as the technologies, insights and understandings evolved for the first time ... The evolving Blue Streak concepts set the pace for ... ABM studies'.[234]

Battlefield nuclear weapons

In 1958, as we have seen, the War Office had revised its doctrine for fighting on the NATO central front to include the widespread use of tactical nuclear weapons on the battlefield. Although this doctrine later became politically controversial, detailed plans were naturally made to procure the necessary weapons. Corporal, an American surface-to-surface guided missile with a range of 70 miles, was to provide BAOR with its first atomic capability. Although a British warhead had at one time been planned for Corporal, since 1957 the assumption had been made that US warheads would be available under similar terms – US peacetime custody and dual control – to the RAF's Project E. A BAOR Corporal regiment was formed at Dortmund during 1958 but did not, initially, have warheads available locally; instead, plans were made to transport them in emergency from storage sites in the American sector of West Germany. Local storage was only agreed in August 1959, and was presumably not provided in practice until later still; this must be the reason some accounts say nuclear warheads for BAOR did not arrive until 1960.[235] A second Corporal regiment was moved to Germany in 1961, and a total of 100 British Corporal missiles is given by one source.[236] Corporal had a number of operational limitations. As a 1959 report noted, based on experience with test firings at a range in the Outer Hebrides, guidance and propulsion took a long time to set up: 'The electronic "matching" of the guidance system with each missile is a long and complicated process lasting some hours'. The missile followed a radio beam, transmitted by a guidance unit set up some distance to the rear of the launcher, and liquid propellant had to be loaded before firing. Set-up and countdown might not proceed flawlessly and it would be difficult to alert friendly forces to the exact time of launch: 'it will be impossible to warn troops when to cover their eyes to avoid flash blindness, neither can the air force be warned to clear a certain area at a certain time'. Targets of opportunity could not, realistically, be engaged. Although eight of 12 test firings had met range and accuracy requirements, four had fallen short. The warhead would not have armed in such an accident, in a real scenario, but there would still have been radioactive debris and propellant fires at the crash site, and the report argued that 'the risk of its falling among our own troops is unacceptable'. Worse, electronic countermeasures might be able not simply to jam but to 'divert' the guidance beam.[237]

Partly to replace Corporal, the War Office planned to acquire a British missile, originally of somewhat shorter range. This was Blue Water, and two versions were eventually planned with low- and high-yield warheads of around ten and 100kt respectively. The low-yield warhead was originally to have been Indigo Hammer, and later Tony. Service entry was hoped for in 1965, and the intended targets included enemy missile and rocket sites, dug-in infantry, bridges, defiles, corps or divisional headquarters, forward airfields, beachheads or paratroop dropping zones. The missile and its mobile erector-launcher were to be air-transportable, making use outside Europe a practical proposition. Rapid launch was required, and inertial guidance; Blue Water would not have the limitations of Corporal.[238] The Blue Water project was given to English Electric – soon to merge with Vickers and Bristol as the British Aircraft Corporation (BAC) – who built up design teams at Luton and Stevenage. The missile, in its final form, weighed around 5000lb and measured 25ft long by two feet in diameter. It had mid-section wings for control with a span of six feet nine inches, and large tail fins for stability. A twin-chamber solid propellant motor was designed, and static firings began in 1958. Test flights at Aberporth in Wales began in 1960. Scale models were meanwhile also fired at Woomera, where larger instrumented test facilities were prepared.[239]

As time went by, the War Office was to urge repeatedly the need for the high-yield version of Blue Water, although this requirement was never formally agreed. A low-yield warhead of 10kt or less, the War Office felt, would be inadequate for attacks on dug-in targets or armoured penetrations along fronts of more than about 600 yards.[240] By 1959, plans had been drawn up to procure 50 low-yield missiles with Tony warheads, and 70 high-yield missiles with Una. Blue Water's range was now given as 65 miles.[241] The following year, the War Office decided to make common cause with the Air Ministry over the high-yield warhead, judging that its approval might be eased if a single requirement could be issued for a warhead of up to 300kt for Blue Water and the RAF's planned high-yield Red Beard replacement. At this point, a 'phase two' longer-range Blue Water was under discussion, although still awaiting Treasury approval. The maximum design range of the weapon had originally been 30 miles, but with improvements in propulsion a range of 75 miles was now possible. The DRPC approved work on a longer-range version in May 1960, and in November the Army Council decided this would be their main focus.[242] In early 1961, the Defence Committee gave the Blue Water project its blessing.[243] Approval for the high-yield warhead, given the MoA reference number GM462, was, however, no closer, and now explicitly tied up with the ongoing strategic debates on NATO tactical nuclear weapons. The case for even a low-yield British warhead was also being questioned, for the Defence Committee had decided in October 1960 not to plan for ground-based nuclear weapons outside Europe. This being the case, a warhead under American custody, *à la* Corporal, might be acceptable. Blue Water nevertheless survived a further Defence Committee review in November 1961.[244] One reason was that it was seen as an export opportunity for BAC, rivalling a US missile known as Sergeant, and in this context there were somewhat far-fetched discussions of giving Blue Water warheads to West Germany under dual-key custodial arrangements, or even fitting Blue Water with a French warhead.[245]

A third nuclear missile of interest to the army – or rather an unguided *rocket*; a missile, strictly speaking, should be guided – was the American Honest John. Honest John was one of several weapons BAOR was theoretically committed to procure under NATO Military Committee document MC 70. It was a simple weapon to operate, of a similar size to Blue Water but with a shorter range of up to 15 miles. A US offer to supply the weapon, with warheads under American custody, was made in 1958 and the War Office seized upon Honest John as an interim measure until Blue Water could be made available. Early in 1959, the chiefs agreed that a BAOR unit should be equipped with the rocket, and after more than a year of Whitehall squabbling over funding, the weapons arrived in the autumn of 1960. One regiment at Nienburg (later Paderborn), one at Sennelager and one at Menden were reequipped for the nuclear role, each with two Honest John batteries and two M115 eight-inch nuclear artillery batteries; 120 Honest John and 36 artillery warheads were apparently made available by the US.[246] The guns reflected another long-standing War Office requirement; there had been discussion of nuclear artillery as early as 1955. For a time, a British nuclear artillery warhead project Yellow Anvil had been pursued, but in late 1958 it was abandoned. The DRPC's atomic sub-committee recorded that this had been 'a research project only and should be dropped since the US had tried the approach and found it wanting'.[247] Using an American weapon, with warheads under US custody, was the only sensible alternative.

Two final War Office requirements need to be mentioned: the atomic demolition munition (ADM) Violet Mist, and the atomic mortar Davy Crockett. Violet Mist was the successor to an earlier project, originally Brown Bunny and later Blue Peacock, to put a large Blue Danube warhead on the back of an army lorry and use it as an ADM.[248] Violet Mist was originally to have used a Red Beard warhead, although the possibility of a lighter US-designed warhead was raised in late 1958. The requirement was to create a major obstacle for an invading Soviet army, perhaps in a valley, harbour or river, and where conventional sabotage methods might be too difficult. Operationally, an ADM might have been sunk in up to 50ft of water.[249] Davy Crockett meanwhile was a curious American project: a very light mortar with a sub-kiloton warhead, designed to be man-portable for use in very close combat indeed, down to as little as 1000ft range – where most people thought it would have been lethal to the troops firing it. This weapon was of interest to the War Office because of its extreme mobility on the dispersed nuclear battlefield envisaged in this period, and a requirement for an astonishing 1275 Davy Crocketts was discussed.[250] Nyman Levin, the Director of AWRE, felt confident that a British sub-kiloton warhead – alternative solutions included a low-yield version of Tony, or another still smaller warhead known as Wee Gwen – could be produced. Between July 1959 and at least June 1961 this warhead was on the DRPC's list of possible nuclear projects under assessment, being given the MoA reference number BQ267.[251] The case for Violet Mist was weak, especially with the growing controversy in this period over battlefield nuclear weapons, and the project was abandoned some time in 1961. By February 1962, there was also no British requirement for Davy Crockett.

The future

As debates about future strategic deterrent systems waxed and waned, various practical efforts were made in the service ministries, the MoA, private industry and the research establishments to draw up requirements, begin project action on weapons systems in the UK or at least track the progress of work in the US. Polaris and TSR.2 were only the two most important future nuclear systems needing to be covered in this way; others, to be considered here, included new strategic bomber aircraft and cruise-type missiles.

As with Skybolt, the origins of Polaris lay in the US, and the background to its story can be found in the bitter controversy over the creation of the USAF and the roles and missions of the services in the late 1940s. During these struggles, the US Navy conceived a keen interest in the delivery of strategic nuclear weapons from aircraft carriers. Defeated in Congress in 1949, and thereafter limited to a nuclear delivery role against targets of strictly naval interest such as ships at sea, submarine pens and port facilities, the US Navy nevertheless continued to experiment with potential nuclear bombers and missiles. Modified German V-1 and V-2 cruise and ballistic missiles, for example, were launched from aircraft carriers and submarines in 1947 and 1948. A larger cruise missile, Regulus, was deployed on submarines in the mid-1950s but in fact enjoyed few advantages over the V-1: range was unimpressive, launch was from the surface and Regulus had to be guided to its target by up to two other submarines. Guidance was very susceptible to ECM, and the missile itself flew at subsonic speeds, making interception relatively easy. Naval aviators, like their USAF brethren, strongly preferred aircraft and this preference certainly undermined Regulus. Ballistic missile research for the US Navy meanwhile languished completely, until in 1955

Admiral Arleigh Burke became Chief of Naval Operations. Burke called almost at once for the creation of a fleet ballistic-missile (FBM) programme, and the US Navy's Special Projects Office (SPO) was created in November 1955. SPO initially found itself, as a result of inter-service politics, responsible for a sea-launch system for the army's liquid-fuelled Jupiter IRBM. But the technical difficulties involved in using such a large – nearly 60ft long – liquid-fuelled missile at sea led to investigations of a smaller and simpler system. Almost straight away, SPO was in touch with Aerojet and Lockheed about the possibility of solid-fuelled missiles. As in the UK, solid fuel was at first assumed to mean less power and payload, but good news began to filter in: lighter guidance systems were possible, said a team at the Massachusetts Institute of Technology (MIT); the navy's own researchers came up with ideas on solid propellants with much greater specific impulse (a measure of thrust to weight); and at the Nobska conference in the summer of 1956, Edward Teller famously predicted that a much smaller warhead would be available by the time the missile became operational: 'Why use a 1958 warhead in a 1965 weapon system?'[252] Acting on all of this new information, navy scientists now conceived Polaris, a relatively small solid-fuelled missile, equal in range and destructive power to Thor and Jupiter, but only a quarter or a fifth as heavy. Here was a weapon that could feasibly be launched from a submerged submarine. Burke was keen on Polaris partly because, like Mountbatten, he was an instinctive moderniser, but also because he felt the navy's 1949 defeat keenly and personally, and wished to reassert a strategic role for the navy.

Polaris faced opposition within the US Navy: 'As a major innovation in naval weapons, the FBM would be certain to alter career opportunities within the officer corps, favouring particular types of training over others. It is not surprising that naval officers tied to outmoded technologies found it difficult to appreciate the benefits of an innovation which challenged their role in life'.[253] Money was tight; other missile programmes suffered, and even the carrier and SSN felt the pressure as Polaris came close to absorbing ten per cent of the navy's budget in the peak year, 1962. But Polaris succeeded: partly because it was differentiated as strategically unique, an invulnerable second-strike retaliatory weapon; partly because of skilful public and political advocacy; partly because of a willingness to sacrifice technical elaboration on the altar of cost and time; but mostly because 'the Polaris was devised and built by true believers'.[254] Because Polaris was a minimum-deterrent system, Burke's strategic vision included savings in other nuclear systems – for example those of the USAF – to fund improvements in conventional forces. This vision was set out in an influential article in September 1959:

> the sort of unlimited, chase-your-tail philosophy which we are following ... is an ... ultimatum which permits neither us nor the Russians any room for manoeuvre. It leads directly to a spiralling arms race ... With a manageable ... upper limit on the relatively invulnerable forces necessary to implement a national policy of finite deterrence we then can afford not only to keep them at peak efficiency, but also to provide and maintain those [forces] necessary to successfully handle limited wars.[255]

This kind of thinking had a considerable appeal to Mountbatten, Zuckerman and indeed Watkinson in the UK.

Polaris test launches began in September 1958, initially without much success. The first five launches were outright failures, and of the first 17 flights, only four reached even 700 miles range. But the launches were away from the harsh glare of publicity and SPO was able to declare all but one of the 17 a 'partial' success. In September 1959 test flights of A-1X missiles, very similar to operational hardware, began. These were guided, from January 1960, and ranges extended at times to 1000 miles. Thrust termination – more difficult for solid-fuelled than liquid-fuelled missiles – continued to be a problem, with the second stage sometimes bumping the RV. On 20 July 1960, however, USS *George Washington*, the first American bomber submarine, successfully fired two A-1 missiles in succession to full range. Polaris was operational.[256]

The A-1 version of Polaris was a two-stage solid-fuelled missile, 28ft six inches long by 54 inches in diameter. It weighed 28,800lb, and was capable of carrying its single Mk.47 warhead, 600lb in weight and structurally integral to the 850lb heat-sink type RV, to a range of 1200nm. Accuracy of two nautical miles circular error probable was expected. Air- or ground-burst was possible. The design yield was one megaton, apparently not because the US Navy believed this was necessary to attack the Polaris's targets but because without it, air chief LeMay 'would laugh us out of this business'.[257] The earliest Mk.47 warheads gave perhaps half a megaton. The missile was built by Lockheed, the motors by Aerojet. The propellant, polyurethane with a powdered aluminium additive, had a similar specific impulse to the liquid fuel of Blue Streak, and each motor had a steerable nozzle for control. The inertial guidance system, progressively improved over time, was developed by the Draper laboratory at MIT and built, like the RV, by General Electric. The FBM programme did not just involve a missile: the submarine, its inertial and auxiliary navigation systems, fire-control system, launch tubes and ejection system, operational cycles with twin 'blue' and 'gold' submarine crews – all were new. The operation of the Polaris system will be described in more detail in Chapter 4.

Submarine-launched strategic missiles had been suggested independently in Britain, soon after the war. Amongst a series of naval ideas on the atomic bomb, solicited in September 1945, was a suggestion from the Director of Naval Operational Research: 'It seems probable that no fleet of surface ships could remain afloat within the sphere of action of land-based aircraft carrying atomic bombs ... three submarines capable of surfacing for a short time and launching three V-1s against an enemy port may have a better chance of success than a surface fleet'.[258] Mountbatten's arrival gave the idea new life. 'Amenable to any scheme which stood to project the fleet into the future',[259] Mountbatten was soon outlining 'my plan', as he described it, 'for the launching of ballistic rockets from nuclear-powered submarines in the Barents Sea, Persian Gulf and possibly the Pacific ... it seems that we should design our nuclear-powered submarine around the medium-range ballistic rocket'.[260]

By 1958, a great deal of information was available on Polaris in the UK. A delegation from the joint US/UK Ballistic Missile Advisory Committee, for example, visited Aerojet, Lockheed and the US Navy ordnance bureau and reported in detail on such arcana as propellant compositions, air-burst heights, fuzing arrangements, airflow experiments around the RV and the surface roughness of its beryllium heatshield.[261] The Admiralty mentioned Polaris briefly and indirectly in its public statement on the naval estimates in 1958, and a working party was established 'to examine and report on the strategic case for Polaris ... [and] to consider the possibility of a programme of Polaris submarines'.[262] The party was led by the Deputy Chief of the Naval Staff, the splendidly named Admiral Sir Manley Power. Power was enthusiastic; and so, for a time, were their lordships. They concluded, however, that the time was not ripe for a paper on the subject to go beyond the Admiralty: 'In reaching this conclusion the Board were influenced not only by the bitter opposition which the Air Ministry must be expected to offer to the substitution of the seaborne Polaris for the land-based Blue Streak; but also by the risk that if too great an enthusiasm were shown prematurely for the Polaris project, the Admiralty would be pressed to realise it without any addition to navy votes'.[263] Replying to an encouraging letter from Burke, Mountbatten confided that 'what we are aiming to do at the moment is to keep the Polaris pot boiling over here'. At this point Burke offered Mountbatten the chance to post a liaison officer to SPO; Commander Michael Simeon arrived in the US in October.²⁶⁴ Continuing studies in the Admiralty were low-key, partly because in mid-1959 the Board was advised by James Mackay to wait a full ten years before returning to Polaris. Papers were passed, sometimes with little enthusiasm, to the BNDSG machinery. In 1960, a report on the possible Admiralty headquarters organisation for a Polaris programme was produced by rising star Admiral Mike Le Fanu. In February 1961, a mission to the US under Sidney Palmer, the Admiralty's top submarine designer, produced a positive report with a recommendation that five Polaris submarines be built in the UK, based on the design of the SSN HMS *Valiant*. But Simeon's successor recalled that 'up to this point the Royal Navy's interest in Polaris had been largely academic, and there were a good many key figures in the navy who wanted it to stay that way' – evidently including the head of the design team working on the SSN HMS *Dreadnought*, who described Polaris to Palmer as 'completely bloody daft'.²⁶⁵

The contrast with Air Ministry attitudes to the TSR.2 could not have been more striking. TSR.2 – standing for tactical strike and reconnaissance – was the great hope of the future, for the RAF and for much of the aircraft manufacturing industry, whose consolidation into a smaller number of firms was beginning. Because of its cancellation in 1965, the history of the TSR.2 project has become extraordinarily controversial. The most impartial, factual account is in Wynn's official history, on which this account therefore relies heavily.²⁶⁶ The draft requirement for an aircraft to replace the Canberra was first circulated in 1956, and issued a year later. TSR.2 was to be a large aircraft intended for transonic operation at low level. From the outset, it was intended as a nuclear-capable system, able to deliver Red Beard and if necessary supplement the deterrent power of the V-bombers. Conventional weapons could also be carried. The Air Ministry had belatedly recognised, after a number of false starts, that low-level penetration of air defences, at least on the central front in Europe, was essential. The airframe, engines and avionics were new and very advanced – especially the navigation and attack system for low-level operation, incorporating a moving-map display, terrain-following radar, digital computer, and an inertial guidance platform with updates from doppler and sideways-looking radar. Combat radius was to be over 1000nm on internal fuel, and penetration of air defences to and from the target would be at 200ft. Weight and complexity was added by the need to operate from rough airstrips, requiring a new undercarriage. The targets listed in a 1959 document give some indication of the roles envisaged for the aircraft: bridges, blast-resistant and reinforced-concrete buildings, radio stations, airfield runways, parked aircraft, thin-skinned and armoured vehicles, small ships, guided-missile sites and even 'tribal forts', for TSR.2 would not just be used in Europe.[267]

After almost a year of pressure from the Air Ministry, Sandys and the Treasury approved an initial design contract in December 1958 which was placed with Vickers and English Electric (later BAC). In May 1959, the Air Ministry's TSR.2 requirement was reissued as OR.343. The aircraft was now to replace the SACEUR-assigned Valiants as well as the RAF's Canberras at home and abroad. Watkinson, doubtless influenced by Mountbatten, was sceptical about TSR.2, although attracted somewhat by the idea of its secondary deterrent role, carrying not just bombs but perhaps some kind of stand-off missile. Thus, by the time Watkinson secured the Defence Committee's agreement to an airframe development contract for TSR.2 in September 1960, work was underway on possible missile armament. Blue Steel would be too heavy; Skybolt had to be guided and launched from altitude; Blue Water, carried externally, would reduce range and target coverage; but a new missile might be worth investigating.[268] The improved kiloton bomb to OR.1177, offering a lay-down delivery mode, was also now being considered for TSR.2.

As early as 1958, a long-running and bitter competition had begun in Whitehall between the TSR.2 and the shorter-range, subsonic naval NA.39, later called the Buccaneer. NA.39 was intended to replace the Fleet Air Arm's Scimitar strike aircraft, and had the advantage over TSR.2 of a head start and a less taxing requirement. It was designed for low-level delivery of Red Beard, although from time to time the Admiralty also expressed interest in a megaton weapon for NA.39, partly to make 'cross-decking' operations between Royal Navy and US Navy carriers easier, and partly to annoy the Air Ministry by undermining one of the TSR.2's competitive advantages, the secondary deterrent mission, which was raised many times but never fully accepted. The Buccaneer first flew in 1958, and began carrier trials in January 1960 on HMS *Victorious*.[269] Until the S.2 version arrived in the late 1960s, the Buccaneer was under-powered; this fact, its relatively primitive navigation and attack systems, and its association with the navy in general and Mountbatten in particular, made it wholly unacceptable to the RAF and Air Ministry.

Indeed, far from being prepared to adopt unsatisfactory naval aircraft for nuclear strike roles, the Air Ministry had in mind throughout this period the objective of a new generation of bomber aircraft. Mindful of Sandys's cancellation of the Avro 730 project in 1957, the ministry proceeded with great caution. As we have seen, however, the subject had been raised in Zuckerman's Air Ministry Strategic Scientific Policy Committee during 1959. A confused draft requirement was considered containing a number of far-fetched and contradictory provisions: vertical or very short take-off and landing, endurance of 15 or 20 hours, a 20-minute turnaround on the ground, perhaps Mach 2 dash performance, low-level penetration, a 100,000ft ceiling, variable geometry and even nuclear propulsion.[270] In December 1959, the requirement was given a wider circulation; long endurance and the ability to carry Skybolt were now seen as its most important aspects. A short-term solution using a modified transport aircraft was suggested, then for the longer term a completely new aircraft. Vertical take-off, or at least reduced reliance on large fixed air bases, was still under consideration.[271] Thinking began to crystallise around a new large transport, the VC-10, as a deterrent weapons carrier for the 1970s. Pike, the new air chief, was 'said to hold the view that a system based on the VC-10 transport would largely fill the requirement'.[272] Vickers, the makers of the VC-10, were already looking at possibilities, although the installation of Skybolt navigation and computer equipment, and the performance requirements of the draft OR – especially the need to be able to use short runways – were a challenge. A total of 60 aircraft was contemplated, carrying 240 Skybolts with the then-current light Mk.47 warhead for long range; these numbers were progressively reduced to make the system more competitive with Polaris on cost grounds.[273] By November 1960, more exotic solutions were again being discussed: a new 'HP.117 laminar flow aircraft', proposed by Handley Page, and a variable-geometry design. A 'stage three' modification of the Victor showed some promise as a future Skybolt carrier, but apparently the VC-10 now fell 'far short of the operational requirement ... The development of a new, high performance vehicle would give us far greater strategic, tactical and political flexibility'.[274] Thus, at a time when its political energies might better have been spent justifying the Skybolt/VC-10 combination as a reliable and cost-effective alternative to Polaris, the Air Ministry could not resist dreaming up a more exciting new aircraft. This train of thought was at least partly inspired by the belief in air circles that an ABM defence was in prospect and that fast low-level penetration, *à la* TSR.2, would be the only reliable means of attacking Soviet targets in future. By January 1961, ACAS(OR) was looking for 'a long endurance supersonic replacement aircraft' with a 'variable contour' (or cruise) missile.[275]

The latter requirement was probably inspired by work at Bristol during the second half of 1960 on 'a new family of cruise type missiles for TSR.2 and Vulcan' which, after discussion with Air Ministry representatives, quickly led to the issue of a new operational requirement, OR.1182. This called for a long-range air-to-surface missile, for service entry if possible in 1966. The missile was to have Mach 2 performance at low level, 'a variable trajectory, the ability to perform jinking, a low-level terminal phase of at least 100nm and terrain following not higher than 300ft', and a Skybolt type warhead.[276] In proposing such a weapon, Bristol were taking advantage of their own experience with Bloodhound in ramjet propulsion and associated aerodynamics and structures. As part of BAC, they were also now able to capitalise on English Electric's work on Blue Water inertial guidance and Ferranti (Edinburgh) work on terrain-avoidance radar for the TSR.2. Ministers quickly showed an interest in OR.1182.[277] A joint Air Ministry/MoA working party reported at the end of December, rejecting a proposal from Avro for a rocket-powered weapon with no low-level capability, known as W130, but concluding that studies of OR.1182 were promising and should continue.[278] A specific proposal from Bristol, known as Pandora or X-12, remained in the field, and another was now commissioned from Avro for a similar weapon, W140. A long RAE report in the spring of 1961 discussed their merits.[279] X-12 was a ramjet missile, 33ft long with a body diameter of 28 inches and a narrow delta configuration with a wingspan of nine feet. It weighed 10,500lb with extra wrap-around rocket boosters. The Avro missile was turbojet-powered, similar in shape to X-12, slightly longer, but lighter at 8200lb and with a wingspan of only six feet six inches. RAE felt that neither missile would quite have the performance, range or accuracy stated in the operational requirement, or be available in the stated five-year timescale. A paper was submitted to the DRPC in June,[280] but the Air Ministry now accepted that the political prospects for OR.1182 were poor. It would clearly be a major undertaking, and timescale in particular told against it. Zuckerman, Sir Steuart Mitchell, and the Admiralty and War Office were opposed; also, as at least one senior official pointed out, it had become politically dangerous to suggest that an alternative or successor to Skybolt was necessary at all.[281] In August 1961 Zuckerman was informed of the 'death of X-12, or OR.1182'.[282]

The sheer variety of British nuclear-weapons requirements and projects in these years is striking. Applications for nuclear warheads were considered from underwater to the fringes of outer space, and from close quarters in the battlefield to cities deep in the Soviet Union. There were no quick wins, however; nuclear-weapons projects took considerable time, treasure and ingenuity. Even the relatively unambitious Blue Steel, for example, had been in development for seven years by the autumn of 1961, involving big defence industries, leading-edge manufacturing techniques and long series of trials at home and abroad. Requirements shifted, as Bomber Command changed its readiness levels and tactics. Resources were limited, and projects took longer – often much longer – than first thought. Political uncertainty had a significant impact at working level, for example as the fortunes of Blue Streak waxed and waned, and as the Red Beard replacement project was put on hold for more than a year. Impatience on all sides, and poor relationships between government and industry, are painfully apparent from the documentary record. Progress should not be underestimated. Aldermaston and Bomber Command, in particular, were growing in confidence. Enough British nuclear weapons were now available, for example, to equip every front-line V-bomber for at least one sortie. British scientists and engineers were, if not always at the forefront, then at least heavily engaged in most fields of importance to the cold-war arms race. The Blue Streak cancellation, however, had been a significant blow, and reality was to bite further in the following years.

The second-generation kiloton bomb Red Beard undergoing vibration trials, probably at RAE Farnborough. Red Beard struggled through these and other environmental tests, delaying service entry and leading to pressure for a more modern and robust replacement weapon.

Source: Crown Copyright, via Doug Bateman.

The second guided Blue Water round on its transporter/launcher, shortly before its test flight at Aberporth, March 1962. The weapon was abruptly cancelled by Defence Minister Thorneycroft a few months later.

Source: photo courtesy of Imperial War Museum, Aberporth 3281/1.

Drawings and photographs of Blue Streak usually show the blunt-nosed space launch vehicle of the 1960s. This is an attempt to present the missile as it would have appeared in RAF service, including a late-design re-entry vehicle (RV). In fact, the RV design had not been finalised at the time of cancellation, so the missile's overall size and shape remain speculative.

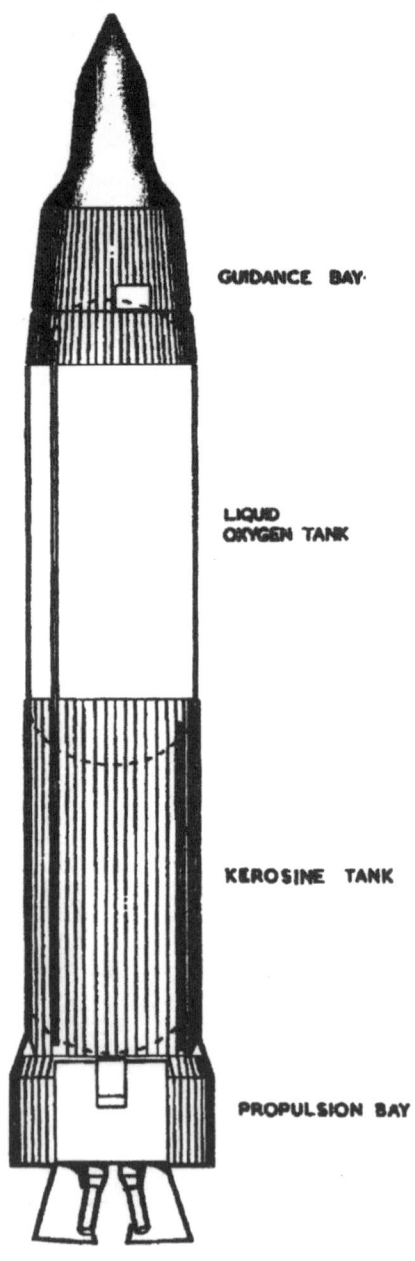

Source: author, composite of other images.

A Blue Steel missile receiving attention under a Vulcan at RAF Scampton in the mid to late 1960s. The second Vulcan in the background is painted in low-level camouflage, and the protective clothing in use gives some idea of the hazards faced by Blue Steel ground crews in servicing the high-test peroxide-fuelled weapons.

Source: photo courtesy of Imperial War Museum, RAF-T 4841.

Harold Watkinson, Defence Minister between October 1959 and July 1962. Watkinson was an industrialist, who trained originally as an engineer. Somewhat unsuccessful attempts at defence diplomacy in the US, and failure to achieve economies, led to his departure: 'had I been a shrewder politician', he later reflected, 'I should have been more aware of my increasingly exposed position'.

Source: National Portrait Gallery, X165632.

Sir Dermot Boyle (left) and Sir Thomas Pike (right), successively Chiefs of the Air Staff between 1955–59 and 1960–63. Both waged a tireless battle to protect manned aircraft projects, especially the TSR.2, but cared less for Blue Streak and could not save Skybolt.

Source: photo courtesy of Imperial War Museum, HU 63229; Crown Copyright, RAF Museum.

The Chief of the Defence Staff, Earl Mountbatten of Burma, watches a Seacat missile launch aboard the carrier HMS *Eagle* in October 1964. Mountbatten's boyish enthusiasm for high technology is in evidence.

Source: photo courtesy of Imperial War Museum, A 34867.

Sketch by an unknown hand showing an early version of the Skybolt missile, spring 1959.

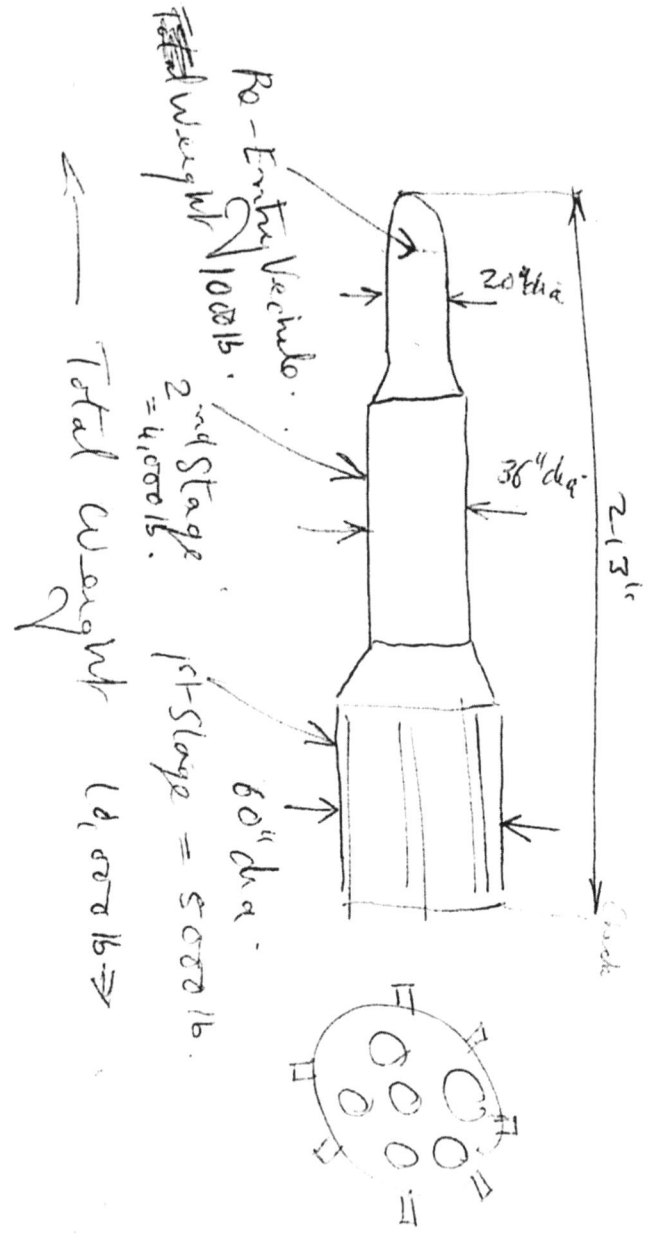

Source: PRO, AIR 2/15261.

Missile compartment of one of the Royal Navy's four Polaris submarines.

Source: photo courtesy of Imperial War Museum, TR 28637.

Mountbatten and his close political ally Sir Solly Zuckerman, Chief Scientific Adviser at the Ministry of Defence, sip their drinks conspiratorially at Serudong Laut in the Borneo jungle in March 1965.

Source: photo courtesy of Imperial War Museum, A 34932.

Part II
Nuclear Reality

3
Policy-making 1961–64

If the period between 1958 and 1961 was one of political success for the British government's nuclear defence policy, with growing American links and the domestic political opposition in disarray, the succeeding three years were not so happy. The Macmillan government was weakened by economic difficulties and political scandal, and in October 1963 the Prime Minister was forced to resign for health reasons. The impressive series of Anglo-American defence agreements reached under Eisenhower, including the atomic bilateral, remained in force. The new Kennedy administration, however, resolved officially and specifically to discourage Britain's nuclear ambitions. Although Macmillan came to enjoy a cordial and even friendly relationship with Kennedy, his major diplomatic achievements *vis-à-vis* the US – the Polaris deal of December 1962 and the successful pursuit of a partial nuclear test-ban in 1963 – came at a political price, and necessarily involved the defeat of powerful bureaucratic interests in Washington. Polaris, as we shall see, was seen in some quarters as a very visible blow to Britain's independence, and the deal infuriated the State Department. Acute pressure to agree to join the NATO MLF was to follow. On the way to the partial test-ban, Britain was made to look slightly ridiculous at ministerial meetings in Moscow, and the deal was bad news to the Pentagon and the nuclear-weapons laboratories in the US. Moreover, the French and West Germans now increasingly complicated British diplomacy, both in NATO and bilaterally with the US.

At home, the Labour party regrouped in the aftermath of the leadership's victory over the party rebels in October 1961, and after Gaitskell's death took up an increasingly confident position of opposition, not to nuclear weapons in all their forms, but to the Conservative 'pretence' of independent deterrence in particular. Labour charged that the deterrent was no longer independent, as it had been before the Blue Streak cancellation; that it was no longer credible, in the face of improvements in Soviet air defences; that it detracted from necessary expenditure on conventional forces; and that strategic rationales for its use were weak. The government found its policy harder and harder to defend, partly because Macmillan and his ministers privately recognised all of these criticisms. Despite concerns about Skybolt, a long series of investigations, in the BNDSG and elsewhere, failed to find a convincing and affordable alternative with a greater measure of independence and the ability to penetrate targets in the Soviet Union. Ministers had to listen mutely to criticism from Secretary McNamara in his 1962 speeches at Athens and Ann Arbor. At the end of the year, McNamara secured the cancellation of Skybolt, and the basis for Britain's future nuclear defence seemed to have been cut away entirely.

Above all, Macmillan was failing in these years in the search for a priority decision that might relieve pressure on the defence budget. He was unable to abandon Britain's worldwide commitments, either east of Suez or, in the face of stiff American and European opposition, in NATO. Mountbatten and others continued to drive the debate on conventional defence, pressing for credible alternatives to overseas bases in Singapore and Aden, which might not be available by the end of the decade. Little progress was made over NATO strategy. Ministers agreed more or less with McNamara's criticisms of the massive-retaliation policy of the Eisenhower administration, but were unable to face the implication of greater expenditure on conventional forces – too expensive, and too obvious a break with the Sandys policy of 1957–58. Nevertheless, in January 1962, Macmillan decided that the long-term defence costings should be based on the assumption that the V-bomber/Skybolt deterrent force would *not* be replaced at the end of the decade. This was unilateral nuclear disarmament in the making. As events at the end of the year made clear, however, Macmillan was ultimately quite unable to abandon the deterrent.

In this chapter I shall cover, in turn: cabinet changes; the international politics of the test ban and NATO strategy; the search for a credible east of Suez defence policy and the implications for NATO and the deterrent; the continuing internal debate over deterrent delivery systems; the fate of Skybolt; the Nassau talks of December 1962; subsequent Anglo-American difficulties over the MLF and the Polaris sales agreement; and finally party politics and the run-up to the October 1964 election.

Change at the top

In the summer of 1962, Macmillan's government was beset in particular by economic difficulties. Most historians agree that Selwyn Lloyd, the chancellor, was out of his depth. His deflationary budget of 1961 was deeply unpopular with middle-class voters, and a number of by-election defeats followed. After Gaitskell's triumph at the October 1961 party conference, the Labour opposition was meanwhile reviving. Macmillan looked to Lloyd for reflationary measures ahead of a possible 1963 election, but the chancellor stubbornly refused. Party chairman Iain Macleod, chief whip Martin Redmayne, and possibly also Sir Norman Brook, pressed Macmillan for a ministerial reshuffle. In a series of emotional meetings on 12 July 1962, Macmillan sacked a full third of his cabinet, including the distraught Lloyd. This was a 'night of the long knives', and some historians see it as the beginning of the end for Macmillan himself. Watkinson was one casualty. There is no agreement over the background to his departure; some report that he had been planning for some time to return to private industry – he later became chairman of Cadbury-Schweppes – while others emphasise his sense of hurt and betrayal at the circumstances.[1] As Macmillan's official biographer records, however, the Prime Minister 'had not been unduly impressed' by Watkinson's performance.[2] The Defence Minister had been unsuccessful in his attempts at personal diplomacy, for example with Gates during the Polaris and Holy Loch discussions in the summer of 1960, and subsequently, as we shall see, with the French. On top of his clumsiness in Washington, the policy ideas he had put forward to Macmillan in September 1961 were unwelcome, and he was failing to make headway with economies or the (intractable) issue of priority between NATO and east of Suez. His own later assessment was candid: the Prime Minister 'wanted a close and friendly relationship with President Kennedy. Feuding between the Pentagon and Storey's Gate was not part of this scenario ... had I been a shrewder politician, I should have been more aware of my increasingly exposed position as one of the largest spenders in the government'.[3]

Watkinson's replacement was Thorneycroft, in confident mood after a fairly successful period as Minister of Aviation, and charged by Macmillan with achieving cuts and reorganisation. Thorneycroft remained ambitious, and despite his later reputation as a proto-Thatcherite, he was considered pro-European.[4] In Peter Hennessy's words, here was 'at least one clearing in the forest of late-imperial sentimentality and economic half-reality'.[5] Thorneycroft was disinclined to be pushed around, in particular by the Americans. Julian Amery moved to the MoA, and was replaced at the Air Ministry by the relatively junior Hugh Fraser. Macmillan left Carrington at the Admiralty and John Profumo at the War Office – little thinking that it would be the latter, hitherto unremarkable, whose resignation the following year would further, and perhaps fatally, undermine his premiership. The Profumo affair, linking the Secretary of State for War with call-girls and Soviet agents, exposed the very seedy side of 1960s London high society. After lying to parliament, Profumo had no choice but to resign on 5 June 1963.

Thorneycroft's plans for defence reorganisation proceeded apace. As Michael Howard notes, 'it was an open secret that much of the initiative and many of the ideas came from Lord Mountbatten'.[6] Mountbatten envisaged a single Ministry of Defence, absorbing the Ministry of Aviation as well as the single-service ministries. Defence would have a Secretary of State and functional, rather than service-based, ministers: one for personnel, and one for research. The Chief of Defence Staff would be more than just first among equals: the other chiefs would be his deputies, their roles as professional heads of the services given instead to commanders-in-chief. By November 1962, Macmillan had been briefed on Mountbatten's revolutionary proposals, and gave his general backing. The Prime Minister despaired of the emergence of strategic commonsense or economies from the endless Whitehall competition between the services; he was later to plead with Thorneycroft: 'I beg you to take an axe to all this forest of prejudice and interest'.[7]

Mountbatten had been sorry to see Watkinson go: 'Said sad goodbye to dear Harold Watkinson ... who has been sacrificed in the massacre', he confided to his diary, and then, 'Thorneycroft. He is going to be difficult'.[8] The CDS managed, however, to forge a working alliance with his new minister. Reorganisation was no trivial exercise. In Ziegler's rather dramatic words it 'involved the destruction of institutions that had stood the test of centuries, the elimination of innumerable vested interests, a confrontation with entrenched opposition as determined as any [Mountbatten] had met at war'.[9] Of these latter-day Japanese, it was Tom Pike, the air chief, who led the opposition to reform. Caspar John was a moderate – as was Dick Hull, who looked one day to succeed Mountbatten as CDS – but the chiefs were united in opposition to Mountbatten's original proposals. He was 'utterly at loggerheads' with them, Sir Ian Jacob recalled: 'they seemed to hate him'.[10] Scott, the MoD Permanent Secretary, and Zuckerman, on the other hand, were supporters. A stalemate threatened, until the idea emerged of an enquiry into defence reorganisation by the impeccably independent team of Lord Ismay,

Churchill's personal chief of staff during the war, and Jacob, who had been one of Ismay's deputies. Their report, in February 1963, supported the idea of a single ministry in a single building, but stopped short of a reorganisation by function, and preserved the powers and prerogatives of the chiefs. On the basis of the Ismay-Jacob report, agreement was finally reached in the summer of 1963. The independence of the Ministry of Aviation was preserved, but the service ministries would move bodily to the neutral MoD main building, with a Navy Department at the Horse Guards end, an Army Department in the middle, and an Air Force Department to the south, in the existing Air Ministry accommodation. The service ministers heading these departments would be confined to 'whatever responsibilities the Secretary of State may delegate to them from time to time'. The Defence Committee would be replaced by a Defence and Oversea Policy Committee, of which only the Secretary of State for Defence would be a member by right; the junior service ministers might attend by invitation. The Board of Admiralty and the Army and Air Councils would be merged into a Defence Council, and the single-service staffs into a defence staff, reporting to the chiefs and, through CDS, to the Secretary of State. The DRPC would be replaced by a Defence Research Committee and a Weapons Development Committee, both under the chief scientist. For the first time a single post was recommended, the assistant CDS for operational requirements, authorised to comment on the *validity* of requirements coming out of the single services. Previously not even the chief scientist had this authority – 'although he might, and in Sir Solly Zuckerman's case usually did, ask a number of embarrassing questions'.[11] The cabinet gave its approval, a formal white paper was issued in July,[12] and the changes took effect on 1 April 1964.

By the time this revolution took place, however, Macmillan himself had left office. Ill and politically threatened, especially by the Profumo affair, Macmillan was near to collapse at the cabinet on 8 October 1963. As his colleagues departed the same afternoon for the party conference in Blackpool, Macmillan, needing urgent surgery on his painfully enlarged prostate gland, decided to resign. Home travelled north to convey a message to this effect to the conference; ten days later, to general surprise, he had secured the succession. Something of an unknown quantity, the Foreign Secretary had to renounce his earldom to take office as Prime Minister, and did not appear in the House of Commons until 8 November, after a contrived by-election. An intelligent and likeable man, with the image of a gentleman amateur and the temperament of an old-school Tory grandee, Sir Alec Douglas-Home, as he now became, began with no discernible defence or nuclear policy of his own. On the contrary, he had been closely involved with Macmillan's policies, for example at Nassau. One of Home's first prime-ministerial duties was to attend Kennedy's funeral; he therefore also faced a new American President, Lyndon Johnson, and one with considerable domestic preoccupations. Butler now became Foreign Secretary, but Reginald Maudling remained Chancellor. Thorneycroft stayed at defence, and Amery at aviation. The change of administration led to no real shift in nuclear policy. As we shall see, however, a change of emphasis could be discerned during the long election campaign of 1964, when Home showed himself more concerned to assert nuclear independence than his predecessor.

Nuclear testing

When we left the story in Chapter 1, the nuclear test-ban talks in Geneva had been adjourned awaiting the Kennedy administration's arrival. Initially, although the talks resumed in March 1961, little movement could be discerned. Home reported gloomily to the cabinet that 'no progress was now being made in the negotiations ... The attitude of the Russians had hardened, and the prospects of securing a settlement appeared to be deteriorating'.[13] Kennedy's strong advice at home, from the joint chiefs and the USAEC, was that it was more important to resume testing than to gaze thirstily at the mirage of test limitation. Initially, Kennedy was not easily convinced by the nuclear-weapons lobby's arguments on the need for neutron bombs, 'clean' fusion weapons and ABM research, but after the failed June 1961 summit meeting with Khrushchev at Vienna he became, in the words of USAEC chairman Glenn Seaborg, 'more inclined to think that the resumption of testing was inevitable'.[14] Plans were therefore drawn up for a propaganda campaign to accompany a resumption of testing around February 1962: 'Looking towards resumption ... the administration would in the meantime cultivate international sympathy for its test-ban position and encourage tolerance of American tests if and when they eventually took place'.[15] In the absence of progress at Geneva, the British government seemed happy enough at this point to defer to American positions, and in early August 1961 Kennedy began to prepare the ground with Macmillan for the resumption of testing:

> I remain most reluctant to take a firm decision to resume testing – the stakes are high and the consequences not easily predicted. So I propose to send Dean [Rusk] back to Geneva, about August 24, with instructions to make one more strenuous effort to move the Soviets

... Meanwhile, I shall be forced to consider a decision to resume testing. I am still reviewing the evidence, and in any event I do not expect that there need be any US tests in 1961. But I am not very hopeful that it will be possible to wait much beyond the first of the year. If we do resume, it will be underground, unless and until the Soviets resume atmospheric tests. We are considering one further possibility, which is that at the UN and in a general campaign for some time thereafter – and before we resume testing – we should offer to join in an unpoliced agreement to give up all tests which can cause fallout. We believe that it may be possible to get wide public understanding of 'fall-out testing' as bad, and underground testing as reasonable – and this would give us the assurance of parity with the Soviet Union which cannot exist at present. May I hear how all this strikes you?[16]

The Soviet announcement on 30 August of a new series of tests – probably related, at least in its timing, to events in Berlin – interrupted the calm of this rather slow-paced period of diplomacy. For Kennedy, the resumption of testing was now inevitable, and the only question was whether to test in the atmosphere, as well as underground. In Britain too, correspondence began immediately on the possibility of resumption. Zuckerman speculated on the reasons for the Soviet announcement in a letter to Macmillan in early September, and Scott asked Makins at the UKAEA for an assessment of what the UK might wish to do: perhaps develop new weapons, improve knowledge of existing types, or advance scientific knowledge on test detection. Caccia, the ambassador in Washington, also noted the need, as an atomic ally, to share the odium of any western test resumption with the US.[17] On 3 September, the UK and US responded jointly to the Soviet resumption with a public offer to end atmospheric testing, the US following this with the announcement of a series of underground tests. On 9 September the Geneva talks were again suspended.[18]

The question of nuclear testing was now complicated, for the British government, by American interest in the use of British test facilities at Christmas Island. US atmospheric testing of large-yield weapons in the Pacific had taken place between 1946 and 1958 at Bikini and Eniwetok, two atolls in the Marshall Islands, but the facilities there were in a state of disrepair. Furthermore, the Americans were now sensitive to criticism in the United Nations of the use of the Marshall Islands, a UN trust territory. Christmas Island suggested itself as an easier alternative, although it left the US in an unfamiliar situation of near-dependence on the

British: 'If this requirement did not give Macmillan a veto over American testing plans, it nevertheless exposed those plans to a searching British critique, informed by the Prime Minister's paradigm of modern international behaviour'.[19] Underground testing meanwhile was limited to low-yield warheads, and as a discipline it was in its infancy. Alone, it was not enough to satisfy the US nuclear lobby, or indeed the President, who wished to send an unambiguous signal that he was not surrendering any advantage in the nuclear-weapons field to the Soviets. 'The logistical difficulties of underground testing ... were preventing Kennedy from making the swift and unequivocal expression of American power that he would have wished'.[20] During September, Seaborg and Makins discussed a request for US testing at Christmas Island, and UK testing underground in Nevada. An obvious deal was in prospect, swapping the one for the other, but Macmillan, although willing to join the Americans in testing underground, told the cabinet he was still optimistic that atmospheric testing could be avoided.[21] In parliament at the end of October, he explained that he could support testing only for safety reasons, or to develop a new weapon such as an ABM.[22]

On 3 November, Macmillan formally asked Kennedy's permission to stage an underground test in Nevada, and on 7 November US ambassador David Bruce asked Home in return for permission to use Christmas Island, if atmospheric testing should be necessary. Rather than link the two requests explicitly, Kennedy quickly agreed to the test in Nevada; but the pressure on Macmillan was nevertheless increased.[23] By December, Penney and other British scientists were being briefed by the Americans on the tests they intended to carry out, focusing on the ABM problem. Although there was still some scepticism – shared now, for example, by Watkinson, doubtless under Zuckerman's influence – there was nobody on the British side who could contemplate an outright refusal to share Christmas Island. Ministers were told US tests would focus on further improvements in yield-to-weight, doubtless to facilitate re-entry system improvements including penetration aids and multiple independently targeted re-entry vehicles (MIRV); warhead hardening; ABM warheads; safety; and nuclear-weapons effects including on electronics and communications.[24] Although there were references to sharing information on the test results, this seems not to have been of central interest to British officials, whose own testing ambitions at this point, as we shall see in Chapter 4, were more modest. Penney, to whom Macmillan often deferred in these matters, was no warmonger, but he did incline to the view that 'there was always something that can be learned from testing' – which, as even Zuckerman was forced to recognise, was a 'manifestly sound' proposition.[25]

Meeting Kennedy in December in Bermuda, Macmillan found himself with less and less room to manoeuvre; all he could extract was a commitment to launch an unspecified new disarmament initiative to sugar the pill of more tests.[26] This new initiative was thrown together hastily by the State Department, and when it appeared in January it was 'only just on the meaningful side of verbosity'. Nevertheless Macmillan linked the use of Christmas Island to this initiative in another discussion in parliament on 8 February 1962.[27] Zuckerman travelled to Washington, where his usual interlocutors, notably the President's science adviser, Jerry Wiesner, shared his view that atmospheric testing was unjustified, and specifically that an ABM breakthrough was unlikely. Zuckerman recalled that:

> More than anyone else, it had been Jerry who had instilled in me a total disbelief in the strategic value of anti-ballistic-missile systems, in the same way as I had converted him to my views about the lack of any military utility of so-called battlefield or tactical nuclear weapons. We shared the same fears that a renewal of the nuclear arms race would add nothing to the security of either side. But the political fact that we both had to accept was that President Kennedy had been forced to say that now that the Soviet Union had broken the moratorium, America would resume testing.[28]

It was now politically impossible for Macmillan to make use of Wiesner's and Zuckerman's arguments, or indeed to revert to the conditions he had tried to lay down the previous October. British public opinion remained in general strongly opposed to testing; in June 1961, for example, 22 per cent favoured and 58 per cent opposed the resumption of testing in the absence of progress in Geneva; in spring 1962, opinion on whether to associate the UK with US testing was finely balanced.[29] The American public, however, took the opposite view: two thirds now favoured atmospheric testing. On 4 March, Kennedy announced that US atmospheric testing would indeed resume in six weeks' time.[30]

During the spring and summer of 1962, the eight non-aligned members of the 18-nation disarmament conference made much of the running in Geneva, rejecting the over-elaborate control proposals of the 1958 conference of experts and suggesting a much simplified system. This was hardly designed to appeal to the US, where concessions on control were fraught with domestic political difficulty; the whole internal debate in the US continued to focus on the issue of Soviet cheating. A draft partial test-ban treaty began to circulate in Washington, but the control-system issue frustrated any progress towards a comprehensive ban. Only in August was a new western initiative, as requested by Macmillan to coincide with the resumption of atmospheric testing, ready for presentation in Geneva. Kennedy and Macmillan announced new draft comprehensive and partial test-ban treaties, with a preference for the former, and conceded that although international inspections were still required, there need be no control posts actually on Soviet territory. Optimism grew that, once current US and Soviet test series were complete, there might be progress. At independent and informal Pugwash meetings of Soviet and American scientists, possible concessions and deals on the number of inspections were aired. This 'good season' for talks was nevertheless eventually a missed opportunity, partly because it was punctuated by international crises. After Cuba, in particular, Khrushchev was in no position to make further damaging concessions to the US. In early 1963, a new US underground test series was underway and the Soviets introduced a non-aggression treaty proposal in Geneva, which became the focus of any diplomatic energy they were prepared to devote to disarmament.

By May 1963, however, the political atmosphere between east and west was once again on the mend, and Khrushchev sent a letter inviting high-level representatives to visit Moscow for talks. The prospects for a ban on atmospheric testing seemed especially good. At a Chequers meeting, Home urged the revival of this proposal, noting that fall-out was the real nub of public concern. A US Senate resolution was passed on similar lines, and Dobrynin, the Soviet ambassador in Washington, seemed interested. Macmillan, on the other hand, was sceptical that Khrushchev would be able to agree to such a deal, noting that if underground testing remained possible, the Americans, with more experience in the field, would have a technological edge.[31] On 10 June, the prospects for agreement nevertheless improved further when Kennedy made his so-called 'peace speech' at the American University in Washington, reported extensively in *Pravda*, and announcing a unilateral commitment to end atmospheric testing. The public mood in the US was less hawkish now, in the aftermath of Cuba. Towards the end of the month, the President and Prime Minister met at Birch Grove, Macmillan's Sussex home, agreeing a general line for their representatives, Averell Harriman and Lord Hailsham, to take in Moscow in July. Harriman was a diplomatic veteran, having been ambassador in Moscow during the war, and would be backed by a strong team of seasoned arms-control negotiators. Hailsham was a somewhat eccentric choice; as Zuckerman pointed out, he knew 'nothing whatever about ... disarmament' and 'was regarded by certain members of the US delegation as a bit of a joke'.[32] On 2 July, although confirming that he was still unprepared to conclude a comprehensive test-ban treaty because of the inspections issue, Khrushchev did publicly state his support for an atmospheric ban; he also made no reference to any linkage between this and a moratorium on underground testing.

The Moscow meetings went well, although British involvement was peripheral, and a ban on testing in the atmosphere, outer space and underwater was initialled on 25 July, coming into effect in October. In retrospect it seems odd that the long and sometimes tedious proceedings of the test-ban talks had not been short-circuited in this way earlier. A partial ban – far easier to verify, and therefore to agree, than a comprehensive ban – dealt with the over-riding environmental and health issue of worldwide fall-out. Although the possibility had been raised at least four years earlier, none of the leaders involved made significant efforts in this direction. For all Macmillan's patient advocacy, for which he deserves admiration, the testing issue was dominated by domestic American and Soviet concerns, and credit for such progress as was achieved, including the partial ban, must surely go to Eisenhower, Kennedy and Khrushchev for their respective struggles against internal lobbying and the cold-war mindset.

NATO and the central front

As we have seen, early discussions between British officials and the incoming US administration in 1961 had revealed disagreements on NATO strategy. Kennedy and McNamara did not seek to re-write MC 14/2, but in working within existing NATO strategy they were anxious to improve two things in particular: conventional force levels, and command and control arrangements for nuclear weapons. Both preoccupations arose from their fundamental interest in developing more flexible and controllable strategies than the 'massive retaliation' of the SIOP, although here as elsewhere some disconnect between illusion and reality has been perceived by historians. Flexible strategies were slow to emerge in a form meaningful to real military operational commanders. The Berlin crisis of August 1961, in particular, left the President feeling an urgent need for sub-strategic options. Berlin had been an irritant for many years, especially since Khrushchev in late 1958 threatened to sign a separate peace treaty with East Germany and end the four-power occupation arrangements in the former German capital.[33] Berlin was also a problem for Anglo-American relations, as Macmillan's sympathy for the Soviet position – and unwillingness to risk precipitate action – was tantamount, for some in the US, to appeasement. During 1959 and 1960, the US, UK and France had drawn up plans for limited operations with conventional forces to keep access to West Berlin open in an east-west crisis. The ground component of these plans went under the codename Live Oak.[34] On the recommendation of Dean Acheson, Kennedy began to contemplate the use of nuclear weapons as part of the Live Oak planning, and at this point the British became extremely concerned. Discussions of the earlier Mottershead conclusions on tactical nuclear weapons had revolved around a retaliatory scenario – nuclear weapons as a counter to a massive Soviet invasion. Did the US now contemplate, for example, the deliberate first use of nuclear weapons by an allied column travelling up the autobahn to West Berlin? With the building of the Wall and the subsequent arrival of US troop reinforcements backed by Vice-President Johnson and the hero of 1948 in Berlin, General Lucius Clay – and even more so with the stand-off at Checkpoint Charlie in October 1961 – these fears became, for a time, very real. US officials were meanwhile disappointed with Britain's far from robust response to events in Berlin.[35]

Concerns over Berlin contingency planning were a microcosm of the wider debate in succeeding years about flexible response for NATO. It became clear to US policy-makers during the Berlin crisis that no realistic sub-strategic nuclear options yet existed. In October 1961, Kennedy issued two policy directives to try to address this: a national security action memorandum on Berlin 'which laid the groundwork for a series of graduated conventional and nuclear responses in a Berlin crisis', and a national strategic targeting and attack policy 'as guidance for redesigning the SIOP'. The new SIOP, to enter into force on 1 August 1962 – and introduced over the objections of SAC – included five options. These were subsequently criticised, however, as 'five options for massive retaliation'.[36] To the European allies, meanwhile, the very search for such options was dangerous: the more options existed, the greater the (equal and opposite) risks of inappropriate US escalation and withdrawal. With massive retaliation, at least everybody knew where they stood. At the December 1961 and 1962 NATO council meetings, and especially at the ministerial meeting in Athens in May 1962, McNamara put pressure on the European allies to face these problems.[37] Intellectually, British officials and strategists had few difficulties in accepting McNamara's position, although they tended to worry more about war by miscalculation than US planners, and in some ways this concern amounted to an implicit criticism of the new thinking. Practically, however, there was no prospect of finding the money for improvements to conventional forces on the continent. British planners and policy-makers therefore continued to resist attempts to modify NATO nuclear strategy for the central front, and only under Labour after 1964 was there any significant UK policy shift towards flexible response. Indeed, there is room for a good deal of scepticism about the practical impact of the new NATO doctrine even in later years, and even as it affected US forces.[38]

At sea, too, the British were uncomfortable with NATO strategy during these years. In May 1962, the Vice-Chief of the Naval Staff, Admiral Varyl Begg, produced a report on NATO maritime strategy which highlighted the outdated assumption in SACLANT's emergency defence plan – also inconsistent with planning for the land battle – that a future war would begin with an all-out strike, of which there would be little warning, and comprise 'a relatively short initial phase of intensive nuclear attack' followed by 'operations of indeterminable length and of lesser intensity'.[39] Maritime shield forces should be introduced, thought Begg, and a post-nuclear justification for a conventional balanced navy replaced with a pre-nuclear one. Caspar John discussed these ideas enthusiastically with the US Chief of Naval Operations, Admiral George Anderson, and got them on to the chiefs' agenda.[40] In correspondence with Lord Carrington, at the height of the Cuban missile crisis, he also noted that 'the events of the last few days' might have dispelled doubts about the possibility of pre-nuclear operations at sea.[41] The JPS made a similar point at the end of the year:

> There are other and perhaps yet more serious forms of aggression [than the use of sea power alone] which can be halted or deterred by the judicious use of maritime shield forces. This has been forcefully demonstrated by the recent events in Cuba, where the timely use of United States naval forces, in conjunction with the deterrent power of the United States strategic forces and the known capability of destroying the missile sites, played a significant part in helping to frustrate the Soviet attempt to alter the balance of power. In this particular case diplomatic pressure and economic boycotts seemed likely to prove ineffective and the application of some form of military force was indispensable.[42]

This analysis was not necessarily correct, but the interesting point is that Cuba was reinforcing a belief that conventional shield forces were an important part of a balanced deterrent, further undermining the massive retaliation strategy of the 1950s. The joint planners' paper was approved by the chiefs and sent to Thorneycroft.[43]

France, West Germany and Europe

So far in this study, I have ignored the political and diplomatic situation in NATO Europe, concentrating on Anglo-American angles. To understand British nuclear policy as it developed during and after 1961, however, this is no longer adequate. France in particular, and its leader General Charles de Gaulle, became more and more important to Macmillan's nuclear policy as time went by.

The French government of Pierre Mendès-France had secretly taken the decision to develop nuclear weapons in December 1954, a decision confirmed by de Gaulle on coming to power in the political crisis of May–June 1958. In February 1960, a French atomic device was tested in the Algerian desert at Reggane; the world officially had a fourth nuclear power. De Gaulle had already made clear that he was interested in a 'big three' system of US/UK/French talks at the heart of NATO. Eisenhower was also now favourably disposed towards some kind of atomic agreement between the US and France, akin to that reached in 1958 with the UK, although Washington officials were less impressed by the idea. There were suggestions, for example, in June 1960 – at the time of Watkinson's ultimately unsuccessful talks with Gates about Polaris – of a Polaris force for the French. The administration decided, however, that, as with the British, they would insist on full participation in the NATO MRBM force as a condition of any such deal. De Gaulle was also interested at this time in some kind of deal with the UK to secure access to Blue Steel and/or Blue Streak technology, including information on guidance and re-entry systems.[44]

The issues of possible Anglo-French, or US-French, or even tripartite nuclear cooperation had already been raised therefore when, in July 1961, the British cabinet took the momentous decision to apply for membership of the EEC. Suddenly Anglo-French cooperation in particular was an important problem, for it offered one possible political *quid pro quo* for French support in the entry negotiations, which began in October. Anglo-French staff talks were also now underway; Watkinson had begun a series of meetings with his French counterpart, Pierre Messmer; and Thorneycroft was pressing for the release of Blue Streak technology in the context of the new European space launcher development organisation. Watkinson apparently even raised the possibility of talks on joint nuclear targeting.[45] Kennedy was not ready at this stage to countenance any such close Anglo-French cooperation, making clear to Macmillan that he opposed any moves to pass nuclear information to the French, and reminding the Prime Minister that not all British nuclear secrets were his own to pass on.[46]

Various motivations were in play. Both the British and US governments wished to explore ways of influencing and perhaps controlling the nuclear ambitions of de Gaulle; elements in the US administration also wished to further their project for a European nuclear force. But Kennedy could never quite contemplate working as closely with France as with the UK. This was not simply a matter of personal antipathy to de Gaulle and friendship with Macmillan. As recently as 1958, the French government and constitution had altogether collapsed; the French communists were strong; in April 1961 there had been a failed military coup in Paris, widely reported in France as having a CIA connection. This was hardly an atmosphere conducive to nuclear cooperation. De Gaulle's motivations in the matter have not been investigated closely, but he gave little indication that he was interested in anybody else's support for his independent nuclear striking force. In spring 1962, he and Kennedy traded negative comments by press conference, and American resolve was strengthened: any nuclear cooperation with France would be in the context of a NATO force.[47]

At just the same time, on the other hand, Macmillan was putting out diplomatic feelers once again for an atomic deal with France, apparently thinking this to be an important card to play in the EEC negotiations. The subject attracted questions in the House of Commons.[48] Watkinson and Messmer now talked about the possibility of an Anglo-French independent submarine force as an alternative to Skybolt, and Macmillan had to warn his Defence Minister to proceed with caution.[49] Watkinson's military advice from the chiefs was always hostile to any nuclear cooperation with the French. This opposition was justified on practical grounds, although it no doubt also had a basis in difficult wartime military relations, and frank prejudice. Between July and September, there were lengthy Whitehall discussions of the supply of a heat exchanger and associated reactor parts for a French SSN, eventually resolved in favour of a sale, despite the risk of annoying Admiral Rickover. Macmillan and de Gaulle also made rather ambiguous comments on nuclear cooperation at their meetings in June and again in December, shortly before Nassau.

West Germany, under Chancellor Konrad Adenauer, was committed by treaty not to produce its own nuclear weapons, but there were persistent fears on all sides – British, French, American and especially Soviet – that the Germans would nevertheless get their finger on the nuclear trigger. The Germans themselves, deeply divided over nuclear weapons – for reasons, as Beatrice Heuser puts it, of 'sin and redemption' – were terrified equally by the prospect of a real war on the central front and by the prospect of American abandonment and isolationism.[50] In this context, it is easy to sympathise with their unhappiness at British and American attempts to clarify and understand NATO nuclear strategy, and at the British troop withdrawals begun by Sandys. The US sought to sublimate German nuclear ambitions through involvement in a joint force and, as we have seen, this was a key political motivation behind the NATO MRBM force and later the MLF, which was initially received favourably in Germany. For the British, although the point was usually unspoken, opposition to any West German nuclear-weapons capability was a strong motivation. Bitter memories of two world wars were fresh, and affected serious political discourse; in 1960, for example, the train-drivers' union introduced a motion at the Labour party conference thus: 'This conference believes that the ideology of the Nazi party is still predominant in the minds of many of the Bonn administration, and it therefore opposes the rearming of Western Germany, especially with rockets and nuclear weapons'.[51]

British politicians – indeed British people generally – were not, in the 1960s, well disposed towards the French or Germans, whose prosperity and growing political importance they envied. This served as a largely unspoken political spur to the British nuclear-weapons programme. How could any British politician seriously suggest abandoning or even reducing Britain's nuclear capability when that of the French was growing, and that of the Germans might be around the corner? Macmillan found it harder than Kennedy to influence his European allies, and did not in any sense enjoy an easy relationship with Adenauer or de Gaulle; nor did the Foreign Office, at this time, have a pro-European reputation. On the occasion of a meeting between the two European elder statesmen in September 1962, they were described, hardly diplomatically, by the British ambassador in Bonn as 'aged jesuitical devils'.[52] Although the French and Germans, through their different interests especially in US and NATO nuclear affairs, became more important to British policy-makers in this period, British diplomatic efforts to woo the Europeans were generally ineffective. In 1963, de Gaulle's veto over EEC entry and the conclusion of a Franco-German treaty of friendship rounded off an unhappy period for British diplomacy.

Defence policy east of Suez

In October 1961, as we have seen, Macmillan submitted one of his discursive and questioning papers on future policy to the Defence Committee. Watkinson was also interested at this point in reviewing the fundamentals of defence policy, intending to produce a new and significant white paper early in 1962 to mark the fifth anniversary of the Sandys review. In this context, and building on previous work comparing fixed overseas bases with air and sea mobility, the JPS embarked on a study of British strategy in the 1960s.⁵³ This study retreated from earlier work on mobility by proposing fewer naval and more army and air force units. The Prime Minister had ruled that the study must assume the continued availability of bases in the Mediterranean, Aden, Malaya and Singapore. A section on the 1970s still, however, made the contrary assumption, that by then only Britain and Australia could be relied upon as bases. This opened the way for Watkinson and Mountbatten to continue to press for greater mobility, and larger naval forces, in the long term. Watkinson therefore described the JPS paper on British strategy in the 1960s, endorsed by the chiefs and circulated to the Defence Committee in January 1962, as 'transitional'.⁵⁴ As Watkinson acknowledged, 'it had proved extremely difficult to devise a strategy which, while adequately directed to the objectives laid down, remained within the cost specified, [but] he could see no alternative to the strategy proposed, which marked the first step towards reliance on seaborne and airborne forces using forward operating facilities rather than bases in the traditional sense'. The strategy provided, amongst other things, for replacing the current generation of aircraft carriers – but *not* for replacing Skybolt and the V-bombers to maintain an independent British contribution to the deterrent. Pressed by the chancellor on where savings might be found within the programme described, Watkinson conceded that manpower, nuclear materials and the research and development programme would have to be reviewed. Macmillan, summarising the committee's discussion, noted that 'as regards the strategic deterrent, our efforts should be directed towards maintaining the effectiveness of a system based on Skybolt for as long after 1970 as possible and no plans should be based at present on the assumption that we should provide for ourselves a future generation of strategic nuclear weapons. It would, however, be open to ministers to reconsider this question at any time in the next two years'.⁵⁵

The Defence Committee's conclusions allowed Watkinson to produce a white paper which contrasted, in a number of ways, with the Sandys papers of 1957 and 1958. The focus was on limited war and the defence of Britain's friends and allies in the wider world; a long section detailed these commitments in the middle east, Africa and the far east. A broad spectrum of deterrence was envisaged, not an inevitable first use of nuclear weapons:

> In 1957 the west had undoubted superiority in the capacity to deliver strategic nuclear weapons. Today the west still has superiority but each side has the capacity to inflict upon the other a degree

of devastation which has never before in human history been either possible or imaginable. An armed clash involving the vital interests of either side is, therefore, likely to lead to the virtual destruction of both and not merely to conquest or defeat. This truth must increasingly condition the attitude of powers to the use of force as an instrument of policy, for governments can no longer choose to have either a full-scale conventional war or a limited war without risking the use of nuclear weapons ... We must continue to make it clear to potential aggressors ... that we should strike back with all the means that we judge appropriate, conventional or nuclear. If we had nothing but nuclear forces, this would not be credible. A balance must be maintained ... to deter every form of aggression and military threats.[56]

Unsurprisingly, no mention was made of the decision not to commit to a strategic deterrent in the 1970s; instead the paper glossed over the question, saying only that 'the efficacy of our deterrent will ... be maintained throughout the 1960s by using our V-bombers and fitting them with stand-off weapons, Blue Steel in the first instance and later Skybolt'.[57] The paper stated commitments to a number of specific hardware projects, not all of which were uncontroversial: for example new carriers, TSR.2 and the first VC-10 transports. It also referred to continuing nuclear commitments to CENTO and SEATO.

Two set-piece Defence Committee discussions of future policy were postponed in the succeeding months, and then Watkinson was replaced, so the issue of bases and mobility received little attention during the rest of 1962. As we shall see, however, Watkinson dutifully pursued significant savings in the nuclear-warhead programme during the spring and summer. A wider defence policy discussion was not held at Chequers until February 1963.[58] Instead, the incoming Thorneycroft addressed himself in July to a series of difficult short-term economy measures. The resulting cancellation of the army's Blue Water missile was a sudden and serious blow to the War Office and indeed BAC, leading to considerable short-term job losses. The ostensible reasons for cancellation – valid enough in themselves – were that there were plenty of tactical nuclear weapons in Europe already, and that TSR.2 could cover many of the targets the army had in mind for Blue Water. Unusually, Thorneycroft joined with the chancellor, Maudling, in submitting a paper to the Defence Committee, stating his underlying motivation more plainly:

> The truth is that we are overstretched. The attempt from a small island with limited resources to maintain our role in Europe, our

contribution to the deterrent and a worldwide military presence is proving too much for us … Obviously we cannot immediately contract out of our worldwide obligations, but from now on a substantial part of our overloaded research and development programme will be devoted to meeting requirements which assume that our commitments ten years hence will be substantially the same as they are now, and for this reason we believe that radical review of those commitments is urgently needed.[59]

During the autumn, the chiefs were duly asked to consider British strategy for the 1970s. Thorneycroft's efforts to make sense of long-term defence policy were hampered by disagreement between his most important advisers. Scott saw NATO as overridingly important; Mountbatten was more concerned about east of Suez. The first serious shots were also fired in what was to become a long-running campaign over the means of implementing a mobile strategy east of Suez, the Air Ministry pushing their idea of a network of island bases against the navy's carriers. By November 1962, Thorneycroft was ready with a paper for the Prime Minister stressing the need to choose between NATO and east of Suez; he marginally favoured the latter, no doubt at Mountbatten's urging: 'I believe we can make a greater contribution to the free world by maintaining forces outside Europe than by continuing to keep forces in Europe on the present scale'. The need to choose would become still more urgent if the current nuclear assumption were to change, because expenditure on a Skybolt successor would then be necessary.[60]

These urgent, economy-driven and politically fraught discussions were a most important backdrop to the Skybolt crisis and the Nassau meeting. Unpalatable decisions already faced ministers at the end of 1962 – even before the whole basis of deterrent policy was undermined, adding upwards of £200 millions to the projected cost of defence during the 1960s. It even seems possible that, if the Skybolt cancellation had not come when it did, Britain would have been forced out of the deterrent business. On 22 October, a couple of weeks before he became aware of the Skybolt cancellation, and despite several years of working-level toil on the subject, Thorneycroft was still looking somewhat uncertainly to Macmillan for a ruling 'that we must possess a significant nuclear capacity after the period covered by the V-bomber/Skybolt force'.[61] Looking at the 1970s, the joint planners, and then the chiefs, did recommend that 'we see a continuing military requirement for a strategic nuclear capability under our own sovereign control'.[62] But only when

Skybolt was taken away did the decision to continue the deterrent become unavoidable. Indeed, it now also became impossible to cut NATO conventional commitments – upon which, as we shall see, Kennedy and McNamara set great store at Nassau. Attention therefore turned east of Suez, and to the carrier programme. The chiefs produced an appreciation early in 1963 of the likely implications of a choice between NATO and east of Suez. If Britain plumped for the former, the carriers and long-range air transport would have to be cut; if the latter, army manpower and TSR.2 would bear the brunt. The positions of the service ministries and the individual chiefs can easily be imagined; no coherent advice on the subject was available to Thorneycroft from within his ministry.[63]

Two meetings of the full cabinet in July 1963 discussed the carrier programme. In a written submission, Maudling summed up the defence dilemma nicely, protesting that 'every time we look at defence in the round, we decide that our commitments in total are too great. Every time we look at one or other commitment in isolation, we decide that it is inescapable. The net result is that we go on planning to do more than we can or should afford'. The sum of between £300 and £400 millions spent annually on defence in the far east, for example, was 'half of the total cost of the schools or of the hospital services'.[64] This kind of comparison, more familiar to readers of twenty-first-century newspapers, gives a clear idea of the defence burden felt in the last months of Macmillan's premiership. Even so, the cabinet found the cancellation of the carrier programme impossible, agreeing instead to perpetuate a three-carrier force through the 1970s and to order a new ship to replace HMS *Ark Royal*.[65] The Conservative government showed a resilient ability to continue to promise all three of its major defence commitments: the deterrent, NATO and east of Suez.

Deterrent systems

At the beginning of 1962, despite long and occasionally ill-tempered discussion in the BNDSG and its technical sub-committee, the question of *which* long-term replacement for Skybolt should be selected – if the decision were made – was still unresolved. Scott noted impatiently, in a draft BNDSG report for Watkinson, that 'for some months we have been considering strategic deterrent policy against Russia after the period covered by present plans [i.e., for the 1970s]. Two possible successor systems have been studied, submarine launching vehicles armed with Polaris missiles and aircraft launchers armed with Skybolt. We have failed to reach agreement on which is superior or even on the criteria by which to establish superiority. Protracted and difficult costing exercises have shown no clear cut advantage either way'.[66] Scott evidently discounted the possibility that Skybolt would *not* be replaced. He became convinced, instead, that it would be necessary to revise downwards the criterion for a 'significant contribution' to the western deterrent, which stood at 50 per cent damage to 40 cities. In this, he appears to have been encouraged by a new assessment from the Joint Intelligence Committee that the destruction of just five Soviet cities would be a sufficient deterrent. A figure of 20 cities was also discussed, before Scott decided to write to ministers suggesting ten.[67] On 7 March, Macmillan met with Watkinson, Scott, Home and Sir Norman Brook to discuss this, having been briefed that production orders for Blue Steel and Skybolt needed to be placed and that 'Brook also thinks it would be helpful if you asked him to arrange for the Future Policy Committee to make a study of the political and military advantages of maintaining an independent British contribution to the deterrent of the west in the 1970s'.[68] Ministers directed the BNDSG to examine the possibility of revising the damage criterion down to 15 cities, a figure seemingly plucked out of thin air as a compromise. Moscow and Leningrad would be two of the cities.[69]

The Vice-Chief of the Air Staff, Sir Edmund Hudleston, saw dangers in this new thread of discussion. For example, because the production order for Skybolt had yet to be agreed by ministers, it might now be reduced. Worse, the capital expense of a Polaris solution depended in large part on the number of submarines required, and if this were reduced then Polaris would look a great deal more attractive. He therefore recorded his fundamental disagreement with the approach, arguing on the basis of wartime evidence that 'Russia can absorb a lot of punishment'.[70] This view misunderstood the political context of the independent deterrent. Alone, Britain would hardly be waging a war of conquest and unconditional surrender against the Soviet Union, as Hitler had done, but rather seeking to deter Soviet action in a crisis by threatening a level of damage disproportionate to any likely political objective. Alternatively, if Bomber Command were operating jointly with the Americans, there would be no doubting the potential of the west to inflict complete devastation. Although Macmillan at first agreed only to *study* a new city-targeting criterion of 15 cities, this does seem to have been adopted as official Bomber Command policy by October 1962.[71] The BNDSG seems not to have met between April and October 1962, and instead calculations of the likely numbers of nuclear weapons required were revised and debated at the Defence Committee.

As we have seen, a review of the nuclear warhead programme had meanwhile been underway for a considerable time, ever since the October 1960 Chequers meeting of the Defence Committee at which Thorneycroft had volunteered to look into the subject. During the summer of 1962, the review's conclusions finally began to surface at ministerial level. In April, first the chiefs and then the Defence Committee discussed the review, evidently endorsing a recommendation that no further tactical nuclear weapons with a yield above ten kilotons be produced.[72] In June, a series of papers, indicating serious political disagreement about the size and scope of the warhead programme, was prepared for a further Defence Committee meeting. The first paper, from Watkinson, proposed a series of reductions in warhead numbers. Julian Amery, the Secretary of State for Air, submitted one response calling for more warheads; Henry Brooke, the Chief Secretary to the Treasury, submitted another calling for still fewer; finally Hailsham, the minister responsible for UKAEA, submitted a more neutral paper on the implications for fissile material production. The main disagreement was over Skybolt numbers. Although a firm order had not been placed with the US, then-current plans called for 170 missiles and 158 warheads. Watkinson now suggested 100 and 90; the Chief Secretary 70 and 60. Amery, even on the basis of calculations for an airborne alert force made against the suggested 15-city criterion, was not prepared to contemplate fewer than 128 and 112. He also now challenged the earlier decision to cancel the requirement for a high-yield kiloton warhead for the Red Beard successor, arguing slightly curiously that a ten-kiloton bomb 'could not in all circumstances be dropped from the TSR.2 with enough accuracy to ensure the destruction of difficult targets such as bridges'. The total cost of the proposed programmes varied by as much as £43 millions, and as we shall see significant changes in fissile material production and in the research and development programme at Aldermaston were implied.[73] The importance of the discussions can be gauged by the fact that Amery, travelling in the far east, kept in touch with the Air Ministry Permanent Secretary by signal via the British embassy in Bangkok.[74] Meeting again on 8 July 1962, the committee managed to defer a decision on the high-yield kiloton warhead but, after hard bargaining overnight on 2/3 July, Zuckerman and Hudleston agreed an initial purchase of 100 missiles against an eventual requirement for between 110 and 130. This could therefore be confirmed.[75]

Skybolt

As we have seen, on taking office, the Kennedy administration initially favoured Skybolt with a modest increase in funding while Secretary

McNamara dealt with more important issues, in particular the need to revise US nuclear strategy to increase the elements of control and choice. Power and LeMay, the air force leaders, both argued for the preservation of a first-strike option; as LeMay put it, typically uncompromisingly, 'the capability of a first strike – of initiating nuclear war ... [is] absolutely necessary if the United States is to prevail'.[76] McNamara disagreed, wishing to be able to use nuclear weapons 'in a cool and deliberate fashion and always under the complete control of the constituted authority'.[77] The SIOP was revised, and it is claimed that Moscow was taken *off* the Americans' initial target list in late 1961 'to provide the Soviet Union with the option of fighting a "controlled" nuclear war'.[78] This is interesting in the context of the *increasing* British focus on Moscow, and the US administration's continuing opposition to small national deterrents. McNamara developed options for counter-force targeting against military targets, and counter-value targeting against cities. As time went by, these options were elaborated into damage-limitation and assured-destruction strategies respectively. The term 'flexible response' came to be associated with the Kennedy/McNamara strategy.

During 1962, and especially as the fiscal year 1964 budget build began in Washington, Skybolt costs came into sharp focus. The Pentagon became suspicious, in particular, that the air force's first bid for production funds hid a further escalation in development costs, pegged since the previous year at just under $500 millions. The table reproduced below, from one of Group Captain Fryer's reports, was of little immediate concern to his Whitehall readers, who were not paying; it was of great interest, however, to McNamara and his whiz-kids.

Skybolt coat escalation[79]

$M	Feb 60	Aug 60	Nov 60	Feb 61	Jun 61	Jul 61	Dec 61	Feb 62	May 62	Jul 62
R&D	220	372		391			492.6			
Production			989		1124	1260		1424	1517	1771
No. of msls			1000		1122	1319		1141	1137	1077

Desmond Ball estimates that June 1961 was the tipping-point at which Skybolt became more expensive to complete than to replace with the equivalent number of Minuteman ICBMs.[80] MIRV technology was on the agenda by 1962, and provided an opportunity for McNamara to cap the hitherto endless growth in delivery system numbers.[81] MIRV was impossible, however, on the light-payload Skybolt. Skybolt had 'priced itself out of the defence-suppression market',[82] especially as the 200 or so air-defence targets in the USSR could be more than covered by shorter-range Hound Dog cruise missiles, which were already in service. Skybolt's cost escalation was not unusual, but its position relative to other programmes was now different. As William Kaufmann, one of McNamara's circle, put it, 'Skybolt would very likely have become nearly a $3bn programme, not counting the additional cost of warheads'.[83] The US could afford $3bn programmes – Polaris and Minuteman had been equally costly – but why would it want another? Whereas at the start of 1961 Polaris and Minuteman had still seemed shaky, by the end of 1962 a fair proportion of the costs of these programmes was in the past.

At this inauspicious moment, as we shall see, things began to go wrong with Skybolt. The first five test-launches of the missile during 1962 were unsuccessful. This was not an unusual record; the early Polaris and Minuteman launches had been equally problematic. Polaris had five successive failures in 1958–59; Minuteman yet more in 1959–60.[84] But these problems were behind them and the missiles were in service. Importantly, neither missile had a track record of adverse scrutiny and opposition within the administration. Skybolt did not even get as far as its third launch before these opponents were sharpening their knives again. In August, Pentagon financial controller Charles Hitch and research and development chief Harold Brown reported to McNamara that 'the risk that Skybolt will fail to work at all is very low; the risk that it will not be a highly reliable ... system until the late 1960s is quite large'.[85] Hitch, Brown and McNamara discussed tactics to secure a December cancellation, although word did not begin to reach a wider Washington audience until some time in October.[86]

On 31 October, Fryer signalled to the UK his fear that cancellation was imminent on the basis of McNamara's reaction, not to budgetary or strategic issues, but to the failure of the fourth launch. He went on to explain that extraordinary measures were being taken to ensure the success of the fifth (and first guided) launch.[87] On 7 November, however – before this launch could take place – McNamara recommended cancellation to Kennedy at a face-to-face meeting. He proposed to delay an announcement until the adjournment of Congress towards the end of the month.[88] 'It had become apparent that this very complex weapon system could not be completed within the cost estimates or the time limits that had been projected when the programme was begun. It was also clear that Skybolt was as much a way to keep the air force's manned bombers usefully employed as a way to improve the US deterrent'.[89] McNamara duly briefed the British ambassador, Ormsby-Gore, who apparently returned to the embassy in shock, 'like a man who'd learned the bomb was going to drop, the end of civilisation, and he doubted he could stop it'. On 23 November 1962, Kennedy agreed to cancel.[90]

The rest is well recorded history. There were angry exchanges between LeMay and McNamara after cancellation, and senator Russell complained bitterly but impotently that 'we were comforted with a lollipop that the Skybolt would assuage our concern over the cutback of the ... B-70, and now we have had that lollipop taken from us without any compensating factor'.[91] In the UK, Thorneycroft had been told of the cancellation by McNamara on 9 November, but initially kept quiet, possibly uncertain what to do or in whom to confide. His first thought was to secure Polaris in exchange for Skybolt, although he knew what a storm this would provoke in Whitehall. His private secretary wrote to Macmillan's that 'the Prime Minister may wish to know that the minister's thoughts are moving towards, at least, two of the present generation of complete Polaris submarine systems (less warhead) and the right to manufacture the next generation'.[92] A few officials in the MoD, MoA, Admiralty and Air Ministry were instructed to examine alternative lines of action in the UK, including the further development of Blue Steel – an idea that never quite seemed to go away – the TSR.2, or the acceleration of the SSN programme and the production of dual-role submarines with Polaris-type missiles. It was also claimed, in what must have been a misunderstanding, that McNamara had offered, both to Ormsby-Gore and to Thorneycroft, 'to supply the United Kingdom with missiles such as Minuteman or Polaris, without political strings'.[93] Press stories on Skybolt cancellation began towards the end of the month.[94]

McNamara travelled to London to meet Thorneycroft on 11 December, carrying an aide-memoire which appeared to account for the cancellation decision on technical grounds. An ill-tempered meeting resulted.[95] Thorneycroft was badly taken aback by McNamara's unwillingness to offer Polaris except in the context of the MLF. McNamara in turn was astonished that the British 'hadn't done their homework ... They had made no plans ... They obviously hadn't given any thought to what would be satisfactory for them and how to get it and how to present it publicly ... I'd given them a perfectly good warning and it was obvious they'd made no use of it'.[96] This appears to have been a little unfair; Thorneycroft had written to Macmillan several days previously about his tactics for the meeting, which were to press for Skybolt, in case the decision on its continued development was not yet final; but otherwise to press for Polaris without strings, *plus* 'the loan ... of two or three complete Polaris carrying submarines for a period of years until our own submarines are ready'. He also highlighted the Admiralty's recommendation, which was to build seven dual-purpose 'hybrid' SSNs with eight Polaris missile tubes, and gave outline costings.[97] Macmillan had told Thorneycroft, however, that he thought 'the right course would be to take a very cagey line'. His own feeling – not shared with his Minister of Defence – was apparently that 'our best plan would be to try and play Skybolt along for another year ... It was clearly in our interests to get on to a Polaris deterrent at some stage but we had made a number of statements about Skybolt and it would be a little easier if that continued for the time being'.[98] If Macmillan perhaps wished in early December that the problem would go away, he cannot be accused of complete ignorance.

Further progress would have to await the summit meeting at Nassau, just before Christmas. The Americans now engaged in frantic staff-work on proposals. Secretary of State Dean Rusk made it clear that the relationship with Britain was important: 'We have to have *somebody* to talk to in the world ... we can't talk to de Gaulle ... or Adenauer'.[99] McNamara and the Pentagon felt the same way, and were inclined to an offer of Polaris. State Department officials were a good deal less willing to help the British in this way. The prospects for agreement were not necessarily good; in the run-up to Nassau, as one historian has put it, the British party were 'uncommonly irritated' by the whole business.[100]

Explaining the Skybolt crisis

If they were seeking to minimise adverse reaction from the UK, the Americans appear to have made a tactical mistake in justifying the cancellation primarily on technical grounds. Thus McNamara's aide-memoire emphasised the problems of guidance, data processing and display, and overall system reliability.[101] This emphasis was understandable in one sense. The original Skybolt agreement of June 1960 had stated explicitly that the United States government would 'make every reasonable effort to ensure the successful and timely completion of Skybolt development and the compatibility of the missile with Royal Air Force Mark II V-bombers', but that the sale would go ahead only 'if the missile is developed successfully'.[102] If the missile had failed technically, therefore, all bets were now off. Moreover, to admit that the decision had been political and financial would have been to devalue Britain's importance as a US ally. I have found no source – even Zuckerman and his Washington counterparts – to suggest the Skybolt system had completely insuperable technical problems, as opposed to concerns about reliability. As one British assessment put it, 'There is no part of the Skybolt programme that can be singled out as technically infeasible ... It is reasonably well based on techniques with which the US already have experience, in this respect it is better off than Polaris was at the start. On the other hand a lot of difficult or complicated techniques are involved and this is bound to cause difficulties ... in ... reliability'.[103] Because guidance had always been a focus of this reliability concern, the first guided launch did take on special significance. It was highlighted to Zuckerman by Pentagon research chief Brown, his deputy John Rubel *and* Wiesner,[104] and as noted above Fryer reported on the extraordinary measures taken effectively to fix the outcome of the test. But Skybolt's supporters in the UK felt, and were probably right to feel, that McNamara was lying to them about the missile's technical prospects. Lighthill, the Director of RAE, had a long conversation at Nassau with Rubel – who 'lacked solid arguments to substantiate DoD doubts on reliability' – and concluded that 'the evidence is that the DoD damning of Skybolt on technical grounds was a trumped-up affair'.[105]

There is no room for doubt that the system was cancelled for US political and financial reasons. George Ball, one of Rusk's Under-Secretaries of State, recalled that it was the cost-effectiveness argument that weighed most heavily with McNamara, who had 'a moral horror of inefficiency and waste. Skybolt offended him morally'.[106] Moreover, based on copious technical and political reporting, it is now clear that genuine information was flowing from the US to the UK, including on the many problems of Skybolt. There was perhaps the occasional inaccuracy, but there was little real room for misunderstanding. Interestingly, McNamara's efforts to justify the cancellation on technical grounds also made it impossible for Macmillan to accept the continuation of the missile's development for the UK, either as sole customer or on a 50-50 basis, when this offer was made to him at Nassau.

Another particular goad to the British was the well founded suspicion that the US administration was keen to limit its ally's nuclear independence. On June 1962, McNamara made a speech on nuclear strategy at the University of Michigan, Ann Arbor, arguing that:

> Relatively weak national nuclear forces with enemy cities as their targets are not likely to be sufficient to perform even the function of deterrence. If they are small, and perhaps vulnerable on the ground or in the air, or inaccurate, a major antagonist can take a variety of measures to counter them. Indeed, if a major antagonist came to believe there was a substantial likelihood of it being used

independently, this force would be inviting a pre-emptive first strike against it. In the event of war, the use of such a force against the cities of a major nuclear power would be tantamount to suicide, whereas its employment against significant military targets would have a negligible effect on the outcome of the conflict. Meanwhile, the creation of a single additional national nuclear force encourages the proliferation of nuclear power with all its attendant dangers.

In short, then, limited nuclear capabilities, operating independently, are dangerous, expensive, prone to obsolescence, and lacking in credibility as a deterrent.[107]

Despite McNamara's protests that the speech had not been aimed at the British, there *was*, as we have seen, an official US policy, agreed by the President in April 1961, to ease the British out of the strategic nuclear-weapons business. Thorneycroft perceived 'a great deal of Americans working jolly hard to do away with the British deterrent',[108] and key advisers drew his attention to the 'cardinal feature of [Kennedy's] policy to deny his allies independent nuclear forces'.[109] On the American side too, LeMay, for example, attested to the 'quietly held purpose ... to denuclearise either or both of the existing European nuclear powers, France and England'.[110]

Finally, the RAF and USAF Skybolt lobbies had made tactical mistakes too – generally involving not making enough fuss. As Ken Young puts it, 'it was not in the interest of the British to openly acknowledge the uncertainties, as this would only weaken their bargaining position if it came to cancellation'.[111] More than that, to imply to the US that the British were any less committed would weaken their bargaining position *now*. If Zuckerman, for example, were to cast doubt in American minds, then surely the US opposition to Skybolt would take too much heart. 'While the Skybolt project was still alive, [the British] naturally could not do anything to prejudice its chances by canvassing an alternative to it'.[112] Or, as Defence Minister Watkinson had put it: 'I do not want to throw too much cold water on it, because there is still just a chance of its getting through'.[113] This, it seems, led to one or two decisions to keep quiet and hope the problem went away. The USAF also seemed shy of raising the temperature over Skybolt, either because in the early days it had bigger fish to fry with the B-70, or later because LeMay and others felt Congress would come to their rescue. The air attache in Washington signalled home in December 1962 that 'General LeMay ... confirmed ... that the end of SAC as a manned deterrent force is in sight if Mr McNamara has his way ... in the circumstances his equanimity in discussing these problems is surprising. I suspect that he is relying on a major congressional battle when the budget comes up for approval'.[114] On this occasion, Kennedy and McNamara were too smart for Congress.

Cuba

The history of the Cuban missile crisis is now a familiar one, and somewhat peripheral to our story. To describe the events of October 1962, as they affected the British government, will, however, still provide some insight into Anglo-American relations, and indeed into the political management of a nuclear crisis. Large numbers of bombers and weapons, including the Thor missiles, were now available to the RAF; in addition, SAC bombers were present in the UK in large numbers. If not necessarily at the heart of decision-making, Britain did seem therefore to be on the nuclear front line, and the British aspects of the crisis have generated an interesting literature.[115]

Britain's political part in the developing crisis did not begin until Sunday 21 October, when ambassador Ormsby-Gore was invited in to see the President. Gore was a close friend of the Kennedys, but the date in itself is significant: several daily meetings of Kennedy's executive committee or 'ExComm' had already been held. During the brief conversation, Gore offered the unremarkable opinion that air strikes or an invasion of Cuba were inadvisable, and a blockade might be more sensible. Kennedy then wrote in general terms to keep Macmillan informed of progress, the message arriving late at night. The next day, 22 October, Macmillan met the ambassador in London, David Bruce, assuring him of British support; at around the same time, Dean Acheson had a similar conversation with de Gaulle. Toying with the idea of recommending an invasion 'and have done with it', Macmillan eventually thought better of offering Kennedy any specific advice at this point, and confined himself to a message of support. Kennedy announced the imposition of a blockade or quarantine on television that evening, shortly after telephoning Macmillan – the first of a series of calls during the crisis, mostly in the early evening (US time; late at night in the UK).[116] Macmillan had also conferred during the day with Norstad, the two men agreeing not to pursue alert measures in NATO, such as the call-up of reservists. US forces outside NATO command, however, including SAC bombers in the UK, had been put on a worldwide 'Defcon 3' alert. US Polaris submarines slipped out of Holy Loch, and on Wednesday 24 October, SAC's alert state was increased to 'Defcon 2'. Bomber Command staff were aware of these preparations. The quick-reaction alert status of the SACEUR Valiants was also increased on 24 or 25 October as the quarantine of Cuba came into force, and according to one account this meant for practical purposes that Britain was given control of the Valiant's US nuclear weapons.[117]

At 11am on Saturday 27 October, Macmillan met Pike and told him that no overt preparations for action were to be made by Bomber Command; this message was relayed to the other chiefs, and to Sir Kenneth Cross, the Bomber Command AOC-in-C. In the afternoon, as the chiefs were gathering to meet, Cross ordered a move to alert condition three. As we saw in Chapter 2, this meant only unobtrusive preparations, and was at Cross's own discretion. It is likely that such measures had already been taken at a number of bases.[118] The chiefs considered that V-bomber dispersal should only follow if the US looked set to invade Cuba.[119] We now know this was the day Kennedy and Khrushchev moved back from the brink, probably acting on a deal suggested between ambassador Dobrynin and the President's brother. On the morning of 28 October, Khrushchev's radio announcement of the dismantling of the missile bases in Cuba made the relaxation of tension public. Cross also now finally met with Pike face-to-face to discuss instructions to the bomber force, and additional V-bombers were ordered onto 15-minute quick-reaction alert, effective the following morning, Monday 29 October. An impressive 59 out of 60 Thor missiles were brought to an equivalent readiness level. Alert condition three was maintained until 5 November.[120] But as the atmosphere of crisis reduced, David Bruce, the American ambassador in London, suggested happily that 'now perhaps a number of people immobilised during this emergency can devote future weekends to depleting the game-birds who are ravaging British agriculture'.[121]

It is clear that – on alerting and other matters – Macmillan, the British chiefs and indeed Norstad were less hawkish during the crisis than, for example, the joint chiefs in the US. Some historians have been inclined to talk up the British contribution to the crisis, for example suggesting that it was Gore who drove the publication of U-2 photographs demonstrating that the missile bases were in place, and who bought a little more time for the 'back channel' with Dobrynin by suggesting that the quarantine line be moved closer to Cuba. May and Zelikow, rather melodramatically, give Macmillan and Gore the status of honorary ExComm members.[122] It seems clear, however, that the influence of any British figure over US policy was limited. In Gore's own estimation, the importance of Kennedy's conversations with himself and Macmillan was limited: 'I can't honestly think of anything said from London that changed the US action – it was chiefly reassurance to JFK'.[123] Diplomatic initiatives including a Prime Ministerial trip to Washington and a trade involving the Thor missiles had been discussed in Whitehall, and the latter was mentioned by Macmillan to Kennedy, but not pursued. In Rab Butler's opinion, Macmillan's 'most praiseworthy achievement ... was to do so little. He was continually tempted to "take an initiative", to propose a summit talk or any other device to clear tension ... He was well advised by Alec Home to confine himself to the message supporting the Americans'.[124] Still, it is probably fair to say that clear public support for America – from Britain and other allies – was important to Kennedy. It is also perfectly respectable to argue that Macmillan's frequent foreign-policy discussions with Kennedy in the past had influenced and moderated the President's thinking on nuclear war and therefore his overall response to events in Cuba.

Public, press and parliamentary reactions to the crisis in Britain were somewhat muted. It surprised the CND, and other observers, that events in Cuba led to no great resurgence in unilateralist sentiment or even apocalyptic concern about war. On the contrary, following a week in which the world seemed on the brink of Armageddon, the public seemingly became more stoical, and even optimistic. There were crowds outside the American embassy, but Lord Russell suggested it had become 'too late to protest against something that may occur in a matter of minutes; and if a man expects himself and his family shortly to become a digit in a megadeath, he tends to prefer the intimacy of his family circle to the effect – itself dehumanising – of being caught up in an aimless, chattering crowd ... After Cuba, demonstrations began to be left to people who happened to enjoy them'.[125] Although CND made a lasting contribution to a 'culture of protest' in the UK, activism and sense of urgency declined sharply after Cuba; one sympathiser recalled a dawning realisation that 'we could well go on living like this for two or three hundred years'.[126] Britain's irrelevance to the superpower competition had moreover been underlined; did it matter any longer whether Britain disarmed? Interestingly, the crisis coincided with the release of the first of Albert R Broccoli's James Bond films, *Dr No*, also set partly in the Caribbean. The public was now thinking of a very different cold war.[127]

The Nassau meeting

Macmillan and Kennedy had recently arranged a meeting at Nassau in the Bahamas, then still a British colony, to talk about arms control and other foreign-policy issues. The venue was a villa called Bali-Hai, on Lyford Cay at the western tip of New Providence Island.[128] If Kennedy was looking forward to a few days' relaxation and amicable discussion in the sun after his exertions over Cuba, however, he was to be disappointed. In the aftermath of cancellation, Skybolt entirely dominated the meeting. The official record of the talks was extremely full, and has been a gold-mine for diplomatic historians.[129]

Macmillan began, on the morning of Wednesday 19 December, with an eloquent lecture on the history of Anglo-American nuclear collaboration and European politics. A member of the US delegation recalled 'the "chintzy" atmosphere in the room where the conference took place; the smell of roses drifting in through the window; intimate British country atmosphere. And Macmillan's dramatic statement ... like being in a girl's bedroom with something going on that shouldn't happen there'.[130] The Prime Minister ended with a threat: the bad feeling so far 'would be as nothing to the difficulties which would follow if the United States seemed to be using the Skybolt decision as a means of forcing Britain out of an independent nuclear capacity'. Kennedy, who had decided before the meeting to offer Polaris to Macmillan if necessary, at first ignored the Prime Minister's attempts to equate Skybolt and Polaris, offering Britain the right to continue with the airborne missile but saying that 'Polaris should be dealt with if at all in a much more European atmosphere'. Macmillan wittily dismissed Skybolt: 'while the proposed marriage with Skybolt was not exactly a shot-gun wedding, the virginity of the lady must now be regarded as doubtful. There had been too many remarks made about the unreliability of Skybolt for anyone to believe in its effectiveness in the future'. Kennedy also offered Hound Dog. After a long and inconclusive discussion, focusing mostly on the British opposition to a NATO multi-lateral force, the principals adjourned for four and a half hours for lunch.[131]

By the late afternoon, the US delegation had already come up with the bare bones of the final deal. Kennedy suggested an offer of Polaris, 'assigned' to NATO, but conceded that 'in the last resort, in a case of real emergency, of mortal peril, the force could revert to United Kingdom control'. Macmillan predictably replied that 'a great deal depended on what was meant by "assigning" forces to NATO ... we must be able in the last resort to control our own force'. The Foreign Secretary, Home, 'wondered how these words would apply to the case in which, say, Mr Nehru asked for British Polaris submarines to be sent to the Bay of Bengal. President Kennedy replied that this was not the kind of situation he had in mind ... He meant a direct attack on the United Kingdom'. This was the nub of the discussion. Home also mentioned 'the defence of Kuwait and its oil wells', and Macmillan a possible threat to Singapore. But the

Americans certainly did not envisage allowing independent nuclear action outside Europe; instead they reminded Macmillan about Dunkirk. The two delegations were surely talking, in a roundabout way, about Suez. With their concern for sensible, centralised nuclear decision-making, would Kennedy and McNamara really want American-supplied missiles to be brandished in response to Soviet or other threats by a future Anthony Eden? The scenario was too awful to contemplate: Britain as rogue state. Macmillan retreated, but not very far. Kennedy had said that 'British Polaris forces could be withdrawn from multi-lateral command only in the case where the very survival of the United Kingdom was at stake. But that meant taking away from the United Kingdom the right of trying to influence events by means of these weapons'.[132] The talks were once again adjourned; during the evening, the principals had two further conversations, on the Congo and Berlin. One wonders whether Kennedy envisaged attempts by Macmillan 'to influence events' in either of these places with his nuclear diplomacy.

On Thursday morning, 20 December, Macmillan returned to the charge, this time daring to say out loud the word 'Suez'. Kennedy made it clear that nuclear weapons 'should certainly not be used for a Suez type operation to intimidate President Nasser'. Macmillan 'nodded assent'. This airing of unspoken fears seems to have eased the way to an agreement, and the President and Prime Minister fell to discussing public statements.[133] By lunchtime, however, an acceptable formula had still not been found to describe the degree of Britain's independence, and Macmillan turned to emotional blackmail: 'critics of the United States draft would say that it revealed an American purpose to keep the "little people" quiet while controlling the reality themselves'. (No doubt the critics would have been right). 'Much as he regretted it', Macmillan continued, 'if an agreement was impossible, the British government would have to make a reappraisal of their defence policies throughout the world'. On this dramatic note, the President and Prime Minister adjourned once again, and Thorneycroft and McNamara got to work, for the first time producing the words that would appear in the final joint statement: 'The Prime Minister made it clear that [Polaris] will be used for the purposes of international defence of the western alliance in all circumstances, except where Her Majesty's government may decide that supreme national interests are at stake'.[134] This text was sent to London, and Kennedy and Macmillan spent the afternoon discussing India and Pakistan. On Friday lunchtime, 21 December, Macmillan and Kennedy finalised their joint statement, incorporating some minor drafting changes suggested by the cabinet in London.[135]

The worm's-eye view of Air Vice-Marshal Christopher Hartley, meanwhile, is interesting, partly because it is the most atmospheric account I have found of the Nassau meeting.[136] It gives some idea of the conditions in which Anglo-American relations and nuclear strategy were discussed:

> In the course of a partridge shoot near Coltishall on Monday 17 December, I was given a message at 1400hrs that I was to accompany the Minister of Defence and his party to Nassau to represent the air staff, leaving London Airport at ... about 2130 in a Comet IV of 216 Squadron. The journey was relatively uneventful, except that I was told firmly by the Private Secretary (Mr Hockaday) that I was not required at the Minister's table, the fourth seat being reserved for him ...
>
> We reached Nassau at about 0700 local, Tuesday 18 December, and assembled for our first advisors' meeting at 1045, in the cottage next to the PM's house, where the main meetings were to be held. Apart from the signals and cypher office, which was housed in another building, this cottage appeared to be the only roof under which the UK delegation could operate. It consisted of three relatively small rooms and one hallway ... as follows:-
>
> (a) Smallest room: typing pool.
>
> (b) The large room: Minister's conference room, overflow from typing pool, and bar (because it had a sink).
>
> (c) Smaller room: apparently reserved for FO and PM's staff: penetrated by others at their peril in order to reach the only lavatory.
>
> (d) Hall-way: used by Lord Hood and occasionally Sir Robert Scott for private drafting sessions. Tactful advisors used the back door on these occasions.
>
> This cottage was used off and on by up to 40 people: fortunately there was a good verandah, and Nassau weather is delightful. However, it rapidly became one-upmanship (and at times very important) not to be left out in the sun ... In these conditions any system for distributing and handling papers was conspicuous by its absence. It became a matter of initiative to get a sight of papers and of skill verging on subterfuge to retain possession of those which appeared important ... The same problems applied to hearsay information on the progress of the talks, on which I was heavily dependent since I was never once called in to them. This information could be obtained, but usually only by direct questioning of the source; it was seldom volunteered ... I have outlined the

domestic background because I feel it is to some extent relevant to the final agreement.

Hartley and other supporters were in Nassau, we should remember, for a full day before Kennedy and Macmillan. He appears to have taken the proceedings rather more seriously than Zuckerman, who claimed to have spent 'the first day mainly chatting, and the rest of the time ... enjoying the delightful weather, and inventing something to do'.[137] Hartley went on to describe the consideration and rejection of Skybolt cost-sharing and Hound Dog which, as the official record of the meeting confirms, 'was disposed of quickly on the grounds that it could not be fitted to the Vulcan except at great expense'.[138] Thorneycroft believed Skybolt still to be feasible, and refused 'to subscribe to any joint statement which agreed to cancel Skybolt because it was technically unsound'. Hartley also noted his (entirely correct) impression that ministers had decided before leaving London not to fight to change Kennedy's mind over Skybolt, but to get the best Polaris deal they could. Hartley tried to make a point about the likely deterrent 'gap' left by Skybolt between the V-bombers and Polaris, a point that seemed to be brushed aside. He then recounted a conversation between himself, Lighthill and Rubel: 'I was horrified at the thought that the workings of the largest democracy in the west could in any way be influenced by someone so shallow as Rubel'. (Zuckerman noted elsewhere that that Rubel 'was a graduate of Caltech, and had had nearly 20 years of experience in a variety of research and development posts in industry. He was a cultivated and widely read man'.[139] Such were the polarised views generated over Skybolt).

On Tuesday evening, Hartley noted, 'there was a cocktail party at Government House followed by a Press party and barbecue on the beach. I did not attend these'.[140] Formal discussions followed on what for Hartley was the second day of the conference, covering – as outlined above – alternative systems, the issue of 'strings' attached to Polaris, and the Americans' dropping the controversial accusation that Skybolt had failed technically, in favour of an

> indisputable statement that the US were abandoning Skybolt 'because of the availability of alternative weapon systems'.
>
> Attempts at drafting continued during the [Thursday] morning in the PM's house. The situation was confused and I cannot recall who was in or out at any given moment. McNamara and Scott were certainly involved for much of the time. None of the advisors got a

sight of the draft, as far as I can recall, until it appeared in what proved to be almost its final version at 1530. In the course of the morning Thorneycroft gave us some interesting comments on the situation. Apparently it was clear that the US long term aim was indeed to get us out of the independent deterrent. The President had said something like this: 'We did not mind too much about giving you Skybolt because we thought it might not work and in any case it would have been obsolete by 1970. But Polaris is an entirely different matter as it will last much longer'.

When the final draft communique did emerge, Hartley says, 'the general feeling among the advisors was that it was a thoroughly bad agreement ... it proved very much easier to pose awkward questions than to devise convincing answers'. On Friday, Hartley heard of the cabinet's and the chief whip's messages (see below), but was unable to see a copy of either. As Thorneycroft prepared for the subsequent press conference, Hartley intervened again on the question of the deterrent gap: 'It was clear', he said, 'that everyone was determined to indulge in self-deception ... I told the Minister ... I could see no way of maintaining the [V-bomber] force as a fully credible independent British deterrent [until Polaris came along]. The Minister was obviously most displeased ... This concluded both the Nassau talks and my small part in them'.

Certain aspects of the talks were naturally unknown to Hartley. In particular, he said little about conventional forces, the 'Suez' issue, or about Macmillan's domestic political concerns. Indeed, the issue of conventional forces is neglected in most accounts of Nassau, and yet one of the Prime Minister's most important objectives was to avoid any linkage between a Polaris deal and ruinous additional expenditure on non-nuclear forces. For the US team, conversely, one valid reason to help with Polaris was to enable the British to spend more money on conventional defence. To Macmillan, this kind of deal might unravel his whole defence policy. NATO's force goals, laid down in MC 70, were much bigger than Britain could support without a return to conscription. At home, the full cabinet – chaired in the Prime Minister's absence by his deputy, Rab Butler – twice discussed the progress of the talks. On Thursday 20 December, the cabinet confined itself to passing a 'message of encouragement and support' to Macmillan,[141] but the following day the discussion was more substantial. Four telegrams had been received from the Prime Minister, which Butler digested for the benefit of his colleagues, highlighting the successful removal of the words 'an agreement to meet their NATO non-nuclear force goals at the agreed NATO standards' from the draft communique, and the issue of the 'supreme national interests' clause. The cabinet was keen to make the point that independence should mean the freedom to use Polaris in national crises outside, as well as within, the NATO area. Carrington, the First Lord, was invited to speak, and outlined two schemes for Polaris: a force of four 16-missile submarines, costing perhaps £220 millions by 1970; and a force of seven eight-missile boats, costing £290 millions. Either of these would be offset by a Skybolt saving of only £100 millions. The cabinet had not previously been made aware of the considerable additional cost the Nassau deal might represent. Moreover, further increases in expenditure could be expected because spend on the V-bombers would be 'unabated' during the deterrent gap, and the US would expect more money to be set aside for conventional forces. Maudling, the chancellor, was horrified and wished to reserve his position. Butler tried to sum up. There was 'general agreement ... that the Prime Minister and his colleagues deserved their full support for the largely successful efforts that they had made', but in conveying this to the Prime Minister Butler felt he should 'emphasise their view that the government were being asked to pay a heavy price and that for this reason the independent role of Her Majesty's government in the use of nuclear forces' would have to be 'clearly and unambiguously expressed' in any communique.[142]

Interestingly, the Conservative chief whip, Martin Redmayne, also felt moved to send a telegram to the Prime Minister on Friday 21 December: 'I am not sure the cabinet have sufficiently considered the political repercussions of the Polaris decision. Although I realise that you have had a great battle to win any ground, it may well be thought that what you have won is not worth the cost in that it has little prestige value until 1968 at the earliest. Moreover, it will be denigrated because it will have been so hardly wrung from a nation which will be clearly seen to regard it only as a sop to our pride ... Would it not be better to pause and study at leisure here whether there are no practical alternatives which, even if more costly, might well be more acceptable politically?'[143] That the whip had taken the most unusual step of intervening in a matter of international diplomacy is a measure of the political controversy at home among Macmillan's party back-benchers, 127 of whom had apparently signed a letter to him on the subject.[144]

For Macmillan, Nassau had been a balancing act. His own delegation was certainly disunited. Thorneycroft apparently wanted to 'leave in a huff, rally the country, go it alone'.[145] The Skybolt cancellation had hit him badly: 'like Macmillan, he had his political career in mind and was anxious to avoid any accusations of incompetence or worse'.[146] That Zuckerman, Lighthill and Hartley were among Thorneycroft's team guaranteed meanwhile that he would have no single consistent line of advice. The cabinet and party were sniping from a safe distance. On the American side, Kennedy wanted to help, but also to uphold his policy against national deterrents, as he noted in closing the Thursday lunchtime session of the talks: 'The United States had for some years been declaring their opposition to national deterrents and it was difficult to abandon this decision'.[147] Lighthill and no doubt others noted the divisions within the American team: 'A general impression throughout the conference is that the US department of defence was aiming at making concessions to reach agreement, while the US State Department and Mr Bundy were seeking to secure the torpedoing of the UK independent deterrent'.[148] Macmillan's private secretaries, and also Home, were more loyal and helpful, but it seems the Prime Minister's personal political instincts and the courage of his convictions lay behind the final deal.

The French and Germans were a complicating factor: in particular, again and again during the meetings at Nassau, de Gaulle's attitude had been discussed. How pleased would he be at the deal? To be even-handed, Kennedy felt bound to offer him Polaris on the same terms as Macmillan. De Gaulle firmly and publicly rejected this offer at a press conference on 14 January 1963, announcing at the same time his veto over Britain's application to join the EEC. To what extent this attitude was precipitated by the Nassau deal is a controversial point. Although the *force de frappe* remained weak – the Mirage IV bombers to carry France's atomic bomb were not yet in service – de Gaulle had probably long since decided to preserve its independence in the face of any Anglo-Saxon offer of help, and also to keep Britain out of Europe.[149] His mood, however, cannot have been improved by Nassau.

The multi-lateral force

Interest in a NATO ballistic missile force had waned since early 1961 but, during the Skybolt crisis, enthusiasts in the State Department spotted an opportunity to revive the proposal. At Nassau, the discussion of Polaris was intimately bound up with the MLF, which thereby received a 'high-voltage jump-start'.[150] There was an element of clutching at straws; if the Nassau deal was to be at all palatable to other European countries, the Americans had to emphasise its MLF context. That the MLF continued to make way even during 1963, after it was holed below the waterline by de Gaulle on 14 January, is a tribute to State Department damage-control parties led by Kennedy's special representative, Livingston Merchant.

By late January 1963, proposals had been drawn up for an MLF consisting either of eight 16-missile Polaris submarines, or 25 eight-missile surface ships, with costs and manning to be divided among the participating nations under detailed arrangements still to be determined. The surface-ship force was eventually preferred, apparently because of Rickover's blunt refusal to participate. Supporters believed the MLF could head off the danger of resurgent German nationalism and any accompanying demand for access to nuclear weapons, especially as Adenauer was thought to be contemplating retirement. 'With Adenauer gone, Germany might find it impossible to prevent a slide towards nationalism and perhaps nuclearism also'.[151] A sense of political momentum and cohesion through the nuclear-sharing initiative was also thought, by the MLF's advocates, to have a chance of keeping the French in some kind of close association with the NATO allies. The US armed forces were not keen, although McNamara was interested in the concept if it offered greater American control over the nuclear strategy and behaviour of the European allies. Before Merchant left for a tour of European capitals, he was warned by the President not to oversell the proposal, or to pursue it too far if reactions were negative:

> The President's reluctance to embrace the MLF without reservation at this point grew out of his concerns that the project, while attractive enough in American eyes, not only failed to contain enough of the right ingredients to satisfy the Europeans but quite possibly contained more than enough to cause serious concern to the Soviet Union ... The initial sounds coming from Moscow appeared to be more vituperative and hard-line than many of Kennedy's advisers had been expecting.[152]

For the Soviet government, the spectre of German (nuclear) rearmament was in fact a constant source of irritation and fear. Khrushchev refused, during the partial test-ban talks in July 1963, to discuss counter-proliferation while the MLF was still in prospect. For the Europeans, several issues arose. The military requirements of SACEUR still, on paper, included MRBMs; some form of control over any decision to use nuclear weapons was desirable, in case the Americans should ever prove too cautious or too reckless in a crisis. The Europeans also wanted assurance that the Americans wished to integrate their forces in NATO, and not to preserve them in isolation – ready perhaps for a future decision to withdraw from Europe.[153]

In the UK, reactions to the MLF 'ranged from unenthusiastic to hostile throughout the military establishment and in the two principal political parties'.[154] Thorneycroft, Mountbatten and Zuckerman thought it 'military nonsense contrived for political reasons' and Viscount Montgomery, speaking in the Lords, described it as 'utter and complete poppycock'.[155] Considerable tooth-gritting must have been required on the part of Merchant, and later US Admiral Claude Ricketts, when they came to London to discuss the mixed-manning concept. The MLF would also cost a great deal of money – perhaps £100 millions over ten years – and warheads might have to be provided. The Foreign Office, nevertheless, came round to the belief that Britain must support the MLF. The basic objectives of the US – to contain the Germans and make the nuclear defence of the west more credible – were, after all, shared by the British government. When the cabinet discussed the MLF in March 1963, the concept of a 'multi-national' as opposed to a 'multi-lateral' force was favoured by the Foreign Secretary – not, in other words, a force

> which would be genuinely international in the sense that all the participating countries would subscribe contributions, in manpower and resources, which could not be withdrawn even in extreme national emergency, [but] a force to which individual nations with a nuclear capability would contribute without surrendering their ultimate sovereignty over the weapons in question. This concept had been endorsed by the NATO council, apart from the French representative, and we should seek to develop it further, together with the question of the command and administration of such a force, at the council's forthcoming meeting at Ottawa in May.[156]

Home's multi-national concept had been foreshadowed at Nassau, where in the final communique the British had promised to commit the V-bomber force to NATO – in advance of the arrival of Polaris, but subject to the same 'supreme national interests' clause. This commitment, announced in parliament and reaffirmed at the NAC meeting in May, was now described as part of a multi-national Inter-Allied Nuclear Force (IANF), supposedly to supplement the more truly multi-lateral MLF. In reality, its political purpose was to undermine the force the US was now proposing.[157]

At a subsequent cabinet meeting, Home sought to go still further. The MLF, he suggested, would go ahead on a mixed-manned basis with or without the UK's participation, and 'if we did not participate in it, we should be unable to exert any influence'. Moreover 'responsible German political leaders' had indicated that the MLF would enable 'dangerous aspirations to be diverted and contained', and finally 'if we opposed, or refused to support, a project to which the United States government attached great importance, we should subject our relations with them to considerable strain, and they might look with less favour than hitherto on our continued possession of an independent nuclear capability'.[158] In other words, with the Polaris sales agreement not yet signed, this was a bad time to make trouble with the US administration.

During the autumn of 1963, 'an unusually visible Whitehall dispute' ensued between the Foreign Office and the MoD.[159] By September, two international study groups on the MLF had been proposed: one meeting in Washington to consider technical and operational issues, and one meeting in Paris to examine political and legal aspects. Thorneycroft objected even to attending the meetings, now putting the likely cost of the MLF to the UK at £250 millions.[160] The cabinet decided that any participation in the talks should be on a basis 'which would not only make it wholly clear that we remained uncommitted to participate in any multilateral force ... but would also allow us to bring forward for re-examination the broad strategic objections to the concept which had hitherto been ignored by the United States government'.[161]

At this point, Home became Prime Minister, and the terms of his dispute with Thorneycroft were therefore somewhat changed. By December, the Defence Minister was necessarily putting forward more positive ideas on the MLF. Thorneycroft's proposals, announced to a NATO audience on 2 July 1964, involved a massive multi-lateralisation of *all* NATO nuclear aircraft and missiles having an interdiction role – not just V-bombers, but also Canberras, later the TSR.2, American and German F-104s, F-111s, Pershing surface-to-surface missiles and others.[162] Like the IANF, but unlike the MLF, this was a proposal for the reassignment of existing forces, not the creation of new ones. It would therefore be cheaper than the MLF. In a significant concession, however, the Thorney-croft proposals envisaged mixed-manning. Also significantly, they excluded the British Polaris force, whose city targets were strategic. The Air Ministry found an additional role for the TSR.2 politically useful, and the strategic argument was made that the forces now under discussion, targeted against eastern Europe, ought to be the very ones that the European NATO nations were most interested in controlling during the early stages of a nuclear crisis.[163] During 1964, the Royal Navy also participated – despite the absence of a rum ration – in a moderately successful experiment to man the destroyer USS *Claude V Ricketts* with a multinational crew.[164]

Home now found himself in an awkward situation, committed on the one hand to the MLF, but on the other hand, as we shall see, waging an election campaign heavily focused on nuclear independence. With a US election also pending, 'throughout most of 1964 the hard choices on the MLF were held in abeyance since no decision of consequence could be reached'.[165] Whilst US officials, who were threatening to create an MLF bilaterally with the Germans, might hope to persuade a future Home government to accept the MLF, they were under no illusions about the outcome if Wilson won the election. 'The Labour party was even more strongly opposed to the MLF than the Tories or the defence establishment ... Distaste for Germany and of any German nuclear role was at the heart of Labour's opposition'. Wilson announced in parliament that 'the opposition were completely opposed to any suggestion that West or East Germany, directly or indirectly, should have a finger on the nuclear trigger, or any responsibility for deciding that nuclear weapons were to be used'.[166]

Buying Polaris

Not even the dramatic deal reached at Nassau could end the controversy over deterrent systems in the UK. For the RAF and Air Ministry, the cancellation of Skybolt was a slap in the face that was still smarting many years later. Opinions on the missile itself continued to differ markedly, with Charles Hitch and Air Vice-Marshal 'Paddy' Menaul at opposite ends of the spectrum. In 1965, Hitch wrote that 'no responsible military or civilian official in our defense department ... would argue in favour of the Skybolt today'.[167] In 1980, Menaul still fervently believed Polaris was 'a pitiful contribution to a kind of collective deterrent operated by NATO', but that 'if Skybolt had been produced it would have been the least vulnerable and most effective missile system in the world'.[168] One official, in a report summarising the missile's history, used the words of Edmund Burke: on Skybolt, he said, it was 'difficult to speak, and impossible to remain silent'.[169] Embarrassingly, the sixth and final test-launch of Skybolt on 22 December 1962 – the day after Kennedy got back from Nassau – was fully successful.[170]

Unhappiness about Polaris resurfaced immediately. There was no crowing from Zuckerman, for example; on the contrary, he and Scott jointly wrote to Thorneycroft, while they were still in Nassau, about the 'very serious risks' inherent in the Polaris deal: 'We know that to the President it is a cardinal feature of his policy to deny his allies independent nuclear forces'. Polaris would never be independent; it would be committed to the MLF. Also, given recent experience, there were fears of never actually getting the missile. Zuckerman recalled that Scott, no doubt with furrowed brow, typed the note 'with two fingers on his own portable machine'.[171] Macmillan, though satisfied with the outcome of the conference, certainly shared some of these concerns, writing to Thorneycroft on 26 December:

> There are a lot of snags to be watched very carefully here ... we shall have to reserve the right to re-open and clarify the exact terms of our independent rights. I am also anxious as to how [the Americans] can be kept to the mark. It would be a good thing to pay something down on signature, and perhaps to get delivery [sic – of information? of a lend-lease submarine?] as soon as possible for us to study with a view to designing our submarine. We must also be clear that the words 'on a continuing basis' mean that we get the Mark II or Mark III, or whatever it is, to suit us ... In addition, I think we must be prepared for some pressure to be put upon us, and coming to a point where we would threaten to tear up the agreement. For this purpose could you find out from the Minister of Aviation or anybody else whether, if we were driven into a corner, we could, either as a bluff or as a reality, make a Polaris missile, perhaps of a simpler kind, ourselves from our own designs; how long would it take, etc.? There is a further point which we must study. Will there be pressure for a Mark II Blue Steel, and if this is possible, what would this cost?[172]

The weakness of the British opposition to the Nassau deal can be seen in the slow and rather ineffectual search for a cheaper homegrown deterrent as an alternative to Polaris, which will be covered in Chapter 4.

Vice-Admiral Sir Aubrey Mansergh's editorial in the navy's professional journal *Naval Review*, meanwhile, was an extraordinary tirade: 'To prevent war by threatening to slaughter the enemy's population on a vast scale ... is the unpalatable task that the navy seems shortly to be stuck with ... the Admiralty (if such an institution is to survive the changes) is destined to wage a constant, and probably losing, battle against the Treasury to prevent the "deterrent force" swamping and distorting the "balanced fleet" ... If this is a good bargain the writer will eat the editorial hat'.[173] On behalf of the First Sea Lord, Begg wrote to his liaison office in Washington at the start of the Nassau meeting to say that, 'while it would be a great honour for the navy to be given the deterrent role there are obvious long term dangers to be appreciated'.[174] The words of Caspar John, the professional head of the navy, were probably the most significant: '"A filthy week", he recorded in December 1962. "This millstone of Polaris hung round our necks. I've been shying off the damned things for five and a half years. They are potential wreckers of the real navy and my final months [as First Sea Lord] are going to be a battle to preserve some sort of balance in our affairs".'[175] Carrington felt the need, meanwhile, to reiterate to Thorneycroft that 'I trust there could be no question of stopping all building of the urgently needed nuclear hunter/killers while building specialist Polaris boats. I hope we need not contemplate any such crushing blow to our anti-submarine capability ... I am extremely anxious that in taking on this new burden we should avoid distorting and unbalancing the "cold and limited war navy" with its world-wide roles'.[176]

It was too late. Polaris was the deterrent that was politically possible, and in January 1963 Zuckerman found himself leading a technical mission to the US, 'to secure as much information as possible about American plans for Polaris, their experience of operating the submarines, their production problems and how far they would be prepared to assist us with our programme, so that Her Majesty's government would be able to take firm decisions on the shape and size of the British Polaris fleet'.[177] Technical questions included the number of missiles per submarine; the nature of any supplies and technical training needed from the US; and the type of missile to be procured, A-2 or A-3.

Indeed, a great deal was left unclear by the statements agreed at Nassau and, as we have seen, Macmillan soon recognised that he would have to be alert to American back-tracking during the detailed negotiation. The financial arrangements for the sale, for example, were completely unclear. Macmillan appears to have assumed that the deal would be similar to that struck over Skybolt: a straight purchase of finished missiles, minus warheads. McNamara had other ideas, and sought a contribution to ongoing research and development costs; the Polaris programme, although more advanced than Skybolt, was still not complete. This was only resolved when Ormsby-Gore took a personal message to Kennedy from Macmillan, offering a five per cent research and development payment.[178] Other more arcane accounting details had to be resolved 'to average out the cost of missiles and equipment purchased for both countries so that lower priced tail-end orders would bear their share of early learning costs'.[179] The British mission sent in March to negotiate a detailed Polaris sales agreement, led by the Admiralty's James Mackay, also had a difficult job persuading the State Department's lawyers to remove references from the agreement to general mutual defence arrangements which implied a stronger NATO link than the British government wished to accept. Other issues facing the negotiators were the protection of intellectual property and the fact 'there was a refusal to say anything about penetration aids'.[180] The talks on the sales agreement were therefore difficult, and 'that it achieved remarkably favourable terms for the United Kingdom was due to Jim Mackay; a big man in every way, mentally and physically, he was an extremely patient but forceful negotiator'.[181] The agreement was signed on 6 April 1963.[182] Previous accounts of the agreement have failed to mention that several confidential annexes were agreed at the same time, covering responsibility for export licensing, the contract price-averaging arrangement and the exclusion of penetration aids.[183]

Party politics

Hugh Gaitskell's victory over his party's defence policy in 1961 did not mark a return to bi-partisan support for Britain's independent deterrent. On the contrary, as we have seen, Labour was now committed to a policy of abandoning nuclear independence, whilst remaining a member of the nuclear-armed NATO alliance. In effect, Labour's policy was not to replace the V-bombers but to bow out of the strategic nuclear-weapons field 'gracefully' once they became obsolete.[184] With growing confidence, opposition politicians derided the government's loss of independence over Skybolt and the intellectual underpinnings of the deterrent policy. Indeed, at the very time the government was moving privately to emphasise the interdependence of the western alliance – the need for a *contribution*, no more, to the western deterrent – and to rely increasingly on US delivery systems, *independent* deterrence became more and more of a public political issue. The Conservative back benches were greatly concerned by the deal reached at the end of 1962 to acquire Polaris, on less obviously independent terms than Skybolt. As Pierre puts it:

> During the 21 months between the Nassau conference and the October [1964] election – a period which coincided with the longest 'unofficial' election campaign in 50 years – the issue was surrounded with a fog of confusion, distortion, and over-simplification. As the British bomb became the volley ball of the political arena both parties believed that it was in their electoral interest to accentuate the differences between them so that they became, in fact, grossly

exaggerated. Wrongly, the Conservatives became the party of perpetual nuclear independence, and Labour the party which was going to drop the nuclear arms immediately into the Lake of Geneva.[185]

On 18 January 1963, after a sudden illness, Gaitskell died. Harold Wilson, regarded as a left-winger, and certainly no supporter of Gaitskell's, now took over as leader of the opposition. This made a difference at least to the presentation, if not necessarily the substance of Labour policy. The opposition now vociferously criticised the deterrent on practical grounds: for undermining the solidarity of the western alliance and encouraging nuclear proliferation by France, West Germany and others; for duplication and waste; for lack of technical credibility; and for its impact on conventional forces. Labour also made fun of the belief that nuclear weapons alone made Britain a player on the world stage. In January 1964, Wilson waxed eloquent in parliament about the

> so-called independent, so-called British, so-called deterrent ... I trust [the government] are not contemplating another Suez, certainly not a thermonuclear Suez. As I have said, Cyprus and Borneo – and Aden and Hong Kong too – show the utter irrelevance of the so-called deterrent to the kind of problems that we face today ... they underline how the vast expenditure of money and resources upon the deterrent has undermined our ability to deploy urgently needed resources.[186]

To use nuclear weapons independently, for example in a 'catalytic strike' to ensure US involvement in the defence of Europe, was surely unrealistic and wrong: 'I would acquit the Prime Minister of anything so fundamentally evil as that proposal, because if the Americans have decided not to honour the alliance, I am not certain that they will be shamed into it by the fact that we have committed suicide first'. He rounded off the attack with a trenchant commentary on Nassau: 'The right honourable member for Bromley [Macmillan] did not dare come back from Nassau in the then mood of his party without bringing at least a fiction of a deterrent – and he was right. His back benchers would have eaten him alive ... no Conservative leader could survive who did not maintain this pretence'.[187]

Wilson had been developing this theme ever since 1960 when, in the wake of the Blue Streak cancellation, he had taunted Macmillan: 'Like so many other rather pathetic individuals whose sense of social prestige outruns their purse, he is left in the situation ... of the man who dare not admit that he cannot afford a television set and who ... just puts up the aerial instead'.[188] In fact, Wilson was privately cautious about nuclear-weapons policy, and never advocated outright unilateralism. He needed to balance the views of his own supporters on the left wing with the need to appeal to the electorate and indeed the US government as a responsible statesman – a potential Prime Minister. Denis Healey, a serious participant in the intellectual and academic debate on Britain's defence, who was to become Wilson's Defence Minister, also took a cautious line, avoiding a specific commitment to cancel Polaris.[189] Wilson raised instead the prospect of completing the submarines as SSNs: 'before honourable members start spreading threats of unemployment around the shipyards ... let me repeat that in our view ... we shall need more conventional naval vessels, including nuclear power tracker submarines'.[190] This was the background to Labour's much-quoted manifesto commitment in 1964 to 're-negotiate' the Nassau agreement. Specifically, the party manifesto stated:

> The Nassau agreement to buy Polaris know-how and Polaris missiles from the USA will add nothing to the deterrent strength of the western alliance, and it will mean utter dependence on the US for their supply. Nor is it true that all this costly defence expenditure will produce an 'independent British deterrent'. It will not be independent and it will not be British and it will not deter. Its possession will impress neither friend nor potential foe.
>
> Moreover, Britain's insistence on this nuclear pretence carries with it grave dangers of encouraging the spread of nuclear weapons to countries not possessing them, including Germany.
>
> The Government bases its policy on the assumption that Britain must be prepared to go it alone without her allies in an all-out thermo-nuclear war with the Soviet Union, involving the obliteration of our people. By constantly reiterating this appalling assumption the Government is undermining the alliance on which our security now depends ...
>
> A Labour Government's first concern will be to put our defences on a sound basis and to ensure that the nation gets value for money ...
>
> We are not prepared any longer to waste the country's resources on endless duplication of strategic nuclear weapons. We shall propose the re-negotiation of the Nassau agreement. Our stress will be on the strengthening of our conventional regular forces so that we can contribute our share to NATO defence and also fulfil our peacekeeping commitments to the Commonwealth and the United Nations.

We are against the development of national nuclear deterrents and oppose the current American proposal for a new mixed-manned nuclear surface fleet (MLF). We believe in the inter-dependence of the western alliance and will put forward constructive proposals for integrating all NATO's nuclear weapons under effective political control so that all the partners in the alliance have a proper share in their deployment and control.[191]

Although therefore many expected Labour's re-negotiation to mean cancelling Polaris, the way was open for a far subtler approach. Journalists began to suspect, even before the election, that Wilson would keep Polaris and make its assignment and deployment the focus of any re-negotiation. As Pierre concludes, 'Labour's decision to maintain the British nuclear force was implicitly taken before the election of October 1964'.[192]

Home, meanwhile, as Prime Minister from October 1963, believed the opposite to be the case and took a deliberate decision to focus attention on the nuclear issue, appealing to the patriotism of traditional Tory voters and hoping to exploit residual divisions within the opposition. He also wished to divert attention from economic affairs – a field in which Wilson was strong and he personally was weak – and on to what was, for him, more familiar ground of international policy. Home could speak with 'authority and conviction' on the bomb. Without it, he stressed, Britain would lose its place at the top table – recently, if rather curiously, exercised in Moscow at the test-ban talks.[193] The attitude of de Gaulle was also significant for the Conservatives. As one leading backbencher put it, voicing a concern left unspoken elsewhere: 'If the French bring about [a nuclear force] and we have not got a deterrent, where will Britain be? I have seen Britain pushed around enough on other things. If we are allowed to be pushed around by General de Gaulle, that is just about the end'.[194] Earl Jellicoe, the First Lord of the Admiralty, was one of very few Conservatives to express reservations in this period about independent deterrence, noting to Home's embarrassment in March 1964 that 'there might – it is not inconceivable, in my view – come a time when the organic structure of the western alliance was sufficiently strong for us to be able with entire confidence to place our nuclear armoury irrevocably in a common pool'.[195] This was not the position given in the Conservative manifesto for the 1964 election: 'Conservatives do not accept the view that we could never be threatened on our own, or that an enemy will always assume we shall have allies rushing to our side. Britain must in the ultimate resort have independently controlled nuclear power to deter an aggressor. We possess this power today. Only under a Conservative government will we possess it in the future'.[196] After a very close election indeed, it became clear, in the mid-afternoon of 16 October 1964, that this statement was about to be put to the test. Wilson was in power, with an overall majority of just five seats.

4
Policy Execution 1961-64

Britain's nuclear capabilities continued to mature after 1961, although plans for their further development were curtailed in several ways. During the summer of 1962, a much reduced target stockpile of tactical nuclear weapons was agreed. Nuclear Seaslug and Blue Water were cancelled, and the decision was made to end the production of fissile material for use in weapons. Significant reductions in the workforce at Aldermaston were implied by these decisions, but AWRE's services were still in considerable demand, especially when, after the Skybolt cancellation, new warhead designs were once again required. After September 1961, Aldermaston was able to plan on the resumption of nuclear testing. A significant British advance in implosion technology, known by the codename Super Octopus, became the basis for a nuclear device tested underground in Nevada in March 1962. A new family of warheads was planned for use in Skybolt and WE177. At the end of the year, plans were again revised to take account of the Skybolt cancellation, and it was found that the new warhead technology could be modified for use in Polaris.

The RAF's V-bomber force meanwhile continued to expand towards its target strength, and was finally equipped with high-performance Mk.2 aircraft and a full complement of British Yellow Sun Mk.2 and Blue Steel megaton weapons. Blue Steel's development had been protracted and at times difficult, but experience was accumulated after 1963 and reliability was improving somewhat. Some reductions followed in the front-line strength of Bomber Command. In particular, the Thor missiles were withdrawn during 1963; V-bomber numbers were also reduced somewhat by the end of 1964. The cancellation of Skybolt at the end of 1962 was a tremendous blow to the RAF. However, with the move to low-level operation from 1963, and new navigation and ECM equipment as well as new weapons, the V-force's confidence in its ability to penetrate Soviet defences for the rest of the decade was much improved. From May 1963, the V-bomber force was committed to SACEUR under new command and control arrangements, replacing the bilateral Anglo-American plans of the late 1950s. There remained, however, a national plan to attack Soviet cities independently in the event of a disastrous break with the US and NATO.

RAF nuclear weapons were also deployed for the first time to Singapore in 1963, finally giving reality to a SEATO commitment discussed in the mid-1950s. Red Beard, the kiloton successor to Blue Danube, was now fully in service in a Mk.2 version, allowing increased operational flexibility, and the project to provide a successor, WE177, was approved and underway. When the warhead and re-entry system for Polaris were finally chosen, the nuclear-weapons programme was set fair: Aldermaston, the RAF and now the Royal Navy were working towards a set of capabilities that would remain in service, in slightly modified form, until the end of the cold war.

In this chapter, I shall describe the ups and downs along the way to this steady-state programme: the 1962 reductions in the warhead and fissile materials programme; Aldermaston's work on Super Octopus and new warheads, and its new programme of testing; the operation of the V-bomber force, at low level after 1963, and the introduction of the final versions of its megaton weapons; the final months of Skybolt; the run-down of Thor; the travails of TSR.2; and the move of nuclear weapons to the far east. I shall cover some abortive projects for tactical nuclear weapons and deterrent alternatives and stop-gaps, and then describe the Polaris weapons system and the complicated process of choosing, during 1963 and 1964, the missile, re-entry system and warhead. The story is – once again – one of an extraordinary amount of hard work in a great many directions.

Military requirements and fissile material

We have seen that the warhead review begun by Thorneycroft as Minister of Aviation in October 1960 reached the Defence Committee in the summer of 1962, provoking a bitter row about Skybolt numbers. Less politically controversial, but also with implications at working level – at Aldermaston and especially Capenhurst – were parallel decisions about tactical weapons. In May 1962 the NRDC was told of a proposal to produce only 334 kiloton warheads, all of them RO106/Tony. The reduction arose 'by omission of all versions over 10kt and the ... atomic demolition mine, high-yield Blue Water and nuclear shells, all for the army'.[1] The table below summarises the reduced weapons requirements of the period 1961–64, omitting Blue Danube and Yellow Sun Mk.1 which, it seems, were now quickly withdrawn from service.

Reqt. No.	Issued	Service	Description
OR.1127	1953	RN/RAF	Small kiloton bomb (Red Beard)
OR.1132	1954	RAF	100nm-range powered guided bomb (Blue Steel Mk.1) – Red Snow warhead
OR.1136	1955	RAF	Megaton free-fall bomb (Yellow Sun Mk.2) – Red Snow warhead
	c.1955	RN	Seaslug naval SAGW – RO106/Tony warhead (cancelled Jun 1962)
	c.1957	Army	8-inch artillery shell (under discussion until 1962)
	c.1957	Army	Surface-to-surface guided weapon (Blue Water) – low-yield RO106/Tony warhead; high-yield warhead (GM462) under discussion (missile cancelled Aug 1962)
	1957	Army	Atomic demolition munition (under discussion until 1962)
OR.1171	1959	RAF	Common megaton warhead capsule for free-fall or powered bomb (Red Snow)
OR.1172	1959	RN/RAF	Common kiloton warhead capsule for Seaslug, Blue Water (RO106/Tony) (cancelled Aug 1962)
OR.1177	1960	RN/RAF	Lay-down bomb (WE177) – variable (low-yield) warhead to OR.1176 (PT176) and (from 1963) high-yield warhead to OR.1195 (ZA297)
		Army	Sub-kiloton warhead for Davy Crockett atomic mortar (BQ267) (under discussion 1959–61)
OR.1179	1960	RAF	Warhead for Skybolt (RE179) (cancelled Dec 1962)
OR.1187	1961	RAF	Skybolt weapons system (cancelled Dec 1962)
OR.1195	1963	RAF	High-yield warhead for WE177 (ZA297)
	1963	RN	Polaris warhead (ET317)

Not included: (a) requirements for US warheads under dual-key arrangements; (b) political requirement for NATO MLF warhead – not formally issued.

It is unclear, from the surviving documentary evidence directly associated with the warhead review, how the figure of 334 kiloton warheads presented to the NRDC in May had been derived. We may speculate that it included around 50 warheads for Seaslug, at least 50 for low-yield Blue Water, and at least 165 for WE177, of which 102 would have been for TSR.2 and the remainder for the Royal Navy. As we shall see, the nuclear warhead for Seaslug was cancelled by the Admiralty in June, after which Watkinson presumably made proposals to the Defence Committee on the basis of fewer than 300 kiloton warheads. These proposals were accepted, and the committee decided specifically to defer the requirement for a high-yield warhead for the lay-down bomb; Aldermaston was directed to spend no resource on this requirement for the time being.[2]

Only three years previously, the assumption had been that 500 or 600 kiloton weapons would be required by the RAF alone, and decisions on the size of the plant at Capenhurst had been taken in the mid-1950s when as many as 1500 kiloton weapons were envisaged.[3] Hailsham's paper for the Defence Committee made the implications clear:

> From a date sometime in 1963 no supplies of U235 would be required from Capenhurst for weapons. The plant would therefore have to be closed within the next year unless it can be kept going at a minimum level until a civil demand arises ... Capenhurst ... employs over 3000 technical and industrial staff, and closure or a substantial reduction in output would lead to immediate redundancy. In the meantime, it is clear that even the present level of production at Capenhurst is considerably in excess of the requirements of any likely programme. Pending consideration of the future of the plant, the Authority would propose to reduce output to about two-thirds of the current level ...
>
> The development load on ... Aldermaston would remain relatively unchanged until March 1964. Thereafter, if no further weapons projects arise, the load would decrease rapidly ... and in 1967/8 would be at a level of a post design service in support of the nuclear weapons held by the services. The minimum complement needed to provide this support would be about 50 per cent of the existing establishment ... It will be impossible for the Authority to provide a continuing support to the services on a post design basis without an appropriate research and development programme. This programme would also have to take account of the need to maintain an

adequate level for UK/US scientific collaboration, and in the circumstances it will be difficult to preserve the present high quality of scientific work.[4]

The NRDC had already been told, in addition, that the new programme implied no requirement for military-grade plutonium from Calder Hall and Chapelcross after September 1964.[5] The financial implications of closing Capenhurst were significant. Government departments in the 1960s accounted on a cash basis; the UKAEA, on the other hand, had adopted commercial accounting practices and so capital assets like the Capenhurst plant were held on the books and depreciated. Closing the plant, together with Calder Hall and Chapelcross and associated chemical production and extraction facilities, would mean a huge write-off of up to £250 millions. The MoD, which had been paying the Authority's cost of ownership of these capital assets through a 'historic cost' levy on the price of fissile material, might have to find the money. Whitehall officials seem barely to have understood the mysteries of commercial accounting, and Watkinson had already written to the Treasury to ask for an end to the historic-cost levy, which he described as 'unnecessarily difficult' and 'arbitrary'.[6]

A looming surplus of fissile material had been suspected as early as February 1960,[7] and in June 1962 – in advance of final decisions on the warhead programme – a decision was taken by the UKAEA to run the Capenhurst plant at two-thirds capacity.[8] This run-down, which would lead to 500 job losses, was announced in parliament.[9] By October, a further run-down had been agreed: Capenhurst would effectively be moth-balled to run 'at the lowest possible level consistent with keeping diffusion plant technology alive in the UK and with maintaining the plant in a state which would enable full-scale operation to be resumed in the future should further policy changes so require'.[10] A further 1000 job losses were involved, reducing the Capenhurst workforce to around 1500. The trades unions – accustomed to security of employment in a nationally important industry, and naturally unaware of the highly secretive discussions of the weapons programme – were outraged: 'The people responsible for the present position must be aware of the general level of unemployment ... and in particular that on Merseyside ... What hopes had men leaving Capenhurst of getting employment, let alone getting a job which even approximated to the conditions to which they had been accustomed and which would enable them to maintain the standard of living to which they had committed themselves and which they had every right to expect?'[11] A large financial write-off was indeed made, and production of highly enriched uranium for military purposes was brought to a complete halt by March 1963. 'Tick-over' operation continued until a further review of Capenhurst, beginning in 1964, after which the plant found a role in the civil nuclear industry.[12]

Meanwhile the implications for AWRE were elaborated in a further NRDC paper. Staff numbers would be cut from around 8600 to 4800 by 1967/8 (these figures did not include, for example, the ROF at Burghfield). Aldermaston's future role would be to complete existing projects, preserve a post-design capability for as long as nuclear weapons were in service, and conduct effects studies and research on warhead physics, materials and technology. This research would have to be of a sufficiently high standard to maintain collaboration with the US.[13] This appears to have been the first use of an argument which, by the late 1960s and early 1970s, would dominate Whitehall discussion of nuclear weapons. The atomic relationship between Aldermaston and the US labs was no longer just a means to the end of a nuclear-weapons capability, but a thing to be cherished and nurtured in its own right; any reduction in work at Aldermaston had implications for its viability and the value set upon it by the US. Makins made it clear that, in the context of Anglo-American collaboration, the quality of research work at Aldermaston was 'of the first importance'.[14]

Warheads

We saw in Chapter 2 that in the years immediately after the UK/US bilateral agreement, AWRE embarked on a programme of anglicising US warhead designs, and that this was a more difficult exercise than had perhaps been anticipated. We have seen also that British weapons designers were faced with new requirements, for Skybolt and WE177 warheads in particular, which were not to be met simply by producing unmodified US designs. Instead, a series of new investigations began, with the eventual aim of producing a family of warhead designs based on the Skybolt warhead.

When in September 1961 it became clear that nuclear testing would probably resume, a summary of possibilities was produced for UKAEA chairman Sir Roger Makins. This gave an interesting insight into progress at Aldermaston and the situation regarding warhead design. The testing requirements listed included a stockpile version of Tony – 'this we hope would confirm the modifications we propose, enabling us to comply with British standards of safety and employ British materials and British methods of manufacturing with maximum economy, speed and safety'. This was not thought quite as important as a test of the stockpile version of the anglicised primary for Skybolt, yielding around ten kilotons, and/or a 'partial' test yielding around 100kt of the complete Skybolt warhead. Areas of 'joint' research might also be illuminated by testing, including 'nuclear gunshells, light-weight tactical weapons and the long term research into the new techniques which might lead to the development of a neutron bomb'. Pride of place in the wish-list, however, went to a wholly British device referred to as Super Octopus, the principle of which had been 'tested by the UK in 1958 and attracted particular interest in the US'. Super Octopus was said to have immediate applicability to the Skybolt warhead.[15] Aldermaston clearly now had not only anglicised and joint US/UK work on the books, but also set great store by a new and independent British technological development. Further correspondence gave more background: there were 'sharp differences of opinion' between Aldermaston and the US on the safety of the proposed Skybolt primary; 'we can either adopt the proposed American primary which is *based* on a tested device, and uses more sensitive explosive than UK authorities advocate, or use an untested British modification of this particular device. But neither solution seems likely to provide the same assurance of safety and reliability that our labs have been able to provide about Red Snow'. Super Octopus, the new implosion system for lighter and more reliable warheads, suggested a way out of this conundrum.[16]

Britain's wish to test Super Octopus – and for the time being no other device – was put specifically by Macmillan to Kennedy in his request for underground facilities in Nevada in November 1961, with the words: 'As a kiloton weapon and as a primary for Skybolt ... this promises to be safer and more efficient and in every way more satisfactory' than the anglicised US alternative. Makins was told by Leland Haworth, a commissioner of the USAEC, that 'there was increasing technical interest in this device, especially at Los Alamos'.[17] The Super Octopus device was duly tested successfully on 1 March 1962,[18] and indeed it seems, from a retrospective account in a document of 1965, that it was of such interest that it was adapted and tested again, more than once, by the US: 'the Americans have also tested underground at Nevada devices similar to the British primary and have made the full results available to us. (They followed up our initial test with others on a range of devices employing the British principles)'.[19] The precise nature of the advance or advances made with Super Octopus, which was described variously as a device or a principle, remain unclear, but the evidence of further significant British progress in implosion is interesting.

Although the new March 1962 test device had potential, more work was evidently still needed before an entirely satisfactory Skybolt warhead could be produced. Briefings in the summer of 1962, giving an unusually detailed insight into the trade-offs faced by warhead designers at Aldermaston, explained the need for a further test:

> The outstanding problem of the British nuclear warhead development programme is to select an effective design for the primary stage of the Skybolt warhead. One successful step in this direction was the underground firing of a British device ... in Nevada on 1 March 1962. This device proved a new implosion system for the primary, leading to a more rugged, reliable and lighter type of warhead than existing designs ... the British RO106 warhead has been based on the [same] Tsetse design [as the US Skybolt primary]. But in developing RO106 some explosive power was deliberately sacrificed in the interests of using an explosive (EDC11) that is less likely to detonate, in the event of an accident, than the ... explosive used in the US Tsetse. As a result the yield of the RO106 is less than Tsetse, and cannot be used as the Skybolt primary.[20]

Specifically, the RO106 (or Tony) warhead would yield only around 8.5kt, not enough 'to ensure reliable functioning of the secondary'.[21] The Nevada test meanwhile had proved the Super Octopus principle, but to achieve the required yield for a Skybolt primary – completely safely – would mean either reducing the amount of fissile material, but at the same time increasing the size of the high-explosive charge around the device; or using a mechanical safeing technique, something conceptually similar to the steel balls of the earlier Green Grass warhead. The first course was preferred, but to determine just how much the fissile material content of the warhead could be reduced, and how much of an increase in high-explosive was required, would mean another underground test. It was now also stated that 'any other British nuclear warhead is likely to follow this line of development'.[22] Specifically, a high-yield warhead or warheads for the Red Beard replacement could be based on a 'down-graded [Skybolt warhead] ... these modifications would involve reductions in the fissile materials in the secondary, but would not concern the primary, which would remain identical to that used in the Skybolt warhead'.[23] The case for this additional test was strong, and it duly took place on 7 December 1962. Makins reported to the Prime Minister that 'the device was fully up to expectations'. The aspirations of mid-1960 for a family of common warhead designs had now been realised – on the basis of American help, but also a new and specifically British technological advance. When Skybolt was cancelled, the confident expectation was that the current line of development would also provide a suitable primary for a Polaris warhead.[24]

Although the weapons-development programme was now set fair, at least until a Polaris warhead had to be chosen – a process we shall follow in due course – a stimulating and useful programme of research for Aldermaston scientists, partly to add value to collaboration with the US, was also still required. In October 1963, the question of further British tests was therefore debated by the NRDC. None was strictly necessary to meet the stated warhead requirements of the services (a statement conditional, as we shall see, on a particular view of the likely Polaris warhead). A 300lb warhead with 500kt yield was evidently being studied, however, which might eventually require testing, as might new ideas on mechanical safeing.[25] AWRE was asked to draw up a desirable programme, and more testing was approved in principle by ministers by the end of the year. What emerged was a list of nine possible underground tests, designed to explore smaller low-kiloton devices, yield-to-weight improvements for two-stage megaton weapons, 'clean' warheads with low fission yield, warheads 'with high neutron output' and warheads using plutonium from reactors operating on a civil fuel cycle. The first item on the list, the exploration of smaller low-kiloton devices, had potential relevance to Polaris and was therefore the highest priority.[26]

Penney later recalled that 'the programme proposed was chosen as a basis for maintaining an adequate research and development effort at Aldermaston, and an adequate level of collaboration with the US'.[27] Home was told, slightly less explicitly, that 'this programme would not be aimed primarily at the development of specific weapons but would seek to maintain an effective and up-to-date nuclear weapon technology in the United Kingdom'. His approval was sought for two low-kiloton tests during 1964, aimed at improvements to mechanical single-point safety and a further reduction in the size and weight of low-kiloton devices. This, he was told, would be 'a very useful step towards smaller and lighter megaton weapons ... the initial programme is also expected to throw some further light on the possibility of achieving a much higher fusion to fission ratio in nuclear bombs'.[28] The two research tests for 1964 were evidently approved, and on 17 July 1964 one of these went ahead in Nevada. Codenamed Cormorant by the US authorities, it may not have been a success; Penney wrote soon afterwards to the USAEC chairman, Glenn Seaborg, to explain that 'I am afraid the yield is disappointing and we are pressing on with all speed to analyse the results'.²⁹ The second research test was postponed in favour of a Polaris warhead test, as we shall see later.

At Maralinga, the planned experimental programme for 1962 was repeatedly thrown into doubt and confusion by revisions to the warhead programme, and by the ultimately successful test in Nevada in March. In June, the Australian authorities were finally told that there would be no minor trials at Maralinga until 1963. 'It was difficult for the [Australian army] range commandant to maintain morale throughout 1962, but the time was profitably used for a much needed tidying up exercise'.³⁰ During negotiations over the experimental programme for 1963, the Australian government was more assertive than previously, conscious of the domestic political impact of any problems at the range, or of any impression that they had little control over events. Again, the turmoil in weapons and warhead policy intervened to make revisions to the programme necessary, but in March and April 1963, the last Tims and Vixens trials were conducted, relating to the high and low-yield WE177 warheads.³¹ The experiments were judged successful. The Maralinga range had cost £10 millions to set up and extended over 20,000 square miles of desert. The village had accommodation for up to 750 people, laboratories and workshops, a church, a power station, a hospital and facilities including cricket and football pitches and a golf course.³² The future of the range was now in doubt, however, and after the signature of the partial test-ban treaty the British and Australian governments agreed to put Maralinga on a care-and-maintenance basis, capable of being restored to operation in six to nine months after a decision to do so. No such decision came, and the agreement to use the range was terminated in 1967.³³

V-bombers

By the end of 1961, three squadrons of Vulcan B.1s were operational at Waddington, and three of Vulcan B.2s at Scampton; and there were four squadrons of Victors at Cottesmore and Honington. The Valiant was being withdrawn from the front line, but two dedicated strategic bomber squadrons remained, one each at Wittering and Honington, in addition to three at Marham, assigned to SACEUR, and a number of tanker aircraft with a secondary bomber role. Each squadron had a theoretical front-line strength of eight aircraft 'units effective' (UE), meaning the full planned numerical strength of the V-force agreed by the Defence Committee in July 1960, 96 aircraft, had now been reached.³⁴ The force was further strengthened during 1962, however, with the arrival of more of the latest B.2 aircraft: three new Vulcan B.2 squadrons were formed at Coningsby and two Victor B.2 squadrons at Wittering. Ultimately a front-line force of 72 Vulcan B.2s with Skybolt, and 24 Victor B.2s with Blue Steel, was the aim.

The operational life of the V-bombers continued to revolve around readiness and now QRA. In early 1963, the commander-in-chief, Cross, put forward proposals to extend QRA to around 20 per cent of the V-force, partly in compensation for the run-down of Thor. Although these proposals seem not to have been adopted – QRA was a considerable drain on the mental and physical resources of the V-bomber air and ground crews – the Micky Finn series of no-notice dispersal exercises did continue annually. The October 1964 Micky Finn was particularly satisfactory. Alert level two had been declared shortly after three o'clock in the morning. Within four hours, 28 aircraft with freefall (i.e., presumably Yellow Sun) weapons were ready for dispersal; within ten hours, 52 were ready and within the permitted 20 hours 59 out of 61 were ready. Of 30 aircraft armed with Blue Steel, however, only 14 were ready within 20 hours. Blue Steel, the Chief of the Air Staff reported, remained 'a complicated system requiring almost as much effort in preparation as the aircraft itself'.[35]

Targeting arrangements for the V-bombers were changed somewhat during 1962. The UK/US plan, agreed in 1958, had been subsumed within the first US SIOP in 1961, although there is little evidence for practical change at this point. A new targeting plan was adopted in August 1962, however, which as far as the RAF was concerned placed a good deal more emphasis on military counterforce targets: 44 airfields, 28 IRBM sites and ten air-defence centres, but only 16 cities, were now allocated to Bomber Command.[36] The reasons for this are obscure, although they must relate to the entry into force at the same time of a new US plan, SIOP-63. Ian Clark speculates that there was now American pressure to move towards the kind of selective counterforce targeting advocated by McNamara.[37] It seems more likely that Bomber Command was now assigned less ambitious military targets simply because of concerns about its ability to penetrate SAM defences around Soviet cities, and that city targets were assigned instead to the rapidly growing US ICBM force.[38]

Command and control arrangements had been reviewed during 1961, and some weaknesses were addressed. A working group on nuclear retaliation procedures was set up in Whitehall, reporting in February 1962. Sir Norman Brook doubted the need for permanent communications facilities to keep the Prime Minister in touch: 'If there were to be a "bolt from the blue", we must accept that it may not be possible to contact the

Prime Minister before the impact'.[39] A greater degree of pre-delegation of authority was introduced into Bomber Command's directive in September 1962, specifying circumstances in which it would be in order for Cross to order retaliation on his own authority. If it were clear that an enemy nuclear attack on the UK was underway, and if attempts to contact the political authorities and SAC commanders in the UK were unsuccessful, then, Cross was told, 'you are authorised in the last resort to order on your own responsibility nuclear retaliation by all means at your disposal'. Twigge and Scott have speculated that a Soviet 'decapitation' attack might have had the effect of 'devolving nuclear command authority downward within the command structure', and it seems conceivable that if Bomber Command headquarters at High Wycombe had been attacked then the commander of No. 1 Group at RAF Bawtry would have assumed the AOC-in-C's weighty responsibilities.[40] After Cuba, further changes were contemplated, for it seemed possible that decisions might have to be taken during a US-Soviet crisis not directly involving the UK, and draconian emergency legislation was drafted for the running of the United Kingdom in a crisis.[41]

Likely V-bomber attack procedures and tactics have not been discussed in great detail in the open literature, although Andrew Brookes gives a good general account and some interesting details have emerged recently in internet discussion groups.[42] With the order to scramble, 'on airfields everywhere from the north of Scotland to Cornwall 16 engines would have started simultaneously ... Throttles would be opened and four bombers would take off in quick succession ... to comply with the coordinated raid plan laid down by Bomber Command'.[43] Although Brookes says that 'the V-bombers would forge on to enter Soviet airspace anywhere from Novaya Zemlya to the Caspian Sea', it seems that aircraft would have been routed mainly across specific sectors – certainly not over the heavily defended inner-German border, for example, but more likely from the direction of Scandinavia or Turkey. An Air Ministry document of 1961 recorded that:

> The direct routes cross the satellite countries in Europe and the greatest distances over Russian territory and therefore involve the longest crossing of the Russian air defence system. It is essential now, and as the Russian defence system improves it will be vital, to route our bombers tactically so they proceed as far as possible outside the perimeter of the Russian defence system to points from which targets are reached by the shortest penetration. This

involves flying round northern Norway and south-east Europe which increases considerably the distance to be flown.[44]

Brookes acknowledges that 'intelligence sources tried to predict the points where the defences might be weakest'.[45] Any chinks in the long-range SA-2 and later point-defence SA-3 SAM systems would have been followed, and ECM would have assisted penetration. After attack from high level, the aircraft would have headed for home; all sorties were planned from take-off to recovery. Bearing in mind the possible need for manoeuvre within Soviet airspace, including at high speed to avoid fighter and SAM defences, fuel would in most cases have been too short for every aircraft to recover to bases in the UK – should these still exist – and V-bomber aircrew have spoken of plans to return to land in Norway or Turkey.

Brookes makes a convincing argument that, despite undoubted advances in Soviet air defence, many of the bombers would have been able to prosecute an attack successfully in the early 1960s, even at high level – a point of pride for the RAF and its supporters. As time went by, however, the need to penetrate at low level was recognised. In particular, as we have seen, the Defence Committee decided in the aftermath of the Skybolt cancellation to order the V-force to low level to cover the likely deterrent gap between about 1965 and 1968. As Wynn makes clear, this was not a decision taken lightly:

> Changing over a force whose equipment had been designed to operate at 50,000ft so that it could operate at near ground level involved many technological and training factors: modifying the aircraft to endure the greater stresses and hazards they would encounter at, say, 2000ft and below; changing the navigation equipment to include height-above-ground and terrain-avoidance instrumentation, and adapting electronic warning and countermeasures devices to cope with defences likely to be encountered in a low environment; developing new weapons to suit low-level delivery or changing techniques to use existing bombs at the end of a low-level penetration of enemy defences; and training crews to become efficient under the new circumstances, by the arduous practice of low-level navigation and weapon delivery.[46]

Air Vice-Marshal Hartley explained to the DRPC that:

> The considered opinion of the Air Ministry was that the only possible course was to operate the bombers at low level. In consider-

ing the implications of this they had examined first the question of the fatigue life of the aircraft at low level, secondly whether any improvements to the navigational fit would be needed and thirdly what could be done to improve the survival capability of the aircraft. They had concentrated on steps that could be taken quickly.[47]

Vulcan and Victor B.1 aircraft began to exercise at low level, around 500–1000ft, in March 1963, and B.2s followed in 1964; crews were certified for low-level flight as soon as they were proficient. The technical measures required to operate in this regime took a couple of years to perfect. Fatigue life was a concern, especially for the Victor, and navigation, fire control and ECM would require various modifications. Even a new colour scheme was required: hitherto, V-bombers had been painted in all-over anti-flash white; now their upper surfaces were camouflaged. Low-level flight also badly affected range, with implications for targeting and routeing. Both Yellow Sun and Blue Steel had to be modified in varying degrees, even to be delivered from 12,000ft in a 'pop-up' manoeuvre (this was already possible for Red Beard, but it is not clear that Red Beard was any longer in use by the main V-force).[48] Investigations of ideas for brand-new weapons will be described a little later. A final, somewhat reduced programme of modifications to V-bomber navigation and ECM systems for the low-level role was approved by Thorneycroft in July 1964.[49] 'For the rest of the decade', says Brookes – with at least some justification – 'the V-force was unstoppable'.[50]

A recent account by a former V-force navigator suggests that, in the event of war in this later period, much of the bomber force would have headed for the Skaggerak before flying east across Sweden, dropping to low level in the region of Linköping and penetrating Soviet airspace over Latvia or Lithuania.[51] Swedish air defence was evidently not considered a threat to the V-force. Despite its official neutrality, the Swedish government had made a series of secret arrangements to facilitate British and US use of Swedish airspace in wartime, including for the purposes of nuclear attack:

> The [Swedish official Commission on Neutrality Policy of 1994] found that a number of Swedish air bases had been given longer and stronger runways to accommodate very heavy allied aircraft, and concluded that these were intended for recovery landings of bombers damaged during a strike. A former [CINCSAC], Russell Dougherty ... also said that by the mid 1950s, a simple procedure had been set up for aircraft

from SAC to identify themselves to Swedish air controllers, adding that 'we would never dream of being shot at by the Swedes'.[52]

Paragraph six of the Nassau joint declaration had said, on the subject of a NATO nuclear force, that 'for the immediate future a start should be made by subscribing to NATO some part of the forces already in existence. This could include allocations from the United States strategic forces, from United Kingdom Bomber Command, and from tactical nuclear forces now held in Europe. Such forces would be ... targeted in accordance with NATO plans'.[53] The *whole* of the V-force, over and above the three Valiant squadrons at Marham, was therefore committed to SACEUR on 23 May 1963. Home announced the move at a NATO council meeting in Ottawa: 'We are today giving instructions for the immediate formal assignment [of the V-bombers] to SACEUR'.[54]

This arrangement has attracted little comment from historians, and there is not much solid evidence of its practical implications. It seems, however, that this marked the end of the joint Anglo-American Bomber Command/SAC targeting plan. There were some attempts at official level in the Air Ministry to downplay its significance. Anglo-American political talks on the subject, already made complicated enough by the MLF, made little headway at first. In January 1963, the chiefs argued that assignment to NATO should not allow undue NATO control over readiness, deployment, dispersal and logistical arrangements for the V-force, or prevent its use in a conventional role, for example in the far east. The joint staff mission at the Washington embassy was 'seeking to water down these terms and ... suggesting that the less said about them the better'.[55]

The chiefs would have preferred simply to 'earmark' Bomber Command for assignment to SACEUR – a command arrangement similar to that adopted by SACLANT, who had no formal peacetime control over the forces that would be assigned to him in war. Thorneycroft, however, needed further progress in the context of his political proposal for an IANF. A working group of national experts at SHAPE now drew up an inventory of nuclear-capable systems, focusing on those 'pre-targeted' by SACEUR, as opposed to those whose control would be delegated to lower-level commanders for use against mobile and opportunity targets in the land battle.[56] In March, Sir Evelyn Shuckburgh, Britain's Permanent Representative to NATO, reported that, although he had stated and restated Britain's political willingness to assign the V-force to SACEUR, other nations were interested to know what this meant in concrete terms of roles, command structures, operational missions and targeting, certainly before committing any forces of their own in a similar way. The French, unsurprisingly, were resolutely opposed.

Assignment was discussed in April between Thorneycroft, Assistant Defense Secretary Paul Nitze and the new SACEUR, General Lyman Lemnitzer; and again between Thorneycroft and McNamara. By now, working-level discussions appear to have concluded that little operational difficulty would arise from the reassignment of the V-force. Targeting, for example, would not in practice be affected.[57] On 23 May, Mountbatten, as CDS, recorded the formal transfer of command responsibility in a letter to Lemnitzer:

> In the course of discussion with President Kennedy at Nassau last December, the Prime Minister suggested that, as a start to the implementation of new and closer arrangements for the organisation and control of strategic western defence, there should be subscribed to NATO some part of the nuclear forces already in existence, including allocations from the United Kingdom Bomber Command.
>
> Her Majesty's government subsequently decided that, to secure a strong and credible NATO nuclear force, it would be best for the United Kingdom to assign the whole of the V-bomber force to the alliance.
>
> Her Majesty's government, therefore, in implementation of paragraph six of the Nassau communique, assign to you the whole of the V-bomber force with immediate effect.
>
> Bearing in mind, however, the dual role of this force and the United Kingdom's commitments outside NATO for the defence of the free world, Her Majesty's government have decided that:-
>
> (a) they must retain the right to order the use of these British forces at discretion, if they decide that supreme national interests are at stake;
>
> (b) forces must be available to meet national commitments outside NATO in conditions of lesser emergency. Accordingly, the number of aircraft available at any time for their allotted NATO task and their equipment must remain a national responsibility;
>
> (c) states of readiness, deployment and dispersal, logistics and support of the assigned forces, must remain a national responsibility.
>
> The bombers are assigned to you for targeting, planning, coordination and execution of strikes in accordance with your nuclear strike plan. The fulfilment of national commitments by the V-bombers

would not normally be expected to alter the availability of forces sufficient to cover the targets allocated to them by you.[58]

It is clear, given the stipulations of this letter, that the assignment of the V-force was somewhat less clear-cut than the assignment of the Marham Valiant squadrons. SACEUR had no right, for example, to select the weapons to be used by the bombers, which presumably remained Yellow Sun or Blue Steel. He was keen to avoid publicity about these limits to his responsibility, and about the appointment of an RAF officer as air executive to his nuclear deputy, Belgian Air Force Lieutenant-General van Rolleghem. Nevertheless Lemnitzer professed himself impressed and satisfied with his new command following an inspection visit to RAF Scampton in August.[59]

Megaton weapons

In 1962, the number of megaton weapons available to the RAF grew, for the first time, to match closely the number of front-line aircraft, although for the time being not all were the final versions. By March 1962, clearance had been received for all extant V-bombers to use Yellow Sun Mk.2, and the use of Project E weapons for the front-line V-force had been discontinued.[60] Yellow Sun Mk.2 was now the RAF's main strategic nuclear deterrent weapon. Some problems had been encountered with degraded performance of the external neutron initiation unit for the bomb's Red Snow warhead, but short- and long-term solutions were recommended and by the end of the year replacement programmes were well underway.[61] Yellow Sun production had reached 83 by the end of 1962,[62] and almost certainly ended in 1963, when the Mk.2 weapons were also modified by the Bomber Command Armament School for low-level delivery.[63] There had been some correspondence on a new retarded version of Yellow Sun for low-level delivery, but the minor modifications finally agreed related only to fuzing.[64] At around this time, Yellow Sun Mk.1 bombs were in all probability withdrawn from service. The final order for Yellow Suns appears to have been for 96 of the Mk.2 version, although the Air Ministry had considered reducing this to 86.[65]

For 1961 and most of 1962, Skybolt was the RAF's deterrent weapon of the future, and the development of the weapon was therefore followed with keen interest in the Air Ministry and elsewhere. In November 1961, even Zuckerman was reasonably impressed, writing that 'satisfactory solutions have been found to all the technical problems which have so far emerged' and that 'the warhead development programme shows good correlation with the forecast missile deliveries and there is no reason to suppose that any delays will arise on this account'.[66] Building on previous work on Blue Streak, limited studies were being made of decoys and penetration aids for Skybolt.[67] A problem with the so-called header reference system of the Vulcan, affecting the aircraft's ability to provide precise navigational data to the missile and therefore the missile's ability to acquire stars, had been resolved. The RAF wished to be able to launch within 30 minutes of the Vulcan's take-off, but without sufficiently accurate input data from the aircraft, the missile might take three hours to acquire a star. Additional American equipment was procured to remove the problem.[68] In March 1962, Group Captain Fryer circulated the fourth in his irregular series of Skybolt progress reports from Washington. A research and development programme costing $492.6 millions was underway, against a likely US production requirement for a total of 1140 missiles. Skybolt was 'fairly and squarely' Douglas's top priority, the first guided launch was expected in October 1962 and Vulcan squadron service was anticipated in the fourth quarter of 1964. At 920nm, range would more or less meet the requirement. The weight of the pre-launch navigation computer was increasing, but the Skybolt star-tracker was proving its ability at the Mount Palomar observatory.[69] An extensive RAF trials team was also now built up at Eglin Air Force Base in Florida to gain experience with the Skybolt system. Plans were being made to introduce Skybolt to the V-bombers based at Cottesmore, Honington and Waddington.

When test launches began in April 1962, confidence was therefore high. At the first launch, however – a 'programmed' launch, with no functioning guidance system but a series of pre-programmed guidance commands – the missile's second stage failed to ignite. Still, in May, Zuckerman expressed optimism: 'I was much impressed by the progress that had been made', he told Watkinson after a trip to the US; 'everyone I spoke to at Douglas expressed a quiet confidence'.[70] Plans for the Skybolt warhead were also progressing, as we have seen, with the testing of British implosion designs for the primary. The final Skybolt warhead design, known by its MoA reference number RE179, apparently had a design yield of 850kt.[71] In June, at the second programmed Skybolt launch, neither stage of the missile ignited correctly; in September, at the third programmed launch, the second stage separated before first-stage ignition and flew down-range for several minutes; and at the fourth programmed launch, second-stage thrust reversal was premature, reducing range. The missile was now in greater political difficulty and finally, at the very important first guided launch in November – despite the 'extraordinary' measures reported by Fryer to guarantee success – the airframe control system failed, toppling the missile. A faulty gas generator may have been to blame.[72] At this point, as we have seen, the decision had already been taken at a political level to cancel Skybolt.

If Skybolt was doomed, and the development and production of Yellow Sun proceeded calmly to completion, the story of Blue Steel was somewhere between the two. In December 1961, the Defence Committee was told that 27 missiles had been test-fired, but 'with only mediocre success'. Only three had navigated to full range. Engineering defects, often in the motor control and fuel supply systems and the control and guidance electronics, were diagnosed.[73] As we saw in Chapter 2, the missile's internal power supply system had also been especially problematic. Nevertheless the RAF and Air Ministry remained desperate to see Blue Steel in service, to extend the capability of the increasingly vulnerable V-bombers. In January, Thorneycroft reported to the Defence Committee that firings of Blue Steel rounds approximating closely to the operational missiles were about to begin, and would provide a better basis for judging the weapon's potential than previous tests. By April, two more tests had taken place, completely successfully.[74] CA release for Blue Steel to be carried by the Vulcan 'in a national emergency' was achieved in July 1962, although this could hardly be described as a satisfactory operational capability since approval did not in theory extend to launching the missile.[75] By September, the Deputy Chief of the Air Staff felt confident enough to state that 'trials have progressed sufficiently far for the Air Ministry to ... take the risk of launching the missiles should a national crisis justify our overriding the prohibitions which remain. We have examined the clearances given and are satisfied that by cutting corners and taking certain risks we could, if necessary, use Blue Steel in an emergency'.[76] The first operational missile was expected in October, and a squadron of eight might be expected by the end of the year. One important remaining problem was that, if the missile had to be fuelled operationally but was not then used, it would subsequently have to be defuelled and dried out; but drying-out facilities were not yet available. Deliveries of Blue Steel warhead 'pods' incorporating Red Snow were, however, now underway, around 18 being produced in 1962.[77] Representatives of the press were eventually invited to RAF Scampton in February 1963 to mark the official entry into service of Blue Steel, to the annoyance of some Whitehall officials who remained concerned that a true operational capability had still not, in reality, been demonstrated.[78]

Cross wrote to Pike in July 1963 to record his concerns about Blue Steel's readiness and reliability. He complained that, on the basis of experience so far, 'generating' a missile for an operational sortie would take seven hours at best, or more likely between ten and 15. Then 'the chances of a missile being fit for powered launch at the launch point are no better than 40 per cent; the probability of a missile reaching the target after launch is only 75 per cent'. For every six weapons at readiness on the ground, therefore, two or perhaps three could eventually be launched, and one of these would fail to reach the target. The rest would have to be dropped free-fall – rather negating their basic purpose. Cross concluded that Blue Steel had 'so many basic faults ... that it is very doubtful whether they can be overcome'. Pike could only reply that, since Cross's findings were based on research and development firings at Woomera and experience with pre-production missiles at Scampton, things could be expected to improve later.[79]

On 13 May 1963, a new issue of the Blue Steel operational requirement was circulated. This formalised the requirement for the weapon to be carried and released, in line with Bomber Command's new operational concept, 'at the lowest possible level'.[80] In order to operate successfully at low level, a new turbojet motor for Blue Steel was initially contemplated. It was then discovered that the missile's flight-rules computer could instead be modified relatively inexpensively for low-level release, an elegant solution that saved a great deal of time and money.[81] It seems that, as a result of the move to low level, a reduction in missile range had nevertheless to be accepted, although this was not admitted at the time.[82] In October 1963, the necessary modifications were approved by the DRPC. Test firings of Blue Steel from low level at Woomera began in November 1963 and continued until August 1964; a final test launch from high level was made in October.[83] The new Bomber Command AOC-in-C, Air Marshal Sir John Grandy, wrote to the Secretary of State for Air in November 1963 with a more up-beat assessment of the missile's progress. He still recognised, however, the need for a further series of approvals to operate at higher readiness: for example fuelling the missile with the warhead in place, fitting warheads with thermal batteries and dispersing with the live warhead. In July 1964, CA release for low-level Blue Steel, including dispersal with HTP and live warheads, was finally given.[84] Blue Steel now equipped 40 front-line RAF aircraft: two squadrons of Victors at Wittering, and three of Vulcans at Scampton. The original plan to convert a third Victor squadron to Blue Steel operation for a front line of 48 aircraft was reversed by the Air Council in February 1964, probably too late for production orders for missiles or warheads to be reduced.[85]

In May 1962, the Air Council decided to recommend running down the Thor missile force which, with the continued growth in the V-force and its capabilities, was becoming less important. In July, the Defence Committee confirmed the decision. The withdrawal of Thor had been on the cards since at least September 1961, but it seems McNamara gave the discussion some urgency with his announcement to Watkinson on 1 May 1962 that US support for the deployment would end in the autumn of 1964.[86] Although, as we have seen, the Thor force demonstrated an impressive degree of readiness during the Cuban missile crisis, calls for its preservation were resisted. As a liquid-fuelled ground-based missile, Thor was obsolescent and running-cost expenditure on the force could better be spent elsewhere in the RAF. On 3 January 1963, the removal of Thors from their launch emplacements began, at RAF Breighton in Yorkshire, and was complete by August.[87]

In April and October 1962, the Valiant squadrons at Honington and Wittering were withdrawn, and towards the end of our period, in February and October 1964, the two Victor B.1 squadrons at Cottesmore were also withdrawn. Some Yellow Suns were now becoming surplus to requirements, and it seems that some Red Snow warheads were being transferred from Yellow Suns into Blue Steels to match the build-up of the Blue Steel force.[88] Others were no doubt returned to Burghfield to allow fissile material to be recycled into newer warheads for WE177 and Polaris.

Other nuclear forces

In August 1962, Macmillan agreed to the deployment of live Red Beard bombs to RAF Tengah in Singapore. It seems he did so with a certain reluctance, and only on advice from Sir Norman Brook that 'the building of storage at Tengah has apparently excited no remark in Singapore and the proposal at this stage is simply to fly the bombs there for storage'.[89] Anglo-American talks on nuclear coordination in the far east now began, and one document reported that 'the Americans have asked us if we would take on targets in Burma, adjacent parts of China and in Hainan. This we could do reasonably with the Canberras now stationed in Singapore and the V-bombers that we plan to deploy to the theatre in an emergency, and by stationing our strike carrier in the Indian Ocean'.[90] The arrival of Red Beards in the far east finally gave reality to the commitment, discussed in the mid-1950s and confirmed by the Defence Committee in October 1960, to introduce a British nuclear capability for SEATO to fight a limited nuclear war against China. At first, the Red Beards had to remain out of sight in their storage area, although training in the open with dummy weapons could be undertaken. The weapons were earmarked for use by three squadrons of V-bombers, which would deploy to the far east if necessary, and one locally based squadron of Canberras.[91] A total of 48 weapons had long been planned for the far east, and it seems likely this was the number eventually deployed. V-bombers were sent to the far east from time to time throughout the 1960s on SEATO reinforcement exercises.[92] The Canberra squadron at Tengah completed its training in the LABS role in November 1963, and remained in the far east, with the stored Red Beard weapons, until 1970.[93]

Meanwhile, west of Suez, RAF Akrotiri's four Canberra squadrons received new B.15 and B.16 aircraft in 1961–62; during 1962, a full nuclear capability, using LABS, can be said to have become available in support of CENTO. LABS training was conducted on ranges off Cyprus and in Libya. Canberras remained at RAF Akrotiri throughout our period, being replaced by Vulcans from 1969.[94] Four squadrons of Canberras also remained in West Germany, assigned to SACEUR in the same way as the three squadrons of RAF Valiants at Marham. The Canberras continued to use Mk.7 Project E weapons with a yield of 28–43kt, whereas the Valiants used Mk.28s with a yield in the range 60–100kt until early 1963, when these were replaced with Mk.43s suitable for lay-down delivery.[95] The Valiants were a significant capability in themselves, and also pioneered low-level and QRA operation for the rest of Bomber Command. Each Valiant also had a national target assigned in case 'supreme national interests' dictated the force's withdrawal from SACEUR's control.[96]

The Air Ministry remained passionately committed to the TSR.2 project, which maintained a steady forward momentum during 1961 and 1962. Pike, the Chief of the Air Staff, summarised his views: 'TSR.2 was essential to the RAF as a general work horse in replacement of the Canberra, to provide close support for the army with atomic or conventional bombs and for reconnaissance. It was required to meet NATO, CENTO and SEATO commitments ... The plan was to deploy roughly one for every two Canberras, a total of 106 in all'.[97] The Air Ministry also argued that the aircraft could cover most or all of the targets of the army's Blue Water missile, and the case for TSR.2 was therefore materially strengthened by the missile's cancellation in August 1962. By 1962, the TSR.2 was also seen as a likely replacement for the Valiants assigned to SACEUR. Plans for nuclear-weapons carriage by TSR.2 were changing; Red Beard had originally been envisaged, but the WE177 project for a lay-down bomb had now been approved, and TSR.2 would therefore be able to operate at low level all the way to its target, without worrying about pop-up delivery or LABS. Somewhat unenthusiastic consideration was also given to US Project E weapons for the TSR.2.[98]

By early 1963, however, TSR.2 was in serious trouble over cost escalation and delays. Research and development costs were now estimated at £175 millions – nearly twice the budget approved in 1960 – and CA release was now planned for the end of 1967, not 1965 as stated in the operational requirement. Doubtless at Mountbatten's prompting, Thorneycroft offered the view that the order for TSR.2 should be cut to 50 or 60, offset by procurement of an equivalent number of Buccaneers.[99] By June, research and development costs had risen once again, to around £200 millions, and six months later the total was £240 millions; production costs would add £2.8 millions per aircraft.[100] As TSR.2 approached its first flight on 27 September 1964, its political future – and therefore the RAF's continuing ability to meet its nuclear commitments to Britain's various alliances – looked distinctly questionable.

The Royal Navy's carriers continued unobtrusively to carry Red Beard nuclear weapons for possible use in either the North Atlantic, in support of NATO plans, or in the far east in support of SEATO. So, for example, in April 1962 HMS *Hermes* recommissioned after a six-month refit, and sailed to join *Centaur*, the USS *Enterprise* and *Forrestal* and the French *Clemenceau* for an Atlantic striking-fleet exercise. Her Scimitars and Sea Vixens were both, at this time, nuclear-capable. Towards the end of the year, *Hermes* departed for an east-of-Suez deployment, relieving *Ark Royal*. In the summer of 1963 *Victorious*, newly recommissioned after an extended refit of her own, took over east of Suez, carrying the first squadron of Buccaneers to enter service.[101] The Royal Navy's nuclear capability was therefore also maturing, and as planning got underway after 1959 for a new generation of carriers, nuclear weapons were naturally factored in. We have already seen that the carrier programme was politically controversial; the design process was also fraught, with problems around cost and weight. During 1962 and 1963, detailed ship-design work was reported to the Board of Admiralty. The new carrier was known as CVA-01, and the favoured design would carry 20 nuclear weapons, to be delivered by Buccaneers, an Ikara anti-submarine missile launcher and perhaps helicopters. Nuclear weapons for a new fighter aircraft, developed jointly in line with Air Ministry requirement OR.356, were also contemplated.[102] Drawing-office staff in particular were in short supply, and work on the carrier was affected by the demands of the Polaris programme. Meanwhile the many novel features of the design increased cost and risk, to the extent that the project manager for CVA-01 described cancellation in 1966 as 'the happiest day of my life'.[103]

In central Europe, Corporal, Honest John and eight-inch nuclear artillery remained in service and BAOR continued to exercise its nuclear capability. Exercise Spearpoint in 1961 – described as the largest manoeuvres so far of the nuclear era – controversially showed that BAOR would be 'incapable of defending itself even for a short time without nuclear support', indicating the army's 'entire and willing subjection to a completely nuclear philosophy in every circumstance short of the most trivial'.[104] Despite McNamara's enthusiasm for control, despite Zuckerman's belief that he was winning the Whitehall battle against the concept of a tactical nuclear battlefield, and despite Mottershead's concern to delimit carefully the circumstances in which nuclear weapons might be used in Europe, doctrine and training remained thoroughly nuclear. Another gulf, or at least time-lag, between illusion and reality can be discerned. When Whitehall decided to buy something, it took a long time to arrive; similarly, when Whitehall took against a nuclear concept, it took a long time to bring it to an end in practice. As one commentator put it, 'what was disturbing about Spearpoint was the clear implication that BAOR was rather less inhibited about the use of nuclear weapons than [even] current NATO doctrine envisaged'.[105]

WE177

By the end of 1961, 100 or more Red Beard kiloton bombs had been delivered, and the new Mk.2 version had recently been cleared for service. The weapon was well on the way to meeting the full stockpile requirement, apparently 110 for the RAF (plus 17 'spare' warheads for training and maintenance, without the fissile core) and 28 for the Royal Navy (again plus spares).[106] During 1962, most of the remaining weapons were delivered, and many Mk.1 warheads were upgraded to Mk.2 standard.[107] Preparations were nevertheless also already underway for the retirement and replacement of the weapon. Red Beard was expected to remain in service only for another three to five years, at which point fissile material from Red Beard, and indeed Red Snow, warheads would be recycled into newer weapons.[108]

The design of the Red Beard replacement, WE177, now proceeded a little more smoothly than during the fits and starts of 1960–61 described in Chapter 2. Lay-down and ballistic trials of bomb shapes took place at Porton in Wiltshire. The RAE-led feasibility study was complete by summer 1962, offering a number of possible ways forward. A bomb based on the RE179 (Skybolt) warhead could be developed, meeting the staff requirement in all major respects except weight; a bomb based on the RO106 (Tony) warhead, meanwhile, would meet the requirement in all major respects except yield. A new warhead would be needed to meet both the yield *and* weight requirements, for up to 300kt and down to 1000lb respectively, and this solution was recommended. The US Mk.57 could also be used in various ways, although it would not meet the yield requirement; RAE concluded that some US knowledge would be useful, but that the Mk.57 should not be adopted.[109]

As we have seen, the Cabinet Defence Committee approved, around the same time, the production of the weapon in a low-yield version only, reserving judgement on a high-yield version, and making no specific comment on the choice of warhead. For the first time, there was also confirmation 'that the warheads to be developed for the Royal Navy in replacement of Red Beard would be suitable for underwater detonation'.[110] However, disagreements on priority had resurfaced, because although the Air Ministry's focus was still on laydown for the TSR.2, the Admiralty was now talking about a new requirement for a simpler, lighter, 500lb version of the bomb suitable for anti-submarine use from small helicopters and the Ikara missile (see below).[111] This new interest is noteworthy: the Admiralty had been involved in correspondence on nuclear depth-bombs in previous years, but a firm requirement had not appeared, and indeed the Board had recently played down its interest in a (separate) nuclear depth-bomb project.[112] The Air Ministry, meanwhile, remained keen to preserve an option of using yields higher than the ministerial limit of 10kt, and so, when a new version of the OR.1176 requirement was circulated in November 1962, it was stated that:

> Lethality studies by the Admiralty show that the majority of naval tactical targets and submarines could be effectively attacked with weapons having a yield of between 0.5 and 10kt, provided that delivery accuracy is of the high order expected ... The tactical targets envisaged by Air Ministry include airfields, missile sites and general communications in the middle and far eastern theatres. Studies show that most of these targets could best be attacked with weapons in the 50 to 300kt range, allowing for degraded delivery accuracy in the face of defences or weather hazards ...
>
> The naval staff requires a warhead capsule for use in the nuclear bomb to GDA.15/OR.1177 capable of producing three yields of [0.5, 2 and 10]kt, by pre-flight selection. The air staff requires a similar

capsule with a production-set yield of [10]kt. If higher yields are authorised, warheads will be required with production-set yields of up to [300]kt.[113]

A bewildering number of WE177 delivery aircraft and fuzing options was by now specified: the bomb would be capable of delivery free-fall from high level by the Vulcan, Victor, Canberra and TSR.2; dive/toss from medium level by the TSR.2 and OR.356; LABS and laydown, from as low as 50ft, by the Canberra, Buccaneer, Sea Vixen, TSR.2 and OR.356; retarded after a 'pop-up climb from a low-level run-in' by unspecified aircraft; or finally as a depth-bomb by anti-submarine helicopters, Ikara and later OR.357. The bomb and warhead were both required in service in 1965.[114] As we have seen, Aldermaston was now convinced that a new Skybolt warhead primary, based on a device now tested in Nevada using the Super Octopus principle, would also be a suitable warhead for WE177. This was described at one working-level meeting as an 'enlarged Cleo'.[115] The final dimensions of the weapon had not been set. An exact diameter was not specified in late 1962, but length and rear fin diameter were both a matter for concern. Inevitably the services wanted the bomb to be as small and light as possible. Specifically, Ikara could take only a 100in long payload, and dual internal carriage in the TSR.2 implied a maximum rear fin diameter of 24in; the Air Ministry were desperate to avoid any specification changes to the aircraft weapons bay.

At the start of 1963, the debates around Skybolt cancellation and a looming deterrent gap, as we shall see, finally also resulted in the approval of work on a high-yield variant of WE177. Such a weapon, with a yield of 300–450kt, would impose additional research and development costs. At least three possible solutions were discussed at working level, including a substantially new weapon with a yield approaching that of Skybolt, which would delay the introduction of the low-yield WE177A.[116] The Treasury's grudging agreement was noted in February: 'you may take this letter as conveying Treasury authority to the development of the laydown bomb with alternate high and low yields with an estimated total cost of £12 millions'.[117]

The original low-yield weapon now became known as WE177A, although the high-yield WE177B was given higher priority, and would enter service sooner. An RAF requirement for 102 WE177A weapons had been approved, although this appears to have been reduced during 1963 to 84. The Air Ministry also now wished to carry WE177B on TSR.2 and the V-bombers, and an order for 53 of the high-yield bombs was approved.[118] There is some evidence that Aldermaston continued to toy with more than one idea for a high-yield WE177B warhead; different yields were discussed up to at least November 1963.[119] It seems likely that, until it became clear that Blue Steel could be introduced successfully into service, and modified for low-level delivery, the Air Ministry wished to have a warhead for WE177B yielding a full megaton.[120] It later had to settle for less. The Admiralty, meanwhile, was interested in WE177A only, for delivery by naval strike aircraft, helicopters and Ikara. It had stated a requirement for 63 weapons.[121] Dimensions were finally settled in July 1963, indicating continuing design uncertainty to at least this point. The low-yield WE177A would measure 112in long by 16.5in diameter (24.5in over the rear fins); the high-yield version would be 133in long, with the same diameter.[122]

A description of the final WE177 survives in a document produced by Zuckerman in 1965. The new weapon, designed to meet a joint Admiralty/Air Ministry requirement for service entry in 1966, would solve a number of Red Beard's problems: inadequate yield (of 15kt) for some targets; no lay-down mode; incompatibility with some high-performance aircraft; and some remaining safety limitations. WE177 would be used for tactical operations against point targets on land and at sea, in high-level, dive, LABS, lay-down and pop-up delivery modes, and for 'delivery as a nuclear depth charge from both helicopters and anti-submarine guided missiles'. The low-yield WE177A version, weighing 600lb, would have two pre-selected yields of 0.5 and 10kt, the latter being specified for anti-submarine use in shallow water (less than 350ft[123]) and in relatively close proximity to friendly forces. WE177B, with a yield of 450kt and weighting around 950lb, was meanwhile intended for RAF use against strategic targets.[124]

Other tactical nuclear weapons

The Admiralty was now beginning to see the SSN as vitally important to offensive and defensive operations at sea. SSNs were many times more capable than the slow conventional submarines, tied to the surface by their air-breathing main engines, that had nearly defeated Britain in two world wars. The first SSN, USS *Nautilus*, was able to outrun most torpedoes and to exercise with impunity underneath allied carrier groups. The US Navy introduced nuclear depth-bombs into service in the early 1950s, and later also quick-reaction nuclear anti-submarine missile weapons. RAF Coastal Command tried to interest the Air Ministry and Admiralty in a nuclear depth-bomb in 1956, and Air Ministry documents making a number of references to nuclear depth-bombs have survived from 1959 and early 1960.[125] There were several practical problems with nuclear depth-bombs, not least the safety implications for friendly forces and the effects of nuclear explosions on sonar conditions. A US nuclear test in 1962 was designed specifically to 'investigate blast effects on strategic hydroacoustical [i.e., sonar] systems', whose great importance to the cold war at sea was coming to be recognised.[126] Admiralty views on the subject are frustratingly difficult to find, but it seems clear that the Admiralty was now becoming interested in a nuclear depth-bomb capability.[127]

By the early 1960s, the performance of western passive sonars against Soviet submarines was improving to the point where other anti-submarine weapons, especially heavy submarine-launched torpedoes, began to look inadequate in range. The US Navy introduced a weapon known as ASROC which offered a longer range and could respond more quickly than a torpedo. ASROC was an unguided rocket fired from a surface ship, carrying a light-weight homing torpedo or nuclear depth-bomb towards a submarine contact. Ikara was an Australian project for a similar system, and the Admiralty expected to fit the weapon in the large Type 82 destroyers that would escort its cherished new generation of aircraft carriers. Launching a nuclear depth-bomb using Ikara would remove the need for a helicopter to be detached from other duties, and would be less hazardous to friendly forces. The light-weight Wasp helicopter, in particular, was thought to be at some risk from using a nuclear depth-bomb.[128] The Ikara launcher was expensively redesigned to allow nuclear operation: if a nuclear depth-bomb were the payload then Ikara would need to be launched on a much more precise bearing than if a homing torpedo were carried. In a sample tactical study, it was claimed that the 'kill probability' against a Soviet SSN rose from 0.3 using a Mk.44 homing torpedo to 0.75 using a nuclear depth-bomb.[129] Ultimately, however, the requirement to carry WE177A on Ikara was dropped in the later 1960s. The US Navy also at this time had a weapon known as SUBROC, which was fired from a submerged submarine, flew above the water for a time and then dived again to attack the target with a nuclear warhead. The Admiralty had rejected SUBROC, partly because there was no option to use a conventional warhead.[130]

For the Royal Navy, a dual-key Project E arrangement – occasionally referred to as Project N – was never a practical proposition, even for weapons designed exclusively for use in European waters. A warhead-custody detachment of US marines would not have been welcome aboard ship.[131] RAF Coastal Command, on the other hand, although interested in nuclear anti-submarine warfare, did not in the end pursue a requirement for WE177, deciding instead to modify its Shackleton maritime-patrol aircraft to carry US nuclear depth-bombs. This was discussed within the Air Ministry as early as October 1960, and was brought to ministerial attention in the spring of 1961.[132] In June 1962, however, the nuclear conversion of the Shackletons – agreed to by Macmillan only after 'considerable pressure from Washington' – had been delayed.[133] In November, shortly after the Cuban crisis, the US Navy was still urging greater efforts to achieve the capability.[134] Most sources suggest that US nuclear depth-bombs were not introduced until around 1965, with the arrival in service of the 'phase three' Shackleton.[135]

The nuclear version of the navy's Seaslug surface-to-air missile remained in development until June 1962, when the Board of Admiralty reluctantly accepted it as a financial saving.[136] Seaslug Mk.2 went to sea in 1965, in a non-nuclear version. Although the decision to cancel nuclear Seaslug needs to be seen in the context of the warhead review being considered by ministers at around the same time, it appears to have been taken independently. The Admiralty had previously been sceptical of the weapon's value. Cancellation further reduced the number of UK ten-kiloton warheads required, below the 334 mentioned in May 1962. It left the requirement for RO106/Tony resting only on Blue Water which, as we have seen, was soon cancelled in its turn.

A guided Blue Water round had been test-fired at the end of March 1962 and, from a technical perspective, development was proceeding fairly happily. As conceived in 1962, the weapon would have been carried on a three-ton Bedford lorry acting as a mobile erector-launcher. This in turn would have been carried by the planned AW681 transport aircraft to a rough airstrip in the forward battle area, then driven to the launch site. The launch crew would have stabilised and erected the missile, and aligned the guidance system manually by theodolite. The Blue Water launch computer, dealing with targeting, was in an accompanying Land Rover, and technical support was provided by mobile workshops in two more three-ton lorries. Blue Water had a twin-chambered motor with an eight-second boost phase at high thrust and a longer sustain phase at relatively low thrust, but it was not a staged missile; the boost motor did not fall away when spent. Also, unlike a strategic ballistic missile such as Blue Streak, Skybolt or Polaris, Blue Water had no separating warhead following a ballistic trajectory to the target; the missile would only reach 60,000ft and atmospheric re-entry was not a concern. Blue Water would remain in one piece and fully guided and controlled until impact or airburst, which at full range would be around three minutes after launch.[137]

The War Office continued until May 1962 to press for a high-yield warhead of at least 100kt for 46 of its Blue Waters, a requirement that was never accepted.[138]

When Blue Water itself was cancelled by Thorneycroft at the start of August – seemingly an entirely economically and politically motivated decision – RO106/Tony was suddenly not required at all. The warhead had been about to go into production, and scientists at Aldermaston were disappointed and frustrated.[139] Although the War Office continued to stress that its requirements for the European nuclear battlefield stood, including ADMs and a replacement for Corporal, it was forced to accept that, if procured at all, the warheads for these weapons would be supplied by the US under dual-key arrangements.[140] As we have seen, the Defence Committee had also decided in 1960 that ground forces outside Europe would not be equipped with British nuclear weapons, and the War Office was unable to challenge this decision seriously.[141] When Corporal was finally withdrawn in 1966, BAOR did not immediately get a replacement, although Honest John and eight-inch nuclear artillery remained in service.

In October 1961, Sir Steuart Mitchell asked Bill Penley, wartime radar pioneer and now Director of the Royal Radar Establishment at Malvern, to head a working party 'to consider and give their views on the potential merits of possible systems of ABM defence'. Penley's committee agreed essentially with the BNDSG technical sub-committee's down-beat report, quoted in Chapter 2. The difficulties of ABM defence had only increased. It was still 'generally accepted that if no decoys are present then the problem of intercepting and destroying an enemy warhead, at a sufficiently high altitude, is solvable with existing techniques, even against an incoming warhead small in size, travelling up to 24,000ft/sec'. However, 'with small weight penalty the ballistic missile designer can eject decoys which effectively resemble the warhead down to burst altitude making it well nigh impossible for the defence to pick out the dangerous object'. Although the Penley committee knew of no concrete evidence of Soviet experimental work on decoys, they knew that Soviet scientists were well aware of the possibility and now felt 'that any active defence system which is incapable of satisfactory use in a decoy environment is not a worthwhile project on military grounds'. Moreover, the Soviet 50-megaton test of 31 October 1961 had demonstrated the feasibility of very large missile warheads, raising the prospect of attacks against city targets with air-bursts at very high altitude, around 100,000ft. This would give the defence almost no time to react. A defensive missile might – if it found it – be able to destroy an incoming warhead. There was new interest in neutron and X-ray kill mechanisms, which might have long ranges at high altitude, although the committee concluded that 'the damaging effects of X-rays are insufficiently understood to allow us to consider them further here'. But 'an atomic warhead in the defensive missile is expensive and may lead to serious blackout effects on the defensive radar system, apart from any general damage at ground level if the burst is at low altitude'. BMEWS was also now felt to have a number of weaknesses. In certain circumstances it might give less than three minutes' warning, and could not be expected to detect submarine-launched missiles fired towards the UK from the west. An early-warning system like BMEWS was moreover designed only to give an indication that a mass attack was imminent, not to give precise information on the number of incoming missiles and their aiming-points. Meanwhile the problems of decoy discrimination and fire control were more or less insurmountable: 'Dozens of methods of discriminating have been proposed and most have been discarded because it is easy to see ways of combating them by minor changes in decoy construction or methods of ejection'.[142]

Roy Dommett recalls that the Penley committee's report, delivered in 1962, was decisive in ending serious British research into missile-defence systems. Work at Malvern on a discrimination radar, and at Bristol on an aerodynamic test vehicle, was cancelled.[143] The Penley report did, however, underline the importance of further basic research into re-entry phenomena, using Black Knight, and into X-ray phenomena and hardening, through the medium of JOWOGs set up under the bilateral atomic agreement. Black Knight re-entry experiments had begun in 1958 and Dazzle, a new programme starting in Australia in 1962, was sponsored by the TTCP sub-groups on infra-red and ABM. In later years this work was extended by the US, but a British follow-on programme, Crusade, was cancelled in around 1964.[144]

Alternative weapons

The cancellation of Skybolt did not simply result in the substitution of Polaris and an end to all other nuclear ambitions. As we have seen, political events left some in the British defence establishment wary of relying, in future, on American delivery systems. There also loomed a specific gap in the credibility of the British deterrent between 1965, when Skybolt had been expected to enter service, and 1968, when the first Polaris patrol was now envisaged. These factors drove a hurried search for home-grown alternatives to Polaris, focused on the Ministry of Aviation and its powerful suppliers in the aircraft manufacturing industry. Thorneycroft drafted a paper in early January 1963, originally intended for the full cabinet:

> I have been considering, in the light of the Nassau agreement on Polaris, what additional measures should now be taken to maintain the credibility of our nuclear deterrent. My main assumptions are that the credibility of the V-force equipped solely with Blue Steel and free-falling weapons and operating at high altitude as at present would diminish beyond 1965 ... [and] that the defence burden that we face is already so large that we must restrict expenditure on deterrence to the minimum level consistent with credibility ...
>
> Additional measures in the deterrent field could have one or more of the following objectives. Firstly there are those measures which will improve the capability and therefore the credibility of the V-force between 1965 and the time when we expect to have Polaris in service. Secondly, there are the measures which would take so long to implement that they would only become effective very near to or after the time when we expect to have Polaris and which are best considered as supplementing or diversifying the Polaris deterrent. Finally there are measures directed to re-insuring, within our own resources, against a failure to obtain Polaris from the Americans ...
>
> I do not believe that it would make sense either politically or financially for us to work on any other assumption than that the detailed negotiations with the Americans will give us a Polaris force and that this, with the TSR.2, will give us an adequate deterrent. Of course if further negotiation shows that this is not the case we should have to reconsider the whole matter.[145]

As we have seen, these ideas were not new. The TSR.2 was already widely held – at least by the Air Ministry and RAF – to have a secondary deterrent role, and the ministry at once assumed that in the Polaris era this would assume greater importance.[146] The plan for a high-yield lay-down weapon for TSR.2, only recently deferred by the Defence Committee, was immediately dusted off, and the DRPC atomic sub-committee recommended restarting work.[147]

By 15 January, Thorneycroft's ideas on filling the deterrent gap were ready for circulation to the Defence Committee. The idea of 'supplementing or diversifying' the Polaris deterrent, from the minister's earlier draft, was gone; the focus was on short-term measures. The reference to TSR.2

had also been toned down; the aircraft was just 'a useful back-up'. Thorneycroft made two recommendations. First, the V-force would go to low-level operation: 'Trials by Bomber Command and experience with the training of the Valiant squadrons assigned to SACEUR, have convinced the air staff that low-level attack by the V-bombers is practicable operationally'. Second:

> to enable the bomber force to operate at low level, high priority should be given to developing the lay-down bomb being designed for carriage by the TSR.2 and Buccaneer to carry a high-yield warhead (in addition to one of low yield) and using it to arm both the V-bomber and in due course the TSR.2 ... The number of weapons required must be studied further. For the moment, it has only been possible to make some arbitrary assumptions for the purpose of costing the associated warhead programme. The assumptions are as follows: (a) instead of the 90 warheads approved for Skybolt, there will be 90 high-yield warheads for lay-down bombs; (b) in addition, of 102 warheads for lay-down bombs already approved for the TSR.2, about half will now be provided in the high-yield version.

The front-line V-bomber force would still, however, be reduced by 1965, in line with current plans, from the existing strength of 120 aircraft (15 squadrons) to 88 (11 squadrons); and an airborne alert posture was not proposed. The cost of the various measures, including new navigational and possibly ECM equipment for the V-bombers, was estimated at £30 millions over a number of years, although Thorneycroft recognised some uncertainty over fissile material requirements. It seems the Air Ministry gained approval for just 53 high-yield lay-down weapons (WE177B), rather fewer than it required.[148]

On 23 January, the Defence Committee approved Thorneycroft's initial recommendations, and offered to consider further proposals for Blue Steel or other developments as necessary for the period up to 1967.[149] New possibilities were therefore now canvassed at working level. The Ministry of Aviation was already conscious of the possibility of a 'Pandora-like missile', a reference to the OR.1182 proposals of 1960–61, and of a possible deterrent version of Black Knight. It was even looking at the possibility of all-British equivalents to Skybolt or Polaris.[150] RAE produced a 'rush summary paper of possible deterrent development gap fillers' in early January, listing: the lay-down bomb; a stand-off bomb with a range of between 25 and 50 miles, related to Air Ministry requirement OR.1168 for a similar conventional weapon;

longer-range developments of Blue Steel; and Black Knight. The point was made that V-bombers at low level would be flying slowly enough to make them vulnerable to anti-aircraft guns, although 'the higher speeds of TSR.2 and Buccaneer would make these aircraft more or less invulnerable to this'.[151] Companies including Bristol, de Havilland, Avro, BAC and Hawker-Siddeley were offering a range of air-launched cruise and ballistic missiles, from the mundane to the exotic, as deterrent stop-gaps. BAC were interested in resurrecting the cancelled Blue Water for use in air-launched mode from the TSR.2. An air-launched Polaris was even suggested, or a WE177 mounted on the front of an unguided rocket.[152]

Many of these proposals looked rather sketchy or had obvious drawbacks, but some were more promising. The lay-down bomb did have the disadvantage that it required the carrier aircraft to overfly the target, where even TSR.2 or Buccaneer could be vulnerable to SA-3 city defences. A longer RAE paper was produced in February, suggesting the need for a stand-off weapon instead, light enough to carry on Buccaneer or at least TSR.2 but with enough range – between 25 and 60 miles – to avoid the need to penetrate the majority of city defences. Proposals from Bristol and BAC to re-use Bloodhound or Blue Water technology found some favour, although none of the industry proposals so far received quite met RAE's vision. Weapons with a range between 60 and 400 miles offered no particular advantage, because the launch aircraft would still have to enter Soviet airspace. Ballistic missiles with a greater range than this, meanwhile, were effectively Skybolts, and there could be little confidence in their development or the associated timescales.[153] The realisation that Blue Steel could after all be cheaply modified for low-level stand-off operation appears to have determined the outcome of these investigations. Although the Chief of the Air Staff attended an MoA presentation on the subject in March 1963,[154] none of the projects was pursued further. Attention focused instead on WE177B and gaining approval for the low-level modification to Blue Steel.[155]

Choice of Polaris missile

Ever since May 1957, Polaris had been seen in the US as an incremental programme, with an interim Polaris A missile of 1200nm range intended to enter service in 1963, then a 1500nm Polaris B in 1965. Following the launch of Sputnik and the publication of the Gaither report, the in-service date of the interim missile, now known as A-1, was brought forward, first to 1961 and later to November 1960, a deadline that was met successfully.[156] Although the A-1 schedule was of overriding importance to the programme, work continued on a longer-range version, now known as A-2. This would be better engineered and more reliable, and incorporate a new second stage, developed by the Hercules Powder Co., with new steerable nozzles for thrust control. On 6 May 1962, USS *Ethan Allen* successfully launched a Polaris A-1 with a live nuclear warhead towards Christmas Island. Codenamed Frigate Bird, this was the only test the United States ever conducted of any nuclear ballistic missile from launch to detonation. After a 1000-mile flight lasting 12.5 minutes, the warhead exploded at around 11,000ft altitude with a yield of 600kt.[157] Just a month later, Polaris A-2 became operational. Further incremental improvements to the FBM were already planned. Lockheed had been awarded a contract in November 1961, for example, to develop penetration aids for Polaris A-2 including decoys, chaff and jammers. These were flight-tested between July and December 1962, and entered production during 1963, although their deployment was ultimately limited.[158]

To penetrate Soviet ABM defences, SPO put its faith instead in the 2500nm-range Polaris A-3, work on which began in 1959. A-3 would deliver three warheads in a 'claw' configuration over the target, creating a megaton's worth of damage. A new RV was developed, weighing just 300lb with an integral 200kt Mk.58 warhead, and using a nylon-phenolic ablative heat shield in place of the beryllium heat-sink design of the A-1 and A-2 Polaris. The RVs would be ejected forcefully from the missile, removing the need for the troublesome second-stage thrust-termination system. Penetration aids for A-3 were developed, including decoys and chaff but not jammers, and test-flown in 1963 and 1964, although they were never deployed.[159] Significant advances in weight-saving, propellants and guidance were also made. Polaris A-3 was 32ft four inches long by 54 inches in diameter, weighed 35,700lb, and was able to carry its warheads to a range of over 2000nm, where accuracy of half a mile circular error probable was expected. According to Chuck Hansen, the cone/cylinder/flare-shaped RV was 54 inches long, 12 inches in diameter at the head, and twice as wide at the flare.[160] Polaris A-3 was deployed at sea by the US Navy from September 1964.

Admiral Mike Le Fanu, responsible as Controller for all Admiralty procurement activity, was present at Nassau and recorded his rather breathless thoughts after a private discussion with McNamara: 'We are now "in" Polaris in a big way. We are in the big time'. Le Fanu had already made some study of the organisation of SPO in the US and the likely equivalent arrangements necessary in the UK, and advised in particular against MoA involvement: 'The Ministry of Aviation will have to be kept firmly in their place ... the United States Navy would neither understand nor relish working with the ministry'. Because Nassau had been 'a high level political meeting ... there was no member of the United States Navy present; therefore we did not get on to questions such as whether or no [sic] we had the A-2 or A-3 missile'.[161] This, as we have seen, was one of the questions the Zuckerman mission was sent to discuss in January 1963.

Even the A-2 missile had only recently become operational, and A-3 was completely unproven; test flights had only begun in August 1962. Zuckerman found, however, that the A-3 was likely to be the only version in production by 1967, when British missiles would be needed. This would make its adoption much more cost-effective for the UK than reopening a production line for the A-2. A-3 also offered considerably greater range and therefore sea-room for the launching submarine, an important operational consideration. It was not immediately obvious, however, how to fit a British warhead to the A-3. A-2 could accommodate the British Skybolt warhead. If this warhead were to be incorporated into the A-3, however, 'considerable redesign and flight testing' would be needed. A whole new warhead, compatible with the US RV, might be just as viable. Amongst other comments there was also, even at this early date, British speculation on the penetration capabilities of Polaris. 'Due to binding space limitation within the A-3 missile', Zuckerman reported, 'the amount of penetration capability that can be built into any of these systems is severely limited. The effectiveness of these systems ... needs careful study in the light of likely deployments of USSR anti-ballistic missile defence'.[162] Zuckerman seems not to have been especially keen on A-3, because research and development on the missile was still required: 'we do not want to run into another Skybolt disaster'.[163] Moreover, three times as many warheads would be needed for Polaris A-3 than for the equivalent number of A-2 missiles, and this had significant implications for fissile material.

The MoA, meanwhile, had picked up on the possibility of a wholly new warhead and RV, and produced a list of four suggestions, in ascending order of cost and complexity: first, a new British warhead to fit exactly the A-3 RV, for which an underground nuclear test would be necessary; second, a new British warhead to fit the space available on the missile, requiring flight tests if the RV shape were affected, but not necessarily a nuclear test; third, the adaptation of the Polaris nose structure and separation mechanisms to accept a proven US RV, for example that used on Minuteman, but carrying a single British warhead, presumably of the Skybolt type; and finally a completely new RV with an existing British 450kt warhead design, which would need flight testing but not nuclear testing, and which could have a small radar cross-section and carry a suite of decoys.[164] This was an impressive list of options, produced in a short time.

As we have seen, James Mackay noted in his report on the Polaris sales agreement talks a refusal to talk about penetration aids. Indeed, a confidential annexe to the agreement later formally excluded these from the sale. A second mission was in the United States at the same time as Mackay's, looking specifically at the choice between A-2 and A-3. This was led by the MoA's Director-General of Atomic Weapons (DGAW). A-2's disadvantages were still clear: range was short, and production lines were due to close at the end of the year. 'The heavy cost of reinstatement of production facilities would fall on the UK' if A-2 were chosen. On the other hand, A-3 was having problems. Eight of the ten tests so far had been less than fully successful, with RV separation a particular issue. DGAW reported that penetration was 'of great importance', but that 'strict US orders prevented any discussion of the matter'. Unfortunately, the abandonment of thrust-termination in favour of RV ejection left the missile front-end very sensitive to even the tiniest changes in weight distribution, such as might result from the (secret) US work on penetration aids. DGAW concluded that 'the design [of A-3] presses harder on present limits of technology than any other US missile', but still came down in its favour.[165] Mackay, back in the UK, meanwhile reported 'a noticeable reluctance to disclose information about American plans for the A-3 warhead'.[166]

American coyness about penetration aids was to become rather important in later years when the Polaris improvement programme, later Chevaline, was conceived. It is not at all clear where the reluctance had come from. There was probably a good deal to say, given that penetration aids for Polaris A-2 had already been flight-tested and an equivalent programme for A-3 was underway. Perhaps the Americans feared delay to their own programme or the need for modifications to comply with British requirements. Perhaps there was a genuine additional security issue, for the vulnerability (if any) of US systems to ABM defence was exceptionally sensitive. The British seem not to have been involved during this period in discussions with the US on MIRV, which was beginning to be considered by a number of American teams.[167] Perhaps, even, US opponents of British independent deterrence had regrouped and were now seeking to limit the scope of the Nassau agreement. I have found almost no speculation on the subject in the copious British documents of the period, except one marginal note 'USN hold-up?'[168] Carrington, the First Lord, was disinclined to make too much fuss about this; as he wrote to Thorneycroft, 'it will be noted from the confidential minute that penetration aids are excluded from the scope of the agreement. At present we simply do not have the knowledge to assess how far this would impair the value of the missile to us or how it would affect problems of design and proving of the 'front-end'. But I understand that given only partial knowledge of these devices, which we might hope to get after the agreement is signed, we might well be able to help ourselves out of the difficulty. I consider we should not therefore challenge this exclusion at this stage'.[169] Thorneycroft, writing to the Prime Minister, concurred.[170] Penetration aids remained a background issue, however, and so for example Zuckerman sent a paper on the subject to Thorneycroft on 9 April 1964, in response to which the minister minuted 'study authorised limited to [£]50,000 and an attempt should be made to lift US security'.[171] This was presumably the origin of HR169, a little-known research project at Farnborough during 1964 which prefigured some of the later Chevaline work.[172]

Meanwhile, at the end of May 1963, Carrington endorsed the earlier recommendation of Polaris A-3.[173] Assurances had been received on navy-to-navy channels that, if necessary, information on changes to weights and balances as a result of US work on penetration aids *would* be passed to the UK.[174] Following all these discussions, a clear choice of the A-3 missile was made on 10 June, probably by Thorneycroft in consultation with the Prime Minister.[175]

Polaris system and facilities

British base facilities and carriers for Skybolt had already been available, but for Polaris they had to be created from scratch. The earliest American Polaris submarines of the *George Washington* class, displacing around 6700 tons submerged, were significantly larger than any existing British submarine, and later US 'bomber' submarines were still larger. At first, British studies of Polaris, before and after Nassau, made no particular assumption on how closely to follow the US submarine design. 'Hybrid' hunter-killer/Polaris submarines were studied, offering some capability for limited war and causing less disruption to the navy's SSN building programme. In January 1963, the Defence Committee was presented with a choice between building four or five 16-missile submarines on the American pattern, or a larger number of hybrid submarines, perhaps seven, carrying just eight missiles each.[176] The prospect of more submarines was an annoyance to the Air Ministry, and Fraser and Pike were told 'you cannot afford to be squeamish about attacking the cost of the proposals'.[177] In the event, the Defence Committee rejected the hybrid submarine, largely on American advice. The 16-missile submarine would be easier and quicker to build, taking advantage of American experience, whereas an eight-missile fit would need expensive modifications to the weapons system. The operation of a hybrid would also be complicated if its missiles were assigned in normal circumstances, under the Nassau agreement, to NATO. The committee agreed to build four 16-missile submarines, deferring a decision on a fifth.[178] In March, arrangements for the construction of the submarines were announced. Vickers at Barrow-in-Furness would act as lead shipyard, but Cammell Laird at Birkenhead would also be involved. Shipyard facilities had to be expanded, and indeed Vickers took on over 1000 new workers between 1964 and 1967. The Walney Channel, between the shipyard at Barrow and the open sea, had also to be extensively dredged.[179] The submarines were, by some distance, the largest yet built in the UK. Their design was essentially that of the second British SSN, HMS *Valiant*, with a slightly smaller pressure-hull diameter but with a large missile section inserted, adding over 100ft in length.[180] The keel of the first submarine, HMS *Resolution*, was laid in February 1964, and by the end of the year work on another boat, HMS *Renown*, was underway at Birkenhead. Also in February 1964, the cabinet decided that a fifth boat would be built, on the basis that this would make it easier to keep two boats on station. When the new Labour government eventually decided, the following year, to cancel the fifth boat, pressure was put on the refit cycles of the Polaris fleet, but it usually remained possible to have two boats at sea, or three in a crisis.

By the end of March 1963, the choice of a base at Faslane, on the Gareloch, close to the American facility at Holy Loch, had been made. The key consideration was ready access to deep water; other sites at Devonport, Rosyth, Loch Alsh, Invergordon and Falmouth were rejected on various grounds. Submarines were already based at Faslane, but

> a new jetty, with an extensive range of services (including, as a later modification, a heading check test facility for the submarine's navigation subsystem) had to be built; a range of workshops and test bays; emergency power sources; a separate module repair facility for weapon system parts; a calibration laboratory; sleeping, eating, recreational and administrative accommodation; security installations; computer installations; playing fields, and so on – the variety of components to the base was, as [Capt Bomford, the Polaris logistics officer]

reported to one progress meeting, 'as nearly infinite as I can bear to contemplate'.[181]

Missiles and warheads would be stored and serviced at the nearby Coulport armament depot. As accounts of the Polaris programme make clear, the nuclear-weapons business was still a huge national undertaking for the United Kingdom, and we are reminded once again just what practical ramifications there could be when decisions were taken in the rarefied atmosphere of Whitehall, or in this case the Bahamas. A large new Polaris executive organisation, akin to SPO in the US and reporting directly to the Controller of the Navy, was created to manage the programme under Rear-Admiral (later Vice-Admiral Sir) Hugh Mackenzie.

The operation of the Polaris system, and some of its notable support requirements, can be understood from the perspective of the submarine's deterrent patrol. The patrol lasted two months or more, and the submarine's purpose was to remain undetected, to remain in communications with its base, and to remain at 15 minutes' readiness to fire. The submarine could tell whether communications had been received, because the schedule was regular and the messages numbered; communications transmit and receive logs were also compared in port after the patrol. The Admiralty kept in touch with Royal Navy submarines through the very low frequency (VLF) broadcast, using a large transmitter at Rugby in Northamptonshire, and a slightly lower-powered back-up at Criggion in north Wales. VLF could be received by the submarine at 3000nm range from Rugby – i.e., across most of the North Atlantic and Mediterranean – using a buoyant trailing aerial about 20ft below the surface. The submarine itself could stay deep. Given the importance of VLF to nuclear submarine operations, it was decided in the 1960s to rebuild the Rugby transmitter using more modern and powerful equipment, the works being completed by Post Office engineers.[182] Criggion also got new transmission and antenna equipment, completed in time for the early Royal Navy Polaris patrols.[183] Further backups to Rugby and Criggion were possible: NATO facilities were under construction at Anthorn in Cumberland, and at Sainte-Assise near Paris.[184]

To remain at 15 minutes' readiness to fire was more of a challenge, chiefly because of the difficulty of navigating a more or less permanently submerged submarine. Dead-reckoning with the US-supplied ship's inertial navigation system (SINS) was supplemented, in American use, by three back-up systems. The first two were radio-based. Loran-C, a US long-range low-frequency navigation system, remains in operation today, using the same basic triangulation concepts as Bomber Command's wartime Gee system. Britain's shorter-range Decca system was a commercial competitor to Loran-C, and this made the British government disinclined to host a Loran-C station in the UK.[185] Loran-C coverage was available, however, by the early 1960s across the Mediterranean and North Atlantic, and this effectively delimited the patrol areas used by the US Navy's first Polaris boats. Meanwhile a whole new satellite-based navigation system was 'conceived in the early 1960s to support the precise navigation requirements of the navy's fleet ballistic missile submarines', and funded by the Polaris SPO. This system, known as Transit, became operational in 1964 when, thanks partly to extensive research work on a new gravitational model of the earth, accuracy greater than 0.1nm could be claimed. At this point, errors in estimation of submarine speed, and those due to RV separation events, came to dominate missile accuracy.[186] The submarine needed to come to periscope depth to receive Loran-C, and break the surface with an antenna to receive signals from the Transit satellites. It is remarkable how much money the Americans poured into these support systems; Transit was also a milestone in satellite navigation and an important precursor to today's GPS.

HMS *Resolution's* first commanding officer, Commander Michael Henry, has written, however, that on her first patrol Loran-C was off air and that 'satellite navigation came later', so *Resolution* relied for updates to her SINS equipment on the third back-up system, bottom contouring.[187] It is not widely appreciated that, for all their intended stealth of operation, Polaris submarines used *active* sonar for navigation, parts of the ocean bottom in the patrol areas having been surveyed in enough detail to reveal suitable navigational features. The American BQN-4 sonar used for bottom contouring used very low power and highly directional signals. To provide accurate charts for bottom-contour navigation, the Royal Navy invested in three new survey ships, the *Hecla* class, to survey large parts of the North Atlantic for nuclear submarine operation. These ships entered service in 1965 and 1966.

To launch her missiles, the submarine had to hover accurately at low speed. This was no mean feat, and required a special system to keep the boat steady in the water. Any water speed over the missile hatch above three knots would damage the missile on ejection; much less speed than this, however, and the submarine would be impossible to control. One document suggested that launch was possible in sea states of up to seven – which is defined as a fresh gale with wind speeds of up to 40 knots, waves of up to 58ft crest to trough, and large amounts of spray in the air affecting visibility. Another source has said that launch was something of an art, that the crew could 'catch the hover' when roll was at a minimum, but that sea state six was a practical limit: 'there would have been periods when sea and weather conditions would have reduced the chance of a successful launch of all 16 missiles'. At launch depth, around 100ft, the submarine's motion would have been relatively subdued, even in such rough weather; weather studies and post-patrol analysis tended to show that crews underestimated the severity of surface and atmospheric conditions.[188]

Dummy targets were dialled into Polaris missiles whilst alongside at Holy Loch (or later, in service with the Royal Navy, at Faslane). When the patrol began, operational targets from the SIOP would be dialled in to the fire-control system by hand. New targets, including targets of opportunity, could apparently also be signalled to the boat at any point during the patrol, and their latitude and longitude entered manually. The fire-control computer would then read in details for each target from a magnetic tape and, based on constant electronic input from navigational systems, would keep a current firing solution in memory. Early Polaris A-1 submarines required a library of punched paper cards, holding computerised firing solutions for arbitrary grid points in the patrol area, to help the fire-control system in its finer calculations, but by the time the Royal Navy's Polaris boats entered service these cards were no longer required. With a firing solution in memory, the submarine could be at 'station quarters two' (2SQ, or 15 minutes' readiness).

Missiles could be fired one by one, or in a preset ripple. The order of firing was important: as part of the SIOP, everything would be in a specific time window and each bomb and missile would have been carefully deconflicted from all others. On receipt of the fire order, the boat would have taken all 16 missiles through a series of range and bearing calculations and the guidance system in each would have been initialised with the local vertical and bearing to target, thereby bringing the missiles to one or two minutes' readiness. Then, two missiles at a time, internal batteries would have been fired up and a series of finer guidance calculations performed, including a complex process of refining vertical by means of a beam of light, passed from the submarine to the guidance system of each missile through a window in the launch tube and missile body, and reflected by a heavy trolley traversing rapidly fore and aft between launch tubes in the upper level of the missile compartment. The missile would then be deemed 'assigned' to target and the warhead fuzing and arming sequence would begin. In line with a two-man rule, the submarine's captain (or in his absence his executive officer) and Polaris systems officer (or weapons engineering officer) would manually have fired each missile, having already, at various stages, cross-checked each other's authentication of the firing order and target information. The missile would have been ejected from the launch tube, the first-stage motor firing more or less as it surfaced, depending on depth. The second stage would separate about a minute later, the nose fairing would be ejected after another 20 seconds, and RV ejection, laterally and forwards, would be at around 145 seconds or 80 miles, depending on range to target. The RVs would have proceeded ballistically to impact or air-burst.[189]

British officials were well aware, from an early date, of the operational weaknesses of Polaris, including its reliance on a very few vulnerable shore communications facilities, its need to risk detection by updating its inertial navigation systems as often as three times a day, and limitations on patrol areas due to the characteristics of the ocean floor.[190] The Air Ministry, for whatever reason, failed to make these weaknesses the basis of a concerted attack on the credibility and effectiveness of the system.

Polaris warheads and Aldermaston

Following the definitive choice of the A-3 missile, a UK/US joint re-entry systems working group (JRSWG) was set up to discuss the fine details of warhead and RV, meeting for the first time in June 1963 and again in September.[191] The UK members of JRSWG reported in December 1963, having assessed various options for warheads and RVs and soliciting a choice early in the new year. Modifications to the Polaris A-3 re-entry system were underway in the US to incorporate penetration aids – in fact, as we have seen, these were not deployed – but JRSWG had been told this would *not* affect the interface between the missile and a UK warhead. The choice of warhead lay between a close copy of the US Mk.58 warhead and 'a modified version which would match the ballistic characteristics of the Mk.58, but would have a different firing set and safing mechanism. Such a warhead would be of the same basic type as others already under development and might have production and/or safety advantages'.[192] British scientists and engineers had also considered various British RV schemes, building on the MoA's January 1963 suggestions, including a completely new UK conical RV design with a reduced radar echo, on which the US members of JRSWG had not felt able to comment.

The Admiralty, and later the Navy Department of the MoD, was keen in all discussions relating to Polaris to minimise differences with the US system for simplicity and speed, and ideas of improved RVs will not have impressed naval audiences at all. The dominant assumption in

Whitehall during 1963, heavily influenced by these considerations, was that the British Polaris warhead would be a 'copy' of the US Mk.58,[193] and this assumption underlay the confidence with which the need for future testing of the warhead was dismissed. At some point, however, it became clear that Aldermaston was in fact unable to 'copy' the US Mk.58 warhead without introducing new manufacturing techniques and equipment. During the spring of 1964 a British warhead was therefore chosen – perhaps at the 26 March meeting of the MoD Weapons Development Committee, a successor to the DRPC.[194] Zuckerman wrote to Home in the following terms:

> We have no plans, as yet, for penetration aids because it is difficult to make out a plain case that such aids are necessary ... The US warhead was successfully tested in 1962. The UK had a choice of either copying the US design as closely as possible or of modifying it by substitution of a UK designed primary to be in closer accord with UK practices. The secondary will be the same in both cases. The UK primary is similar to, but smaller than, that used in the British lay-down weapon at present under development. The smaller size requires the introduction of 'mechanical safeing' which has been under development at AWRE for several years, in anticipation of the need in small primaries, and high reliability has been demonstrated ... Arrangements have been made with the Americans to ensure complete compatibility of the British warhead with the American A-3 missile.[195]

By June 1964, plans were being discussed to test this British Polaris warhead in Nevada. The test was justified to Whitehall readers as a 'Polaris economy test', and reference made to the possibility of saving a substantial amount of plutonium,[196] although its true intention may simply have been to test the functioning of the warhead. Held on 25 September 1964, the test was unsuccessful because of problems with US-made neutron-injection equipment.[197] When it was repeated a year later, however, the result was satisfactory.

The replacement of Skybolt with Polaris, and the need at the same time to consider interim arrangements for the likely deterrent gap of 1965–68, called into question the decisions of summer 1962 to run down Capenhurst and Aldermaston. Zuckerman was briefed in January 1963 that the highly enriched uranium situation had become 'very complex'. The type and number of Polaris warheads was unknown, a high-yield lay-down bomb would now be required, and the timetable for the withdrawal of Red Snow warheads from the stockpile was uncertain. On the assumption that five submarines were required with single-warhead Polaris A-2 missiles, and 'provided that we [later] cannibalise our Red Snows and all but 50 of the high-yield lay-down bombs', existing stocks and the barter arrangement with the US would just suffice.[198] Some recovery of fissile material from Red Beards, and some delay to the low-yield lay-down bomb, might also be necessary. And if Polaris A-3 were acquired, three times as many warheads would be needed – in the worst case, 252.[199] Not only this, but each individual Polaris A-3 warhead would require more fissile material than the equivalent Skybolt warhead.[200] In July 1963 the NRDC decided, in line with the new requirements now arising, to order an additional 120kg of UK-produced weapons-grade plutonium in 1964–65.[201]

As early as January 1963, concern was expressed that the new requirements for a Polaris warhead and a high-yield version of WE177 might 'overload' Aldermaston.[202] The Defence Committee was therefore told that recent developments 'would delay somewhat the rundown that would otherwise take place at Aldermaston',[203] although this implication of the Nassau agreement has attracted little attention. One is struck again by the weak and indirect linkage between policy formation and implementation. Could the run-down of Aldermaston, and indeed Capenhurst, really be glossed over so easily at ministerial level? By the start of the following year, the Chief Secretary to the Treasury, now John Boyd-Carpenter, had also noticed the effect the new programme for warheads and research tests was having at AWRE. In 1962, he pointed out, it had been thought 'there might be a substantial rundown' at the establishment; he wondered now whether and how this decision had been reversed, consciously or unconsciously.[204] Penney reported in December 1964 that the number of staff employed at Aldermaston on weapons work had reduced by 20 per cent since 1962, although this may have been a slight exaggeration, and a reduction to 4800 staff was no longer envisaged.[205]

Some myths about the British nuclear-weapons programme in these years can be laid to rest. It is clear, for example, that atomic insiders were not driving British nuclear-weapons development with a mad arms-race logic; Zuckerman's perceptions, in this regard, were too heavily influenced by his American friends. It is clear, too, that British scientists were making an independent contribution in warhead design, and not simply copying US drawings. Norris, Burrows and Fieldhouse suggest, for example, that WE177 used a copy of the US Mk.57 or Mk.61 warhead, and UK Polaris a copy of the Mk.58.[206] Although AWRE certainly had information on at least the Mk.57 and Mk.58, it is clear from the documentary evidence now available that the primaries for these warheads were British designs. The assumption that the absence of a long series of British tests is conclusive evidence for the adoption of US designs is wrong; British scientists were able to extrapolate from previous tested designs and used full-scale testing more frugally.

Britain's attempt to keep pace with the leaders in the arms race had seemed, to politicians and the public, to be at an end when Blue Streak was cancelled. Two years later, service requirements for nuclear weapons were thinned out significantly and even the most enthusiastic officers in the requirements branches of the service ministries had been made to see that a baroque arsenal, from sub-kiloton battlefield weapons to megaton ABM warheads, was, for Britain, unattainable. Solly Zuckerman, for one, took considerable satisfaction from this new state of affairs. His likeminded American friends may have aspired, as he did, to curb the wilder excesses of the arms race, but they had less success at home. Britain did not, however, turn from the bomb in these years. On the contrary: British nuclear forces became increasingly capable, both in pure numerical terms and in performance, training and exercising. By the end of our period, Aldermaston was evidently once again very busy.

Conclusions

The story of Britain's nuclear-weapons programme is a complex one, and a great deal happened during the six years covered in this study. Some distillation is required before we can address, for example, the motivations behind Britain's massive effort to achieve and maintain a credible nuclear capability. Several essentially political issues were central to the story: the long quest for a measure of nuclear test limitation; concern over American bases in the UK, reaching a peak during the Holy Loch negotiations; and the twin cancellation crises of Blue Streak in 1960, and Skybolt in 1962. Each of these issues made the achievement of a credible nuclear capability more difficult, and each was solved with American help. The test moratorium of 1958–61, for example, made it impossible in the short term fully to engineer, for weapons use, the advanced British nuclear warhead designs of the Grapple-Z series. British scientists had mastered tritium boosting and the two-stage H-bomb using radiation implosion, but without testing they could take that theoretical knowledge only so far. President Eisenhower was sympathetic enough to modify the US Atomic Energy Act and authorise the July 1958 bilateral agreement to allow Britain to use engineered US warhead designs. American atomic scientists were meanwhile interested and impressed enough by British progress to forge a productive relationship with Aldermaston over the following several years. During 1958, Britain's deliverable nuclear arsenal increased from around 50 to over 150 warheads. This increase came not as a result of the bilateral, but because of other Anglo-American agreements – reached before the launch of Sputnik – to make American nuclear weapons available to the RAF and later the army. At this stage, a final total of up to 1500 British nuclear weapons was envisaged. Concern over the use of American bases in the UK was met by the US, to the extent politically possible, by the Murphy-Dean agreement, later reconfirmed and extended to the Polaris force operating out of Holy Loch. The US made the use of its nuclear forces based in the UK a matter for 'joint decision'. Finally, and importantly, Blue Streak was replaced by Skybolt, and Skybolt by Polaris – although the latter deal in particular came at some political cost to both the US and UK.

Britain's nuclear policy had essentially been successful. A British strategic nuclear force and a ban on atmospheric nuclear testing, for example, were undeniably in place, in line with the wishes of the majority of the British electorate. Two of the Prime Minister's three key defence objectives – a close Anglo-American relationship, and defence reorganisation to reduce the power of the single services – were also achieved. Reorganisation was extremely important in the struggle to curtail individual defence projects, including nuclear projects. Broader defence economies, on the other hand, were harder to find, at least partly because Macmillan found the necessary hard political choices unpalatable. It was Wilson's government which, in the devaluation crisis of 1967, would finally be forced to accept withdrawal from bases east of Suez. Zuckerman and others were able, however, to attack many nuclear procurements on strategic and cost grounds. During 1962, ministers made important decisions to cancel Blue Water and make deep cuts in the nuclear warhead programme. In time, these decisions resulted in a minimum-deterrent posture at the strategic level, permanent reliance on the US for battlefield nuclear weapons, and – when it became clear that the British would not be working on a full range of nuclear warhead projects in future – a certain loss of American enthusiasm for cooperation with Aldermaston. Great efforts would be made in the 1970s to recover this situation. For the time being, however, despite a reduction in staff, Aldermaston had a great deal of work to do on the warheads for Polaris and two variants of WE177.

Unfortunately for Macmillan, because the Americans had readily and repeatedly come to his aid in nuclear matters, he came to be seen as more and more heavily dependent on their goodwill. With growing confidence, notably during the 1964 election campaign, the Labour opposition criticised this dependence. The rhetoric of Duncan Sandys was also softened in the early 1960s. It became clear, during long and difficult discussions of NATO nuclear defence policy, that the policy of massive retaliation could not be sustained intellectually or practically. In 1961, Mottershead and others made some progress towards an intellectually coherent policy for the central front, but many observers felt any plans for the use of nuclear weapons were worse than useless in the context of the defence of West Germany. Zuckerman in particular began a long campaign against tactical nuclear weapons, although as we have seen BAOR exercised and remained practically committed to a strongly nuclear posture for many years longer than he would have wanted. Long discussions of the MLF, which appeared by turns a nonsense or a further concession to the dominant US, failed to reassure critics of government defence policy. Continued investment in conventional forces was required – a point made forcefully in Whitehall by Mountbatten and his army counterparts, and indeed more widely by civilian strategists. Macmillan had broadly achieved what he set out to do in defence, but perceptions of this success were, at best, mixed.

Paradoxically, although Conservative nuclear policy came to be seen as weaker and less coherent, these were the years in which Britain's investment in creating a meaningful nuclear capability began to yield a practical dividend. Navies, armies and air forces can only truly do the things they are equipped, trained and exercised to do. At the time of the Sandys white paper in 1957, or the drafting of the army's doctrine for the nuclear battlefield in 1958, few nuclear weapons were available and little nuclear training and exercising was in place. Aldermaston knew the science, but Britain's real operational nuclear capability was somewhat illusory. By 1964, however, BAOR had a full range of integrated tactical nuclear weapons – Corporal, Honest John and eight-inch artillery, all with American warheads under dual-key control – and had based its exercising for several years on the early use of these weapons. The V-bomber force was at full strength and training hard to penetrate the USSR at low level. Now with modern weapons and ECM, it probably stood a good chance of success. The Royal Navy had embarked nuclear weapons on board ship, cleared for use by a range of aircraft. British nuclear weapons were stored in Cyprus and Singapore. Although external commentators assumed – and some continue to assume – that Aldermaston had become little more than an American outpost, there is concrete evidence that new research and design work was underway, and that the anglicisation of American designs was no mean feat in itself. Problems with the engineering reliability and operational flexibility of early British nuclear weapons were being overcome, and Aldermaston's knowledge was still increasing. By the end of 1964, Britain's nuclear capability was mature – in the real and meaningful sense that the armed forces had available precisely the number of nuclear weapons deemed necessary by the government. 1964 was the first year since 1953 in which no new nuclear weapon was delivered to the British armed forces. Britain's nuclear stockpile had reached a plateau. This pause in the arms race had nothing to do with the election of a new Labour government, with an ambivalent attitude to nuclear weapons; it had been planned since 1962.

Britain and the United States

As Macmillan made clear to the Defence Committee in 1958, and as the Future Policy Committee reiterated in 1960, the most important overt political motivation for the British nuclear-weapons programme was to impress the Americans. Macmillan clearly felt that making a substantial contribution to the western deterrent increased his influence with Eisenhower. The Air Ministry and RAF also felt it won friends in SAC and the Pentagon. Were they correct? It is too easy to assume, reading Whitehall documents and looking from the British end of the telescope, that the Americans took care at all times to think of their allies. It is absolutely clear that domestic concerns in Washington, and not just crude realist international politics, set American nuclear policy affecting the UK, for example over nuclear testing and the Skybolt cancellation. Britain's interests were essentially peripheral to those of a number of powerful groups within the US. It is interesting, for example, that the relationship between Mountbatten and Arleigh Burke, which has been highlighted by a number of British writers, is hardly mentioned by Burke's American biographers.[1] US policy-makers also understood perfectly well that Britain was no longer the great power of the past. Nevertheless, it is hard to argue that Eisenhower, or for that matter LeMay or Power, felt that Britain's nuclear weapons were entirely negligible, politically or militarily. SACEUR also seems to have valued the British increment to his nuclear striking power. In this sense, at least, nuclear weapons were important to the overall Anglo-American relationship. There is little evidence, however, that Britain's standing in American eyes – or its value to the western alliance – lay *solely* in its possession of nuclear weapons. This is what made Macmillan's defence budgeting dilemma so difficult. In 1962, for example, the Americans made perfectly clear they valued the contribution Britain was able to make in NATO and east of Suez. Britain's whole defence posture – not simply its nuclear capability – was the basis of its international importance and value to the US. There were over 60,000 British soldiers and airmen in Germany, and over 75,000 east of Suez.[2]

Another vexed question of Anglo-American relations is that of British nuclear independence – or the lack of it. At the end of 1958, more American than British weapons were available to the V-bombers, and the Project E agreement gave Eisenhower a measure of physical control over their use. Indeed, by the end of 1960, the British armed forces had three times as many American nuclear weapons, under dual-custody arrangements, as British-made equivalents. Four years later, on the other hand, Britain's strategic nuclear deterrent was – in strictly physical terms – more independent. Every strategic nuclear weapon in service was now a British-made Blue Steel or Yellow Sun Mk.2. The Red Snow warheads in these weapons were certainly based on an American design – incidentally better engineered for reliability and flexibility of use than anything the British had produced alone – but this on its own gave the Americans no veto over the operational use of the weapons.

Britain's *political* freedom of action in nuclear matters – already limited in the mid-1950s, as the Suez crisis had shown – was somewhat further reduced between 1958 and 1964. Macmillan had exercised some influence over both Eisenhower and Kennedy in arms control policy. Home, and later Wilson, were in a different position, and Cuba marked the beginning of a purely bilateral superpower dialogue in such matters. The 1958 atomic agreement, and later the sale of Polaris, meanwhile made it difficult or impossible for Britain to pursue its own initiatives in nuclear diplomacy with Australia or France. The Kennedy administration pursued policies designed purposely to extend American influence over Britain's nuclear forces. In the 1950s, Britain had pretended to an independent relationship with the USSR and an independent (and stridently nuclear) strategy. It had waged bloody post-imperial wars in Africa and Malaya, exercised a not entirely benign influence in the middle east, and been a potential nuclear proliferator. As time went by, this rogue behaviour was brought under greater control, and Britain became – in American eyes – a more responsible member of the international and European communities.

The Americans also, however, found themselves with somewhat reduced freedom of action. The Anglo-American relationship could not be described as *interdependent* by the dictionary definition; the US did not *depend* on the UK in nuclear matters. However, Kennedy found himself curiously drawn to talk to Macmillan, for example about NATO nuclear policy, de Gaulle, and even Cuba. The President's ability to use bases in the UK was also limited, in theory and practice, by a web of formal and informal cooperation. The concession that in some circumstances the use of nuclear weapons would be 'a matter for joint decision' appears to have been made by the US only to the UK and France, among the very many countries hosting US nuclear forces.[3] Macmillan made a great play of domestic political difficulties over American bases during the Holy Loch negotiations. This reflected long-standing public and official concern, at a new peak in these years, over the possibility of high-handed or inappropriate US military action. This fear was strongest over Berlin and the far east, and in both of these areas, Britain was able – at least partly because of its own nuclear involvement – to initiate detailed and ultimately somewhat reassuring discussions with the Americans on the potential use of nuclear weapons. A note prepared in 1961 for Kennedy's National Security Adviser, McGeorge Bundy, recorded a commitment to 'consult with [the British] before using nuclear weapons anywhere, if possible' – an honour accorded to no other foreign government, not even the French.[4]

The degree of formal and informal cooperation and consultation between the US and UK also affected the way that military officers, in particular, responded to and implemented British nuclear-weapons policy. A certain similarity of outlook is apparent from the way debates in Washington came to be mirrored in London. This became important, for example, around the time of the Blue Streak cancellation, when the SAC leadership's visceral dislike of ballistic missiles and preference for manned bombers surely influenced RAF responses. There is plentiful evidence that, during the competition between Skybolt and Polaris, USAF and US Navy interests were supplying information and at times openly lobbying the opposing sides in Whitehall. Although British officers would not necessarily have been comfortable to admit it, closeness with the Americans also to some extent begot covetousness, and this too affected British debates on nuclear weapons. British officers wanted the capabilities enjoyed by their American counterparts; Mountbatten had a particular interest in the contents of the jars in the American technological sweetie-shop.

Not all British attitudes to nuclear weapons were developed in slavish admiration of things American, however, and two counter-balancing tendencies can be seen. One was commercial and industrial. The American and British aircraft manufacturing industries, in particular, were in keen competition for access to overseas markets in these years. In addition, the US and British governments were from time to time in serious disagreement over monetary policy and the defence of their respective currencies. Recent research has begun to explore these aspects of the Anglo-American relationship, both of which affected defence relationships directly.[5] Macmillan showed, on occasion, great annoyance at the depredations of the American aircraft industry, for example when Blue Water lost out to its US competitor Sergeant for a West German order. Later, when an American SAM was sold to Israel ahead of Bloodhound, Macmillan wrote an extraordinarily intemperate letter to Kennedy: 'I cannot believe that you were privy to this disgraceful piece of trickery. For myself I must say frankly that I can hardly find words to express my sense of disgust and despair. Nor do I see how you and I are to conduct the great affairs of the world on this basis'.[6] The Prime Minister appears to have nurtured the eccentric belief that his understanding with Eisenhower would lead to a suspension of the operation of twentieth-century capitalism, and that a series of gentlemen's agreements could carve up the global arms market. Watkinson – a businessman first, and a politician second – made a more mature assessment: 'that little or nothing came of [interdependence] was because of the pressure of the American arms lobbies and a desire on the part of the Kennedy administration to recover a large share of the cost of policing the world by selling American arms and equipment'.[7] The distant echoes of these disputes can be seen too in the nuclear field, where the agreement to transfer a submarine propulsion reactor had considerable commercial ramifications, and where the Polaris sales agreement was burdened with provisions on export control and the protection of intellectual property.

Some in the defence hierarchy and especially the defence industry saw American commercial motives behind all manner of British defence decisions – motives operating, it was thought, through Zuckerman, who was especially well connected in Washington. It was certainly quite convenient to American industry that key figures in the Pentagon, with whom Zuckerman liaised closely, believed with McNamara in limiting both Britain's nuclear independence and the extensive battlefield use of tactical nuclear weapons. The cancellation of Blue Streak, Blue Water and several less well advanced projects, and the run-down of British fissile materials production, also suited American industry. Above all the TSR.2 was – at least in the mythology of British aircraft enthusiasts, for whom Zuckerman is a hate-figure – 'a threat to the American aviation industry'.[8] This aspect of the Anglo-American relationship deserves much closer study, for the students of transatlantic summit diplomacy, poring over the files of the Foreign Office and Prime Minister, do not see it in action.

A second counter-balance was more psychological. Just occasionally, British technology was equivalent or even superior to that available in the US. Probably slightly more often, British defence scientists and engineers *perceived* this to be the case. First, therefore, an almost childish delight could be seen at British achievements, as when Macmillan confided to his diary that American atomic scientists had been impressed by their first contacts with Aldermaston, and when Zuckerman was briefed on Blue Streak re-entry work and decoys. Second, a 'not invented here' tendency was very often at work, especially in the MoA and some of its research establishments. Hence, in 1959, Blue Steel Mk.2 was preferred in some quarters to Skybolt, and hence too the fascinating series of proposals for all-British 'insurance' or 'stop-gap' deterrent systems between 1960 and 1963. This tendency could also be seen at work in early studies of ABM penetration. It seems not to be the case, however, that a sinister military-industrial complex was in operation, lobbying powerfully for British jobs and British industrial solutions. On the contrary, opinions of British industry and especially its management were usually low in Whitehall, and *vice versa*. So for example in 1960, looking at proposals for a future deterrent aircraft, an Air Ministry official commented that the 'phase III' Victor looked promising, but that 'the past record of Handley Page gives no confidence that they could undertake this task in the timescale required'.[9] Similarly, in 1958, the Ministry of Defence felt de Havilland's 'managerial resources were not equal to the load' of Blue Streak and a number of other projects.[10] This is one reason behind the efforts made by successive governments in the 1960s to reorganise the aircraft industry, for example creating the BAC and Hawker-Siddeley groups. The literature on the British aircraft industry, meanwhile, is full of equally condescending references to the civil service and its never-ending bureaucracy. Over TSR.2, for example, 'the Ministry [of Aviation] also superimposed control, or what could perhaps better be described as a sort of amorphous general influence, by setting up a hierarchy of committees'.[11] Graham Spinardi has specifically investigated the charge that, in relation to Britain's nuclear-weapons programme, a powerful internal lobby was generating work, and finds Aldermaston and Whitehall generally not guilty.[12] The suspicion of jobs for the boys remains strong, however,[13] and the developing relationship between the British and American defence industries and their customers is another potentially fruitful area for further research.

Other nuclear motivations

Serious historical writing on British nuclear weapons has been almost entirely dominated by academic experts on international relations and strategic studies, interested in diplomacy and the formulation of theories of deterrence. It is hardly surprising that their explanations focus therefore on international – and especially Anglo-American – relations and the strategic 'need' for forces to deter a nuclear attack on the UK. The desire to impress the United States, and to deepen where possible certain elements of the relationship, was clearly extremely important.

Technical credibility and cost, however, are also recurring themes in the documentary evidence.

Britain's nuclear capability was profoundly shaped by a belief in the need for credibility. This belief, along with professional pride and self-interest, is what drove the participants in the endless debates on delivery systems. Almost every point made in discussion between ministers, the chiefs, the Air Ministry and Admiralty related to the technical ability of systems to press home an attack, or their technical vulnerability to pre-emption or counter-attack, and the cost of any necessary improvements. Only Zuckerman could occasionally be found voicing the opinion that the bomb was purely a political weapon, and that its elaboration was unnecessary. No minimum deterrent was acceptable unless it could believably do its job – whether against 40 cities, or 15, or just Moscow. The system had to be credible, first and foremost, in the eyes of British officials, scientists and military officers, and second in the eyes of the Americans; the Soviets were incidental. This perfectionism seems to have been deeply rooted in British defence scientific and engineering culture, and undoubtedly contributed to the cost of deterrence, the timescales involved in introducing new weapons and the adverse reaction to any which had teething problems or operational shortcomings. The RAF was certainly not content with the outward appearance of a nuclear capability; it had to introduce ECM, low-level flight, dispersal, no-notice exercising, QRA and so forth. Without detailed study of foreign documentary evidence, it is impossible to be sure, but I have an idea that this tendency was more marked in the development of the British nuclear capability than, say, in France, the Soviet Union or certainly China. If the Anglo-American relationship was the major *political* factor in the genesis and growth of Britain's nuclear-weapons programme, I would venture to suggest that the search for technical credibility was the major practical factor operating at working level, and therefore determining the precise form the British nuclear force would take. This is not to argue that Blue Streak or Skybolt were cancelled because they were technically unsound. On the contrary, both were purely political decisions. Rather, the need for credibility motivated the implementation of policy and incidentally, from time to time, set the agenda within Whitehall. Sandys and Watkinson, for example, would not have urged the continuation of Blue Steel at various times if it had not been seen by the Air Ministry as crucial to the penetration of Soviet city defences after 1962. Macmillan and Thorneycroft would have been happy enough with Polaris after Nassau, and would not have had to put the V-force into action at low level, or plan a high-yield version of

WE177, if these suggestions had not surfaced from the Air Ministry and MoA in response to their enquiries.

What Britain's nuclear-weapons programme actually cost between 1958 and 1964 is all but impossible to determine accurately. All financial figures used at senior levels in Whitehall in this period were forward-looking: plans, not records of expenditure. In an age unaccustomed to cost-benefit analysis or reporting against past performance, retrospective out-turn costs were of little interest. Further extensive research, and a familiarity with government accounting practices of the time, would be necessary before any British 'atomic audit' could be produced to approach in quality that of Stephen Schwartz and his collaborators in the US.[14] In October 1958, figures for a study of the cost of the deterrent between 1959 and 1964 were collected by the Air Ministry.[15] The total capital and running cost of the V-force, plus associated research and development cost, was put at £141 millions for financial year 1959/60, rising to £199 millions in 1961/62 before falling again to £167 millions in 1963/64. On the most expensive assumption, the defence of the deterrent would add another £49 millions in 1959/60, rising to £101 millions in 1961/62. The Air Ministry's mastery of figures is illustrated by the presence of a line in the spreadsheet labelled 'adjustment for reasons unknown', but this series of estimates does put the cost of Britain's strategic deterrent – tactical nuclear weapons were excluded – at between £200 and £300 millions, or up to 20 per cent of an annual defence budget of around £1500 millions. Significant cuts in expenditure on air defence were to follow in 1960, and the 1958 projections cannot be taken as an indication that these monies were actually spent. Indeed, when the cost of the deterrent was reviewed again in 1960, it was (or was made to appear) lower: less than ten per cent of the defence budget, or £544 millions for the four years to 1964/65, including warheads but now excluding air defence.[16]

In two important respects, these figures were certainly underestimates. Today, government accounting takes account of the cost of ownership of large capital assets, but in the 1950s it did not. Had it done so, it would more truly have reflected the macro-economic cost of tying up a great deal of land and manufacturing capacity in nuclear deterrence. Instead, the ministry effectively counted only the marginal cash costs directly attributable to the deterrent and some of its defence. A different approach might have attributed to the deterrent front-line some proportion of the fixed costs of defence, such as pensions, basic training, communications, headquarters staffs and brass bands. The Air Ministry's 'other' costs alone were put in 1958 at around £130 millions annually; had they not been ignored for the purposes of the calculation, they would have added tens of millions more to the deterrent bill. Second, fissile material costs were calculated separately, and included an element of historic costs, as explained briefly in Chapter 4. I make these points not to support any argument that the deterrent was, or was not, *worth* the cost, but to demonstrate that the cost was large – and indeed probably somewhat larger than the ten per cent of the defence budget often quoted at the time. That it was also *difficult to afford*, and that the Treasury jealously guarded every penny, cannot be doubted by anyone who has read the Whitehall documents of the period.

Since Andrew Pierre's landmark study of nuclear politics, there has been almost no historical work on the mainstream domestic political discourse on nuclear security policy. Only the historians of decline, or of radical political protest at the margins of the debate, have shown a consistent interest. In one sense, this neglect is justified. Because of secrecy, the relative weakness of parliament in defence matters and the small 'market for strategic ideas' in Britain, even the mainstream of public political debate affected British nuclear policy only indirectly. Having looked in detail at the documentary evidence for the development of nuclear-weapons technology and its political context between 1958 and 1964, we are well placed to assess the explicit motivations behind nuclear policy. We should also bear in mind, however, the implicit and indirect. Looking somewhat beyond the evidence presented in these pages, I should like to make a small number of additional comments on the relative importance of scientific and political drivers in setting military nuclear policy, and finally the relevance to this story of Second World War experience and some elements of popular culture.

Technology, strategy and politics

Histories of science and technology, especially during the cold war, often seek to understand the relative balance of scientific and political drivers in the advance of technology. Many people felt, at the height of the cold war, that science had visited a curse upon humanity, developing nuclear weapons that nobody wanted, and that nobody could control. It seems reasonably clear, however, that the Prometheus of nuclear science was safely bound in the UK during these years. Whether his fire was too expensive for a great power in economic difficulties, or whether some of the classically educated aristocrats and officials at the heart of Macmillan's 'warfare state' looked down on him as a tradesman, is an interesting question. But I believe the stories, for example, of the Blue Streak cancellation, ABM research, OR.1182 and WE177 serve to demonstrate that political possibilities were ultimately more important than technical ones in arriving at defence decisions. Like war itself, defence technology seems to have been an expression and continuation of politics, with no independent logic of its own. The British did not, in the end, pursue every elaboration of the technological arms race. To explain this, we should look to politics as well as finance. British technologists did not have the political and commercial strength of their American counterparts; British opponents of the arms race, notably Mountbatten and Zuckerman, conversely had more success than their opposite numbers.

As we have seen, the demise of Blue Streak is frequently put down to technical or strategic factors, but there are problems with these explanations. Blue Streak was manifestly a technical possibility. Broadly similar weapons were developed elsewhere, the project was more or less on schedule at cancellation, and for a time it enjoyed a relatively successful afterlife as a satellite launcher. To condemn it as a 'fire-first' weapon, vulnerable to pre-emption, required some peculiar strategic assumptions about the weight of Soviet attack in an unbelievable future political scenario. Perhaps a future Suez was envisaged, with the US abandoning the UK and withdrawing the tens of thousands of its own citizens and military personnel in the British Isles, and in those neighbouring parts of Europe that would be affected by fall-out from 300 or more megaton weapons exploding over southern England? If so, nobody was prepared to say so; indeed there is ample evidence that officials inside the debate knew that the strategic arguments against Blue Streak were weak. A political explanation for the demise of Blue Streak, based on the known positions of interested parties, in particular the Air Ministry, is far easier to accept. The project simply lacked support.

ABM research in the UK was very limited after 1962, following the recommendations of Dr Penley's committee. Certainly Penley was downbeat about the technical prospects for ABM. But it was not that there was *no* possibility of a technically credible defence in certain scenarios. On the contrary, Penley stated that a missile like Skybolt – or perhaps the Soviet SS-3 or SS-4? – carrying a single warhead on a ballistic trajectory, without decoys or penetration aids, would one day be vulnerable to ABM.[17] Nor was it the case that there were no interesting avenues of technical research or prospects of collaboration with the US. However, unlike in the United States, where exceptionally powerful military-industrial lobbies ultimately frustrated efforts to end ABM research, in Britain there was no meaningful political support for work on ABM. Instead Zuckerman, finding himself in complete agreement with York, Rubel, Wiesner and others in the US who despaired of the momentum and mentality of the arms race, was minded to oppose any 'weaponeers' he saw pushing the case for ABM or penetration work in the UK.[18] The story of the cruise-type missile requirement OR.1182 is another of technological possibilities – not immediately promising, but not in the realms of fantasy – falling foul of political possibilities. The situation was very different in the United States and indeed the Soviet Union, where these and other technologies were explored vigorously. It seems that bureaucratic debate in the UK on weapons systems was but a pale shadow of the equivalent struggles in America, where Kennedy and McNamara had the greatest of political difficulty cancelling weapons projects, and where political opposition from the services was played out in Congress and elsewhere. British opposition to the test-ban negotiations was also notably meek compared to that in the US from the services and the Atomic Energy Commission. Reading measured submissions on the Whitehall issues of the day from Penney, Plowden or Boyle hardly calls to mind Teller, Strauss or LeMay.

A final example, this time of a weapon that was later successfully introduced, the WE177, again shows firm political control at work in the UK. Just because new American warhead designs, or later the British Super Octopus implosion system, or a parachute-retarded laydown bomb casing, were possible, did not mean immediate development approval and production orders for an improved kiloton bomb. Instead there was a rather lengthy period of discussion of the requirement for a more operationally flexible successor to Red Beard, from the end of 1958 until July 1962 when approval was finally given for work – and on a low-yield version only, despite much lobbying from the Air Ministry and War Office. Only in early 1963 was approval given for the high-yield WE177B – and then only because this was a relatively cheap and cheerful option to plug the 'gap' before Polaris.

It is interesting too that domestic, and not simply international political factors affected these decisions. German historians of the 1960s, writing of their country's rise to the first rank of international power in the late nineteenth and early twentieth centuries, popularised the idea of *der Primat der Innenpolitik*, or the primacy of domestic politics. Specifically, they argued that economics – for example the need for raw materials and markets for German industry – drove political expansionism overseas and the developing Anglo-German antagonism. There had been a tendency previously to study Germany's rise as an aspect of Victorian diplomatic history or realist international relations. Recent attempts to explain de Gaulle's international politics in similar terms – highlighting the needs of

French agriculture, rather than principled geopolitical opposition to the dominance, in NATO, of the Anglo-Saxon powers – have met with considerable controversy.[19] I should not like to argue that Macmillan based his nuclear policies on the needs of Britain's farmers, or even of its aircraft manufacturing industry. It is clear, however, that, as an explanation of either the generality or the specifics of the British nuclear-weapons programme, crude geopolitics or the maximisation of international 'interests' will not do either. Even the need to impress the United States, either by sharing current research into ballistic or cruise missiles or by demonstrating independent national technological prowess, could not save Blue Streak, the OR.1182 studies or the research programme of nuclear tests in the mid-1960s. Neither were strategic arguments decisive. Cost, and internal Whitehall politics, were ultimately more important.

Over arms control, meanwhile, Macmillan found himself driven by domestic political opposition to nuclear testing – with which, it should be said, he seems personally to have agreed. Twentieth-century politicians, with the possible exception of Henry Kissinger, have not approached international relations as a closed academic field in which there is no need to take account of domestic opinion. Students of diplomatic history, however, like many journalists, tend still to look down on domestic motivations, and to see politicians like Macmillan as trimmers – as though it were somehow improper, in a parliamentary democracy, to reflect the will of the majority of the electorate in a government's foreign policy. I hope, at least, that the attempt here to present practical and technical details of policy implementation on the 'home front' alongside the international political aspects of Britain's nuclear-weapons programme will encourage attempts to draw parallels and linkages between the two – attempts of the kind John Walker has now made for Britain's arms-control policy.[20]

Wartime experience and nuclear culture

A final key explanation for Britain's cold-war nuclear defence policy can be found in the years before 1945. Nuclear histories, and histories of the cold war more generally, tend almost always to regard the end of the Second World War, and the use of the atomic bombs at Hiroshima and Nagasaki, as a clean break. In some senses, it was clear in 1945 that nothing would ever be quite the same again; that a qualitatively different weapon had been developed by the United States – truly, in the badly overused phrase, a weapon of mass destruction. Certainly, efforts were being made to create a new world order in the ruins of the old. Although the British were, strictly speaking, undefeated, the European colonial empires would now give way in the international system to the new superpowers.

But it cannot possibly be argued that everything that had come before 1945 was therefore forgotten. On the contrary, I believe the roots of Britain's nuclear-weapons policy are to be found in wartime and prewar experience. At a personal and national level, the experience of the Second World War, in particular, had been both shattering and formative. It is difficult, for example, to understand Mountbatten's postwar preoccupations without pausing to consider his experience during the war. How could he, of all people, support the assumption that fixed bases would always be available east of Suez – especially in Singapore, when he had taken the Japanese surrender there himself, after a humiliating occupation, less than 20 years previously? How could he not advocate carriers and especially amphibious forces instead, when he had been Churchill's wartime Chief of Combined Operations? Had the Canadians he sent to Dieppe died in vain? How could Dermot Boyle and Tom Pike, meanwhile, sit by and watch Sandys replace the RAF's manned aircraft with guided missiles? Had the bomber aircrew of 83 Squadron, led in person by Boyle over Bremen, Wilhelmshaven and Düsseldorf,[21] also died in vain? Sandys's own preoccupation with guided weapons reflected in part his involvement in the activities of the wartime Crossbow committee.

Many other aspects of nuclear strategy were prefigured in wartime and prewar discussions. The concept of deterrence, for example, was not new in 1945, but had been discussed a great deal between the wars in the context of the threat from conventional bombing, the original 'weapon of mass destruction'.[22] Many more specific ideas of nuclear targeting harked back to debates between British and American air commanders during the war. The interdiction targets of Canberra and TSR.2 aircraft, in Europe and indeed the far east, were based on the 'successful' experience of isolating the Normandy theatre from German reinforcements. SAC's emphasis on targeting the war-making capacity of the Soviet Union was also an echo of US wartime strategy in both Europe and the Pacific.

At a corporate and national level, too, explanations for Britain's general and specific behaviour and the assumptions made during the cold war are to be found in previous experience. Airmen had seen that strategic bombing worked – no matter that many others disagreed with them – and they now had a new and absolute weapon to reinforce their argument. Soldiers had seen that a hard and bloody slog across the middle east, Italy and eventually northern Europe was necessary to defeat a determined enemy. Now they had an enemy whose prowess in such a slog nobody could deny. Sailors had seen that prewar plans went wrong, and had rediscovered the need to be ready for anything, especially in the grim struggle of the North Atlantic convoys. Defence scientists had seen their stock rise markedly. In the mythology of many, the Second World War was a boffin's war. Radar, fighter control, intelligence and now nuclear weapons made defence a field in which British technical cleverness could play an important part. Even the civil service had had a good war; sensible organisation, committees, proper paperwork and a spirit of compromise helped Britain to remain indomitable; to refuse to lose the war. Should it now lose the peace? Should it admit to weakness in the face of American power (or, perhaps worse, French power)? Should it admit to an inability to stand drinks at the bar of the nuclear club?[23]

At the highest level, perhaps partly at the behest of Sir Norman Brook, Macmillan repeatedly questioned the need for British nuclear weapons. It seems that Macmillan cannot be accused of clinging to nuclear weapons as a substitute for great-power status. On the contrary, it almost seems that nuclear weapons were clinging to Macmillan, for the answer given to the Prime Minister was always the same: the need was valid. Intellectual and strategic arguments were marshalled duly and appropriately, but something more visceral was at work. The self-image of Britain as a 'militant and technological nation' remains little understood, but the atomic bomb – an expression of both international political power and technological prowess – was precisely the kind of thing necessary to support this self-image in the 1950s and 1960s. Britons saw their country as a force for good in the world, sustained equally by brave and undefeated sailors, soldiers and airmen, and by the boffins in its laboratories. Amongst the positive stereotypes in postwar British popular culture, special places are reserved for military officers and clever, argumentative grammar-school boys with a scientific bent. Both are closely associated with the national pursuit of muddling through. In film, affectionate caricatures abound: Sidney Stratton in *The Man in the White Suit* (1951), Group Captain Lionel Mandrake in *Dr Strangelove* (1964), Sir Sydney Ruff-Diamond in *Carry On Up The Khyber* (1968). These men were sometimes ridiculous; not everything they did was sensible or even believable; but their intentions were always the best. The same seemed to be true of their real-world counterparts. Views of Mountbatten, Boyle, Pike, Zuckerman and Penney, for example, were coloured as a result. To the majority of British voters, in the hands of such men, nuclear weapons felt right.

Weapons development timeline

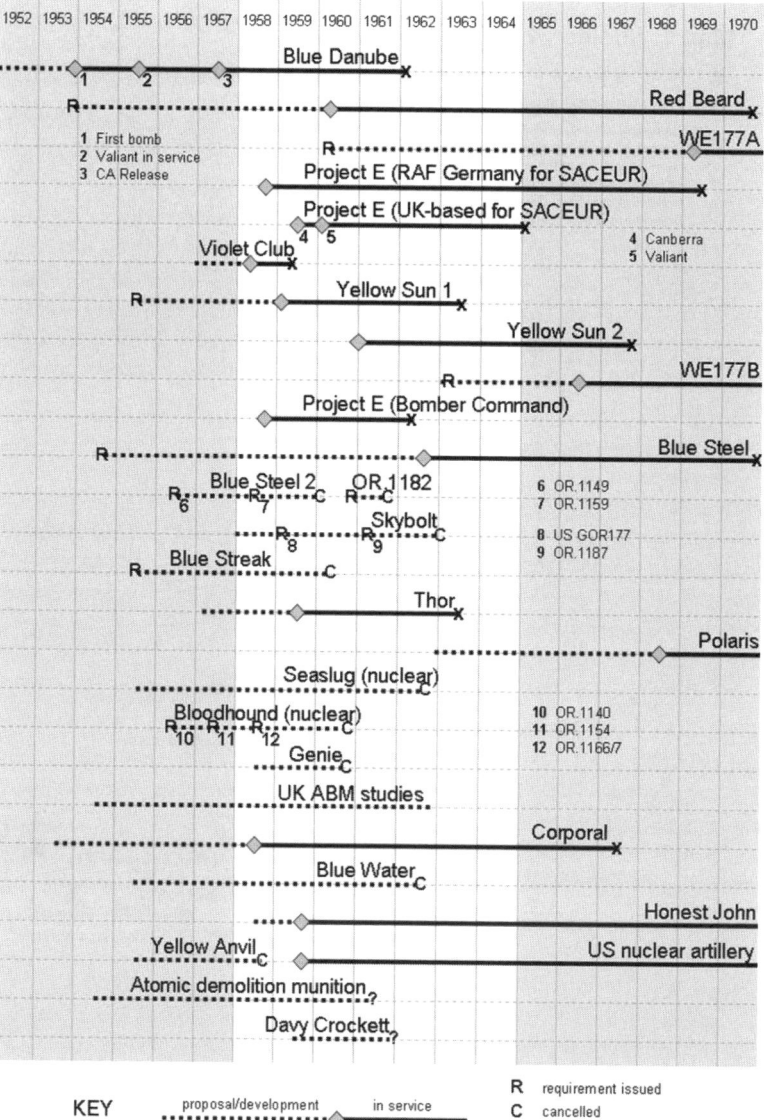

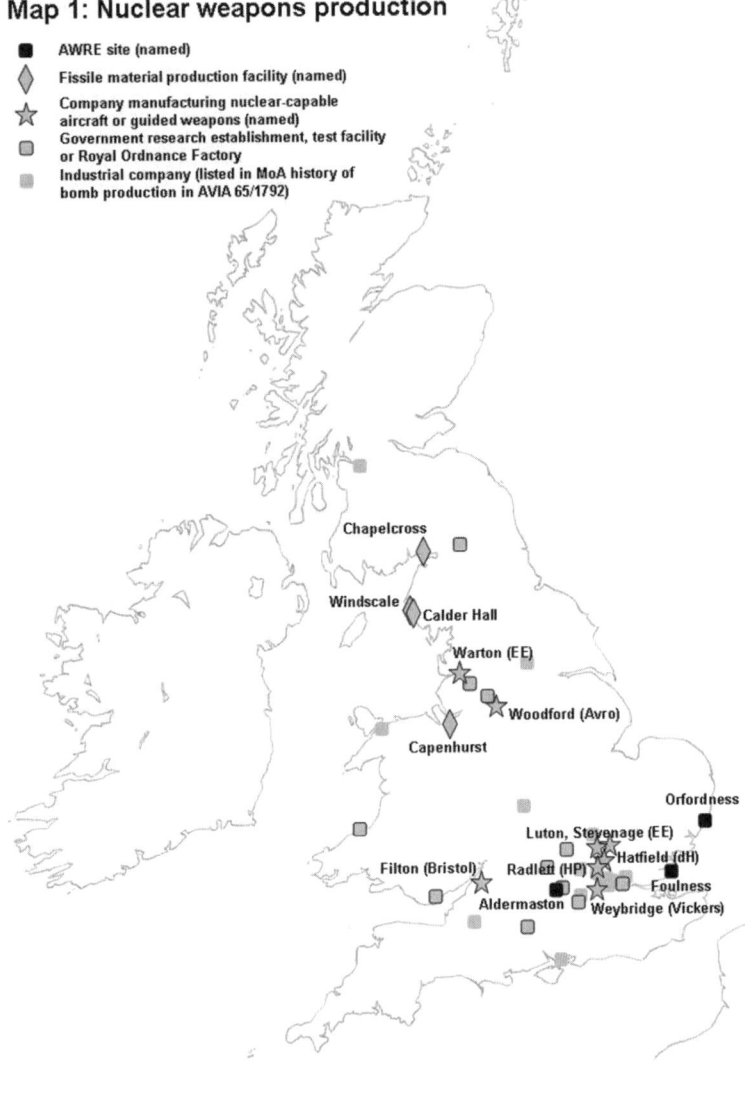

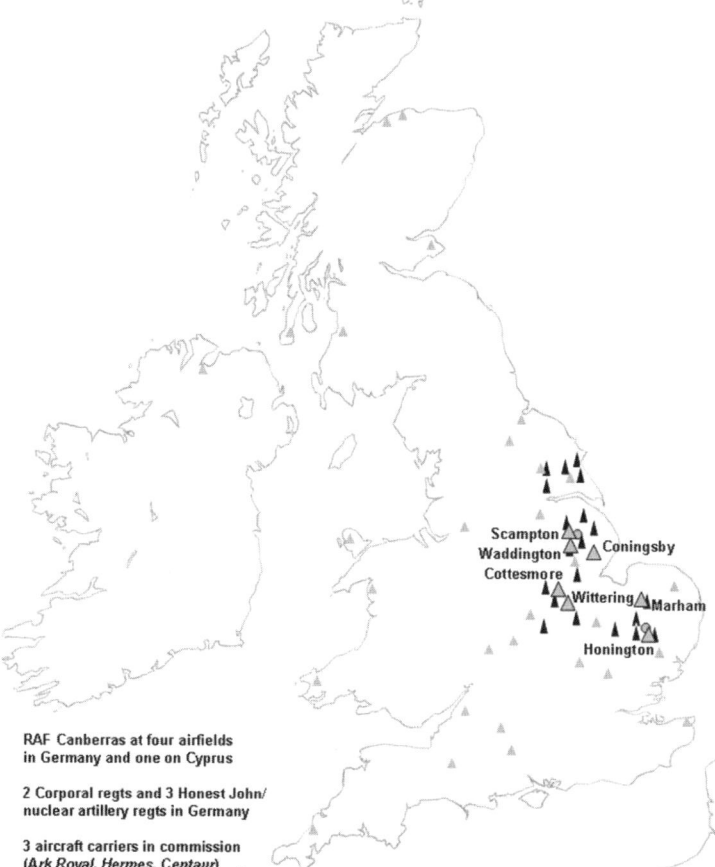

Appendices

Appendix 1: Estimated deliverable nuclear weapons stockpile

at year end	1958	1959	1960	1961	1962	1963	1964
Blue Danube	58	58	58	10	0	0	0
Violet Club	5	0	0	0	0	0	0
Yellow Sun Mk.1	0	13	29	37	0	0	0
RAF Red Beard	0	0	49	90	110	110	110
RN Red Beard	0	0	3	11	20	28	28
Yellow Sun Mk.2	0	0	0	43	83	86	86
Blue Steel	0	0	0	0	9	40	40
Total British	**63**	**71**	**139**	**191**	**222**	**264**	**264**
Mk.5 (V-bombers)	72	72	48	24	0	0	0
Thor	0	40	60	60	60	0	0
Mk.7 (Canberra)	48	96	48	48	48	48	48
Mk.28 (Valiant)	0	0	48	48	48	0	0
Mk.43 (Valiant)	0	0	0	0	0	48	48
Corporal	50	50	50	100	100	100	100
Honest John	0	0	108	108	108	108	108
8-in howitzer	0	0	36	36	36	36	36
Total US	**170**	**258**	**398**	**424**	**400**	**340**	**340**
Ratio British:US	1:2.7	1:3.6	1:2.9	1:2.2	1:1.8	1:1.3	1:1.3
Grand total	**233**	**329**	**537**	**615**	**622**	**604**	**604**

Notes

'Deliverable stockpile' is estimated total capable of assembly and delivery to target by aircraft and/or missiles. It does not include 'spare' or training weapons, or correspond necessarily with production totals for various components. Sources are generally discussed in the text. Brian Burnell has argued (pers. comm. 7 Oct 2007, based on papers in PRO, AIR2/13695) that only 50 Blue Danube were deliverable. This is believable, although the figure of 58 is given in more than one other PRO document. Mk.7 totals based on one bomb for each of 16 UE aircraft with 3 Bomber Command squadrons in the UK, and one for each of 12 UE aircraft at four RAF Germany squadrons (*pace* Norris *et al.* (p. 122), it seems weapons *were* stored at Geilenkirchen and Wildenrath – see e.g., http://forum.keypublishing.co.uk/showthread.php?t=75988 [accessed Dec 2007]).
Figures for Corporal, Honest John and 8-inch howitzer are based on creation of associated army units in Germany.

Appendix 2: Estimated fissile materials stockpile

kg at financial year end	58/59	59/60	60/61	61/62	62/63	63/64	64/65
Pu production[1]	619.1	769.4	1040.9	1477.1	1963.2	2252.6	2690
Pu net available for weapons[2]	618.5	744.9	1017.8	1412.7	1843.7	1956.1	2473.3
U-235 from Capenhurst[3]	2250	3700	5150	6600	7600	7600	7600
U-235 from US	0	0	0	0	0	0	500
U-235 available for weapons[4]	1575	2590	3605	4620	5320	5320	5820

Notes

[1] Calculated from UK Ministry of Defence, 'Historical accounting and plutonium' and 'Plutonium and Aldermaston: an historical account' (MoD 2000) available from: http://www.mod.uk/DefenceInternet/AboutDefence/CorporatePublications/DefenceEstate andEnvironmentPublications/UKNucWeaponsProg/ (accessed August 2007). Cumulative total from table 2, 'from Sellafield' column. Believed to represent UK weapons-grade plutonium production.

[2] Calculated from UK Ministry of Defence, 'Historical accounting and plutonium' and 'Plutonium and Aldermaston: an historical account' (MoD 2000) available from: http://www.mod.uk/DefenceInternet/AboutDefence/CorporatePublications/DefenceEstate andEnvironmentPublications/UKNucWeaponsProg/ (accessed August 2007). Cumulative totals from tables 2–5, 'from Sellafield, Dounreay, Winfrith, Harwell' columns, less cumulative totals from 'to Sellafield, Dounreay, Winfrith, Harwell' columns. Believed to represent UK weapons-grade plutonium stockpile available for weapons use, net of transfers for research purposes to UKAEA establishments and recycling/recovery of scrap material to Sellafield.

[3] Cumulative production calculated on the basis of original Capenhurst plant producing 400kg/yr from 1956/7; and 50 per cent, IMD and civ extensions producing 350kg/yr each from 1957/8, 1958/9 and 1959/60 respectively (see papers in PRO, AB 16/4189).

[4] Assumes UK production divided according to 70:30 agreed ratio between weapons and civil use, but US barter material purely for weapons use.

Notes

Introduction

1 Norman Dombey and Eric Grove, 'Britain's thermonuclear bluff', *London Review of Books*, 22 Oct 1992, pp. 8–10; Lorna Arnold, *Britain and the H-bomb* (Palgrave 2001), pp. 222–4; John Baylis, *Ambiguity and deterrence: British nuclear strategy 1945–64* (Oxford, Clarendon Press 1995), pp. 262–8.
2 White paper Cmnd. 363, *Report on defence*, Feb 1958.
3 Harold Wilson, speaking in parliament: House of Commons debates (hereafter HoC debs.), vol. 687, col. 437 (16 Jan 1964).
4 Margaret Gowing, *Independence and deterrence: Britain and atomic energy, 1945–52* (Macmillan 1974), Vol. 1: *Policy making*; Vol. 2: *Policy execution*.
5 Solly Zuckerman, *Nuclear illusion and reality* (Collins 1982), p. x.
6 See e.g., Correlli Barnett, *The collapse of British power* (Eyre Methuen 1972); C J Bartlett, *The long retreat: a short history of British defence policy 1945–70* (Macmillan 1972); John Baylis, *Anglo-American defence relations 1939–84* (Macmillan, 2nd edn, 1984); Duncan Campbell, *The unsinkable aircraft carrier: American military power in Britain* (Michael Joseph 1984); William Louis and Hedley Bull, eds., *The special relationship: Anglo-American relations since 1945* (Oxford, Clarendon Press 1986); Michael Carver, *Tightrope walking: British defence policy since 1945* (Hutchinson 1992).
7 In the overall context of decolonisation, even the more 'successful' campaigns, for example in Malaya, Cyprus, Kenya and (in 1961) Kuwait, have been seen not as counter-examples but exceptions to prove the rule; or else historians have produced accounts of late-imperial brutality. See e.g., Phillip Darby, *British defence policy east of Suez 1947–68* (Oxford UP/RIIA 1973); William Louis, *The British empire in the middle east 1945–1951: Arab nationalism, the United States, and postwar imperialism* (Oxford, Clarendon Press 1984); William Louis and Roger Owen, eds., *Suez 1956: the crisis and its consequences* (Oxford, Clarendon Press 1989); Saki Dockrill, *Britain's retreat from east of Suez: the choice between Europe and the world?* (Palgrave 2002); David Anderson, *Histories of the hanged: Britain's dirty war in Kenya and the end of empire* (Weidenfeld and Nicolson 2004).
8 Andrew Pierre, *Nuclear politics: the British experience with an independent strategic force 1939–70* (Oxford UP 1972); A J R (John) Groom, *British thinking about nuclear weapons* (Frances Pinter 1974); Lawrence Freedman, *Britain and nuclear weapons* (Macmillan/RIIA 1980).
9 Ian Clark and Nicholas Wheeler, *The British origins of nuclear strategy 1945–55* (Oxford, Clarendon Press 1989); Martin Navias, *Nuclear weapons and British strategic planning 1955–58* (Oxford, Clarendon Press 1991); Ian Clark, *Nuclear diplomacy and the special relationship: Britain's deterrent and America 1957–62* (Oxford, Clarendon Press 1994); Stephen Ball, *The bomber in British strategy: doctrine, strategy and Britain's world role 1945–60* (Oxford, Westview 1995); Baylis, *Ambiguity and deterrence*.

10 Graham Spinardi, 'Aldermaston and British nuclear weapons development: testing the Zuckerman thesis', *Social Studies of Science* 27 (1997), pp. 547–82.
11 Jan Melissen, *The struggle for nuclear partnership: Britain, the United States and the making of an ambiguous alliance* (Groningen, Styx 1993); Timothy J Botti, *The long wait: the forging of the Anglo-American nuclear alliance 1945–58* (New York, Greenwood 1994); Septimus H Paul, *Nuclear rivals: Anglo-American atomic relations 1945–52* (Ohio State UP 2000).
12 Kendrick Oliver, *Kennedy, Macmillan and the nuclear test ban debate 1961–3* (Macmillan 1998); Constantine A Pagedas, *Anglo-American strategic relations and the French problem 1960–63* (Frank Cass 2000); Donette Murray, *Kennedy, Macmillan and nuclear weapons* (Macmillan 2000); Nigel Ashton, *Kennedy, Macmillan and the cold war: the irony of interdependence* (Palgrave 2002); E Bruce Geelhoed and Anthony O Edmonds, *Eisenhower, Macmillan and Allied Unity, 1957–61* (Palgrave 2003); Ashton, 'Harold Macmillan and the "golden days" of Anglo-American relations revisited, 1957–63', *Diplomatic History* 29/4 (Summer 2005), pp. 691–723.
13 See e.g., Alain Enthoven and Wayne Smith, *How much is enough? Shaping the defense program 1961–69* (New York, Harper and Row 1971); Ted Greenwood, *Making the MIRV: a study of defence decision-making* (Cambridge Mass, Ballinger 1975); Desmond Ball, *Politics and force levels: the strategic missile program of the Kennedy administration* (Univ of California Press 1980); Michael E Brown, *Flying blind: the politics of the US strategic bomber program* (Cornell UP 1992).
14 See e.g., Desmond Wettern, *The decline of British seapower* (Jane's 1982); Derek Wood, *Project cancelled: the disaster of Britain's abandoned aircraft projects* (2nd edn, Jane's 1986); the many books on TSR.2, including those cited in Chapter 2; and Stephen Twigge, *The Early Development of Guided Weapons in the United Kingdom 1940–60* (Chur, Switzerland, Harwood 1993).
15 See e.g., John Simpson, *The independent nuclear state: the United States, Britain and the military atom* (2nd edn, Macmillan 1986); Eric Grove, *Vanguard to Trident: British naval policy since world war II* (London, Bodley Head 1987); Graham Spinardi, *From Polaris to Trident: the development of US fleet ballistic missile technology* (Cambridge UP 1994); Arnold, *Britain and the H-bomb*. An increasing number of enthusiasts' books on military hardware are also based on archival research with a sound policy aspect, e.g., Norman Friedman, *British destroyers and frigates: the second world war and after* (Chatham 2006); Chris Gibson and Tony Buttler, *British secret projects: hypersonics, ramjets and missiles* (Midland Counties 2007).
16 Richard Moore, 'The real meaning of the words: a pedantic glossary of British nuclear weapons', *Prospero* 1 (Spring 2004), pp. 71–90. A version with some formatting errors can be found at the Mountbatten Centre's website: http://www.mcis.soton.ac.uk/Site_Files/pdf/nuclear_history/Working_Paper_No_1.pdf (accessed Jan 2007).
17 Alistair Horne, *Macmillan: the official biography* (2 vols, Macmillan 1988–9) remains the best starting point. Anthony Sampson, *Macmillan: a study in ambiguity* (Allen Lane 1967) is still used by historians, no doubt because his judgement of Macmillan's premiership – 'as with de Gaulle, some measure of national deception seemed called for' (p. 256) – remains appealing. Of more recent works, Richard Aldous and Sabine Lee, eds, *Harold Macmillan*

and Britain's World Role (Macmillan 1995); *eidem*, eds, *Harold Macmillan: Aspects of a Political Life* (Macmillan 1999); and Peter Hennessy, 'Quiet, calm deliberation: Harold Macmillan, 1957–63', *The Prime Minister: the office and its holders since 1945* (Penguin 2000) are all authoritative and useful.

18 From a speech at Bedford Town's football ground in 1957, and originally intended as a warning: see Peter Hennessy, *Having it so good: Britain in the fifties* (Allen Lane 2006), pp. 533–4.

19 The 10th Earl of Selkirk, speaking at a witness seminar in July 1988: Michael Kandiah and Gillian Staerck, eds., *The Move to the Sandys White Paper of 1957* (Institute of Contemporary British History 2002), p. 23. Other speakers at the seminar agreed with Selkirk.

20 Cmnd. 124, *Defence: outline of future policy*, April 1957, para 3; HoC debs., vol. 568, col. 1759 (16 Apr 1957).

21 Aldous and Lee, 'Staying in the game: Harold Macmillan and Britain's world role', *eidem.*, eds, *Harold Macmillan and Britain's world role*, p. 150.

22 Macmillan to Kennedy, 5 Jan 1962, quoted in Ashton, *Kennedy, Macmillan and the Cold War: the irony of interdependence* (Palgrave Macmillan 2002), p. 193.

23 Quoted in Peter Hennessy, *Whitehall* (Secker and Warburg 1989), p. 145.

24 *ibid.*, p. 147. See also Kevin Theakston, 'Norman Craven Brook, Baron Normanbrook (1902–67)', *Oxford Dictionary of National Biography*.

25 Simon Heffer, '(George Edward) Peter, Baron Thorneycroft (1909–94)', *Oxford Dictionary of National Biography*.

26 HoC debs., vol. 580, col. 1295 (23 Jan 1958).

27 N Piers Ludlow, '(Edwin) Duncan Sandys, Baron Duncan-Sandys (1908–87)', *Oxford Dictionary of National Biography*.

28 *Sunday Express*, 11 May 1958 (emphasis in original). MRAF Sir Dermot Boyle took a fancy to this article, and kept a copy in his scrap-book, where it can still be seen: RAF Museum, Boyle papers, MF 10101/2.

29 Ludlow, 'Duncan Sandys'.

30 'Brittle'. See *ibid.*, and Dominic Sandbrook, *Never had it so good: a history of Britain from Suez to the Beatles* (Little Brown 2005), p. 84.

31 Geoffrey Goodman, 'Aubrey Jones (1911–2003)', *Oxford Dictionary of National Biography*.

32 UK National Archives (Public Record Office), Kew (hereafter PRO), Watkinson to Sir Robert Scott, 7 Dec 1961 in DEFE 13/617.

33 John Mackintosh, quoted in Hennessy, *The Prime Minister: the office and its holders since 1945*, p. 56.

34 HoC debs., vol. 578, cols. 1274–9; vol. 579, cols. 212–17, 607–10, 1071–4, 1418–36.

35 HoC debs., vol. 622, cols. 211–324 (27 Apr 1960); Nicholas Hill, *A vertical empire: the history of the UK rocket and space programme, 1951–70* (Imperial College Press 2001), p. 113.

36 William P Snyder, *The politics of British defence policy 1945–62* (Ohio State UP 1964), pp. 44–7; Laurence Martin, 'The market for strategic ideas in Britain: the "Sandys era"', *American Political Science Review* 56/1 (Mar 1962), pp. 35–7.

37 PRO, numerous references in index to CAB 128 and 129 volumes. There were probably further references to the subject, for example in general discussions of Anglo-American relations.

38 PRO, D(58)15th mtg 25 Jul 1958, 16th mtg 1 Aug 1958, 18th mtg 10 Sep 1958, 21st mtg 15 Oct 1958, 24th mtg 5 Nov 1958, 26th mtg 18 Nov 1958, 27th mtg 20 Nov 1958, 28th mtg 26 Nov 1958, all in CAB 131/19. Some of the minutes of other meetings around the same time have not been fully declassified, and may also contain discussion of nuclear-weapons issues.
39 PRO, D(60)1 of 1 Jan 1960, covering note of the previous day's meeting in CAB 131/23.
40 Michael Howard, *The central organisation of defence* (RUSI 1970), p. 8.
41 Cmnd. 476, *Central organisation for defence*, July 1958, quoted by Howard, *The central organisation of defence*, p. 10.
42 PRO, DB(58)1 of 23 Jul 1958 in DEFE 30/1.
43 PRO, ND(60)1 of 23 Jun 1960 in AVIA 65/1771.
44 Sir Frederick Brundrett, 'Rockets, satellites and military thinking', *Journal of the RUSI* 105 (Aug 1960), pp. 332–43.
45 Richard Powell, 'Sir Frederick Brundrett (1894–1974)', *Oxford Dictionary of National Biography*.
46 Solly Zuckerman, *From apes to warlords: an autobiography 1904–46* (Collins 1978); *Monkeys, men and missiles: an autobiography 1946–88* (Collins 1988); Richard Maguire, 'Scientific dissent amid the United Kingdom government's nuclear weapons programme', *History Workshop Journal* 63/1 (Spring 2007), pp. 113–35.
47 Harold Watkinson, *Turning points: a record of our times* (Salisbury, Michael Russell 1986), p. 109.
48 Howard, *The central organisation of defence*, p. 17.
49 Richard Moore, *The Royal Navy and nuclear weapons* (Frank Cass 2001).
50 Ken Young, 'The Royal Navy's Polaris lobby', *Journal of Strategic Studies* 25/3 (Sep 2002), pp. 56–86.
51 Zuckerman archive, correspondence of summer 1960 in SZ/CSA/95.
52 Michael Carver, 'Sir Gerald Templer (1898–1979)', *Oxford Dictionary of National Biography*.
53 John Cowley, 'Sir Francis Festing (1902–76)', *Oxford Dictionary of National Biography*.
54 Denis Brogan, quoted in Snyder, *The politics of British defence policy*, pp. 129–30.
55 Zuckerman, *Monkeys, men and missiles*, pp. 291–6, 380–1.
56 VAdm Sir Peter Gretton, 'A maritime strategy for British defence', *Journal of the RUSI* (Nov 1965), pp. 301–10.
57 AVM Stewart Menaul, *Countdown: Britain's strategic nuclear forces* (Robert Hale 1980); Simon Ball, *The bomber in British strategy*; Humphrey Wynn, *The RAF strategic nuclear deterrent forces: their origins, roles and deployment 1945–64* (HMSO 1994).
58 Hew Strachan, 'The British way in warfare revisited', *Historical Journal* 26/2 (Jun 1983), pp. 447–61; Alex Danchev, 'Liddell Hart and the Indirect Approach', *Journal of Military History* 63/2 (Apr 1999), pp. 313–37.
59 See recently, for example, Jörg Friedrich, *The fire: the bombing of Germany 1940–45* (English translation, Columbia UP 2006); Robin Neillands, *The bomber war: Arthur Harris and the allied bomber offensive 1939–45* (John Murray 2001); Mark Connelly, *Reaching for the stars: a new history of Bomber Command in world war II* (I B Tauris 2001). The official histories, though old, are still useful and

balanced accounts, especially of the high-level strategic-bombing debates during the war: Sir Charles Webster and Noble Frankland, *The Strategic Air Offensive Against Germany 1939–45 Vol. 1: Preparation, Vol. 2: Endeavour, Vol. 3: Victory; Vol. 4: Annexes and Appendices* (HMSO 1961; new pbk edn Naval and Military Press 2006).

60 Col Mike Worden USAF, *Rise of the fighter generals: the problem of air force leadership 1945–82* (Maxwell AFB, Air University Press March 1998), p. 243.
61 Gen Sir William Jackson and FM Lord Bramall, *The chiefs: the story of the United Kingdom Chiefs of Staff* (Brassey's 1992), p. 294.
62 Snyder, *The politics of British defence policy*, pp. 137–8.
63 Zuckerman archive, AMSSPC/P(59)12 of 22 May 1959 in SZ/AMSSP/3.
64 Guy Finch, 'The air staff and the deterrent 1943–63', presentation to the British Rocketry Oral History Project conference at Charterhouse, April 2006.
65 David Edgerton, *England and the aeroplane: an essay on a militant and technological nation* (Macmillan 1991).
66 George Hicks (ed. Roy Dommett), 'History of RAE and nuclear weapons', *Prospero* 2 (Spring 2005), pp. 155–78.
67 Sidney Pollard, quoted in Hennessy, *Whitehall*, p. 8.

Chapter 1

1 Cmnd. 124, *Defence: outline of future policy*, Apr 1957, paras. 13–15.
2 Cmnd. 363, *Report on defence*, Feb 1958, paras. 12–13.
3 *ibid.*, para. 38.
4 Cmnd. 952, *Report on defence*, Feb 1960, para. 3.
5 The July 1958 Defence Committee paper in which this creed was set down, D(58)33, has not been declassified, but the extract was quoted subsequently for the benefit of a wider official readership, e.g., in DB(58)10 of 29 Oct 1958 in PRO, DEFE 30/1. Kate Pyne has pointed out that these points match closely those used by the Chiefs of Staff to justify the production of thermonuclear weapons in 1954 (pers. comm. 8 Jan 2008).
6 PRO, D(58)24th mtg 5 Nov 1958 in CAB 131/19.
7 *ibid.*
8 PRO, 'Study of future policy: record of a meeting held at Chequers on 7 Jun 1959' in AIR 8/1961.
9 *ibid.* This was MRAF Sir Dermot Boyle's copy of the paper, and the marginalia indicate that it was he who made the 'suggestion' that Britain would still need an independent nuclear capability.
10 See Peter Hennessy's account of the future policy study in *Having it so good*, pp. 576–86.
11 PRO, FP(60)1 of 24 Feb 1960, quoted in 21 Dec 1960 paper in AIR 20/10067. (The FPC report also became a cabinet paper C(60)35 of 29 Feb 1960 in CAB 129/100, where these passages appear in paras 38–40).
12 Pierre, *Nuclear politics*, p. 170.
13 Martin, 'The market for strategic ideas in Britain', p. 37.
14 Timothy Raison, quoted in Pierre, *Nuclear politics*, p. 177.
15 Geelhoed and Edmonds, *Eisenhower, Macmillan and Allied Unity*, pp. vi–vii.
16 Ashton, *Kennedy, Macmillan and the Cold War*, pp. 6–7.

17 Quoted in Geelhoed and Edmonds, *Eisenhower, Macmillan and Allied Unity*, p. xxxi.
18 US Dept of State, *Department of State Bulletin* 11 Nov 1957, pp. 739–41.
19 Botti, for example, describes British historians' accounts of interdependence, specifically in the nuclear field, as 'startlingly foolish self-delusion' (*The long wait*, p. 241).
20 John Newhouse, *The nuclear age: from Hiroshima to star wars* (Michael Joseph 1989), p. 117. Donald N Michael, on the other hand, noted a fairly stoical reaction away from Washington among the American public: 'The beginning of the space age and American public opinion', *The Public Opinion Quarterly* 24/4 (Winter 1960), pp. 573–82.
21 Writing on 6 October, and quoted in Clark, *Nuclear diplomacy*, p. 80.
22 PRO, papers in AIR 2/14711.
23 PRO, papers in AVIA 65/1564.
24 Quoted in 'Some historical comments and background on TTCP', paper from the Canadian embassy in Washington prepared for the 25th anniversary meeting of the non-atomic military research and development principals, 12–13 October 1983: http://www.dtic.mil/ttcp/history25.htm (accessed July 2007).
25 See Margaret Gowing, *Britain and atomic energy 1939–45* (Macmillan 1964); Ferenc Morton Szasz, *British scientists and the Manhattan project: the Los Alamos years* (Macmillan 1992).
26 Simpson, *The independent nuclear state*, ch. 6; Arnold, *Britain and the H-bomb*, ch. 14; Clark, *Nuclear diplomacy*, ch. 3; Melissen, *The struggle for nuclear partnership*; Botti, *The long wait*; John Baylis, 'Exchanging nuclear secrets: laying the foundations of the Anglo-American nuclear relationship', *Diplomatic History* 25/1 (Winter 2001), pp. 33–61.
27 Clark, *Nuclear diplomacy*, pp. 85–6.
28 Cmnd. 537, *Agreement for cooperation on the uses of atomic energy for mutual defence purposes*, 3 July 1958.
29 Simpson, *The independent nuclear state*, pp. 144–9; Clark, *Nuclear diplomacy*, pp. 92–7.
30 Cmnd. 859, *Amendment to the agreement for cooperation on the uses of atomic energy for mutual defence purposes of 3 July 1958*, 7 May 1959.
31 Stephen Twigge and Len Scott, *Planning Armageddon: Britain, the United States and the command of western nuclear forces 1945–64* (Amsterdam, Harwood 2000), pp. 115–19 and appendix 4; William Burr, *Consultation is presidential business: secret understandings on the use of nuclear weapons, 1950–74*, National security archive electronic briefing book no. 159: http://www.gwu.edu/~nsarchiv/NSAEBB/NSAEBB159/ (accessed July 2007). Botti denied the existence of this agreement (*The Long Wait*, p. 239).
32 Macmillan to Eisenhower, 2 Jan 1958 in US Dept of State, *Foreign Relations of the United States 1958–60*, vol. VII, p. 796.
33 *ibid*.
34 Clark, *Nuclear diplomacy*, p. 202.
35 Byron R Fairchild and Walter S Poole, *History of the Joint Chiefs of Staff: the Joint Chiefs of Staff and national policy 1956–60* (Washington DC, Office of the Chairman of the JCS 2000), p. 64.
36 Clark, *Nuclear diplomacy*, pp. 201, 210.

264 *Notes to pages 38–42*

37 Listed in more detail in PRO, Geneva to London telegram, 12 May 1959 in PREM 11/2861.
38 PRO, Press to Macklen, 15 Nov 1958 in DEFE 19/5.
39 Peter Goodchild, *Edward Teller: the real Dr Strangelove* (Weidenfeld and Nicolson 2004), pp. 280–1.
40 John Walker, *Britain, the United States, weapon policies and nuclear testing, 1954–73: tensions and contradictions* (forthcoming).
41 US Dept of State, *Foreign Relations of the United States 1958–60*, vol. VII, pp. 828–47.
42 James Killian, Eisenhower's science adviser, quoted in Clark, *Nuclear diplomacy*, p. 213.
43 Clark, *Nuclear diplomacy*, p. 207; HoC oral answers, vol. 610, col. 676 (30 July 1959).
44 Oliver, *Kennedy, Macmillan and the nuclear test ban debate*, p. 14. Fairchild and Poole, *The Joint Chiefs of Staff and national policy*, p. 67.
45 PRO, Selwyn Lloyd to Macmillan, 22 April 1960 in PREM 11/3162.
46 Geelhoed and Edmonds, *Eisenhower, Macmillan and allied unity*, p. 118.
47 Martha Smith-Norris, 'The Eisenhower administration and the nuclear test-ban talks, 1958–60: another challenge to 'revisionism'', *Diplomatic History* 27/4 (Sep 2003), pp. 503–41.
48 Fairchild and Poole, *The Joint Chiefs of Staff and national policy*, p. 72.
49 Clark, *Nuclear diplomacy*, p. 209.
50 H W Brands, 'The age of vulnerability: Eisenhower and the national insecurity state', *The American Historical Review* 94/4 (Oct 1989), pp. 963–89.
51 Quoted in Fairchild and Poole, *The Joint Chiefs of Staff and national policy*, p. 70.
52 Quoted in Hennessy, *Having it so good*, p. 612.
53 Walker, *Britain, the United States, weapon policies and nuclear testing*.
54 Samuel R Williamson Jr and Steven L Rearden, *The origins of US nuclear strategy 1945–53* (New York, St Martin's Press 1993), p. 163.
55 Richard E Neustadt, *Report to JFK: the Skybolt crisis in perspective* (Cornell UP 1999), p. 121.
56 Quoted in Brown, *Flying blind*, p. 197.
57 Peter J Roman, 'Strategic bombers over the missile horizon', *Journal of Strategic Studies* 18/1 (Mar 1995), p. 199.
58 Gen Curtis E LeMay USAF with MacKinlay Kantor, *Mission with LeMay: my story* (New York, Doubleday 1965), p. 308.
59 Anon., 'A nuclear-powered plane?', *Time* 13 Jan 1958. (Herbert York rendered this quotation still more obscurely as 'a shitepike' in *Race to oblivion: a participant's view of the arms race* (New York, Simon and Schuster 1970), p. 64).
60 Finch, 'The nuclear deterrent and the air staff'.
61 Wynn, *RAF strategic nuclear deterrent forces*, pp. 373–4.
62 PRO, D(58)47 of 8 Sep 1958, CAB 131/20.
63 PRO, D(58)18th mtg 10 Sep 1958 in CAB 131/19; Clark, *Nuclear diplomacy*, pp. 170–1.
64 PRO, report of Sandys's visit to the US 21 Sep–5 Oct 1958 in DEFE 11/360.
65 PRO, record of talks on cooperation on missile development in the US, 23/4 Sep 1958 in DEFE 13/180; on NATO ballistic missiles, see below.

66 PRO, DB(58)8 of 15 Oct 1958 in DEFE 30/1.
67 PRO, DB/C(58)1st mtg conclusions (extract) in DEFE 24/11.
68 PRO, 1L to 1SL 17 Oct 1958 in ADM 205/202. The reference was to the 'nuclear sufficiency' argument, which was discussed at great length between Sandys and the service chiefs a few days later, although Selkirk also no doubt had Polaris at the back of his mind.
69 PRO, Selkirk to Macmillan, 4 Nov 1958 in DEFE 24/11.
70 PRO, D(58)57 of 3 Nov 1958, D(58)63 of 17 Nov 1958 in CAB 131/20; D(58)24th mtg, 5 Nov 1958 in CAB 131/19; Wynn, *RAF strategic nuclear deterrent forces*, pp. 382–6.
71 PRO, COS(59)1st mtg, 1 Jan 1959 in DEFE 4/115; Clark, *Nuclear diplomacy*, p. 174.
72 PRO, Sabatini (Sandys's private secretary) to Powell, 4 Jun 1959 in DEFE 13/617; summary of Chequers discussions, 7 Jun 1959 in AIR 8/1961; Wynn, *RAF strategic nuclear deterrent forces*, p. 387.
73 Kenneth Nash, Head of M [Military] Branch (I) in the Admiralty, referred to the BNDSG as such, for example, in briefing notes of 24 Oct and Dec 1961 in PRO, ADM 1/31023, although there is no particular reason to believe he invented the term.
74 PRO, BND(SG)(59)19(Final) of 31 Dec 1959 in DEFE 7/1328.
75 PRO, Ronald Kent (Air Ministry AUS(A)) note of 25 Sep 1959 in AIR 2/17371. 'Damage' was a slightly ambiguous term, often used loosely but perhaps retaining its strict wartime meaning relating to dehousing German workers: 50 per cent damage would equate to 50 per cent of houses made uninhabitable by blast. Empirical study during the war had shown that rather less damage than this was needed to 'knock out' a city economically, but only later did the JIGSAW group began to refine the concept of 'breakdown'. All calculations would have taken into account probabilities for accuracy and ability to reach the target point, but would have underestimated the likely damage from fire and fallout, less reliable phenomena than blast. I am grateful to John Coker and Dr Edgar Anstey for their comments on the subject (pers. comm. 20 Jan 2008 and 24 Nov 1996, respectively).
76 PRO, BND(SG)(59)19(Final) of 31 Dec 1959 in DEFE 7/1328.
77 MCIS, Slater archive, unref (originally PRO) paper Kent to VCAS, 2 Nov 1959.
78 PRO, BND(SG)(59)19(Final) of 31 Dec 1959 in DEFE 7/1328.
79 PRO, BND(SG)(59)9th mtg, 19 Nov 1959 in DEFE 7/2301.
80 PRO, SA/AC paper of 12 Nov 1959 in DEFE 7/2216.
81 PRO, Zuckerman to Watkinson, 19 Feb 1960 in DEFE 7/2247.
82 PRO, Chilver to Watkinson, 22 Jan 1960 in DEFE 7/2247.
83 Zuckerman archive, AMSSPC/P(59)11 of May 1959 in SZ/AMSSP/3.
84 Zuckerman archive, AMSSPC/P(59)16, undated (after Sep 1959) in SZ/AMSSP/3.
85 Wynn, *RAF strategic nuclear deterrent forces*, pp. 389–93; quote from p. 392.
86 Clark, *Nuclear diplomacy*, p. 178.
87 Upavon parish-council website: http://www.upavonpc.co.uk (accessed July 2007).
88 Richard Maguire, 'Cancelling Blue Streak', presentation to the British Rocketry Oral History Project conference at Charterhouse, April 2006.

89 PRO, papers in AIR 2/14711.
90 PRO, BND(SG)(59)19(Final) of 31 Dec 1959 in DEFE 7/1328.
91 PRO, brief for CDS, 22 Jan 1960 in DEFE 7/2278; Wynn, *RAF strategic nuclear deterrent forces*, p. 406.
92 Writing on 27 Jan 1960 and quoted in Wynn, *RAF strategic nuclear deterrent forces*, p. 407. The list of Ward's interlocutors is interesting; they could hardly have given a downbeat assessment. See also PRO, SofS's mtg of 21 Jan 1960 in AIR 8/2256.
93 PRO, COS(60)8th mtg, 2 Feb 1960 (confidential annexe) in AIR 8/2256; COS(60)28 of 5 Feb 1960 in AVIA 66/1.
94 Clark, *Nuclear diplomacy*, pp. 181–3.
95 HoC debs., vol. 621 cols. 1265–6; Hill, *A vertical empire*, pp. 110–13. The *Guardian* newspaper described the scenes in the House of Commons as 'bedlam' (14 Apr 1960, p. 1).
96 Sir Frederick Brundrett, 'Rockets, satellites and military thinking', *Journal of the RUSI* 105 (Aug 1960), pp. 339–40.
97 PRO, Nash note of 1 Apr 1960 in ADM 1/31023.
98 PRO, 1SL's weekly mtg, 17 Sep 1958 in ADM 205/172.
99 Mountbatten's files on deterrent policy from this time are in PRO, DEFE 25/13 and Hartley Library, MB1/J311. His silence on Blue Streak was in marked contrast, for example, to his persistent and vocal opposition to TSR.2.
100 PRO, Lambe to Selkirk, 25 May 1959, ADM 1/27389.
101 PRO, Couchman to Thistleton-Smith, undated draft and final letter 26 Apr 1960 in ADM 1/27389.
102 Clark, *Nuclear diplomacy*, pp. 288–90.
103 PRO, Strath to Playfair, 10 Feb 1960 in DEFE 7/2247.
104 Martin, 'The market for strategic ideas in Britain', p. 28; ACdre Henry Probert, *High Commanders of the Royal Air Force* (HMSO 1991), p. 54.
105 RAF Museum, Boyle papers: *My life: an autobiography by MRAF Sir Dermot Boyle* (privately published, 1989), pp. 108–9; also transcripts of recollections in MF 10101/17.
106 Wynn, *RAF strategic nuclear deterrent forces*, p. 408; PRO, Dean's introductory note to his personal papers on 'The Skybolt story' in T 325/88.
107 PRO, Pike to DCAS, 19 Feb 1960 in AIR 8/2256.
108 For example in Watkinson's memoirs: *Turning points*, pp. 122–5.
109 PRO, Watkinson to Sandys, 9 Feb 1960 in AVIA 66/1 (and reproduced in Charles Martin, *De Havilland Blue Streak: an illustrated story* (British Interplanetary Society 2002), pp. 207–8). The remark is somewhat enigmatic, although it does seem to point to some direct measure of blame on Boyle for the cancellation. T C G James notes that 'once CAS was committed to the collective advice of the Chiefs of Staff [on the military inutility of Blue Streak] it was not practical politics for the Air Ministry to argue the contrary case' – although the chief who had endorsed this conclusion was Pike, rather than Boyle (*Defence policy and the RAF 1956–63*, PRO, AIR 41/86, p. 245).
110 Christopher Driver, *The disarmers: a study in protest* (Hodder and Stoughton 1964), p. 12.
111 ibid., pp. 51–3; Richard Taylor, *Against the bomb: the British peace movement 1958–65* (Oxford, Clarendon Press 1988), pp. 26–7.

Notes to pages 51–56   267

112 Quoted in Driver, *The disarmers*, p. 72. Marquand was an academic political scientist, and later became a Labour MP.
113 *ibid.*, p. 55.
114 *ibid.*, pp. 98/9; Snyder, *The politics of British defence policy*, p. 60; George H Gallup, ed., *The Gallup International Public Opinion Polls: Great Britain 1937–75* (New York, Random House 1976), p. 604.
115 Sandbrook, *Never had it so good*, p. 257.
116 Quoted in Driver, *The disarmers*, p. 125.
117 'Britain Belongs to You: The Labour Party's Policy for Consideration by the British People', http://www.labour-party.org.uk/manifestos/1959/1959-labour-manifesto.shtml (accessed July 2007).
118 Quoted in Driver, *The disarmers*, p. 67.
119 See references in the *Guardian* newspaper's reports of the 1960 and 1961 Labour party conferences (6 Oct 1960, p. 5; 5 Oct 1961, p. 3), and of the 1962 House of Commons debate on the defence white paper (7 Mar 1962, p. 2). See also Taylor, *Against the bomb*, pp. 291–2.
120 Pierre, *Nuclear politics*, p. 201.
121 The best short accounts of Labour's difficulties over nuclear weapons in this period are Pierre, *Nuclear politics*, pp. 201–7; and J P G Freeman, *Britain's nuclear arms control policy in the context of Anglo-American relations 1957–68* (Macmillan 1986), ch. 3.
122 Brian Brivati, *Hugh Gaitskell* (Richard Cohen 1996), p. 354.
123 *ibid.*, p. 371.
124 A vote on the party's official policy and on two rival unilateralist resolutions, one sponsored by the transport and general workers and one by the amalgamated engineering union.
125 K Hindell and P Williams, 'Scarborough and Blackpool: an analysis of some votes at the Labour party conferences of 1960 and 1961', *Political Quarterly* 33/3 (Jul–Sep 1962), pp. 306–22.
126 Driver, *The disarmers*, p. 182; Matthew Grant, presentation to the British Rocketry Oral History Project conference at Charterhouse, April 2004; Cmnd. 363, *Report on defence*, Feb 1958, quotes a figure of half a million involved in civil defence.
127 Freeman, *Britain's nuclear arms control policy*, p. 45.
128 Pierre, *Nuclear politics*, p. 207.
129 MC 14/2 (Revised) (Final Decision) of 23 May 1957 in Gregory W Pedlow, ed., *NATO strategy documents 1949–69* (SHAPE Historical Office, 1997): http://www.nato.int/archives/strategy.htm (accessed July 2007).
130 Richard Moore, *The Royal Navy and nuclear weapons* (Frank Cass 2001), ch. 2.
131 MC 14/2 (Revised) (Final Decision) of 23 May 1957.
132 Ralph Dietl, 'In defence of the west: General Lauris Norstad, NATO nuclear forces and transatlantic relations 1956–1963', *Diplomacy and Statecraft*, 17 (2006), pp. 347–92.
133 PRO, General staff training publication 'The corps tactical battle in nuclear war' Apr 1958 in WO 279/279; Gen Sir Hugh Beach and Nadine Gurr, *Flattering the passions: the bomb and Britain's bid for a world role* (IB Tauris 1999), p. 82.
134 Sean M Maloney, 'Berlin Contingency Planning: Prelude to Flexible Response, 1958–63', *Journal of Strategic Studies*, 25/1 (Mar 2002), p. 101.

135 John Duffield, *Power rules: the evolution of NATO's conventional force posture* (Stanford UP 1995), p. 133.
136 Such an assessment remains extremely controversial today. See Walt Rostow's *Pre-Invasion Bombing Strategy: General Eisenhower's Decision of March 25, 1944* (Univ of Texas Press 1981) and Solly Zuckerman's opposed account in *From Apes to Warlords*, ch. 12–15. Zuckerman's involvement in the controversy during the war, and his later involvement in British nuclear-weapons policy, are significant.
137 Duffield, *Power rules*, p. 130.
138 Quoted in James, *Defence Policy and the RAF*, p. 119, PRO, AIR 41/86.
139 As described in PRO, Annex B to COS(61)230 of 19 July 1961 in DEFE 13/427.
140 PRO, Mountbatten to Watkinson, 17 Nov 1960 in DEFE 13/425.
141 Moore, *The Royal Navy and nuclear weapons*, p. 148 note 53.
142 Hartley Library, Mountbatten's 12 Mar 1957 redraft of his opening address for the Fairlead conference, MB1/I143.
143 PRO, Board of Admiralty memo B.1211 of 11 July 1958 in ADM 167/152.
144 PRO, DB(58)1st mtg 31 Jul 1958 in DEFE 30/1.
145 PRO, Dickson to Sandys, 18 Sep 1958 in DEFE 7/2300.
146 PRO, Stratton to Festing, 29 Oct 1958 in WO 216/934.
147 PRO, minutes of meeting MOM/56 of 28 Oct 1958 (dated 20 Nov 1958) in DEFE 7/2300. Mountbatten objected to the record of the meeting (note of 28 Nov 1958 in same file).
148 PRO, paper attached to Board of Admiralty memo B.1231 of 23 Sep 1958 in ADM 167/152.
149 PRO, Board of Admiralty memo B.1273 of 22 Jun 1959 in ADM 167/153.
150 PRO, Board of Admiralty minute 5328 of 25 Jun 1959 in ADM 167/155.
151 LtGen Sir John Cowley, 'Future trends in warfare', *Journal of the RUSI* 55/617, pp. 4–16.
152 Martin, 'The market for strategic ideas in Britain', pp. 32–3; papers in PRO, CAB 21/3900.
153 Richard Moore, 'A JIGSAW puzzle for operational researchers: British global war studies, 1954–62', *Journal of Strategic Studies* 20/1 (Jun 1997), pp. 75–91; also Peter Hennessy, *The secret state: Whitehall and the cold war* (Penguin 2002), esp. pp. 151–4.
154 PRO, COS(58)2nd mtg 7 Jan 1958 (confidential annexe) in DEFE 4/103.
155 PRO, COS(59)255 also COS(JGW)(59)11(Final) of 20 Oct 1959 in DEFE 5/96.
156 PRO, quoted passages from successive drafts of COS(JGW)(60)9 between Oct and 2 Nov 1960 in DEFE 10/403; see also Zuckerman to Mountbatten, 24 May 1960, covering a brief on the subject, in DEFE 7/2236.
157 Hartley Library, record of informal UK-US talks on atomic weapons, 14–19 Jul 1960 in MB1/J314.
158 Invitation list in Zuckerman archive, SZ/CSA/32/2; Dr Edgar Anstey, pers. comm. 24 Nov 1996.
159 Zuckerman, *Monkeys, men and missiles*, p. 280.
160 Zuckerman archive, SZ/CSA/32/4.
161 Zuckerman archive, SZ/CSA/32/10. Zuckerman recalled that the model had been borrowed from the Home Office and actually represented outer London (*Monkeys, men and missiles*, p. 295).

162 Zuckerman archive, SZ/CSA/32/8.
163 Zuckerman archive, SZ/CSA/32/5.
164 Zuckerman archive, SZ/CSA/32/9.
165 Zuckerman, *Monkeys, men and missiles*, p. 295.
166 See e.g., Zuckerman's address to the SHAPEX symposium in May 1961, published as 'Judgment and control in modern warfare' in *Foreign Affairs* in Jan 1962, and reprinted in his collection of essays *Scientists and war* (Hamish Hamilton 1966), pp. 101–21; Mountbatten's speech to the following year's SHAPEX, in Hartley Library, MB1/M33; Zuckerman, *Nuclear illusion and reality* (Collins 1982), ch. 4; Maguire, 'Scientific dissent amid the United Kingdom government's nuclear weapons programme', p. 125.
167 Robert J Watson, *History of the Office of the Secretary of Defense vol. IV: Into the missile age 1956–60* (Washington DC, Office of the Secretary of Defense, 1997), p. 516.
168 Security resources panel of the [Presidential] Science Advisory Committee, *Deterrence and survival in the nuclear age* (Washington, 7 Nov 1957): http://www.gwu.edu/~nsarchiv/NSAEBB/NSAEBB139/nitze02.pdf (accessed Aug 2007).
169 Watson, *Into the missile age*, p. 525; PRO, paper of 2 Feb 1959 (from Sandys?) in DEFE 7/2247.
170 Fairchild and Poole, *The Joint Chiefs of Staff and national policy*, p. 106.
171 Watson, *Into the missile age*, p. 547; Fairchild and Poole, *The Joint Chiefs of Staff and national policy*, pp. 107–8.
172 Dietl, 'In defence of the west', p. 359.
173 Watson, *Into the missile age*, pp. 548–9; Dietl, 'In defence of the west', pp. 360–1; Fairchild and Poole, *The Joint Chiefs of Staff and national policy*, p. 109.
174 PRO, Watkinson draft memo of 30 Sep 1960 in AIR 8/2288.
175 PRO, COS(60)256 of 14 Sep 1960 in DEFE 13/425.
176 Quoted in James, *Defence policy and the RAF*, p. 121, PRO, AIR 41/86.
177 PRO, Annex to COS.1394/26/10/60 of 26 Oct 1960 in AIR 8/2288.
178 PRO, COS.211/14/2/61 of 14 Feb 1961 in DEFE 13/426.
179 *ibid.*
180 Watson, *Into the missile age*, p. 562; PRO, Nov 1959 papers in ADM 205/222; Watkinson to Macmillan 14 Dec 1959 in PREM 11/2940.
181 Clark, *Nuclear diplomacy*, p. 270.
182 Clark, *Nuclear diplomacy*, pp. 258–80; Ronald D Landa, 'The origins of the Skybolt controversy in the Eisenhower administration', in Roger G Miller, ed., *Seeing off the bear: Anglo-American airpower cooperation during the cold war* (Washington DC, USAF 1995), pp. 117–31.
183 Watson, *Into the missile age*, pp. 562–3; Herter to Eisenhower, 27 Mar 1960 in US Dept of State, *Foreign Relations of the United States 1958–60*, vol. VII, pp. 860–1.
184 Watson, *Into the missile age*, p. 563.
185 US Dept of State, *Foreign Relations of the United States 1958–60*, vol. VII, pp. 861–5 (the inclusion of the Skybolt memorandum of understanding on p. 864 of the *FRUS* volume is slightly misleading; this was not formally concluded until 6 June during Watkinson's visit to Washington).

186 PRO, Burke to Lambe, 27 Mar 1960 and related correspondence in ADM 1/27389.
187 PRO, Watkinson to Mountbatten, 3 May 1960 and reply of 10 May 1960 in DEFE 13/295.
188 US Dept of State, *Foreign Relations of the United States 1958–60*, vol. VII, p. 864; PRO, C(60)97 of 20 Jun 1960 in CAB 129/101.
189 Watson, *Into the missile age*, pp. 564–6.
190 PRO, Watkinson to Macmillan, 7 Jun 1960 in CAB 21/4979.
191 PRO, draft paper of 9 Jun 1960 (not eventually submitted) in DEFE 13/295.
192 PRO, note of a meeting between Macmillan, Watkinson, Selwyn Lloyd, Playfair, Zuckerman and Sir Patrick Dean, 15 June 1960 in DEFE 7/2063.
193 Moore, *The Royal Navy and nuclear weapons*, p. 161.
194 PRO, C(60)97 of 20 Jun 1960 in CAB 129/101; CC(60)35 of 20 Jun 1960 in CAB 128/34.
195 PRO, C(60)98 of 20 Jun 1960 in CAB 129/101 and CC(60)35 of 20 Jun 1960 in CAB 128/34.
196 PRO, Macmillan to Eisenhower, 24 Jun 1960 by telegram in PREM 11/2940.
197 Geelhoed and Edmonds, *Eisenhower, Macmillan and allied unity*, pp. 146–7; PRO, Eisenhower to Macmillan, 30 Jun 1960 and 15 Jul 1960 in PREM 11/2940.
198 Brian Lavery, 'The British government and the American Polaris base in the Clyde', *Journal for Maritime Research* (Sep 2001): http://www.jmr.nmm.ac.uk/server/show/ConJmrArticle.2/setPaginate/No (accessed July 2007).
199 HoC debs., vol. 629, col. 37 (1 Nov 1960); HoC oral answers, vol. 629, cols. 830–42 (8 Nov 1960); HoC debs., vol. 632, cols. 739–840 (16 Dec 1960).
200 Memorandum of conference Eisenhower, Goodpaster, Bowie, 16 Aug 1960; memorandum of conference Eisenhower, Goodpaster, Bowie, Norstad, 12 Sep 1960, both in US Dept of State, *Foreign relations of the United States 1958–60*, vol. VII, pp. 611–14, 628–32.
201 Fairchild and Poole, *The Joint Chiefs of Staff and national policy*, pp. 110–11.
202 Presidential National Security Action Memorandum 40, 'NATO and the Atlantic nations', 20 Apr 1961 (approved by Kennedy 21 Apr) in US Dept of State, *Foreign relations of the United States 1961–3*, vol. XIII, pp. 285–91.
203 Fred Kaplan, *The wizards of armageddon* (New York, Simon and Schuster 1984), pp. 271–2; Ball, *Politics and force levels*, p. 119.
204 Robert S McNamara, 'The military role of nuclear weapons: perceptions and misperceptions', *Foreign Affairs* 62/1 (Oct 1983), pp. 59–80.
205 Ashton, *Kennedy, Macmillan and the cold war*, pp. 1–4; idem, 'Harold Macmillan and the 'golden days' of Anglo-American relations revisited'.
206 PRO, draft of Defence Committee paper D(61)24 of May 1961 in DEFE 13/427.
207 J W Boulton, 'NATO and the MLF', *Journal of Contemporary History* 7/3–4 (Jul–Oct 1972), p. 279.
208 Pierre, *Nuclear politics*, p. 244.
209 Martin Navias, *Nuclear weapons and British strategic planning 1955–58*, pp. 39–51; Karl Hack, *Defence and decolonisation in south-east Asia: Britain, Malaya and Singapore 1941–68* (Richmond, Curzon 2001), pp. 206–10.
210 James, *Defence policy and the RAF 1956–63*, PRO, AIR 41/86, p. 196.

211 PRO, COS(60)1st mtg of 5 Jan 1960 in DEFE 4/124.
212 James, *Defence policy and the RAF 1956–63*, PRO, AIR 41/86, p. 197 (and see more generally pp. 196–204); the final paper was COS(60)200 of 5 Jul 1960 in DEFE 5/105.
213 PRO, COS.1519/3/12/59 of 3 Dec 1959; JP(60)16(Final) of 3 Apr 1960; JP(60) Note 28 of 27 Jun 1960 all in DEFE 7/2231.
214 PRO, JP(60)16(Final) App B (Revised) of 28 Jun 1960 in DEFE 7/2231.
215 James, *Defence policy and the RAF 1956–63*, PRO, AIR 41/86, p. 202.
216 PRO, SofSAir to Macmillan 26 Jul 1962 (retrospective account) in PREM 11/4475.
217 James, *Defence policy and the RAF 1956–63*, PRO, AIR 41/86, pp. 206–8.
218 *ibid.*, p. 209.
219 See most recently Ken Young, 'The Skybolt crisis of 1962: muddle or mischief?', *Journal of Strategic Studies* 27/4 (Dec 2004), pp. 614–35.
220 PRO, Zuckerman to Minister, 1 Nov 1960 in DEFE 13/408; and Skybolt historical summary of June 1960 in AVIA 65/2019. A fairly comprehensive account of the missile's chequered political history in the US can be found in Roman, 'Strategic bombers over the missile horizon', and *idem*., *Eisenhower and the missile gap* (Cornell UP 1995), pp. 161–3.
221 PRO, Defence Research Staff newsletter 1 Jan 1963 in T 325/88.
222 PRO, Skybolt historical summary of June 1960 in AVIA 65/2019.
223 The PSAC missile panel's report ('The Skybolt Air Launched Ballistic Missile Programme' of 21 July 1960, doc. no. NSA00508 in *US Nuclear History: Nuclear Arms and Policy in the Missile Age 1955–68* (National Security Archive microfilm document series, Chadwyck-Healey 1998)), recommended that 'serious consideration should be given to cancelling Skybolt before more effort and money is expended' and Zuckerman quoted this passage, reversing only the order of 'money' and 'effort' – PRO, Zuckerman to Minister, 1 Nov 1960 in DEFE 13/408 and DEFE 19/76.
224 Ball, *Politics and force levels*, p. 22.
225 York, *Race to oblivion*, p. 155.
226 Quoted in Ball, *Politics and force levels*, p. 227.
227 *ibid.*, p. 183.
228 PRO, Zuckerman to Minister, 8 Aug 1962, DEFE 7/2160.
229 Neustadt, *Report to JFK*, p. 33. See also the Washington air attaché's account of 'the damage which Sir Solly has done': PRO, Emson to CAS, 2 Nov 1962 in AIR 19/1036.
230 Zuckerman archive, undated paper *c*. Nov 1960, SZ/CSA/192/39.
231 Zuckerman archive, Zuckerman to Watkinson, 16 June 1960, SZ/CSA/192/17.
232 PRO, Kent to VCAS, 9 Mar 1960 in AIR 2/13708.
233 PRO, brief for CAS on COS(60)48 of 25 Feb 1960 in AIR 8/2256.
234 PRO, BND(SG)(60)3 of 12 Apr 1960 in DEFE 7/1328.
235 PRO, drafts of 5 Sep 1960 for BND(SG)(60)6 on Blue Steel and BND(SG)(60)9 on TSR.2 in DEFE 7/2302.
236 PRO, BND(SG)(60)10(Final) of 30 Sep 1960 in DEFE 7/2302.
237 PRO, draft briefing from Playfair to Watkinson, 11 Oct 1960 [not sent] and note of mtg MM.51/60 (Watkinson, Playfair, Mountbatten, Zuckerman), 27 Nov 1960 in DEFE 7/2302.

238 PRO, Constant to VCAS, 9 Mar 1961 in AIR 20/11530.
239 PRO, Lighthill to Zuckerman, 27 Jun 1961 in AIR 20/11530.
240 PRO, BND(TSC)(61)15(Final) of 27 Jul 1961 in DEFE 13/617.

Chapter 2

1 PRO, AM Geoffrey Tuttle to Brundrett, 4 Mar 1958 in AIR 2/13213.
2 PRO, A/ACAS(Ops) note of 4 Mar 1959 in AIR 2/13678.
3 PRO, AC(59)47 of 29 May 1959 in AIR 6/117.
4 PRO, brief for DRP(AES) mtg 12 Jul 1961 in DEFE 7/1888; PM's brief of 13 Mar 1961 in PREM 11/3724.
5 Margaret Gowing, *Independence and deterrence, Vol. 2* provides an account of the early years; of the later books, Simpson's *The independent nuclear state* makes most of the linkages between civil and military programmes.
6 Simpson, *The independent nuclear state*, app. 4; David Albright, Frans Berkhout and William Walker, *Plutonium and highly enriched uranium 1996: world inventories, capabilities and policies* (OUP/SIPRI 1997), p. 63.
7 UK ministry of defence, 'Historical accounting and plutonium' and 'Plutonium and Aldermaston: an historical account' (MoD 2000) available from: http://www.mod.uk/DefenceInternet/AboutDefence/CorporatePublications/DefenceEstateandEnvironmentPublications/UKNucWeaponsProg/ (accessed August 2007).
8 Simpson, *The independent nuclear state*, p. 262 (quoting 10,000lb in kg gives a spurious precision to this estimate); Albright *et al.*, *Plutonium and highly enriched uranium*, pp. 117–18.
9 PRO, numerous papers in AB 16/4189, esp. 1 Nov 1962 paper and attachments on apportionment of capital costs. The Capenhurst plant's original capacity was 400kg/yr, rising by 350kg/yr on three separate occasions, following a programme of expansions agreed for military purposes early in 1954 and 1955 and for civil purposes at the end of 1955. Assuming these expansions to have come on line in March 1957, 1958 and 1959, with the known run-down in 1962/63, gives the figure of 7600kg.
10 See PRO, brief of May 1956 in AVIA 65/1114, for one assessment that existing requirements for U235 could not be met until the year 2043! An Air Ministry official took pleasure in describing a number of naval weapons requirements as 'grossly extravagant in fissile material' at the end of 1955: note of 8 December 1955 in AIR 2/13693. On the fissile material situation in 1958, see also Sandys to Macmillan, 22 May 1958 in WO 32/17182.
11 PRO, Brundrett to Tuttle, 1 May 1959 in AIR 2/15261.
12 Don McIntyre, 'Project Crystal: lithium-6 for H-bombs', presentation to the British Rocketry Oral History Project conference at Charterhouse, April 2007; PRO, note of 14 Jun 1961 in AVIA 65/2332.
13 PRO, note of 21 Jul 1961 in AVIA 65/2332.
14 PRO, ND(62)15 in AVIA 65/1771; Makins to Seaborg, 26 Jun 1961 in AVIA 65/2332.
15 In the words of one nuclear insider, 'the Aldermaston/Burghfield interface was not an easy one to manage' – Frank Panton, pers. comm. 18 Jan 2008.

16 Lorna Arnold, *Britain and the H-bomb*, p. 78; Brian Cathcart, 'William George Penney, Baron Penney (1909–91)', *Oxford Dictionary of National Biography*.
17 Arnold, *Britain and the H-bomb*, pp. 78–9; John Challens, 'Sir William Richard Joseph Cook (1905–87)', *Oxford Dictionary of National Biography*; William Penney and V H B Macklen, 'William Richard Joseph Cook', *Biographical memoirs of fellows of the Royal Society* 34 (1988), pp. 44–61.
18 Carey Sublette, *Nuclear weapons frequently asked questions*, §4.5: http://nuclearweaponarchive.org/Nwfaq/Nfaq4-5.html (accessed Aug 2007); data from Dominic test series: http://nuclearweaponarchive.org/Usa/Tests/Dominic.html (accessed Aug 1997).
19 Simpson, *The independent nuclear state*, 2nd edn, p. xxiv.
20 The subject is dealt with at length in Arnold, *Britain and the H-bomb*.
21 The best accounts are in Robert S Norris, Andrew S Burrows and Richard W Fieldhouse, *Nuclear weapons databook, Vol. 5: British, French and Chinese nuclear weapons* (Oxford, NRDC/Westview 1994), pp. 46–9; Arnold, *Britain and the H-bomb*, pp. 201–14.
22 PRO, planning papers in AVIA 65/1352.
23 PRO, Cook to DGAW, 19 May 1958 in AVIA 65/1441.
24 PRO, DRP(AES)/M(58)2 of 11 Nov 1958 in AVIA 65/1116.
25 PRO, NT(58)7th mtg of 5 Dec 1958 in CAB 134/2274.
26 PRO, briefs for Macmillan of 7 January and June 1959 in DEFE 13/150.
27 PRO, D(59)23 of 7 July 1959 in CAB 131/22; DGAW note of 10 July 1959 in AIR 2/13753.
28 Richard Moore, 'British nuclear warhead design 1958–66: how much American help?', *Defence Studies* 4/2 (Summer 2004), pp. 207–28.
29 Arnold, *Britain and the H-bomb*, pp. 214–15.
30 PRO, minutes of mtg 9 Jun 1959 in AVIA 65/2332, gives a figure of half a dozen Red Snow components. There is other information in AVIA 65/1064 which suggests a wider set of components at least potentially to be purchased in the US, and I am grateful to Brian Burnell for pointing this out to me, although I am not sure the US high-explosive cyclotol was, in the event, procured in this way.
31 PRO, Macklen brief of 4 Dec 1958 in DEFE 7/2380.
32 PRO, papers in PREM 11/2852.
33 Peter Jones, 'Overview of history of UK strategic weapons', *History of the UK strategic deterrent: proceedings of the Royal Aeronautical Society symposium 17 March 1999*, pp. 2.1–10.
34 PRO, DRP(AES)/M(58)2 of 11 Nov 1958 in AVIA 65/1116.
35 Norris *et al.*, *British, French and Chinese nuclear weapons*, p. 49.
36 *ibid*. Some idea of the breadth of work at Aldermaston can also be gained from the PRO class list for AWRE technical reports in the ES10 series, most of which remain classified.
37 PRO, brief for Prime Minister 13 March 1961 in PREM 11/3724.
38 Frank Bongiorno, 'The price of nostalgia: Menzies, the "Liberal" tradition and Australian foreign policy', *Australian Journal of Politics and History* 51/3 (2005), pp. 400–17; Wayne Reynolds, *Australia's bid for the atomic bomb* (Melbourne UP 2000).
39 Walker, *Britain, the United States, weapon policies and nuclear testing*, ch. 3.

40 Lorna Arnold and Mark Smith, *Britain, Australia and the bomb: the nuclear tests and their aftermath* (Palgrave 2006), p. 222.
41 *ibid.*, pp. 215–17.
42 Australian Government Publishing Service, *Report of the Royal Commission into British nuclear tests in Australia*, Vol. 2 (Canberra, AGPS 1985), pp. 505, 414.
43 PRO, tables of minor trials programme for 1958 phase 2 in ES 12/270; for 1959 in ES 12/271.
44 Norris et al., *British, French and Chinese nuclear weapons*, p. 47. Kate Pyne has pointed out that although in-service British nuclear warheads were not by design *inherently* one-point safe, they had in practice an equivalent or greater level of safety through in-flight insertion or other mechanical means (pers. comm. 8 Jan 2008).
45 Peter Morton, *Fire across the desert: Woomera and the Anglo-Australian joint project 1946–80* (Canberra, AGPS 1989).
46 *ibid.*, p. 439.
47 *ibid.*, p. 441.
48 *ibid.*, pp. 441–3.
49 Jim Walsh, 'Surprise down under: the secret history of Australia's nuclear ambitions', *The Nonproliferation Review* (Fall 1997), pp. 1–20; Reynolds, *Australia's bid for the atomic bomb*.
50 Quoted in Walsh, 'Surprise down under', p. 3.
51 *ibid.*, pp. 4–5.
52 Reynolds, *Australia's bid for the atomic bomb*, p. 206.
53 Walsh, 'Surprise down under', pp. 8–9.
54 *ibid.*, p. 5.
55 Wynn, *RAF strategic nuclear deterrent forces*, p. 300.
56 LeMay with Kantor, *Mission with LeMay*, pp. 429–30 (emphasis in original).
57 Wynn, *RAF strategic nuclear deterrent forces*, p. 442.
58 Brookes, *V-force*, p. 71.
59 Quoted in Wynn, *RAF strategic nuclear deterrent forces*, p. 337.
60 Brookes, *V-force*, p. 84.
61 Wynn, *RAF strategic nuclear deterrent forces*, pp. 300–3/8.
62 *ibid.*, p. 313.
63 *ibid.*, pp. 334–5.
64 The best histories of the V-bomber force are Wynn, *RAF strategic nuclear deterrent forces* and Andrew Brookes, *V-force: the history of Britain's airborne deterrent* (Jane's 1982). In addition there are many useful books and websites on the V-bombers produced by aircraft enthusiasts.
65 Wynn, *RAF strategic nuclear deterrent forces*, pp. 150, 298. The Finningley Vulcan squadron moved to Waddington in 1961.
66 *ibid.*, p. 327.
67 PRO, Amery to Watkinson 28 Sep 1961 in AIR 8/2382; also quoted in Wynn, *RAF strategic nuclear deterrent forces*, p. 210.
68 Ken Delve, Peter Green and John Clemons, *English Electric Canberra* (Leicester, Midland Counties 1992), pp. 46–7, 59–64.
69 PRO, Air Ministry note of 1 Apr 1958 on locations in Germany in AIR 2/13736.
70 Delve et al., *English Electric Canberra*, pp. 46–7; Wynn, *RAF strategic nuclear deterrent forces*, p. 369.

71 By March 1961 there were 'gauntlet safes' for Red Beard warhead cores at Coningsby; see note of 8 Mar 1961 listing storage locations in PRO, AIR 2/13775. Wynn, however, in *RAF strategic nuclear deterrent forces*, pp. 124, 258, 571–2, records that Canberras in Bomber Command were supplied with Mk.7, and this is confirmed by the operations record book for the Coningsby Supplementary [i.e., Nuclear] Storage Area for 1959–61 (AIR 29/3103). Wynn is not clear (pp. 364, 495) how many Canberras were eventually assigned to SACEUR in the nuclear role; although 64 had been planned, it seems possible only 48 were eventually made available. I have found no evidence to suggest there were any nuclear storage facilities at Upwood, although several nearby USAF bases might have been used.
72 Wynn, *RAF strategic nuclear deterrent forces*, pp. 367–8. (Confusingly, the term Mk.28 denotes both a US free-fall bomb, available in several versions, and a warhead, used not just in bombs but also in missiles. The megaton version of the Mk.28 warhead was anglicised and produced in the UK; the Mk.28 bomb was not, although it was cleared for carriage by British aircraft in one of its original US versions, probably with a sub-megaton yield; see also the section on Red Beard replacement later in this chapter).
73 *ibid.*, p. 128; PRO, ACAS(Ops) draft brief for VCAS Mar 1960 in AIR 2/13736.
74 The technical and operational history of the Thor force is well described by John Boyes in 'Project Emily: the Thor IRBM and the Royal Air Force 1959–63', *Prospero* 4 (Spring 2007), pp. 7–39, and in his new book *Project Emily: Thor IRBM and the RAF* (Stroud, Tempus 2008); see also Wynn, *RAF strategic nuclear deterrent forces*, ch. 17, 21; Twigge and Scott, *Planning Armageddon*, pp. 109–19.
75 Wynn, *RAF strategic nuclear deterrent forces*, p. 294; John Boyes, *Project Emily*, pp. 88–94. Official coyness was partly because Thor was still being tested in the US, and partly because Macmillan was nervous about publicly avowing a new strategic capability while arms-control talks were underway.
76 Wynn, *ibid.*, p. 357.
77 Moore, *The Royal Navy and nuclear weapons*.
78 PRO, note of DAArm mtg, 8 Dec 1959 in AVIA 65/1166; Hartley Library, Mountbatten to Thistleton-Smith, 6 Apr 1959 in MB1/I586.
79 Twigge and Scott, *Planning Armageddon*, p. 71.
80 Clark, *Nuclear diplomacy*, pp. 132–3.
81 Twigge and Scott, *Planning Armageddon*, pp. 105, 113.
82 From a document preserved in the US national archive, and quoted by Twigge and Scott in *Planning Armageddon*, pp. 76–7, and in 'Learning to love the bomb: the command and control of British nuclear forces, 1953–64', *Journal of Strategic Studies* 22/1 (Mar 1999), pp. 38–9.
83 Twigge and Scott, *Planning Armageddon*, pp. 66–8.
84 *ibid.*, pp. 54–5.
85 *ibid.*, p. 83.
86 *ibid.*, pp. 112, 206; Boyes, 'Project Emily', p. 22; Philip Nash, *The other missiles of October: Eisenhower, Kennedy and the Jupiters 1957–63* (Chapel Hill NC, Univ of North Carolina Press 1997), p. 86.
87 PRO, papers incl. Ordnance Board terms of reference circulated 31 Jan 1958 and description of release procedures of 13 Mar 1959 in AVIA 65/778.

88 PRO, NWSC/P(59)1 of 6 Nov 1959, terms of reference and composition, in DEFE 7/2294.
89 PRO, correspondence of Dec 1958–Apr 1959 in AIR 2/13705.
90 *RAF Historical Society Journal* 26 (2001), p. 96. Brian Burnell argues convincingly (pers. comm. 26 Aug 2007) that this was an accident with Violet Club, rather than Yellow Sun Mk.1, on the basis of the number and size of the steel balls.
91 Wynn, *RAF strategic nuclear deterrent forces*, p. 250; DAArm comments on AC(58)30 of 13 May 1958 in AVIA 65/775.
92 George Hicks (ed. Roy Dommett), 'History of RAE and nuclear weapons', *Prospero* 2 (Spring 2005), p. 167.
93 PRO, DRP(AES)/M(58)2 of 11 Nov 1958 in AVIA 65/1116.
94 PRO, DAWDP note of 7 Jul 1959 in AVIA 65/878.
95 Hicks, 'History of RAE and nuclear weapons', pp. 168–9.
96 Writing in Nov 1958, quoted in Wynn, *RAF strategic nuclear deterrent forces*, p. 251.
97 PRO, D Ops(B&R) to AOC-in-C Bomber Command, 17 Nov 1958 in AIR 2/13705 (plans had earlier been made for up to 16 Violet Clubs).
98 PRO, D Ops (B&R) brief to DCAS of 6 Apr 1959 in AIR 2/13678; PM's brief of 13 Mar 61 in PREM 11/3724 recording 31 Dec 1959 decision on 11 more Green Grasses; draft of OR.1142 issue 3 of Dec 1958 in AIR 2/13746.
99 PRO, AC(59)47 of 29 May 1959 in AIR 6/117. (The Air Council were being ambitious; political debates on Blue Streak were based around a deployment of only 60).
100 PRO, AC(59)88 of 31 Oct 1959 in AIR 6/117; AC(61)29 of 31 May 1961 in AIR 6/151; production graphs in AVIA 65/1792.
101 Wynn, *RAF strategic nuclear deterrent forces*, pp. 186–9.
102 *ibid.*, p. 191.
103 For more technical details of the missile development, see R H Francis, 'The development of Blue Steel', *Journal of the Royal Aeronautical Society* 68 (May 1964), pp. 303–22; John E Allen, 'Blue Steel and developments', *History of the UK strategic deterrent: proceedings of the Royal Aeronautical Society symposium 17 March 1999*, pp. 4.1–25; Hill, *A vertical empire*, ch. 4.
104 Wynn, *RAF strategic nuclear deterrent forces*, pp. 195–7.
105 *ibid.*, p. 202.
106 PRO, DCAS to Ward, 15 Dec 1959 and brief for Ward of 21 Dec 1959 in AIR 8/2256; BND(SG)(59)11th mtg of 30 Nov 1959 in DEFE 7/2301.
107 PRO, note by MoA on Blue Steel improvements of 5 Sep 1960 in DEFE 7/2302.
108 PRO, MoA note of 8 Nov 1960 in AVIA 65/911.
109 Quoted in Wynn, *RAF strategic nuclear deterrent forces*, p. 205.
110 Morton, *Fire across the desert*, p. 347; PRO, papers in AIR 8/2382.
111 PRO, 'History of nuclear warhead production in UK' of Jan 1963 in AVIA 65/1792, p. 35.
112 For accounts of the technical history of Blue Streak, see papers in *History of the UK strategic deterrent: proceedings of the Royal Aeronautical Society symposium 17 March 1999*; Roy Dommett, 'The Blue Streak weapon', *Prospero* 2 (Spring 2005), pp. 7–33; Hill, *A vertical empire*, ch. 5–6; Wynn, *RAF strategic*

nuclear deterrent forces, ch. 23; Morton, *Fire across the desert*, ch. 22; Martin, *De Havilland Blue Streak*.
113 The 2000nm range made Blue Streak, by US standards, an IRBM, but the term 'medium-range ballistic missile' was used consistently to describe it in the UK.
114 Morton, *Fire across the desert*, p. 436.
115 Wayne Cocroft and Roger Thomas, *Cold War: building for nuclear confrontation 1946–89* (English Heritage 2003), pp. 46–7.
116 RAE archive, Farnborough, Minutes of the 4th mtg of the joint UK/US medium-range ballistic missile advisory committee, 20/21 Jun 1957 (with thanks to Roy Dommett). The image of British and American officials, scientists and industrialists discussing these 'bonkers' (presumably intended to 'bonk' the missile in flight) around the conference table is somehow appealing. There is another account of the flight and guidance of Blue Streak in Anon., 'Guiding Blue Streak', *Flight International* 28 Mar 1963, pp. 438–9.
117 PRO, CWP/P(58)3 of 16 Apr 1958 in AVIA 65/1428.
118 *ibid.*, and RAE archive, Farnborough, Minutes of the 4th mtg of the joint UK/US medium-range ballistic missile advisory committee, 20/21 Jun 1957 (with thanks to Roy Dommett).
119 PRO, draft OR.1142 issue 3 of Dec 1958 in AIR 2/13746. I am mystified by the reference to a 'successor' for Yellow Sun Mk.2.
120 PRO, AC(59)88 of 31 Oct 1959 in AIR 6/117.
121 Roy Dommett, 'Ballistic missile defence', lecture to the guided flight group of the Royal Aeronautical Society, 28 Apr 1994.
122 Roy Dommett, 'The development of Blue Streak and Black Knight re-entry heads', *History of the UK strategic deterrent: proceedings of the Royal Aeronautical Society symposium 17 March 1999*, pp. 11.1–10. There are illustrations of the evolution of the RV shape in this paper, also reproduced in Martin, *De Havilland Blue Streak*, p. 104.
123 Hill, *A vertical empire*, ch. 9.
124 PRO, Cornford to Zuckerman, 18 Jan 1962 in DEFE 19/115.
125 PRO, papers in AVIA 13/1283.
126 PRO, Cornford to Zuckerman, 18 Jan 1962 in DEFE 19/115.
127 PRO, minutes of a meeting at RAE 30 Sep 1959 in AVIA 13/1283.
128 PRO, RAE radio dept progress report of 17 Apr 1959 in AVIA 13/1283.
129 PRO, notes of a meeting on decoys, 17 Feb 1959 in AVIA 13/1283.
130 PRO, Cornford to Zuckerman, 18 Jan 1962 in DEFE 19/115.
131 Quoted in Hill, *A vertical empire*, pp. 135–6.
132 PRO, Air Ministry note of 30 Jan 1958 and R J Penney note of 10 Feb 1960, both in AIR 2/13774; undated (mid-1959) note on nuclear weapons ordered by RAF from MoS in AVIA 65/878; ms. correction to original figure of 57 in MoS note 'Red Beard delivery programme' of 9 Feb 1960 in AIR 2/13773.
133 SqnLdr Michael Hely, at the RAF Historical Society seminar at Hendon, 11 Apr 2001. (This phrase did not appear in the printed record of the meeting in *Journal of the RAF Historical Society* 26, but is in the notes I made at the seminar).
134 PRO, DRP(AES)/P(56)20 of 29 Nov 1956 in AVIA 65/1114.

135 PRO, Emson note of 2 Jul 1957 recording CA release in AVIA 65/1153.
136 By January 1962, 'disposal of existing stocks [was] well under way' – PRO, correspondence in AVIA 65/1155.
137 PRO, data for May 1960 given in AIR 2/17780.
138 For the early history of Red Beard, see Moore, *The Royal Navy and nuclear weapons*, pp. 99–106.
139 See PRO file AB 16/2307 on the curious case of Mr J R V Dolphin's claim for an *ex gratia* payment in respect of his contribution to the design.
140 PRO, AW.330/OR.1127 issue 4 of 21 Apr 1958 and draft issue 5 of 5 May 1958 in AIR 2/13728.
141 Wynn, *RAF strategic nuclear deterrent forces*, p. 259. It remains unclear whether the 'E' in Project E ever stood for anything, although other 'E' names were used for aspects of RAF/USAF cooperation: Emily stood for the Thor deployments, and Encircle for joint Bomber Command/SAC strike planning.
142 Wynn, *RAF strategic nuclear deterrent forces*, pp. 265–7.
143 PRO, mtg at MoS 17 Oct 1958 in AIR 2/13774; MoA note 'Red Beard delivery programme' of 9 Feb 1960 in AIR 2/13773.
144 In *The Royal Navy and nuclear weapons*, pp. 139–40, I suggested that *Victorious* did embark Red Beard in 1959 or 1960, but further research has shown that this was not the case. HMS *Hermes* was the navy's first nuclear-capable carrier.
145 PRO, 'History of nuclear warhead production in UK' of Jan 1963 in AVIA 65/1792, pp. 21/4.
146 PRO, papers in AVIA 65/775.
147 PRO, DRP(AES)/M(58)2 of 11 Nov 1958 in AVIA 65/1116.
148 PRO, AC(59)47 of 29 May 1959 in AIR 6/117.
149 PRO, 'History of nuclear warhead production in UK' in AVIA 65/1792, p. 25.
150 PRO, Coles (Head of Armament Dept, RAE) to ACdre Emson (Director Air Armaments, MoA) 30 Oct 1959 in AVIA 65/775; AC(59)88 of 31 Oct 1959 in AIR 6/117.
151 PRO, DAWD paper 'Red Beard delivery programme' of 9 Feb 1960 and record of meeting 15 Feb 1960 in AIR 2/13773.
152 PRO, note of 10 Feb 1960 in AIR 2/13774; DAWD paper 'Red Beard delivery programme' of 9 Feb 1960 and record of meeting 15 Feb 1960 in AIR 2/13773. In *The Royal Navy and nuclear weapons* (p. 204), I suggested a figure of between 20 and 28 Red Beards; evidence unearthed more recently suggests at least the higher figure, and perhaps 34 (paper of 29 May 1966 'The Navy's requirement for WE177A' in DEFE 19/103), although it is unclear whether the Navy's weapons all had fissile cores to match; like the RAF, it may have had a number of spares (refs. above, also 'History of nuclear warhead production in UK' in AVIA 65/1792).
153 PRO, Admiralty signal to HMS *Hermes* 6 Feb 1961 in ADM 1/27827; Ordnance Board report on Valiant B.1 and Vulcan B.1/B.1(A) of 14 Oct 1960 in AIR 2/13775; 1SL note of 25 Oct 1960 in DEFE 32/6.
154 PRO, 'History of nuclear warhead production in UK' in AVIA 65/1792, p. 30.
155 *ibid.*, p. 34; Annexe to AC(62)12 of 28 Mar 1962 in AIR 6/151.

156 PRO, notes on bidders' conference, circulated 1 Apr 1959 in AVIA 65/1661.
157 PRO, record of SofSAir's mtg of 21 Jan 1960 in AIR 20/10697.
158 PRO, brief to VCAS of 10 Feb 1959 in AIR 2/14711; sketch of spring 1959 in AIR 2/15261.
159 White repeatedly referred at the start of 1960, including in Congressional testimony, to the missile 'which I call the Sky Bolt [sic]' (Library of Congress, Thomas D White papers, box 36, summary of DoD official statements on Skybolt dated 15 Sep 1960).
160 PRO, GCapt Stanley Bonser's report of 10 Aug 1959 in AIR 2/15637 (various papers here and in AVIA 65/1661 give fuller details of the missile's configuration changes).
161 PRO, papers of June 1959 in AVIA 65/1661.
162 PRO, papers in AIR 2/15262, and historical summary dated June 1960 in AVIA 65/2019.
163 PRO, copy of Defense Department approval of 1 Feb 1960 obtained by Zuckerman in DEFE 7/2063.
164 PRO, British trip report of May 1960 in AVIA 65/1262.
165 RAE archive, Farnborough, DSR(L) note of 16 Feb 1960 (with thanks to Roy Dommett).
166 RAE archive, Farnborough, GW Dept 'Examination of Skybolt system proposals' 16 May 1960 (with thanks to Roy Dommett).
167 PRO, Fryer, 'Skybolt progress report no. 1' of 13 Jan 1961 in DEFE 13/408; papers in DEFE 19/77.
168 PRO, Zuckerman to Minister, 16 May 1962 in DEFE 7/2160; report from ACdre Russell circulated 29 Nov 1962 in AVIA 65/1851.
169 Chuck Hansen, *US nuclear weapons: the secret history* (Arlington TX, Aerofax 1988), pp. 203–5; Spinardi, *From Polaris to Trident*, pp. 53–5; http://www.globalsecurity.org/wmd/intro/miniaturization.htm (accessed Aug 2007).
170 PRO, Brundrett to Pelly, 26 May 1959 in AIR 2/15261.
171 PRO, Mitchell to Min of Aviation, 24 May 1960 in AVIA 65/912; Mitchell to DGAW, 21 Apr 1960 in AVIA 65/1262; and DGAW to Mitchell, 13 May 1960, preserved in both of these files.
172 PRO, BJSM Washington signal to Brundrett, 21 Jan 1959 in AIR 2/14711.
173 PRO, DGAW note of meeting, 20 May 1960 in AVIA 65/912; Apr 59 draft of Ministry of Aviation R&D Board paper RDB/P(59)24 in AVIA 65/1661; and 7 and 14 Apr 1959 drafts of DRP/P(59)38 in AIR 2/15261. All repeat 'four times' the fissile material.
174 PRO, briefing note of 15 Feb 1960 in AIR 2/13708.
175 PRO, DRP(AES)/M(59)2 of 15 Dec 1959 in AVIA 65/1116.
176 PRO, DRP(AES)/M(60)1 of 12 Jul 1960 in AVIA 65/1116.
177 PRO, DGAW to CGWL, 13 May 1960 in AVIA 65/912 and AVIA 65/1262.
178 PRO, Mitchell to Min of Aviation, 24 May 1960 in AVIA 65/912.
179 PRO, DDOR1 note of 9 May 1960 in AIR 2/15637; DGAW note of meeting 20 May 1960 in AVIA 65/912; and brief for Min of Defence, 25 May 1960 in DEFE 7/2063, where the light warhead is specifically identified as Mk.47.
180 Norris *et al.*, *British, French and Chinese nuclear weapons*; Duncan Campbell, *The unsinkable aircraft carrier*, p. 103.
181 PRO, DGAW note of mtg, 20 May 1960 in AVIA 65/912; note of mtg, 17 Jun 1960 in AVIA 65/1262.

280 Notes to pages 120–123

182 PRO, DAWD note, 21 Oct 1960 in AVIA 65/2019, mentions Filbert 1A and 1B.
183 Fife is mentioned alongside Acorn in PRO, Zuckerman to Watkinson, 16 Jun 1960 in DEFE 7/2063, and described in BJSM Washington to DGAW, 25 Aug 60 in AVIA 65/1262.
184 PRO, DGAW note of 9 Jun 60 in AVIA 65/2019; DGAW note of mtg, 20 May 1960 in AVIA 65/912.
185 PRO, DCAS note of 27 Jun 1960 in AVIA 65/1262.
186 PRO, Skybolt technical and financial agreement of 27 Sep 1960 in AIR 20/10830; correspondence on this file shows that this issue reached the Prime Minister.
187 PRO, DGAW notes of 19 Jan and 13 Feb 1961 in AVIA 65/2019; also Hansen, *US nuclear weapons*, p. 184.
188 PRO, DGAW note 13 Feb 1961 in AVIA 65/2019.
189 It is clear, from this and other evidence, that Aldermaston was working on British thermonuclear primary designs; whether there was independent work on secondaries is very difficult to say on the basis of the currently available evidence. See my 'British nuclear warhead design 1958–66: how much American help?', pp. 223–4.
190 PRO, GCapt Fryer's Progress Report no.2 of 29 Mar 1961 in DEFE 19/77; and no.3 of 31 May 1961 in DEFE 13/408.
191 PRO, GCapt Fryer's Progress Report no.4 of 14 Mar 1962 in DEFE 13/408.
192 PRO, Cornford to Zuckerman, 16 Nov 1961 in DEFE 19/87.
193 PRO, Treble (MoA) to Marshall (Treasury), 24 Dec 1958 in AVIA 65/775.
194 PRO, numerous papers in AVIA 65/775.
195 PRO, DOR(C) letter, 30 Jun 1959 in AIR 2/13735.
196 PRO, Gray to Emson (MoS), 7 Jul 1959 in AVIA 65/775.
197 PRO, Coles to Emson, 28 Jul 1959 and notes of mtg, 20 Aug 1959 in AVIA 65/775.
198 PRO, DRP(AES)/M(59)2 of 15 Dec 1959 and DRP(AES)/M(60)1 of 12 Jul 1960 in AVIA 65/1116.
199 PRO, undated (May 1960) draft DCAS note for DRP(AES) sub-committee, and brief for DCAS on DRP(AES)/P(60)2 dated 11 Jul 1960, both in AIR 2/17322; comments on AC(60)9 dated 22 Feb 1960 in AVIA 65/775.
200 PRO, draft OR.1177 circ. 18 Aug 1959, and OR.1176 circ. 6 Aug 1959, in AIR 2/17322. A note of DOR(C)/AWRE discussions on Red Beard on 25 Sep 1959, in the same file, made the link between OR.1176 and Una explicit.
201 PRO, paper 'Naval philosophy in the selection of a weapon to replace Red Beard' under cover of DGD to DOR(C), 28 Apr 1960 in of AIR 2/17322. It is interesting that the need for an underwater capability did not relate solely to ASW use.
202 PRO, GDA.10/OR.1177 submitted by DOR(C) to CA (MoA) on 30 May 1960, OR.1176 on 31 May 1960, both in AIR 2/17322.
203 PRO, brief on DRP(AES)/P(60)2 dated 11 Jul 1960 in DEFE 7/1888.
204 PRO, Aug 1960 weapons data in AIR 2/17780; ref to OR.1176 yield in notes of War Office mtg, 23 Nov 1960 in WO 32/17067.
205 PRO, DRP(AES)/M(59)2 of 15 Dec 1959 and DRP(AES)/M(60)1 of 12 Jul 1960 in AVIA 65/1116; also brief on DRP(AES)/P(60)2 dated 11 Jul 1960 in DEFE 7/1888.

206 PRO, DRP(AES)/M(60)1 of 12 Jul 1960 in AVIA 65/1116.
207 PRO, DDOR2 note of 3 Nov 1961 in AIR 2/17324.
208 PRO, MoA note on retarded/lay-down bomb for the TSR.2 in the deterrent role of 14 Dec 1960 in DEFE 7/2217; reports of visit in AIR 2/17323.
209 PRO, DRP/P(61)4 of 16 Jan 1961 in DEFE 10/418.
210 PRO, note of MoD approval 8 Sep 1961 in AIR 2/17324.
211 PRO, note of mtg at RAE 19 Dec 1961 and note on security precautions of 28 Feb 1962, both in AIR 2/17324.
212 PRO, undated note (mid-1961), enc. 42 in AVIA 65/2284; note on security precautions of 28 Feb 1962 in AIR 2/17324.
213 PRO, DDOR2 note of 3 Nov 1961 in AIR 2/17324, records the likely size of the lay-down bomb as 144in long by 18in diameter and 1600lb weight, with further reduction possible to 115in long.
214 PRO, War Office internal letter of 4 Apr 1961 in WO 32/17067.
215 PRO, briefs by Dr Bob Press for mtgs 12 Jul and 1 Aug 1961 in AVIA 65/1116.
216 Richard Moore, 'Surface-to-air guided weapons for UK air defence in the 1950s', *Prospero* 2 (Spring 2005), pp. 193–212.
217 PRO, report by Henderson (Air Ministry scientific adviser) 'The use of nuclear warheads for SAGW against manned aircraft' of 20 Feb 1957 in AIR 2/13761.
218 PRO, DRP(AES)/M(57)5 of 30 Jul 1957 in AVIA 65/1116.
219 PRO, DRP(AES)/M(58)2 of 11 Nov 1958 in AVIA 65/1116.
220 PRO, note of 10 Feb 1959 in WO 286/39; Kate Pyne, 'Warheads and rockets – UK nuclear warheads for almost anything with a point at one end and a flame at the other', presentation to the British Rocketry Oral History Project conference at Charterhouse, April 2003.
221 James, *Defence policy and the RAF*, PRO, AIR 41/86, pp. 143/9/52/8.
222 PRO, note of 12 May 1959 in DEFE 13/351.
223 Quoted in James, *Defence policy and the RAF*, PRO, AIR 41/86, p. 151. Australian interest may have kept the weapon in mind for a short time: Walsh, 'Surprise down under', pp. 7–8.
224 James, *Defence policy and the RAF*, PRO, AIR 41/86, p. 155.
225 *ibid.*, pp. 160–3; PRO, D(60)47 of 10 Oct 1960 in CAB 131/24. Pike wrote to his US counterpart soon afterwards informing him of the decision about Genie (Library of Congress, Thomas D White papers, box 37, letter White to Pike of 9 Nov 1960).
226 David Brown and George Moore, *Rebuilding the Royal Navy: warship design since 1945* (Chatham 2003), pp. 37–8; PRO, Nash to 1SL, 1 Dec 1960 in ADM 1/27876.
227 PRO, DRP/P(59)93 of 15 Sep 1959 in DEFE 10/357; Board minute 5411 of 20 May 1960 in ADM 167/156.
228 Jeremy Stocker, *Britain and ballistic missile defence 1942–2002* (Frank Cass 2004), pp. 71, 247–9.
229 *ibid.*, p. 79. The missile was OR.1155 and the warhead OR.1157 (ref. in PRO, extract of DRP/P(59)50 of 29 May 1959 in AVIA 65/1114).
230 PRO, RRE Malvern draft R&D programme of 9 Jan 1958 in AVIA 65/1772. Some of the thinking on operational scenarios for ABM defence can be gathered from Gibson and Buttler's account (*British secret projects*, ch. 5).

282 Notes to pages 129–133

231 PRO, A/ACAS(Ops) draft report on nuclear weapons requirements of 4 Mar 1959 in AIR 2/13678; AC(59)47 of 29 May 1959 in AIR 6/117.
232 PRO, DRP/P(59)1 in DEFE 10/356; DRP/P(60)62 of 20 Jul 1960 in DEFE 10/382 and AVIA 65/1772; papers of interdependence sub-group F in AVIA 65/1564.
233 RAE Archive, Farnborough, BND(TSC)(61)3 of 18 Jan 1961 (with thanks to Roy Dommett).
234 Roy Dommett, 'Ballistic missile defence'.
235 PRO, papers in WO 32/17131; Pierre, *Nuclear politics*, p. 167.
236 Norris *et al.*, *British, French and Chinese nuclear weapons*, p. 82. The two Corporal units were 27 and 47 (Guided Weapons) Regiments (Royal Artillery). There is a summary of BAOR nuclear-capable units at the US 59th Ordnance Brigade's website: http://www.usarmygermany.com/units/Ordnance/USAREUR_59thOrd Bde%201.htm#IUKCorps (accessed Aug 2007).
237 PRO, report of Oct 1959 in AIR 8/2204.
238 PRO, draft military characteristics for a medium-range SSGW, 1 Aug 1957, WO 32/17067.
239 Missile technical detail from the 'Rockets in Europe' website: http://fuseurop.univ-perp.fr/bwater_e.htm (accessed August 2007); Morton, *Fire across the desert*, pp. 345–6; Gibson and Buttler, *British secret projects*, pp. 126–31.
240 PRO, letter of 17 Dec 1957 in WO 32/17067.
241 PRO, note of 21 Sep 1959 in WO 32/17067.
242 PRO, note of meeting 23 Nov 1960 in WO 32/17067; papers in WO 32/21044.
243 PRO, D(61)1st mtg 16 Jan 1961 in CAB 131/25; letter of 14 Apr 1961 in WO 32/17067.
244 PRO, D(61)15th mtg, 22 Nov 1961 in CAB 131/25.
245 PRO, questions of 9 Feb 1959 in WO 32/17067; note from BAC 16 Mar 1962 in AVIA 65/2029.
246 The regiments involved were 24, 39 and 50 (Missile) Regiments (Royal Artillery) respectively. See papers in PRO, WO 32/21248; Anon., 'Honest John', *Windscreen: the Magazine of the Military Vehicle Trust* 111 (Summer 2006), pp. 10–12; Norris *et al.*, *British, French and Chinese nuclear weapons*, pp. 82–3.
247 PRO, DRP(AES)/M(58)2 of 11 Nov 1958 in AVIA 65/1116.
248 One of the two Blue Peacock prototypes completed for training purposes – without fissile material – still exists in the historical collection at AWE Aldermaston; see the article by David Hawkings in AWE's house magazine *Discovery* (Summer 2002): http://www.awe.co.uk/Images/blue_peacock_tcm6-1992.pdf (accessed Aug 2007).
249 PRO, draft military characteristics of Oct 1959 in WO 286/39.
250 PRO, Annex B to War Office paper of 17 Aug 1959 in AVIA 65/1050 (I am grateful to Brian Burnell for drawing my attention to this document).
251 PRO, DRP(AES)/M(59)1 of 28 Jul 1959 in DEFE 10/806; DRP(AES)/M(59)2 of 15 Dec 1959 and DRP(AES)/M(60)1 of 12 Jul 1960 in AVIA 65/1116; DRP/P(61)51 of 27 Jun 1961 in DEFE 10/418; papers in WO 32/19928. Brian Burnell has pointed out to me the likelihood that Wee Gwen was a proposed anglicised version of the American Davy Crockett warhead, known to Los Alamos as Wee Gnat (pers. comm. 26 Dec 2007).

252 Spinardi, *From Polaris to Trident*, p. 30; Goodchild, *Edward Teller*, pp. 265–6.
253 Harvey Sapolsky, *The Polaris system development: bureaucratic and programmatic success in government* (Cambridge Mass, Harvard UP 1972), pp. 34–5.
254 *ibid.*, p. 149.
255 Cdr P H Backus USN, 'Finite deterrence, controlled retaliation', *US Naval Institute Proceedings* 85/3 (Mar 1959), pp. 23–9.
256 Spinardi, *From Polaris to Trident*, p. 59; launches listed at Encyclopedia Astronautica website: http://www.astronautix.com/lvs/polrisa1.htm (accessed August 2007).
257 Hansen, *US nuclear weapons*, p. 204.
258 PRO, DNOR note of 4 Sep 1945 in ADM 1/17259.
259 Adm William J Crowe USN, 'The policy roots of the modern Royal Navy 1945–63', unpublished PhD dissertation (Princeton 1965), p. 256.
260 Hartley Library, Mountbatten to Controller, 17 Aug 1955 in MB1/I586.
261 RAE Archive, Farnborough, Technical Note GW490 of Apr 1958, 'Technical notes on the American ballistic missile programme' (with thanks to Roy Dommett). This paper was based on notes made during a visit to the US in January 1958.
262 Cmnd. 371, *First Lord's statement on the Navy estimates 1958–59*; PRO, H of M note, 14 Jan 1958 in ADM 205/179; report in ADM 1/28949 and under cover of VCNS's Board memo B.1195 of 27 Mar 1958 in ADM 167/152; Moore, *The Royal Navy and nuclear weapons*, pp. 156–7.
263 PRO, Board minute 5216 of 27 Mar 1958 in ADM 167/151.
264 PRO, Mountbatten to Burke, 8 May 1958 in ADM 205/179 and other papers here, in ADM 1/27375 and in Hartley Library, MB1/I447. Simeon's account of his posting is in 'Watching brief 1958–60' in Capt John Moore RN, ed., *The impact of Polaris: the origins of Britain's seaborne nuclear deterrent* (Huddersfield, Richard Netherwood 1999), pp. 34–7.
265 Moore, *The Royal Navy and nuclear weapons*, pp. 159–63. Palmer's report (in PRO, ADM 1/29349) has not been declassified, but he has described it in 'Technical evaluation 1961' in John Moore, ed., *The impact of Polaris*, pp. 42–5 (this is the source for the quote from Rowland Baker, the head of the *Dreadnought* team). See also Wid Graham, 'Watching brief 1961–3', also in John Moore, ed., *The impact of Polaris*, pp. 38–41 (Graham was Simeon's successor).
266 Wynn, *RAF strategic nuclear deterrent forces*, ch. 28. The literature on the TSR.2 cancellation as short-sighted disaster begins with Stephen Hastings, *The murder of TSR-2* (Macdonald 1966). Hastings was a Conservative MP and director of an aircraft manufacturing company, writing in the immediate aftermath of cancellation by a Labour government, but his account has been good enough for most later writers. Menaul's account in *Countdown* is a particular gem for connoisseurs of polemic.
267 PRO, targets for OR.1168 (conventional air-to-surface missile) attached to note of 13 Jan 1959 'Strike weapons for TSR.2' in AVIA 13/1336.
268 PRO, MoA note on strategic weapons for TSR.2, 5 Sep 1960 in DEFE 7/2302.
269 Neil McCart, *HMS Victorious 1937–69* (Cheltenham, Fan 1998), pp. 118–19.
270 Zuckerman archive, draft under AMSSPC/P(59)11, circulated 27 May 1959, in SZ/AMSSP/3.

271 PRO, draft OR.347 of Dec 1959 and associated papers in AIR 2/13382.
272 PRO, note of mtg, 27 Jan 1960 in AIR 2/13382.
273 PRO, papers in AIR 20/10925 and AIR 2/13382.
274 PRO, Air Ministry DOR(A) paper of Dec 1960 in AIR 2/13382.
275 PRO, ACAS(OR) paper of 19 Jan 1961 in AIR 2/13382.
276 PRO, OR.1182 of 16 Nov 1960 in AIR 2/14641. I am very grateful to Brian Burnell for finding papers in this and the related file AIR 20/10638 for me. OR.1182 was issued two days after an air staff discussion with Bristol. See also Gibson and Buttler, *British secret projects*, pp. 114–15.
277 PRO, Amery to Thorneycroft, 18 Nov 1960, Watkinson to Amery, 25 Nov 1960 and Thorneycroft to Amery, 30 Nov 1960 in AIR 2/14641.
278 PRO, report of Nicholson working party, 22 Dec 1960 in AIR 20/10638.
279 PRO, RAE working party report of 21 Apr 1961 in AIR 2/14641.
280 PRO, DRP/P(61)47 of 2 Jun 1961 in DEFE 10/418.
281 PRO, brief to DCAS of 5 Jun 1961 and other papers in AIR 2/14641.
282 PRO, Touch to Zuckerman, 8 Aug 1961 in DEFE 19/87.

Chapter 3

1 Patrick Cosgrave, 'Harold Arthur, Viscount Watkinson (1910–95)', *Oxford Dictionary of National Biography*.
2 Horne, *Macmillan*, Vol. 2, p. 341.
3 The reasons for the sacking, and the 'unpleasant and emotional interview' with Macmillan itself, are covered in Watkinson, *Turning points*, pp. 154–61.
4 Pierre, *Nuclear politics*, p. 222.
5 Hennessy, *Having it so good*, p. 291.
6 Howard, *The central organisation of defence*, p. 14.
7 Writing in April 1963, and quoted in Adrian Smith, 'Command and control in postwar Britain', *Twentieth Century British History* 2/3 (1991), p. 306.
8 Quoted in Ziegler, *Mountbatten*, p. 609.
9 *ibid.*, p. 608.
10 Ian Jacob, quoted in *ibid.*, p. 615.
11 Howard, *The central organisation of defence*, p. 18.
12 PRO, CC(63)45, 11 Jul 1963 in CAB 128/37; Cmnd. 2097, *Central organisation for defence*, Jul 1963.
13 PRO, CC(61)20, 13 Apr 1961 in CAB 128/35.
14 Oliver, *Kennedy, Macmillan and the nuclear test ban debate*, pp. 16–22.
15 *ibid.*, p. 29.
16 Kennedy to Macmillan 3 Aug 1961 in US Dept of State, *Foreign relations of the United States 1961–3*, vol. VII: http://www.state.gov/r/pa/ho/frus/kennedyjf/vii/50950.htm (accessed Aug 2007).
17 PRO, Zuckerman to Macmillan, 6 Sep 1961, Scott to Makins, 8 Sep 1961, and Caccia note of 13 Sep 1961 in DEFE 19/92.
18 Freeman, *Britain's nuclear arms control policy in the context of Anglo-American relations*, p. 110.
19 Oliver, *Kennedy, Macmillan and the nuclear test ban debate*, p. 34.
20 *ibid.*, p. 41.
21 PRO, CC(61)58, 26 Oct 1961, CAB 128/35.

22 HoC debs., vol. 648, col. 37 (31 Oct 1961); Oliver, *Kennedy, Macmillan and the nuclear test ban debate*, p. 41.
23 PRO, Macmillan to Kennedy, 3 Nov 1961, Brook to Macmillan, 7 Nov 1961, and Kennedy to Macmillan, 11 Nov 1961 in PREM 11/3246.
24 PRO, note of a mtg Macmillan/Home/Watkinson/Brook/Zuckerman/Makins, 15 Nov 1961 in PREM 11/3246.
25 Zuckerman, *Monkeys, men and missiles*, p. 318.
26 Oliver, *Kennedy, Macmillan and the nuclear test ban debate*, pp. 52–62.
27 *ibid.*, pp. 71–3; Clark, *Nuclear diplomacy*, pp. 220–1.
28 Zuckerman, *Monkeys, men and missiles*, p. 316.
29 Gallup, ed., *The Gallup international public opinion polls, Great Britain 1937–75*, Vol. 1, pp. 588, 635.
30 Oliver, *Kennedy, Macmillan and the nuclear test ban debate*, pp. 85, 98.
31 *ibid.*, p. 181.
32 Quoted in Ashton, *Kennedy, Macmillan and the cold war*, pp. 216/17; see also Zuckerman, *Monkeys, men and missiles*, ch. 27; Oliver, *Kennedy, Macmillan and the nuclear test-ban debate*, pp. 188–206.
33 For one of the best analyses of the Berlin problem, see Marc Trachtenberg, *History and strategy* (Princeton UP 1991), ch. 5.
34 Sean M Maloney, 'Berlin contingency planning: prelude to flexible response, 1958–63', *Journal of Strategic Studies* 25/1 (Mar 2002), pp. 99–134.
35 Duffield, *Power rules*, p. 161.
36 David A Rosenberg, 'Constraining overkill: contending approaches to nuclear strategy, 1955–65', *Colloquium on Contemporary History Seminar* 9 (1994), US Naval Historical Center: http://www.history.navy.mil/colloquia/cch9b.html (accessed Aug 2007).
37 Duffield, *Power rules*, pp. 164–5.
38 *ibid.*, ch. 5–6; also Francis J Gavin, 'The myth of flexible response: American strategy in Europe during the 1960s', *International History Review* 23/4 (Dec 2001), pp. 847–75.
39 PRO, VCNS paper, 9 May 1962 in ADM 205/188.
40 PRO, COS(62)436 of 12 Nov 1962 in DEFE 7/2031.
41 PRO, John to Carrington (draft not sent), 26 Oct 1962 in ADM 205/188.
42 PRO, JP(62)144(Final) of 19 Dec 1962 in DEFE 7/2031.
43 PRO, COS.13/63 of 10 Jan 1963 in DEFE 7/2031.
44 Pagedas, *Anglo-American strategic relations and the French problem*, pp. 71, 80–2, 95; Clark, *Nuclear diplomacy*, p. 319. I am grateful to Kristan Stoddart and Brian Burnell for additional documents on Anglo-French nuclear relations.
45 Clark, *Nuclear diplomacy*, p. 321.
46 *ibid.*, p. 315.
47 Pagedas, *Anglo-American strategic relations and the French problem*, pp. 194–7.
48 *ibid.*, p. 206.
49 Clark, *Nuclear diplomacy*, pp. 400–1.
50 Beatrice Heuser, *Nuclear mentalities: strategies and beliefs in Britain, France and the FRG* (Macmillan 1998).
51 As reported in the *Guardian* newspaper, 6 Oct 1960, p. 1.
52 Quoted in Pagedas, *Anglo-American strategic relations and the French problem*, p. 244.

53 James, *Defence policy and the RAF 1956–63*, PRO, AIR 41/86, pp. 211–13.
54 *ibid.*, pp. 214–17. The chiefs' paper on strategy for the 1960s was COS(62)1 of 9 Jan 1962 (see PRO, DEFE 5/123), and was circulated to ministers under cover of a short memo from Watkinson, D(62)3. A digest of the chiefs' paper was also circulated to the full cabinet as C(62)24 of 9 Feb 1962 in CAB 129/108.
55 PRO, D(62)1st mtg, 12 Jan 1962 in CAB 131/27.
56 Cmnd. 1639, *Statement on defence: the next five years*, Feb 1962, paras. 7–8.
57 *ibid.*, para. 13.
58 James, *Defence policy and the RAF 1956–63*, PRO, AIR 41/86, pp. 218–19, 224–6.
59 D(62)43, quoted in *ibid.*, p. 219.
60 James, *Defence policy and the RAF 1956–63*, PRO, AIR 41/86.
61 PRO, draft minute Watkinson to Macmillan, 22 Oct 1962 in CAB 21/5125. The word 'that' was underlined by an unknown hand and 'or whether?' was written in the margin.
62 PRO, JP(62)134(Final) of 3 Dec 1962 in DEFE 11/240; COS(62)486 of 19 Dec 1962 in AIR 19/1047.
63 James, *Defence policy and the RAF*, p. 222.
64 PRO, C(63)132 of 19 Jul 1963 in CAB 129/114.
65 PRO, CC(63)48, 25 Jul 1963 and CC(63)50, 30 Jul 1963 in CAB 128/37; Eric Grove, *Vanguard to Trident*, pp. 257/8.
66 PRO, BND(SG)(62)1 of 22 Jan 1962 in DEFE 7/2143. Curiously, although as we have seen the Air Ministry was losing interest internally in the VC-10, this was the aircraft that featured in BNDSG studies of an airborne deterrent as late as Jan 1962.
67 PRO, BND(SG)(62)1st mtg, 24 Jan 1962, extract in AIR 19/999; Scott to Watkinson 6 Feb 1962 in DEFE 13/618.
68 PRO, PM's brief of 7 Mar 1962 in PREM 11/3716. No such study appears to have been attempted, and Brook was soon too ill to continue in office.
69 Clark, *Nuclear diplomacy*, pp. 389–90; Baylis, *Ambiguity and Deterrence*, pp. 309–12; PRO, BND(SG)(62)2nd mtg, 16 Mar 1963, extract in AIR 19/999.
70 PRO, VCAS note of 1 Feb 1962 in AIR 19/999.
71 PRO, note of Macmillan's mtg with Home, Watkinson, Brook, Scott *et al.* of 7 Mar 1962 in DEFE 13/618; ACAS(Ops) to CAS, 'Strategic strike planning by Bomber Command', 5 Oct 1962 in AIR 8/2201. Note, however, that a VCAS paper of 11 Jan 1963 in AIR 20/11578 recorded that the Defence Committee 'last summer' accepted 'the capacity to damage 50 per cent of ten (not 15 – that was the Air Ministry's bid) Russian cities as the criterion for planning the Skybolt Vulcan force'.
72 PRO, brief for NRDC mtg, 31 May 1962 in AVIA 65/1771; ND(62)1st mtg, 31 May 1962 in CAB 134/2239; papers in WO 32/17067, AIR 19/1085, PREM 11/3716.
73 PRO, PM's briefs of 5 Jun and 6 Jul 1962 in PREM 11/3716. Only the Hailsham paper on fissile material has been declassified (D(62)32 of 6 Jun 1962 in CAB 131/27).
74 PRO, Amery to Dean by signal 131315Z Jun 1962 in AIR 19/1085.
75 PRO, MM(62)17, 2 and again 3 Jul 1962 in AIR 19/1085.

76 Gen Curtis E LeMay USAF with MGen Dale O Smith USAF, *America is in danger* (New York, Funk and Wagnalls 1968), p. 163; Ball, *Politics and force levels*, p. 185.
77 William W Kaufmann, *The McNamara strategy* (New York, Harper and Row 1964), p. 53.
78 Ball, *Politics and force levels*, p. 191.
79 PRO, GCapt Fryer's Progress Report no.6 of 30 May 1962, DEFE 19/77. A very similar set of figures is given by Enthoven and Smith (*How much is enough?* p. 255).
80 Ball, *Politics and force levels*, p. 229.
81 Greenwood, *Making the MIRV*.
82 Enthoven and Smith, *How much is enough?* p. 259.
83 Robert Frank Futrell, *Ideas, concepts, doctrine: basic thinking in the United States Air Force 1961–84* (Maxwell AFB, Air University Press 1989), p. 62.
84 Data from Encyclopedia Astronautica website: http://www.astronautix.com/lvs/polrisa1.htm and http://www.astronautix.com/lvs/mineman1.htm (accessed Aug 2007).
85 Quoted in Neustadt, *Report to JFK*, p. 28.
86 *ibid.*, pp. 28–33.
87 Fryer's telegram from Washington 312055Z Oct 62 to Cornford (MoD), CA (MoA) and ACAS(OR) (Air Ministry) is in e.g., PRO, DEFE 7/2161 and AIR 19/1036. Reaction esp. in DEFE 7/2161 shows the significance of the telegram was immediately grasped in Whitehall.
88 Ball, *Politics and force levels*, p. 228; Neustadt, *Report to JFK*, pp. 36–7.
89 Enthoven and Smith, *How much is enough?* p. 251.
90 Neustadt, *Report to JFK*, pp. 37–41.
91 Quoted in Ball, *Politics and force levels*, p. 230.
92 PRO, Godfrey to de Zulueta, 15 Nov 1962 in PREM 11/3716.
93 PRO, unsigned note of 19 Nov 1962 in PREM 11/3716. De Zulueta seems likely to have written this note; it cites Gore's Washington telno. 2832, preserved in the same file, although this did *not* include the phrase 'without strings'.
94 The *Sunday Express* ran a story on 28 November: Neustadt, *Report to JFK*, p. 67.
95 Neustadt, *Report to JFK*, pp. 69–75.
96 Quoted in *ibid.*, p. 75.
97 PRO, Thorneycroft to Macmillan, 7 Dec 1962 in PREM 11/3716.
98 PRO, de Zulueta note for the record, 9 Dec 1962 in PREM 11/3716.
99 Quoted in Neustadt, *Report for JFK*, p. 77.
100 Pierre, *Nuclear Politics*, p. 232.
101 PRO, McNamara aide-memoire of 11 December 1962, Annex 2 to 'The Skybolt story' in T 325/88.
102 Memorandum of understanding of 6 June 1960 in US Dept of State, *Foreign Relations of the United States 1958–60*, vol. VII, p. 864; also in Zuckerman archive, SZ/CSA/192/13.
103 RAE Archive, Farnborough, GW Dept 'Examination of Skybolt system proposals', 16 May 60 (with thanks to Roy Dommett).
104 PRO, Zuckerman to Minister, 16 May 1962 in DEFE 7/2161 and AIR 19/1036.

105 PRO, Lighthill's recollections of the Nassau talks, 2 Jan 1963 in AVIA 65/1840.
106 Quoted in Ashton, *Kennedy, Macmillan and the cold war*, p. 173.
107 Text of speech on CNN website: http://www.cnn.com/SPECIALS/cold.war/episodes/12/documents/mcnamara.no.cities/ (accessed Aug 2007).
108 Quoted in Clark, *Nuclear diplomacy and the special relationship*, p. 301.
109 PRO, Scott/Zuckerman joint letter to Thorneycroft from Nassau, 21 Dec 1962, in DEFE 13/619.
110 LeMay, *America is in danger*, p. 136.
111 Young, 'The Skybolt crisis of 1962: muddle or mischief?' p. 622.
112 Briefing paper to Thorneycroft quoted in *ibid.*, p. 627.
113 Note of 12 Dec 1960 quoted in Clark, *Nuclear diplomacy and the special relationship*, p. 344.
114 PRO, Emson to CAS, by signal 042256Z Dec 62 in PRO, AIR 19/1036.
115 Gary D Rawnsley, 'How special is special? The Anglo-American alliance during the Cuban missile crisis', *Contemporary Record* 9/3 (Winter 1995), pp. 586–601; Peter G Boyle, 'The British government's view of the Cuban missile crisis', *Contemporary Record* 10/3 (Autumn 1996), pp. 22–38; Len Scott, *Macmillan, Kennedy and the Cuban missile crisis: political, military and intelligence aspects* (Macmillan 1999); Twigge and Scott, 'The other other missiles of October: the Thor IRBMs and the Cuban missile crisis', *Electronic Journal of International History* (Jun 2000): http://www.history.ac.uk/ejournal/art3.html (accessed Aug 2007); Ashton, *Kennedy, Macmillan and the cold war*, ch. 4.
116 One of the conversations is available to listen to online: follow instructions from: http://www.jfklibrary.org/jfkl/cmc/pr_jfk_macmillan_phone_call.html (accessed Aug 2007).
117 Scott, *Macmillan, Kennedy and the Cuban missile crisis*, pp. 138–9; Twigge and Scott, *Planning Armageddon*, pp. 126–7.
118 Robin Woolven, 'UK involvement in the Cuban missile crisis', presentation to the British Rocketry Oral History Project conference at Charterhouse, March 2008.
119 PRO, record of the chiefs' mtg 27 Oct 1962 (2.30pm) in DEFE 32/7.
120 Scott, *Macmillan, Kennedy and the Cuban missile crisis*, pp. 143–7.
121 Quoted in Ashton, *Kennedy, Macmillan and the cold war*, p. 84.
122 Ernest May and Philip Zelikow, *The Kennedy tapes: inside the White House during the Cuban missile crisis* (Harvard UP 1997), p. 692; Ashton, *Kennedy, Macmillan and the cold war*, p. 77.
123 Quoted in Boyle, 'The British government's view of the Cuban missile crisis', p. 34.
124 Quoted in Ashton, *Kennedy, Macmillan and the cold war*, p. 88.
125 Quoted in Driver, *The disarmers*, p. 148.
126 Taylor, *Against the bomb*, pp. 89–91.
127 Sandbrook, *Never had it so good*, pp. 558–9.
128 Today, Bali-Hai is an expensive holiday villa: http://www.lyfordcayhomes.com/Listings/ListingDetail.ASPX?LID=790486 (accessed Aug 2007).
129 PRO, papers in PREM 11/4229; a US record of the meetings is in US Dept of State, *Foreign relations of the United States 1961–63*, vol. XIII, pp. 1091–1105/ 9–12. For accounts of the meeting in the secondary literature, see e.g., Clark, *Nuclear diplomacy*, pp. 409–18; Neustadt, *Report to JFK*, pp. 88–98; Zucker-

man, *Monkeys, men and missiles*, pp. 256–64; Ashton, *Kennedy, Macmillan and the cold war*, pp. 176–85; Murray, *Kennedy, Macmillan and nuclear weapons*, ch. 5.
130 William Tyler, assistant secretary of state, quoted in Ashton, *Kennedy, Macmillan and the cold war*, p. 8.
131 PRO, record of a mtg held at Bali-Hai, the Bahamas, 9.50am 19 Dec 1962 in PREM 11/4229.
132 PRO, record of a mtg held at Bali-Hai, the Bahamas, 4.30pm 19 Dec 1962 in PREM 11/4229.
133 PRO, record of a mtg held at Bali-Hai, the Bahamas, 10.30am 20 Dec 1962 in PREM 11/4229. The US record of this key passage of the meeting is subtly different, omitting Kennedy's clear 'should certainly not' statement: Macmillan apparently said the UK wanted a nuclear force 'not only for defence, but in the event of a menace to its existence, which the UK might have to meet, for example, when Khrushchev waved his rockets about the time of Suez, or when [in 1961] that fellow Qassim [the Iraqi Prime Minister] got excited and Kuwait was threatened … The President … assumed that the UK did not have the intention of using nuclear weapons against Qassim.' The implication appears to have been very similar. See US Dept of State, *Foreign relations of the United States 1961–63*, vol. XIII, pp. 1109–10.
134 PRO, records of mtgs held at Bali-Hai, the Bahamas, noon and 12.30pm 20 Dec 1962 in PREM 11/4229.
135 PRO, record of a mtg held at Bali-Hai, the Bahamas, 11.30am 21 Dec 1962 in PREM 11/4229.
136 PRO, annex 19 to 'The Skybolt story' in T 325/88. (Hartley's report was preserved by Air Ministry Permanent Secretary Sir Maurice Dean, who later moved to the Treasury, hence its appearing in a PRO Treasury file).
137 Zuckerman, *Monkeys, men and missiles*, p. 257.
138 This repeated the conclusions of officials in the UK, e.g., ACdre Wheeler to Lawrence-Wilson, 17 Dec 1962 in PRO, DEFE 7/2161; official record of talks 19 Dec 1962, p. 8 in CAB 21/4979. The rather laughable name 'Hound Dog' didn't help.
139 Zuckerman, *Monkeys, Men and Missiles*, p. 203.
140 Hartley missed the performance of a calypso specially composed for the occasion; see PRO, conference timetable in PREM 11/4229.
141 PRO, CC(62)75, 20 Dec 1962 in CAB 128/36.
142 PRO, CC(62)76, 21 Dec 1962 in CAB 128/36.
143 Telegram of 21 Dec 1962, preserved in PRO, DEFE 13/619 with other documents under cover of Scott's note, 22 Dec 1962.
144 See the *Guardian* newspaper's report (2 Jan 1963, p. 1).
145 Neustadt, *Report to JFK*, p. 89.
146 Murray, *Kennedy, Macmillan and nuclear weapons*, p. 149.
147 PRO, record of a mtg held at Bali-Hai, the Bahamas, noon 20 Dec 1962 in PREM 11/4229.
148 PRO, Lighthill's recollections of the Nassau talks, 2 Jan 1963 in AVIA 65/1840.
149 Andrew Priest, *Kennedy, Johnson and NATO: Britain, America and the dynamics of alliance 1962–8* (Routledge 2006), p. 57.

150 Murray, *Kennedy, Macmillan and nuclear weapons*, p. 106.
151 *ibid.*, p. 110.
152 *ibid.*, pp. 114/15.
153 Clark, *Nuclear diplomacy*, p. 311.
154 Pierre, *Nuclear politics*, p. 245.
155 *ibid.*, pp. 246/7; House of Lords debates (hereafter HoL debs.), vol. 250, col. 715 (28 May 1963).
156 PRO, CC(63)18, 25 Mar 1963 in CAB 128/37.
157 Murray, *Kennedy, Macmillan and nuclear weapons*, pp. 132, 192; Twigge and Scott, *Planning Armageddon*, p. 188; Boulton, 'NATO and the MLF', p. 285; PRO, CC(63)34, 23 May 1963 in CAB 128/37.
158 PRO, CC(63)36, 30 May 1963 in CAB 128/37; see also subsequent discussions CC(63)42, 25 Jun 1963, CC(63)43, 27 Jun 1963, CC(63)46, 11 Jul 1963, all in the same file.
159 Pierre, *Nuclear politics*, p. 247.
160 PRO, CC(63)54, 19 Sep 1963 and CC(63)55, 20 Sep 1963 in CAB 128/37. This cost figure appears not to have been a wild exaggeration. Figures given by the US at around this time suggested a whole-life cost for the MLF of around $3 billions (over £1 billion at the then exchange rate), of which the US, UK and West Germany would have had to pay the most substantial contributions. See US Delegation to NATO, 'A concept for the creation and operation of a Multilateral Force', 18 Oct 1963, Table 1 (with thanks to MGen Eric Younson and John Simpson).
161 PRO, CC(63)56, 23 Sep 1963 and CC(63)60, 15 Oct 1963 in CAB 128/37.
162 PRO, UKDEL NATO telno. 280 of 2 Jul 1964 and related correspondence in DEFE 13/727.
163 Pierre, *Nuclear politics*, pp. 248–9.
164 Andrew Priest, 'In common cause: the NATO multilateral force and the mixed-manning demonstration on the USS *Claude V. Ricketts*, 1964–1965', *Journal of Military History* 69/3 (Jul 2005), pp. 759–88.
165 Pierre, *Nuclear politics*, p. 249.
166 Quoted in Boulton, 'NATO and the MLF', p. 287.
167 Quoted in Ball, *Politics and force levels*, p. 230.
168 Menaul, *Countdown*, pp. 130–1.
169 PRO, Defence Research Staff newsletter, 1 Jan 1963 in T 325/88.
170 The launch did not test second-stage thrust termination or RV separation, but post-launch analysis showed that a complete missile would have reached 775nm range with ±2nm accuracy. The guidance system, supposedly the focus of most technical concern, performed especially well, repeatedly acquiring stars: 'daylight star tracking was continuous throughout flight' (Library of Congress, LeMay papers, box B128, folder Office of the Secretary of the Air Force 1962, report on second guided launch under cover of letter from Schriever to LeMay of 26 Dec 1962).
171 PRO, Zuckerman and Scott to Thorneycroft, 21 Dec 62 in DEFE 13/619; Zuckerman, *Monkeys, Men and Missiles*, p. 261. Lighthill, for one, found this letter perplexing – 'the previous evening Zuckermann [sic] had looked very happy with a Polaris agreement' – note of 2 Jan 1963 in AVIA 65/1840.
172 PRO, Macmillan to Thorneycroft, 26 Dec 1962 in AIR 19/1047.
173 VAdm Aubrey Mansergh, editorial in *Naval Review*, Jan 1963, pp. 6–7.

174 PRO, VCNS to BJSM, 18 Dec 1962 in ADM 1/28839.
175 Rebecca John, *Caspar John* (Collins 1987), p. 197.
176 PRO, Carrington to Thorneycroft, 31 Dec 1962 in DEFE 7/1752.
177 PRO, report of Polaris fact-finding mission to Washington, Jan 1963 in DEFE 7/2162, ADM 1/28987.
178 Ashton, *Kennedy, Macmillan and the cold war*, pp. 186–8.
179 Alan Pritchard, 'Negotiating the sales agreement' in John Moore, ed., *The impact of Polaris*, p. 31; Peter Nailor, *The Nassau connection: the organisation and management of the British Polaris project* (HMSO 1988), p. 20.
180 PRO, Mackay's first draft report of the negotiations, 21 Mar 1963 in FO 371/173518.
181 Adm Sir Hugh Mackenzie, 'Setting up the UK project' in John Moore, ed., *The impact of Polaris*, p. 59.
182 Cmnd. 2108, *Polaris sales agreement*, Apr 1963.
183 PRO, agreed minutes and exchange of notes in connection with the Polaris sales agreement, 6 April 1963 in PREM 11/4737.
184 Pierre, *Nuclear politics*, p. 217.
185 *ibid.*, p. 252.
186 HoC debs., vol. 687, cols. 437–44 (16 Jan 1964).
187 *ibid.*
188 HoC debs., vol. 622, col. 330 (27 Apr 1960).
189 Pierre, *Nuclear politics*, p. 264.
190 HoC debs., vol. 687, col. 445 (16 Jan 1964).
191 Labour Party, *The New Britain*: http://www.labour-party.org.uk/manifestos/1964/1964-labour-manifesto.shtml (accessed Aug 2007).
192 Pierre, *Nuclear politics*, p. 284.
193 *ibid.*, p. 253.
194 Sir Arthur Vere-Harvey, HoC debs., vol. 670, cols. 1072–3 (30 Jan 1963). Vere-Harvey was chairman of the Conservative backbench defence committee.
195 HoL debs., vol. 256, col. 720 (17 Mar 1964).
196 Conservative Party, *Prosperity with a purpose*: http://www.conservative-party.net/manifestos/1964/1964-conservative-manifesto.shtml (accessed Aug 2007).

Chapter 4

1 PRO, brief for NRDC meeting 31 May 1962 in AVIA 65/1771.
2 PRO, Hockaday to Bligh, 11 Jul 1962 and preceding papers in PREM 11/3716. Most of the relevant Defence Committee papers for the 18 April, 6 June and 8 July discussions, including Watkinson's full proposals, remain classified.
3 PRO, brief to Brundrett, 22 Jan 1958 in DEFE 7/921.
4 PRO, D(62)32 of 4 Jun 1962 in CAB 131/27.
5 PRO, brief for NRDC meeting 31 May 1962 in AVIA 65/1771.
6 PRO, Watkinson to Brooke, 28 May 1962 in ADM 1/31023.
7 PRO, papers in AB 16/3854.
8 PRO, AEA(62)12th mtg, 21 Jun 1962, extract of minutes in AB 16/4189.
9 HoC written answers, vol. 661, cols. 156–7 (27 Jun 1962).

10 PRO, AEA(62)18th mtg, 4 Oct 1962, extract of minutes in AB 16/4189; HoC written answers, vol. 666, cols. 32–3 (5 Nov 1962).
11 PRO, trades-union side statement attached to Makins to Hailsham, 6 Sep 1962 in AB 16/4189.
12 PRO, ND(63)4 of 25 Mar 1963 in CAB 134/2240; papers in AB 16/4189.
13 PRO, Army Council paper summarising ND(62)13, Oct 1962 in WO 32/17069; ND(62)3rd mtg, 3 Oct 1962 in CAB 134/2239.
14 PRO, draft paper for NRDC of 3 Oct 1962 in AB 16/3977.
15 PRO, Makins to Scott, 18 Sep 1961 in DEFE 19/92.
16 PRO, draft memo by chairman NRDC (Scott), 26 Sep 1961 in DEFE 19/92 (emphasis in original); also draft brief for Min of Aviation, 3 Oct 1961 in AVIA 65/1836.
17 PRO, Macmillan to Kennedy, 3 Nov 1961; Makins to Brook, 7 Nov 1961 in PREM 11/3246.
18 PRO, Makins to Macmillan, undated (Mar 1962) in PREM 11/3706.
19 PRO, brief on parliamentary question, 26 Jan 1965 in PREM 13/222 (I am grateful to Kristan Stoddart for drawing my attention to this document).
20 PRO, briefing of 23 Aug 1962 in PREM 11/3706.
21 PRO, DGAW note of 12 Jul 1962 in AVIA 65/1771 and AVIA 65/1836. This note also identifies the US high-explosive used in Tsetse (but not the anglicised Tony) as PBX-9404.
22 PRO, briefing of 23 Aug 1962 in PREM 11/3706.
23 PRO, DGAW note of 12 Jul 1962 in AVIA 65/1771 and AVIA 65/1836.
24 PRO, Makins to Macmillan, undated (Dec 1962) in PREM 11/3706; ND(63)1st mtg, 7 Feb 1963 in CAB 134/2240.
25 PRO, brief for ND(63)4th mtg, 30 Oct 1963 in AVIA 65/1771. Such a warhead would have been impressive in yield/weight terms – over 3.6 kt/kg.
26 PRO, brief for ND(64)1st mtg, 1 Jan 1964 in AVIA 65/1771.
27 PRO, Penney to Hardman (MoD Permanent Secretary), 21 Dec 1964 in DEFE 24/291.
28 PRO, draft brief for Thorneycroft to send to Home, 8 Jan 1964 in DEFE 24/291.
29 PRO, Penney to Seaborg, 21 Jul 1964 in DEFE 24/291.
30 Arnold and Smith, *Britain, Australia and the bomb*, pp. 231–2.
31 PRO, ND(63)8 of 15 Oct 1963 in AVIA 65/1771 and CAB 134/2240.
32 Arnold and Smith, *Britain, Australia and the bomb*, pp. 232–5.
33 ibid., pp. 238–9.
34 Wynn, *RAF strategic nuclear deterrent forces*, pp. 332–3.
35 ibid., pp. 338–9.
36 Clark, *Nuclear diplomacy*, p. 393; Twigge and Scott, *Planning Armageddon*, pp. 113–14.
37 Clark, *Nuclear diplomacy*, p. 394.
38 For an account of the limited practical difference made by SIOP-63, see Rosenberg, 'Constraining overkill: contending approaches to nuclear strategy'.
39 Quoted in Hennessy, *The secret state*, p. 161.
40 Twigge and Scott, *Planning Armageddon*, p. 88.
41 Hennessy, *The secret state*, p. 166 et seq.

42 Brookes, *V-force*, pp. 103–13; Professional pilots' rumour network website, 'Did you fly the Vulcan??' various authors: http://www.pprune.org/forums/showthread.php?t=111797 (accessed Aug 2007).
43 Brookes, *V-force*, p. 103.
44 Quoted in Alexis Tregenza, 'How capable was the V-bomber force militarily of delivering Britain's nuclear deterrent in the late 1950s and 1960s?', *RAF Air Power Review* (2004), p. 123.
45 Brookes, *V-force*, p. 105.
46 Wynn, *RAF strategic nuclear deterrent forces*, p. 449.
47 PRO, extract from DRP/M(63)1, 11 Jan 1963 in AIR 19/1047.
48 Wynn, *RAF strategic nuclear deterrent forces*, p. 452.
49 *ibid.*, p. 458.
50 Brookes, *V-force*, p. 136.
51 Roy Brocklebank, 'World War III – the 1960s version', *Journal of Navigation* 58/3 (Sep 2005), pp. 341–7.
52 Robert Dalsjö, *Life-line lost: the rise and fall of 'neutral' Sweden's secret reserve option of wartime help from the West* (Santerus, Stockholm 2006), pp. 164–5. Allied bombers had similarly been permitted to overfly neutral Sweden during the Second World War (*ibid.*, pp. 44–6). Somewhat curiously, LeMay was given Sweden's highest military decoration, the Order of the Sword Commander Grand Cross, in 1962 or 1963 (Library of Congress, LeMay papers, box B151, folder Countries S-Z 1963).
53 Statement on nuclear defence systems, 21 Dec 1962, *Department of State Bulletin*, 14 Jan 1963, p. 44.
54 PRO, telegram from Ottawa, 25 May 1963 in DEFE 13/976.
55 PRO, VCAS to Fraser, 29 Jan 1963 in AIR 19/1047.
56 PRO, papers in DEFE 13/722 and inventory attached to COS.3320/16/12/63 of 16 Dec 1963 in DEFE 13/726.
57 PRO, record of Thorneycroft/McNamara talks in London, 10 Apr 1963 in DEFE 13/596; UKDEL NATO telno. 171 of 5 May 1963 and numerous other papers in AIR 20/11579.
58 PRO, Mountbatten to Lemnitzer, 23 May 1963 in DEFE 13/976.
59 PRO, Lemnitzer to Thorneycroft, 16 Aug 1963 in DEFE 13/724. Lemnitzer was pictured at Scampton in the *Guardian* newspaper (10 Aug1963, p. 3).
60 PRO, AC(62)12, 28 Mar 1962 in AIR 6/151. The SACEUR Valiants at Marham continued to use Project E weapons.
61 PRO, 'History of nuclear warhead production in UK' of Jan 1963 in AVIA 65/1792, pp. 36–8.
62 PRO, graph accompanying 'History of nuclear warhead production in UK' of Jan 1963 in AVIA 65/1792 (the text records that over 100 sets of Yellow Sun components were available).
63 Wynn, *RAF strategic nuclear deterrent forces*, p. 452.
64 PRO, papers in AIR 2/13705.
65 PRO, note of 3 Jul 1962 in AIR 2/13705.
66 PRO, Zuckerman to Watkinson, 30 Nov 1961 in DEFE 7/2160 and DEFE 13/409.
67 PRO, RAE guided weapons dept paper of 24 Oct 1961 in AVIA 65/1891; Cornford to Zuckerman, 16 Nov 1961 in DEFE 19/87.

68 PRO, Touch to Zuckerman, 20 Jan 1961 in DEFE 19/77; Watkinson to Sandys 12 Apr 1961 and reply 9 August in DEFE 13/408; also papers in AIR 2/17113.
69 PRO, GCapt Fryer, 'Skybolt progress report no. 4' of 14 Mar 1962 in DEFE 13/409.
70 PRO, Zuckerman to Watkinson, 16 May 1962 in DEFE 7/2160.
71 PRO, brief to SofSAir, 9 Jan 1963 in AIR 19/1047.
72 PRO, papers in DEFE 7/2161 and DEFE 19/78.
73 PRO, Dec 1961 papers in AIR 8/2382.
74 Wynn, *RAF strategic nuclear deterrent forces*, p. 211.
75 *ibid.*, p. 213.
76 Quoted in *ibid.*, p. 214. (DCAS's words should not be misunderstood to imply the Air Ministry had the constitutional right to launch missiles in emergency, merely that such a launch was now, in their judgement, operationally possible).
77 PRO, 'History of nuclear warhead production in UK' of Jan 1963 in AVIA 65/1792, pp. 38–9.
78 PRO, papers in AIR 8/2382. There is an account with pictures from the press day in *Flight International* 21 Feb 1963, p. 250 and 28 Feb 1963, pp. 316–17.
79 PRO, Cross to Pike, 7 Jul 1963 and reply of 9 Jul 1963 in AIR 8/2382; Wynn, *RAF strategic nuclear deterrent forces*, pp. 454–5.
80 Wynn, *RAF strategic nuclear deterrent forces*, p. 452.
81 Allen, 'Blue Steel and developments', p. 4.7.
82 Robert R Rodwell, 'The steel in the blue: last week's glimpse of the V-force', *Flight International* 13 Feb 1964, p. 241. Estimates of range from low level range from 25 to 43 to 50 miles: Wynn, *RAF strategic nuclear deterrent forces*, p. 461; Kev Darling, *Avro Vulcan* (Ramsbury, Crowood Press 2005), p. 128.
83 Wynn, *RAF strategic nuclear deterrent forces*, p. 456.
84 *ibid.*, pp. 457–8.
85 *ibid.*, p. 217.
86 *ibid.*, pp. 358–9; Nash, *The other missiles of October*, p. 108.
87 Wynn, *ibid.*, pp. 361–2; Boyes, 'Project Emily', pp. 32–3.
88 PRO, A/D Ops(B&R) note of 27 Jul 1964 in AIR 2/13705.
89 PRO, de Zulueta to Macmillan 13 Aug 1962 in PREM 11/4475. (Macmillan indicated his agreement on 17 Aug).
90 Twigge and Scott, *Planning Armageddon*, pp. 107–8; see also PRO, COS.339/63 of 4 Oct 1963 in DEFE 5/143.
91 PRO, Amery to Macmillan 26 Jul 1962 in PREM 11/4475. (Macmillan added in the margin: 'I am not quite happy about this. Could we not wait a bit?').
92 Separate detachments of between four and eight V-bombers to bases in Singapore and Malaya were made purely for conventional defence during the 'confrontation' with Indonesia. These aircraft would have carried out conventional air attacks on Indonesian air bases in the event of the conflict's escalating seriously. See Wynn, *RAF strategic nuclear deterrent forces*, ch. 25.
93 PRO, Thorneycroft to Home and Sandys, 15 Nov 1963 in PREM 11/4475; Delve, Green and Clemons, *English Electric Canberra*, p. 106; papers

in AIR 20/12199 record the withdrawal of Red Beard from the far east.
94 Delve, Green and Clemons, *English Electric Canberra*, p. 79.
95 Wynn, *RAF strategic nuclear deterrent forces*, pp. 369–70. Also PRO, note on US weapons for RAF aircraft of 20 Jun 1962 in AIR 2/13702.
96 Wynn, *RAF strategic nuclear deterrent forces*, p. 370.
97 PRO, MM(62)24 of 19 Jul 1962 in DEFE 13/245.
98 PRO, papers in AIR 2/13702.
99 Wynn, *RAF strategic nuclear deterrent forces*, pp. 526–7.
100 *ibid.*, pp. 528–32.
101 LtCdr Tony Dyson RN, *HMS Hermes: a pictorial history* (Liskeard, Maritime Books 1984); McCart, *HMS Victorious 1937–69*.
102 PRO, Board memo B.1456 of 8 Jul 1963 in ADM 167/161; Brown and Moore, *Rebuilding the Royal Navy*, pp. 58–61.
103 Robert Gardiner, ed. dir., *Conway's all the world's fighting ships 1947–95* (Conway's 1995), p. 500.
104 Beach and Gurr, *Flattering the passions*, p. 77; Anthony Verrier, quoted in John Garnett, 'BAOR and NATO', *International Affairs* 46/4 (Oct 1970), p. 676.
105 John Garnett, correspondence in *International Affairs* 47/1 (Jan 1971), p. 269.
106 From figures in PRO, 'History of nuclear warhead production in UK' of Jan 1963 and accompanying tables in AVIA 65/1792.
107 *ibid.*, p. 39.
108 PRO, DGAW paper of 12 Jul 1962 in AVIA 65/1771.
109 PRO, Howell's draft of MoA R&D Board paper, 6 Jul 1962 in AIR 2/17325. Correspondence on the same file shows that both the Air Ministry and Admiralty objected to the use of Mk.57.
110 PRO, ND(62)1st mtg, 31 May 1962 in CAB 134/2239.
111 PRO, notes and minutes of WE177 Working Party mtgs 19 Jan, 15 Mar 1962 in AIR 2/17324; Howell's draft of MoA R&D Board paper, 6 Jul 1962 in AIR 2/17325.
112 PRO, Board memo B.1417 of 7 May 1962 in ADM 167/154. In *The Royal Navy and nuclear weapons*, p. 173, I took this Board memo as a complete disavowal of interest in nuclear depth-bombs, but it now seems clear that the Board was making a subtler point, disowning the requirement for a separate nuclear depth-bomb project at the same time as maintaining interest in an underwater fuzing option for the Red Beard replacement.
113 PRO, draft Issue 3 of GDA.16/OR.1176, sent by DDOR2 to DOR(C) on 7 Nov 1962, in AIR 2/17325. The yields in square brackets were deleted from the released version of the document on declassification, and have been inferred by the author from other papers in this and other Air Ministry files of the period.
114 PRO, draft Issue 3 of GDA.15/OR.1177, sent by DDOR2 to DOR(C) on 7 Nov 1962, in AIR 2/17325. OR.356 was a joint RN/RAF requirement for a supersonic vertical/short-take-off aircraft; the resulting Hawker-Siddeley P.1154 project was cancelled. OR.357 was the requirement for a replacement for the RAF's Shackleton long-range anti-submarine patrol aircraft, which later materialised as the Nimrod.

115 PRO, notes of the 9th WE177 Working Party, 22 Oct 1962, in AIR 2/17325.
116 PRO, 'Bomber Command 1963–70', 17 Jan 1963 in AIR 19/1047.
117 PRO, Treasury letter to Williams (MoA), 12 Feb 1963 in AIR 2/17325.
118 PRO, papers of Dec 1963 in AIR 2/13702. An internal Air Ministry paper (OR19 to DDOR2, 4 Mar 1963 in AIR 2/17325) suggests that the 53 came out of the 102, meaning that only a small number of WE177A (31?) was now required by the RAF.
119 PRO, A/DDOR2 file note to DOR(C) of 12 Jun 1963 in AIR 2/17327; OR19 file note to DDOR2 of 29 Aug 1963 in AIR 2/17328; AD/AArm3 to DDOR2, 7 Nov 1963 and DDOR2 file note of 15 Nov 1963 in AIR 2/17329. Apart from one specific mention of 220kt, the yield figures under discussion have been deleted from the declassified copies of these papers.
120 The requirement for a WE177B warhead – OR.1195 of 13 Mar 1963 in PRO, AIR 2/17326 – used the words 'near megaton yield,' although it is unclear what this meant exactly, and ministerial agreement had probably been secured by mentioning 450kt [only]. The term 'megaton yield' was used elsewhere to cover anything from 500kt upwards.
121 PRO, brief on DRP/P(63)50 in T 225/2793.
122 PRO, 18 Apr 1963 circulation of the GDA.15/OR.1177 requirement and other papers in AIR 2/17326.
123 PRO, OR/P(64)52, undated (1964) in AIR 2/13755.
124 PRO, Zuckerman to Wigg, 15 Jun 1965 in DEFE 19/103.
125 PRO, AC(59)42 of 14 May 1959 in AIR 6/117; internal letter on warheads for tactical weapons, 30 Jun 1959 in AIR 2/13735; DOR(C) to Emson (MoA), 21 Jul 1959 in AVIA 65/775, Emson comments on AC(59)88 dated 5 Nov 1959 and Howell comments on AC(60)9 dated 22 Feb 1960 in AVIA 65/775.
126 United States Defense Nuclear Agency, *Operation Dominic I 1962*, DNA 6040F, 1 Feb 1983, p. 198: http://www.dtra.mil/rd/programs/nuclear_personnel/docs/T24298.PDF (accessed Aug 2007).
127 In *The Royal Navy and nuclear weapons*, I underestimated this anxiety and dated it to the mid to late 1960s. Further research has shown that this was a mistake, although the full story still remains elusive.
128 PRO, OR/P(64)52, undated (1964) in AIR 2/13755.
129 PRO, 'The navy's requirement for WE177A', 19 May 1966 in DEFE 19/103.
130 Moore, *The Royal Navy and nuclear weapons*, p. 173.
131 PRO, Admiralty note to MoA of 26 Jul 1962 in AIR 2/17325.
132 PRO, numerous papers in AIR 20/10058; also Watkinson to Macmillan, 17 Apr 1961 in PREM 11/3253 (I am grateful to Robin Woolven for drawing my attention to this document).
133 PRO, note to PS/VCAS, 27 Jun 1962 in AIR 20/10058.
134 PRO, CINCUSNAVEUR to Pike, 10 Nov 1962 in AIR 20/10058.
135 Norris *et al.*, *British, French and Chinese nuclear weapons*, p. 85; HoC written answers for 26 Oct 1993, col. 529: http://www.publications.parliament.uk/pa/cm199293/cmhansrd/1993-10-26/Writtens-1.html (accessed Aug 2007).
136 PRO, Board memo B.1422 of 19 Jun 1962 in ADM 167/154 and minute 5536 of 20 Jun 1962 in ADM 167/160.

137 Gibson and Buttler, *British secret projects*, pp. 128–30; brochures in PRO, WO 32/18891; Anon., 'Blue Water', *Flight International* 18 May 1961, pp. 657–8 and 2 Nov 1961, p. 703.
138 PRO, note of 13 Oct 1961 and other papers in WO 32/17067.
139 Kate Pyne, 'Warheads and rockets: UK nuclear warheads for almost anything with a point at one end and a flame at the other', presentation to the British Rocketry Oral History Project conference at Charterhouse, April 2003. Kate has elaborated further: 'our lot [at Aldermaston] were gobsmacked at this – the thing was absolutely ready for production' (pers. comm. 8 Jan 2008).
140 PRO, ND(62)3rd mtg, 3 Oct 1962 in CAB 134/2239.
141 PRO, drafts of an Army Council paper on the warhead review, Feb 1962 in WO 32/17069.
142 RAE Archive, Farnborough, Penley committee paper 'ABM defence systems', undated (*c.* Nov 1962) (with thanks to Roy Dommett).
143 Roy Dommett, 'Re-entry observables: the Woomera programmes 1957–67' (unpublished).
144 Hill, *A vertical empire*, pp. 176–86.
145 PRO, draft paper of 7 Jan 1963 (not submitted to the cabinet) in DEFE 7/2145.
146 PRO, Kent to VCAS, 7 Jan 1963 in AIR 19/1047.
147 PRO, DRP/M(63)1 of 11 Jan 1963 in AIR 19/1047.
148 PRO, D(63)2 of 15 Jan 1963 in CAB 131/28; papers of Dec 1963 in AIR 2/13702.
149 PRO, D(63)1st mtg, 23 Jan 1963 in CAB 131/28.
150 PRO, note of mtg 1 Jan 1963 in AVIA 65/1840.
151 PRO, RAE paper of 7 Jan 1963 in AVIA 65/1834.
152 PRO, brief comments on deterrent proposals, 8 Feb 1963 in AVIA 65/1834 (I am grateful to Brian Burnell for drawing my attention to this document). See also Gibson and Buttler, *British secret projects*, pp. 116–17.
153 PRO, RAE memo WE.1054 'Stop-gap deterrent weapons' of Feb 1963 in AVIA 65/1834 (with thanks to Brian Burnell for this document).
154 PRO, brief for CAS presentation, 13 Mar 1963 in AIR 8/2393.
155 PRO, papers of Mar 1963 and later in AVIA 65/1834.
156 Spinardi, *From Polaris to Trident*, p. 37.
157 *ibid.*, p. 65.
158 *ibid.*, p. 66; J P McManus, *A History of the FBM system* (Lockheed Missiles and Space Company, 1989), p. E-24.
159 Spinardi, *From Polaris to Trident*, pp. 67–8; McManus, *A History of the FBM system*, pp. B-19/20, E-24/25.
160 Hansen, *US nuclear weapons*, p. 205.
161 PRO, Le Fanu's recollections, dictated 22 Dec 1962 in ADM 1/28839.
162 PRO, report of Polaris fact-finding mission, Jan 1963 in DEFE 7/2162 and ADM 1/28987.
163 PRO, Zuckerman to Watkinson, 23 Jan 1963 in DEFE 13/734.
164 PRO, brief to Amery on Defence Committee paper D(63)1, 23 Jan 1963 in AVIA 65/1840; also Lawrence-Wilson to Thorneycroft, 7 Mar 1963 in DEFE 13/735.
165 PRO, Williams note, 1 Apr 1963 in ADM 1/28974 and DEFE 13/736.

166 PRO, Mackay's first draft report, circulated 21 Mar 1963 in FO 371/173518.
167 Greenwood, *Making the MIRV*, pp. 27–37.
168 PRO, draft report of inter-departmental steering committee on Polaris, 27 Mar 1963 in DEFE 7/2163.
169 PRO, Carrington to Thorneycroft, 1 Apr 1963 in DEFE 13/736.
170 PRO, Thorneycroft to Macmillan, 3 Apr 1963 in PREM 11/4150.
171 PRO, papers in DEFE 13/295 (Zuckerman's actual paper has been removed from the file).
172 Kate Pyne, 'More complex than expected: the AWRE's contribution to the Chevaline payload', *The history of the UK strategic deterrent: the Chevaline programme*, proceedings of the Royal Aeronautical Society conference on 28 Oct 2004, pp. G2–3.
173 PRO, Carrington to Thorneycroft, 29 May 1963 in DEFE 13/736.
174 PRO, MM(63)6 of 3 Apr 63 in FO 371/173518.
175 Nailor, *The Nassau connection*, p. 35; Simpson, *The independent nuclear state*, p. 168; PRO, papers in DEFE 13/736 and 'Study of a UK re-entry system for the Polaris A3 missile', 24 Sep 1963 in FO 371/173521.
176 PRO, D(63)1 of 15 Jan 1963 in CAB 131/28.
177 PRO, brief for D(63)1st mtg, 17 Jan 1963 in AIR 19/1047.
178 Nailor, *The Nassau connection*, p. 7; Adm Sir Hugh Mackenzie, 'Setting up the UK project', John Moore, ed., *The impact of Polaris*, p. 50; PRO, D(63)1st, 23 Jan 1963 in CAB 131/28.
179 Nailor, *The Nassau connection*, pp. 73–4.
180 Brown and Moore, *Rebuilding the Royal Navy*, pp. 126–7.
181 Nailor, *The Nassau connection*, p. 96.
182 Subterranea Britannica website: http://www.subbrit.org.uk/sb-sites/sites/r/rugby_radio/indexr69.shtml (accessed Aug 2007).
183 *ibid.*: http://www.subbrit.org.uk/sb-sites/sites/c/criggion_radio/ (accessed Aug 2007).
184 PRO, Admiralty note on communications with submerged submarines, 29 May 1961 in DEFE 13/295.
185 PRO, Admiralty note on Loran-C, 17 Sep 1958 in DEFE 13/181; Brook to Macmillan, 11 May 1959 in PREM 11/2640.
186 Federation of American Scientists website: http://www.fas.org/spp/military/program/nav/transit.htm (accessed Aug 2007); RAE Archive, Farnborough, G B Longden, 'Polaris effectiveness and guidance', Technical Report no. 67003 of Jan 1967 (with thanks to Roy Dommett).
187 Cdr Michael Henry RN, 'A CO's story', John Moore, ed., *The impact of Polaris*, p. 249.
188 RAE Archive, Farnborough, G B Longden, 'Polaris effectiveness and guidance', Technical Report no. 67003 of Jan 1967 (with thanks to Roy Dommett); John Coker, pers. comm. 21 Nov 2007. There is also a short account of these problems in Anon., 'Polaris: the destroyer from the deep', *Flight International* 22 Jul 1960, pp. 118–19.
189 I am grateful to John Coker for his considerable help in understanding the operation of the Polaris system, on which this section is heavily based. The description is of the operation of the UK Polaris, and therefore strictly outside the time period covered by this book. The US Polaris A-1, in service from 1960, differed in certain respects, notably (as mentioned briefly in the

text) in the missile itself and RV, and the fire-control system; also as regards available communications and external navigational aids. It was Polaris A-1, with its various shortcomings, which formed the essential basis of UK critiques of the overall system during our period.

190 See e.g., PRO, AVM Sheen brief of 25 Apr 1960 in AIR 20/10057; paper of 20 Dec 1960 in AIR 2/13710.
191 RAE Archive, Farnborough, 1st mtg of the US/UK JRSWG held in Washington 11–14 June 1963, dated 12 Aug 63 (with thanks to Roy Dommett); PRO, 'Study of a UK re-entry system for the Polaris A3 missile', 24 Sep 1963 in FO 371/173521.
192 PRO, 'Study of a UK re-entry system for the Polaris A3 missile', 24 Sep 1963 in FO 371/173521.
193 PRO, ND(63)4th mtg, 30 Oct 1963 in CAB 134/2240.
194 PRO, paper of 8 Apr 1964 in AB 16/3977. Whether the WDC had the authority to make such a decision alone is unclear.
195 PRO, Zuckerman to Home, 16 May 64 in PREM 11/4737.
196 PRO, ND(64)8 of 22 Jun 1964 and ND(64)5th mtg, 25 Jun 1964 in CAB 134/2241; Thorneycroft to Home, 7 Jul 1964 in PREM 11/5172.
197 PRO, ND(65)1 of 20 Jan 1965 in CAB 134/2241.
198 PRO, Lawrence-Wilson to Zuckerman, 17 Jan 1963 in DEFE 7/2162.
199 PRO, DAWD notes on ND(63)4, 28 Mar 1963 in AVIA 65/1771.
200 PRO, ND(63)3rd mtg, 2 Jul 1963 in CAB 134/2240.
201 PRO, undated brief recording NRDC recommendations (Jul 1963) in AVIA 65/1771.
202 PRO, Kent to VCAS, 7 Jan 1963 in AIR 19/1047.
203 PRO, D(63)2 of 15 Jan 1963 in CAB 131/28.
204 PRO, Boyd-Carpenter to Home, 22 Jan 1964 in DEFE 24/291.
205 PRO, Penney to Hardman, 21 Dec 1964 in DEFE 24/291; 7600 staff (88 per cent of the 1962 total) were working for AWRE at Aldermaston, Foulness and Orfordness in April 1964, and a further reduction to 6000 was planned by the end of the decade. This reduction was still underway at the time of the King's Norton enquiry in 1968: see papers in AB 16/3977, ES 13/1.
206 Norris et al., *British, French and Chinese nuclear weapons*, pp. 47, 60/2.

Conclusions

1 See e.g., David A Rosenberg, 'Arleigh Albert Burke', in Richard Love, ed., *The chiefs of naval operations* (US Naval Institute Press 1980), pp. 263–319.
2 Hubert Zimmermann, *Money and security: troops, monetary policy and West Germany's relations with the United States and Britain, 1950–1971* (Cambridge UP 2002), appendix; Hugh Hanning, 'Britain east of Suez – facts and figures', *International Affairs* 42/2 (Apr 1966), p. 253.
3 See Kurt Wayne Schake, 'Strategic frontier: American bomber bases overseas 1950–60', dissertation for the Norwegian University of Science and Technology, Jan 1998 (accessible from: http://handle.dtic.mil/100.2/ADA353633), esp. pp. 121–8 and appendix A4. Schake claims that those with the UK were 'the most permissive base agreements, by far', although this conclusion appears not to be supported by the evidence he cites: other countries wished

to be consulted, before a (unilateral) US decision, or simply expected the US to go ahead without consultation if NATO was at war. For dealings with the French, see US Dept of State, *Foreign relations of the United States 1961–3*, vol. XIII, pp. 666, 672.

4 'Check-list of presidential actions' prepared for McGeorge Bundy on 28 Jul 1961, available from: http://www.gwu.edu/~nsarchiv/nsa/NC/nuchis.html#samp (accessed Jul 2008).
5 See e.g., Jeffrey A Engel, *Cold war at 30,000 feet: the Anglo-American fight for aviation supremacy* (Harvard UP 2007); Zimmermann, *Money and security*; Francis J Gavin, 'The gold battles within the cold war: American monetary policy and the defence of Europe 1960–63', *Diplomatic History* 26/1 (Winter 2002), pp. 61–94; Diane B Kunz, '"Somewhat mixed up together": Anglo-American defence and financial policy during the 1960s', *Journal of Imperial and Commonwealth History* 27/2 (Spring 1999), pp. 213–32.
6 Quoted in Ashton, *Kennedy, Macmillan and the cold war*, pp. 161–2.
7 Watkinson, *Turning points*, p. 149.
8 Frank Barnett-Jones, *TSR.2: phoenix or folly?* (Peterborough, GMS 1994), p. 246.
9 PRO, DOR(A) paper of Dec 1960 in AIR 2/13382.
10 PRO, CWP/M(58)2 of 23 Apr 1958 in DEFE 13/193.
11 Hastings, *The murder of TSR-2*, p. 36.
12 Spinardi, 'Aldermaston and British nuclear weapons development: testing the Zuckerman thesis'.
13 Lewis Page, *Lions, donkeys and dinosaurs: waste and blundering in the armed forces* (William Heinemann 2006).
14 Stephen I Schwartz, ed., *Atomic audit: the costs and consequences of US nuclear weapons since 1940* (Washington DC, Brookings 1998).
15 PRO, 'The cost of the deterrent – January/June 1958', 9 Oct 1958 in AIR 20/11443.
16 PRO, Air Ministry paper of 8 Nov 1960 in DEFE 7/1328; Kent to PS/SofSAir, 11 Nov 1960 in AIR 20/11443.
17 There is very little available information on the penetration capability of Russian ballistic missiles, but a cursory search of the relevant secondary literature has produced no suggestion that missiles introduced before the early 1970s had multiple warheads or penetration aids (Pavel Podvig, ed., *Russian strategic nuclear forces* (Cambridge Mass, MIT Press 2001), pp. 199, 206). British studies seem to have been based on mirroring Blue Streak work, rather than on any solid information of Russian progress.
18 Zuckerman, *Monkeys, men and missiles*, p. 387.
19 See Andrew Moravcsik, 'De Gaulle between grain and grandeur: the political economy of French EC policy 1958–70' (and the several replies thereto), *Journal of Cold War Studies* 2/2 (Spring 2000), pp. 3–43, and 2/3 (Fall 2000), pp. 4–139.
20 Walker, *Britain, the United States, weapon policies and nuclear testing*.
21 Probert, *High Commanders of the RAF*, p. 52.
22 George Quester, *Deterrence before Hiroshima: the airpower background of modern strategy* (New York, John Wiley 1966).
23 PRO, Maudling to Lloyd, 30 Aug 1955 in AIR 19/660.

Bibliography

Primary sources

National Archive (Public Record Office), Kew, London
AB 16: UKAEA London office files: AB 16/2307, AB 16/3854, AB 16/3977, AB 16/4189.
ADM 1: Admiralty correspondence and papers: ADM 1/17259, ADM 1/27375, ADM 1/27389, ADM 1/27827, ADM 1/27876, ADM 1/28839, ADM 1/28949, ADM 1/28974, ADM 1/28987, ADM 1/31023.
ADM 167: Board of Admiralty minutes and memoranda: ADM 167/151, ADM 167/152, ADM 167/153, ADM 167/154, ADM 167/155, ADM 167/156, ADM 167/160, ADM 167/161.
ADM 205: First Sea Lord's papers: ADM 205/172, ADM 205/179, ADM 205/188, ADM 205/202, ADM 205/222.
AIR 2: Air Ministry registered files: AIR 2/13213, AIR 2/13382, AIR 2/13678, AIR 2/13693, AIR 2/13702, AIR 2/13705, AIR 2/13708, AIR 2/13710, AIR 2/13728, AIR 2/13735, AIR 2/13736, AIR 2/13746, AIR 2/13753, AIR 2/13755, AIR 2/13761, AIR 2/13773, AIR 2/13774, AIR 2/13775, AIR 2/14641, AIR 2/14711, AIR 2/15261, AIR 2/15262, AIR 2/15637, AIR 2/17113, AIR 2/17322, AIR 2/17323, AIR 2/17324, AIR 2/17325, AIR 2/17326, AIR 2/17327, AIR 2/17328, AIR 2/17329, AIR 2/17371, AIR 2/17780.
AIR 6: Air Council minutes and memoranda: AIR 6/117, AIR 6/151.
AIR 8: Chief of the Air Staff's department registered files: AIR 8/1961, AIR 8/2201, AIR 8/2204, AIR 8/2256, AIR 8/2288, AIR 8/2382, AIR 8/2393.
AIR 19: Air Ministry private office papers: AIR 19/660, AIR 19/999, AIR 19/1036, AIR 19/1047, AIR 19/1085.
AIR 20: Air Historical Branch papers: AIR 20/10057, AIR 20/10058, AIR 20/10067, AIR 20/10638, AIR 20/10697, AIR 20/10830, AIR 20/10925, AIR 20/11443, AIR 20/11530, AIR 20/11578, AIR 20/11579, AIR 20/12199.
AIR 29: Operations record books, miscellaneous units: AIR 29/3103.
AIR 41: Air Historical Branch narratives and monographs: AIR 41/86
AVIA 13: RAE registered files: AVIA 13/1283, AVIA 13/1336.
AVIA 65: Ministry of Supply (Aviation) registered files: AVIA 65/775, AVIA 65/778, AVIA 65/878, AVIA 65/911, AVIA 65/912, AVIA 65/1050, AVIA 65/1064, AVIA 65/1114, AVIA 65/1116, AVIA 65/1153, AVIA 65/1155, AVIA 65/1166, AVIA 65/1262, AVIA 65/1352, AVIA 65/1428, AVIA 65/1441, AVIA 65/1564, AVIA 65/1661, AVIA 65/1771, AVIA 65/1772, AVIA 65/1792, AVIA 65/1834, AVIA 65/1836, AVIA 65/1840, AVIA 65/1851, AVIA 65/1891, AVIA 65/2019, AVIA 65/2029, AVIA 65/2284, AVIA 65/2332.
AVIA 66: Ministry of Aviation private office papers: AVIA 66/1.
CAB 21: Cabinet Office registered files: CAB 21/3900, CAB 21/4979, CAB 21/5125.
CAB 128: Cabinet minutes: CAB 128/34, CAB 128/35, CAB 128/36, CAB 128/37.

302 Bibliography

CAB 129: Cabinet memoranda: CAB 129/100, CAB 129/101, CAB 129/108, CAB 129/114.
CAB 131: Cabinet Defence Committee minutes and memoranda: CAB 131/19, CAB 131/20, CAB 131/22, CAB 131/23, CAB 131/24, CAB 131/25, CAB 131/27, CAB 131/28.
CAB 134: Miscellaneous Cabinet committee minutes and memoranda: CAB 134/2239, CAB 134/2240, CAB 134/2241, CAB 134/2274.
DEFE 4: Chiefs of Staff minutes: DEFE 4/103, DEFE 4/115, DEFE 4/124
DEFE 5: Chiefs of Staff memoranda: DEFE 5/96, DEFE 5/105, DEFE 5/123, DEFE 5/143.
DEFE 7: MoD registered files: DEFE 7/921, DEFE 7/1328, DEFE 7/1752, DEFE 7/1888, DEFE 7/2031, DEFE 7/2063, DEFE 7/2143, DEFE 7/2145, DEFE 7/2160, DEFE 7/2161, DEFE 7/2162, DEFE 7/2163, DEFE 7/2216, DEFE 7/2217, DEFE 7/2231, DEFE 7/2236, DEFE 7/2247, DEFE 7/2278, DEFE 7/2294, DEFE 7/2300, DEFE 7/2301, DEFE 7/2302, DEFE 7/2380.
DEFE 10: MoD committees and working parties, minutes and memoranda: DEFE 10/356, DEFE 10/357, DEFE 10/382, DEFE 10/403, DEFE 10/418, DEFE 10/806.
DEFE 11: Chiefs of Staff registered files: DEFE 11/240, DEFE 11/360.
DEFE 13: MoD private office registered files: DEFE 13/150, DEFE 13/180, DEFE 13/181, DEFE 13/193, DEFE 13/245, DEFE 13/295, DEFE 13/351, DEFE 13/408, DEFE 13/409, DEFE 13/425, DEFE 13/426, DEFE 13/427, DEFE 13/596, DEFE 13/617, DEFE 13/618, DEFE 13/619, DEFE 13/722, DEFE 13/724, DEFE 13/726, DEFE 13/727, DEFE 13/734, DEFE 13/735, DEFE 13/736, DEFE 13/976.
DEFE 19: MoD scientific staff files: DEFE 19/5, DEFE 19/76, DEFE 19/77, DEFE 19/78, DEFE 19/87, DEFE 19/92, DEFE 19/103, DEFE 19/115.
DEFE 24: MoD secretariat registered files: DEFE 24/11, DEFE 24/291.
DEFE 25: Chief of Defence Staff registered files: DEFE 25/13.
DEFE 30: Defence Board minutes and memoranda: DEFE 30/1.
DEFE 32: Chiefs of Staff committee, secretary's standard files: DEFE 32/6, DEFE 32/7.
ES 12: AWRE miscellaneous reports: ES 12/270, ES 12/271.
ES 13: AWRE Director's private office papers: ES 13/1.
FO 371: Foreign Office general correspondence: FO 371/173518, FO 371/173521.
PREM 11: Prime Minister's correspondence and papers (1951–64): PREM 11/2640, PREM 11/2852, PREM 11/2861, PREM 11/2940, PREM 11/3162, PREM 11/3246, PREM 11/3253, PREM 11/3706, PREM 11/3716, PREM 11/3724, PREM 11/4150, PREM 11/4229, PREM 11/4475, PREM 11/4737, PREM 11/5172.
PREM 13: Prime Minister's correspondence and papers (1964–70): PREM 13/222.
T 225: Treasury defence policy and materiel division: T 225/2793.
T 325: Sir Otto Clarke's papers: T 325/88.
WO 32: War Office registered files: WO 32/17067, WO 32/17069, WO 32/17131, WO32/17182, WO 32/18891, WO 32/19928, WO 32/21044, WO 32/21248.
WO 216: Chief of the Imperial General Staff's papers: WO 216/934.
WO 279: War Office confidential print: WO 279/279.
WO 286: War Office/Ministry of Supply branch registry files: WO 286/39.

Zuckerman archive, University of East Anglia, Norwich

Air Ministry Strategic Scientific Policy Committee: SZ/AMSSP/3.
Chief Scientific Adviser: SZ/CSA/32, SZ/CSA/95, SZ/CSA/192.

Mountbatten archive, Hartley Library, University of Southampton
MB1/I143, MB1/I447, MB1/I586, MB1/J311, MB1/J314, MB1/M33.

RAF Museum, Hendon
Boyle papers: *My life: an autobiography by MRAF Sir Dermot Boyle* (privately published, 1989); MF 10101/2, MF 10101/17.

Library of Congress, Washington DC
Curtis E LeMay papers: boxes B128, B151.
Thomas D White papers: boxes 36, 37.

RAE archive, Farnborough (via Roy Dommett)
Minutes of the 4th mtg of the joint UK/US medium-range ballistic missile advisory committee, 20/21 Jun 1957.
RAE technical note GW490 of Apr 1958, 'Technical notes on the American ballistic missile programme'.
DSR(L) RAE note of 16 Feb 1960.
GW Dept 'Examination of Skybolt system proposals', 16 May 60.
BND(TSC)(61)3 of 18 Jan 1961.
Penley committee paper 'ABM defence systems', undated (*c*. Nov 1962).
1st mtg of the US/UK JRSWG held in Washington 11–14 June 1963, dated 12 Aug 63.
G B Longden, 'Polaris effectiveness and guidance', Technical Report no. 67003 of Jan 1967.

Other unpublished documents
Slater archive, Mountbatten Centre for International Studies, University of Southampton: Kent to VCAS, 2 Nov 1959.
US Delegation to NATO, 'A concept for the creation and operation of a Multilateral Force', 18 Oct 1963 (with thanks to MGen Eric Younson and John Simpson).

UK government white papers and published documents
Cmnd. 124, *Defence: outline of future policy*, April 1957.
Cmnd. 363, *Report on defence*, Feb 1958.
Cmnd. 371, *First Lord's statement on the Navy estimates 1958–59*.
Cmnd. 476, *Central organisation for defence*, July 1958.
Cmnd. 537, *Agreement for cooperation on the uses of atomic energy for mutual defence purposes*, 3 July 1958.
Cmnd. 859, *Amendment to the agreement for cooperation on the uses of atomic energy for mutual defence purposes of 3 July 1958*, 7 May 1959.
Cmnd. 952, *Report on defence*, Feb 1960.
Cmnd. 1639, *Statement on defence: the next five years*, Feb 1962.
Cmnd. 2097, *Central organisation for defence*, Jul 1963.
Cmnd. 2108, *Polaris sales agreement*, Apr 1963.
UK Ministry of Defence, 'Historical accounting and plutonium' and 'Plutonium and Aldermaston: an historical account' (MoD 2000) available from: http://www.mod.uk/DefenceInternet/AboutDefence/CorporatePublications/Defence

EstateandEnvironmentPublications/UKNucWeaponsProg/ (accessed August 2007).

UK parliamentary papers

House of Commons (HoC), Vols. 568, 578–80, 610, 621–2, 629, 632, 648, 661, 666, 670, 687.
HoC written answers for 26 Oct 1993, col. 529: http://www.publications.parliament.uk/pa/cm199293/cmhansrd/1993-10-26/Writtens-1.html (accessed Aug 2007).
House of Lords (HoL), Vols. 250, 256.

UK political manifestos

Labour Party, *Britain Belongs to You: The Labour Party's Policy for Consideration by the British People*: http://www.labour-party.org.uk/manifestos/1959/1959-labour-manifesto.shtml (accessed July 2007).
Labour Party, *The New Britain*: http://www.labour-party.org.uk/manifestos/1964/1964-labour-manifesto.shtml (accessed Aug 2007).
Conservative Party, *Prosperity with a purpose*: http://www.conservative-party.net/manifestos/1964/1964-conservative-manifesto.shtml (accessed Aug 2007).

US government published documents

Department of State bulletin, 11 Nov 1957, 14 Jan 1963.
Foreign relations of the United States 1958–60, Vol. VII.
Foreign relations of the United States 1961–63, Vols. VII, XIII.
Defense Nuclear Agency, *Operation Dominic I 1962*, DNA 6040F, 1 Feb 1983: http://www.dtra.mil/rd/programs/nuclear_personnel/docs/T24298.PDF (accessed Aug 2007).
Text of McNamara's Athens speech: http://www.cnn.com/SPECIALS/cold.war/episodes/12/documents/mcnamara.no.cities/ (accessed Aug 2007).
Audio file of Kennedy's conversation with Macmillan: follow instructions from http://www.jfklibrary.org/jfkl/cmc/pr_jfk_macmillan_phone_call.html (accessed Aug 2007).

Other governments' published documents

Australian Government Publishing Service, *Report of the Royal Commission into British nuclear tests in Australia*, Vol. 2 (Canberra, AGPS 1985).
Canadian embassy Washington, 'Some historical comments and background on TTCP', paper prepared for the 25th anniversary meeting of the non-atomic military research and development principals, 12–13 October 1983, http://www.dtic.mil/ttcp/history25.htm (accessed July 2007).
NATO MC 14/2 (Revised) (Final Decision) of 23 May 1957 in Gregory W Pedlow, ed., *NATO strategy documents 1949–69* (SHAPE Historical Office, 1997): http://www.nato.int/archives/strategy.htm (accessed July 2007).

Other published documents

Security resources panel of the [Presidential] Science Advisory Committee, *Deterrence and survival in the nuclear age* (Washington, 7 Nov 1957): http://www.gwu.edu/~nsarchiv/NSAEBB/NSAEBB139/nitze02.pdf (accessed Aug 2007).

Burr, William, *Consultation is presidential business: secret understandings on the use of nuclear weapons, 1950–74*, National security archive electronic briefing book no. 159: http://www.gwu.edu/~nsarchiv/NSAEBB/NSAEBB159/ (accessed July 2007).

'The Skybolt Air Launched Ballistic Missile Programme' of 21 Jul 1960, document no. NSA00508 in *US Nuclear History: Nuclear Arms and Policy in the Missile Age 1955–68* (National Security Archive microfilm document series/Chadwyck-Healey 1998).

'Check-list of presidential actions' prepared for McGeorge Bundy on 28 Jul 1961, follow links from: http://www.gwu.edu/~nsarchiv/nsa/NC/nuchis.html#samp (accessed Jul 2008).

Secondary sources

Books and articles (published in London unless stated)

Albright, David, Frans Berkhout and William Walker, *Plutonium and highly enriched uranium 1996: world inventories, capabilities and policies* (OUP/SIPRI 1997).

Aldous, Richard and Sabine Lee, eds., *Harold Macmillan and Britain's World Role* (Macmillan 1995).

——, *Harold Macmillan: Aspects of a Political Life* (Macmillan 1999).

Allen, John E, 'Blue Steel and developments', *History of the UK strategic deterrent: proceedings of the Royal Aeronautical Society symposium 17 March 1999*, pp. 4.1–25.

Anderson, David, *Histories of the hanged: Britain's dirty war in Kenya and the end of empire* (Weidenfeld and Nicolson 2004).

Anonymous, 'A nuclear-powered plane?' *Time* 13 Jan 1958.

——, 'Polaris: the destroyer from the deep', *Flight International* 22 Jul 1960, pp. 115–19.

——, 'Blue Water', *Flight International* 18 May 1961, pp. 657–8

——, 'Blue Water', *Flight International* 2 Nov 1961, p. 703.

——, 'Guiding Blue Streak', *Flight International* 28 Mar 1963, pp. 438–9.

——, 'Honest John', *Windscreen* 111 (Summer 2006), pp. 10–12.

Arnold, Lorna, *Britain and the H-bomb* (Palgrave 2001).

Arnold, Lorna and Mark Smith, *Britain, Australia and the bomb: the nuclear tests and their aftermath* (Palgrave 2006).

Ashton, Nigel, *Kennedy, Macmillan and the cold war: the irony of interdependence* (Palgrave 2002).

——, 'Harold Macmillan and the 'golden days' of Anglo-American relations revisited, 1957–63', *Diplomatic History* 29/4 (Summer 2005), pp. 691–723.

Backus, Cdr P H USN, 'Finite deterrence, controlled retaliation', *US Naval Institute Proceedings* 85/3 (Mar 1959), pp. 23–9.

Ball, Desmond, *Politics and force levels: the strategic missile program of the Kennedy administration* (Univ of California Press 1980).

Ball, Simon, *The bomber in British strategy: doctrine, strategy and Britain's world role 1945–60* (Oxford, Westview 1995).

Barnett, Correlli, *The collapse of British power* (Eyre Methuen 1972).

Barnett-Jones, Frank, *TSR.2: phoenix or folly?* (Peterborough, GMS 1994).

Bartlett, C J, *The long retreat: a short history of British defence policy 1945–70* (Macmillan 1972).

Baylis, John, *Anglo-American defence relations 1939–84* (Macmillan, 2nd edn, 1984).
——, *Ambiguity and deterrence: British nuclear strategy 1945–64* (Oxford, Clarendon Press 1995).
——, 'Exchanging nuclear secrets: laying the foundations of the Anglo-American nuclear relationship', *Diplomatic History* 25/1 (Winter 2001), pp. 33–61.
——, 'British nuclear doctrine: the Moscow criterion and the Polaris improvement programme', *Contemporary British History* 19/1 (Spring 2005).
Beach, Gen Sir Hugh and Nadine Gurr, *Flattering the passions: the bomb and Britain's bid for a world role* (IB Tauris 1999).
Bongiorno, Frank, 'The price of nostalgia: Menzies, the "Liberal" tradition and Australian foreign policy,' *Australian Journal of Politics and History* 51/3 (2005), pp. 400–17.
Botti, Timothy J, *The long wait: the forging of the Anglo-American nuclear alliance 1945–58* (New York, Greenwood 1994).
Boulton, J W, 'NATO and the MLF', *Journal of Contemporary History* 7/3–4 (Jul–Oct 1972).
Boyes, John, 'Project Emily: the Thor IRBM and the Royal Air Force 1959–63', *Prospero* 4 (Spring 2007), pp. 7–39.
——, *Project Emily: Thor IRBM and the RAF* (Stroud, Tempus 2008).
Boyle, Peter G, 'The British government's view of the Cuban missile crisis', *Contemporary Record* 10/3 (Autumn 1996), pp. 22–38.
Brands, H W, 'The age of vulnerability: Eisenhower and the national insecurity state', *The American Historical Review* 94/4 (Oct 1989), pp. 963–89.
Brivati, Brian, *Hugh Gaitskell* (Richard Cohen 1996).
Brocklebank, Roy, 'World War III – the 1960s version', *Journal of Navigation* 58/3 (Sep 2005).
Brookes, Andrew, *V-force: the history of Britain's airborne deterrent* (Jane's 1982).
Brown, David and George Moore, *Rebuilding the Royal Navy: warship design since 1945* (Chatham 2003).
Brown, Michael E, *Flying blind: the politics of the US strategic bomber programme* (Cornell UP 1992).
Brundrett, Sir Frederick, 'Rockets, satellites and military thinking', *Journal of the RUSI* 105 (Aug 1960), pp. 332–43.
Campbell, Duncan, *The unsinkable aircraft carrier: American military power in Britain* (Michael Joseph 1984).
Carver, Michael, *Tightrope Walking: British Defence Policy since 1945* (London, Hutchinson 1992).
——, 'Sir Gerald Templer (1898–1979)', *Oxford Dictionary of National Biography*.
Cathcart, Brian, 'William George Penney, Baron Penney (1909–91)', *Oxford Dictionary of National Biography*.
Challens, John, 'Sir William Richard Joseph Cook (1905–87)', *Oxford Dictionary of National Biography*.
Clark, Ian, *Nuclear diplomacy and the special relationship: Britain's deterrent and America 1957–62* (Oxford, Clarendon Press 1994).
Clark, Ian and Nicholas Wheeler, *The British origins of nuclear strategy 1945–55* (Oxford, Clarendon Press 1989).
Cocroft, Wayne and Roger Thomas, *Cold War: building for nuclear confrontation 1946–89* (English Heritage 2003).

Connelly, Mark, *Reaching for the stars: a new history of Bomber Command in World War II* (I B Tauris 2001).
Cosgrave, Patrick, 'Harold Arthur, Viscount Watkinson (1910–95)', *Oxford Dictionary of National Biography*.
Cowley, LtGen Sir John, 'Future trends in warfare', *Journal of the RUSI* 55/617, pp. 4–16.
——, 'Sir Francis Festing (1902–76)', *Oxford Dictionary of National Biography*.
Crowe, Adm William J USN, 'The policy roots of the modern Royal Navy 1945–63', unpublished PhD dissertation, Princeton 1965.
Dalsjö, Robert, *Life-line lost: the rise and fall of 'neutral' Sweden's secret reserve option of wartime help from the West* (Stockholm, Santerus 2006).
Danchev, Alex, 'Liddell Hart and the Indirect Approach', *Journal of Military History* 63/2 (Apr 1999), pp. 313–37.
Darby, Phillip, *British Defence Policy East of Suez 1947–68* (Oxford UP/RIIA 1973).
Darling, Kev, *Avro Vulcan* (Ramsbury, Crowood Press 2005).
Delve, Ken, Peter Green and John Clemons, *English Electric Canberra* (Leicester, Midland Counties 1992).
Dietl, Ralph, 'In defence of the west: General Lauris Norstad, NATO nuclear forces and transatlantic relations 1956–1963', *Diplomacy and Statecraft*, 17 (2006), pp. 347–92.
Dockrill, Saki, *Britain's retreat from east of Suez: the choice between Europe and the world?* (Palgrave 2002).
Dombey, Norman and Eric Grove, 'Britain's thermonuclear bluff', *London Review of Books*, 22 Oct 1992, pp. 8–10.
Dommett, Roy, 'The development of Blue Streak and Black Knight re-entry heads', *History of the UK strategic deterrent: proceedings of the Royal Aeronautical Society symposium 17 March 1999*, pp. 11.1–10.
——, 'The Blue Streak weapon', *Prospero* 2 (Spring 2005), pp. 7–33.
——, 'Re-entry observables: the Woomera programmes 1957–67' (unpublished).
Driver, Christopher, *The disarmers: a study in protest* (Hodder and Stoughton 1964).
Duffield, John, *Power rules: the evolution of NATO's conventional force posture* (Stanford UP 1995).
Dyson, LtCdr Tony RN, *HMS Hermes: a pictorial history* (Liskeard, Maritime Books 1984).
Edgerton, David, *England and the aeroplane: an essay on a militant and technological nation* (Macmillan 1991).
——, *Warfare state: Britain 1920–70* (CUP 2006).
Engel, Jeffrey A, *Cold war at 30,000 feet: the Anglo-American fight for aviation supremacy* (Harvard UP 2007).
Enthoven, Alain and Wayne Smith, *How much is enough? Shaping the defense program 1961–69* (New York, Harper and Row 1971).
Fairchild, Byron R and Walter S Poole, *History of the Joint Chiefs of Staff: the Joint Chiefs of Staff and national policy 1956–60* (Washington DC, Office of the Chairman of the JCS 2000).
Francis, R H, 'The development of Blue Steel', *Journal of the Royal Aeronautical Society* 68 (May 1964), pp. 303–22.
Freedman, Lawrence, *Britain and nuclear weapons* (Macmillan/RIIA 1980).
Freeman, J P G, *Britain's nuclear arms control policy in the context of Anglo-American relations 1957–68* (Macmillan 1986).

Friedman, Norman, *British destroyers and frigates: the Second World War and after* (Chatham 2006).
Friedrich, Jörg, *The fire: the bombing of Germany 1940–45* (English translation, Columbia UP 2006).
Futrell, Robert Frank, *Ideas, concepts, doctrine: basic thinking in the United States Air Force 1961–84* (Maxwell AFB, Air University Press 1989).
Gallup, George H, ed., *The Gallup International Public Opinion Polls: Great Britain 1937–75, Vol. 1* (New York, Random House 1976).
Gardiner, Robert, ed. dir., *Conway's all the world's fighting ships 1947–95* (Conway's 1995).
Garnett, John, 'BAOR and NATO', *International Affairs* 46/4 (Oct 1970).
——, correspondence in *International Affairs* 47/1 (Jan 1971), p. 269.
Gavin, Francis J, 'The myth of flexible response: American strategy in Europe during the 1960s', *International History Review* 23/4 (Dec 2001), pp. 847–75.
——, 'The gold battles within the cold war: American monetary policy and the defence of Europe 1960–63', *Diplomatic History* 26/1 (Winter 2002), pp. 61–94.
Geelhoed, E Bruce and Anthony O Edmonds, *Eisenhower, Macmillan and Allied Unity, 1957–61* (Palgrave 2003).
Gibson, Chris and Tony Buttler, *British secret projects: hypersonics, ramjets and missiles* (Midland Counties 2007).
Goodchild, Peter, *Edward Teller: the real Dr Strangelove* (Weidenfeld and Nicolson 2004).
Goodman, Geoffrey, '(Aubrey Jones (1911–2003)', *Oxford Dictionary of National Biography*.
Gowing, Margaret, *Britain and atomic energy 1939–45* (Macmillan 1964).
——, *Independence and deterrence: Britain and atomic energy, 1945–52* (Macmillan 1974), Vol. 1: *Policy making*; Vol. 2: *Policy execution*.
Graham, Wid, 'Watching brief 1961–3', John Moore, ed., *The impact of Polaris*, pp. 38–41.
Greenwood, Ted, *Making the MIRV: a study of defence decision-making* (Cambridge Mass, Ballinger 1975).
Gretton, VAdm Sir Peter, 'A maritime strategy for British defence', *Journal of the RUSI* (Nov 1965), pp. 301–10.
Groom, A J R (John), *British thinking about nuclear weapons* (Frances Pinter 1974).
Grove, Eric, *Vanguard to Trident: British naval policy since World War II* (London, Bodley Head 1987).
Hack, Karl, *Defence and decolonisation in south-east Asia: Britain, Malaya and Singapore 1941–68* (Richmond, Curzon 2001).
Hanning, Hugh, 'Britain east of Suez – facts and figures', *International Affairs* 42/2 (Apr 1966).
Hansen, Chuck, *US nuclear weapons: the secret history* (Arlington TX, Aerofax 1988).
Hastings, Stephen, *The murder of TSR.2* (Macdonald 1966).
Hawkings, David, 'Blue Peacock: the British army's forgotten weapon' in *Discovery* (Summer 2002): http://www.awe.co.uk/Images/blue_peacock_tcm6-1992.pdf (accessed Aug 2007).
Heffer, Simon, '(George Edward) Peter, Baron Thorneycroft (1909–94)', *Oxford Dictionary of National Biography*.
Hennessy, Peter, *Whitehall* (Secker and Warburg 1989).
——, *The Prime Minister: the office and its holders since 1945* (Penguin 2000).

——, *The secret state: Whitehall and the cold war* (Penguin 2002).
——, *Having it so good: Britain in the fifties* (Allen Lane 2006).
Henry, Cdr Michael RN, 'A CO's story', John Moore, ed., *The impact of Polaris*, pp. 236–50.
Heuser, Beatrice, *Nuclear mentalities: strategies and beliefs in Britain, France and the FRG* (Macmillan 1998).
Hicks, George (ed. Roy Dommett), 'History of RAE and nuclear weapons', *Prospero* 2 (Spring 2005).
Hill, Nicholas, *A vertical empire: the history of the UK rocket and space programme, 1951–70* (Imperial College Press 2001).
Hindell, K and P Williams, 'Scarborough and Blackpool: an analysis of some votes at the Labour party conferences of 1960 and 1961', *Political Quarterly* 33/3 (Jul–Sep 1962), pp. 306–22.
Horne, Alistair, *Macmillan: the official biography* (2 vols, Macmillan 1988–9).
Howard, Michael, *The central organisation of defence* (RUSI 1970).
Jackson, Gen Sir William and FM Lord Bramall, *The chiefs: the story of the United Kingdom Chiefs of Staff* (Brassey's 1992).
John, Rebecca, *Caspar John* (Collins 1987).
Jones, Peter, 'Overview of history of UK strategic weapons', *History of the UK strategic deterrent: proceedings of the Royal Aeronautical Society symposium 17 March 1999*, pp. 2.1–10.
Kandiah, Michael and Gillian Staerck, eds, *The move to the Sandys white paper of 1957* (Institute of Contemporary British History 2002).
Kaplan, Fred, *The wizards of Armageddon* (New York, Simon and Schuster 1984).
Kaufmann, William W, *The McNamara strategy* (New York, Harper and Row 1964).
Kunz, Diane B, '"Somewhat mixed up together": Anglo-American defence and financial policy during the 1960s', *Journal of Imperial and Commonwealth History* 27/2 (Spring 1999), pp. 213–32.
Landa, Ronald D, 'The origins of the Skybolt controversy in the Eisenhower administration', Roger G Miller, ed., *Seeing off the bear: Anglo-American airpower cooperation during the cold war* (Washington, USAF 1995), pp. 117–31.
Lavery, Brian, 'The British government and the American Polaris base in the Clyde', *Journal for Maritime Research* (Sep 2001): http://www.jmr.nmm.ac.uk/server/show/ConJmrArticle.2/setPaginate/No (accessed July 2007).
LeMay, Gen Curtis E USAF with MacKinlay Kantor, *Mission with LeMay: my story* (New York, Doubleday 1965).
LeMay, Gen Curtis E USAF with MGen Dale O Smith USAF, *America is in danger* (New York, Funk and Wagnalls 1968).
Louis, William, *The British empire in the middle east 1945–1951: Arab nationalism, the United States, and postwar imperialism* (Oxford, Clarendon Press 1984).
Louis, William and Hedley Bull, eds, *The special relationship: Anglo-American relations since 1945* (Oxford, Clarendon Press 1986).
Louis, William and Roger Owen, eds, *Suez 1956: the crisis and its consequences* (Oxford, Clarendon Press 1989).
Ludlow, N Piers, '(Edwin) Duncan Sandys, Baron Duncan-Sandys (1908–87)', *Oxford Dictionary of National Biography*.
Mackenzie, Adm Sir Hugh, 'Setting up the UK project', John Moore, ed., *The impact of Polaris*, pp. 46–54.
McCart, Neil, *HMS Victorious 1937–69* (Cheltenham, Fan 1998).

McManus, J P, *A History of the FBM system* (Lockheed Missiles and Space Company, 1989).
McNamara, Robert S, 'The military role of nuclear weapons: perceptions and misperceptions', *Foreign Affairs* 62/1 (Oct 1983), pp. 59–80.
Maguire, Richard, 'Scientific dissent amid the United Kingdom government's nuclear weapons programme', *History Workshop Journal* 63/1 (Spring 2007), pp. 113–35.
Maloney, Sean M, 'Berlin Contingency Planning: Prelude to Flexible Response, 1958–63', *Journal of Strategic Studies*, 25/1 (Mar 2002).
Mansergh, VAdm Aubrey, editorial, *Naval Review* (Jan 1963), pp. 6–7.
Martin, Charles, *De Havilland Blue Streak: an illustrated story* (British Interplanetary Society 2002).
Martin, Laurence, 'The market for strategic ideas in Britain: the "Sandys era"', *American Political Science Review* 56/1 (Mar 1962).
May, Ernest and Philip Zelikow, *The Kennedy tapes: inside the White House during the Cuban missile crisis* (Harvard UP 1997),
Melissen, Jan, *The struggle for nuclear partnership: Britain, the United States and the making of an ambiguous alliance* (Groningen Styx, 1993).
Menaul, AVM Stewart, *Countdown: Britain's strategic nuclear forces* (Robert Hale 1980).
Michael, Donald N, 'The beginning of the space age and American public opinion', *The Public Opinion Quarterly* 24/4 (Winter 1960), pp. 573–82.
Moore, Capt John E RN, ed., *The impact of Polaris: the origins of Britain's seaborne nuclear deterrent* (Huddersfield, Richard Netherwood 1999).
Moore, Richard, 'A JIGSAW puzzle for operational researchers: British global war studies, 1954–62', *Journal of Strategic Studies* 20/1 (Jun 1997), pp. 75–91.
——, *The Royal Navy and nuclear weapons* (Frank Cass 2001).
——, 'The real meaning of the words: a pedantic glossary of British nuclear weapons', *Prospero* 1 (Spring 2004), pp. 71–90.
——, 'British nuclear warhead design 1958–66: how much American help?', *Defence Studies* 4/2 (Summer 2004), pp. 207–28.
——, 'Surface-to-air guided weapons for UK air defence in the 1950s', *Prospero* 2 (Spring 2005), pp. 193–212.
Moravcsik, Andrew, 'De Gaulle between grain and grandeur: the political economy of French EC policy 1958–70' (and several replies thereto), *Journal of cold war studies* 2/2 (Spring 2000), pp. 3–43, and 2/3 (Fall 2000), pp. 4–139.
Morton, Peter, *Fire across the desert: Woomera and the Anglo-Australian joint project 1946–80* (Canberra, AGPS 1989).
Murray, Donette, *Kennedy, Macmillan and nuclear weapons* (Macmillan 2000).
Nailor, Peter, *The Nassau connection: the organisation and management of the British Polaris project* (HMSO 1988).
Nash, Philip, *The other missiles of October: Eisenhower, Kennedy and the Jupiters 1957–63* (Chapel Hill NC, Univ of North Carolina Press 1997).
Navias, Martin, *Nuclear weapons and British strategic planning 1955–58* (Oxford, Clarendon Press 1991).
Neillands, Robin, *The bomber war: Arthur Harris and the allied bomber offensive 1939–45* (John Murray 2001).
Neustadt, Richard E, *Report to JFK: the Skybolt crisis in perspective* (Cornell UP 1999).

Newhouse, John, *The nuclear age: from Hiroshima to star wars* (Michael Joseph 1989).
Norris, Robert S, Andrew S Burrows and Richard W Fieldhouse, *Nuclear weapons databook vol. 5: British, French and Chinese nuclear weapons* (Oxford, NRDC/ Westview 1994).
Oliver, Kendrick, *Kennedy, Macmillan and the nuclear test ban debate 1961–3* (Macmillan 1998).
Page, Lewis, *Lions, donkeys and dinosaurs: waste and blundering in the armed forces* (William Heinemann 2006).
Pagedas, Constantine A, *Anglo-American strategic relations and the French problem 1960–63* (Frank Cass 2000).
Palmer, Sidney John, 'Technical evaluation 1961', John Moore, ed., *The impact of Polaris*, pp. 42–5.
Paul, Septimus H, *Nuclear rivals: Anglo-American atomic relations 1945–52* (Ohio State UP 2000).
Penney, William and V H B Macklen, 'William Richard Joseph Cook', *Biographical Memoirs of Fellows of the Royal Society* 34 (1988), pp. 44–61.
Pierre, Andrew, *Nuclear politics: the British experience with an independent strategic force 1939–1970* (OUP 1972).
Podvig, Pavel ed., *Russian strategic nuclear forces* (Cambridge MASS, MIT Press 2001).
Powell, Sir Richard, 'Sir Frederick Brundrett (1894–1974)', *Oxford Dictionary of National Biography*.
Priest, Andrew, 'In Common Cause: the NATO multilateral force and the mixed-manning demonstration on the USS *Claude V. Ricketts*, 1964–1965', *Journal of Military History* 69/3 (Jul 2005), pp. 759–88.
——, *Kennedy, Johnson and NATO: Britain, America and the dynamics of alliance 1962–8* (Routledge 2006).
Pritchard, Alan, 'Negotiating the sales agreement', John Moore, ed., *The impact of Polaris*, pp. 30–3.
Probert, ACdre Henry, *High Commanders of the Royal Air Force* (HMSO 1991).
Pyne, Kate, 'More complex than expected: the AWRE's contribution to the Chevaline payload', *The history of the UK strategic deterrent: the Chevaline programme*, proceedings of the Royal Aeronautical Society conference on 28 Oct 2004.
Quester, George, *Deterrence before Hiroshima: the airpower background of modern strategy* (New York, John Wiley 1966).
RAF Historical Society Journal 26 (2001).
Rawnsley, Gary D, 'How special is special? The Anglo-American alliance during the Cuban missile crisis', *Contemporary Record* 9/3 (Winter 1995), pp. 586–601.
Reynolds, Wayne, *Australia's bid for the atomic bomb* (Melbourne UP 2000).
Rodwell, Robert R, 'The steel in the blue: last week's glimpse of the V-force', *Flight International* 13 Feb 1964, pp. 241–5.
Roman, Peter J, *Eisenhower and the missile gap* (Cornell UP 1995).
——, 'Strategic bombers over the missile horizon', *Journal of Strategic Studies* 18/1 (Mar 1995), pp. 198–236.
Rosenberg, David A, 'Arleigh Albert Burke', Richard Love., ed., *The chiefs of naval operations* (US Naval Institute Press 1980), pp. 263–319.
——, 'Constraining overkill: contending approaches to nuclear strategy, 1955–65', *Colloquium on Contemporary History Seminar* 9 (1994), US Naval Historical Center: http://www.history.navy.mil/colloquia/cch9b.html (accessed Aug 2007).

Rostow, Walt, *Pre-Invasion bombing strategy: General Eisenhower's decision of March 25, 1944* (Univ of Texas Press 1981).
Sampson, Anthony, *Macmillan: a study in ambiguity* (Allen Lane 1967).
Sandbrook, Dominic, *Never had it so good: a history of Britain from Suez to the Beatles* (Little Brown 2005).
Sapolsky, Harvey, *The Polaris system development: bureaucratic and programmatic success in government* (Cambridge Mass, Harvard UP 1972).
Schwartz, Stephen I, ed., *Atomic audit: the costs and consequences of US nuclear weapons since 1940* (Washington DC, Brookings 1998).
Scott, Len, *Macmillan, Kennedy and the Cuban missile crisis: political, military and intelligence aspects* (Macmillan 1999).
Simeon, Cdr H M, 'Watching brief 1958–60', Capt John Moore RN, ed., *The impact of Polaris*, pp. 34–7.
Simpson, John, *The independent nuclear state: the United States, Britain and the military atom* (2nd edn Macmillan 1986).
Smith, Adrian, 'Command and control in postwar Britain', *Twentieth Century British History* 2/3 (1991).
Smith-Norris, Martha, 'The Eisenhower administration and the nuclear test-ban talks, 1958–60: another challenge to "revisionism"', *Diplomatic History* 27/4 (Sep 2003), pp. 503–41.
Snyder, William P, *The politics of British defence policy 1945–62* (Ohio State UP 1964).
Spinardi, Graham, *From Polaris to Trident: the development of US fleet ballistic missile technology* (Cambridge UP 1994).
——, 'Aldermaston and British nuclear weapons development: testing the Zuckerman thesis', *Social Studies of Science* 27 (1997), pp. 547–82.
Stocker, Jeremy, *Britain and ballistic missile defence 1942–2002* (Frank Cass 2004).
Strachan, Hew, 'The British way in warfare revisited', *Historical Journal* 26/2 (Jun 1983), pp. 447–61.
Szasz, Ferenc Morton, *British scientists and the Manhattan project: the Los Alamos years* (Macmillan 1992).
Taylor, Richard, *Against the bomb: the British peace movement 1958–65* (Oxford, Clarendon Press 1988).
Theakston, Kevin, 'Norman Craven Brook, Baron Normanbrook (1902–67)', *Oxford Dictionary of National Biography*.
Trachtenberg, Marc, *History and Strategy* (Princeton UP 1991).
Tregenza, Alexis, 'How capable was the V-bomber force militarily of delivering Britain's nuclear deterrent in the late 1950s and 1960s?', *RAF Air Power Review* (2004).
Twigge, Stephen, *The Early Development of Guided Weapons in the United Kingdom 1940–60* (Chur, Switzerland, Harwood 1993).
Twigge, Stephen and Len Scott, *Planning Armageddon: Britain, the United States and the command of western nuclear forces 1945–64* (Amsterdam, Harwood 2000).
——, 'Learning to love the bomb: the command and control of British nuclear forces, 1953–64', *Journal of Strategic Studies* 22/1 (Mar 1999).
——, 'The other other missiles of October: the Thor IRBMs and the Cuban missile crisis', *Electronic Journal of International History* (Jun 2000): http://www.history.ac.uk/ejournal/art3.html (accessed Aug 2007).
Walker, John, *Britain, the United States, weapon policies and nuclear testing, 1954–1973: tensions and contradictions* (forthcoming).

Walsh, Jim, 'Surprise down under: the secret history of Australia's nuclear ambitions', *The Nonproliferation Review* (Fall 1997), pp. 1–20.

Watkinson, Harold, *Turning points: a record of our times* (Salisbury, Michael Russell 1986).

Watson, Robert J, *History of the Office of the Secretary of Defense, Vol. IV: Into the missile age 1956–60* (Washington, Historical Office, Office of the Secretary of Defense 1997).

Webster, Sir Charles and Noble Frankland, *The Strategic Air Offensive Against Germany 1939–45 Vol. 1: Preparation, Vol. 2: Endeavour, Vol. 3: Victory; Vol. 4: Annexes and Appendices* (HMSO 1961; new pbk edn Naval and Military Press 2006).

Wettern, Desmond, *The decline of British seapower* (Jane's 1982).

Williamson, Samuel R Jr and Steven L Rearden, *The origins of US nuclear strategy 1945–53* (New York, St Martin's Press 1993).

Wood, Derek, *Project cancelled: the disaster of Britain's abandoned aircraft projects* (2nd edn, Jane's 1986).

Worden, Col Mike USAF, *Rise of the fighter generals: the problem of air force leadership 1945–82* (Maxwell AFB, Air University Press March 1998).

Wynn, Humphrey, *The RAF strategic nuclear deterrent forces: their origins, roles and deployment 1945–64* (HMSO 1994).

York, Herbert F, *Race to Oblivion: a participant's view of the arms race* (New York, Simon and Schuster 1970).

Young, Ken, 'The Royal Navy's Polaris lobby', *Journal of Strategic Studies* 25/3 (Sep 2002), pp. 56–86.

——, 'The Skybolt crisis of 1962: muddle or mischief?', *Journal of Strategic Studies* 27/4 (Dec 2004), pp. 614–35.

Ziegler, Philip, *Mountbatten: the official biography* (Collins 1985).

Zimmermann, Hubert, *Money and security: troops, monetary policy and West Germany's relations with the United States and Britain, 1950–1971* (Cambridge UP 2002).

Zuckerman, Sir Solly, *Scientists and war* (Hamish Hamilton 1966).

——, *Nuclear illusion and reality* (Collins 1982).

——, *From apes to warlords: an autobiography 1904–46* (Collins 1978).

——, *Monkeys, men and missiles: an autobiography 1946–88* (Collins 1988).

Internet material

Encyclopedia Astronautica website: http://www.astronautix.com/lvs/polrisa1.htm and http://www.astronautix.com/lvs/mineman1.htm (accessed Aug 2007).

Federation of American Scientists website: http://www.fas.org/spp/military/program/nav/transit.htm (accessed Aug 2007).

Globalsecurity.org: http://www.globalsecurity.org/wmd/intro/miniaturization.htm (accessed Aug 2007).

Key Publishing Ltd aviation forum: http://forum.keypublishing.co.uk/showthread.php?t=75988 (accessed Dec 2007).

Lyford Cay website: http://www.lyfordcayhomes.com/Listings/ListingDetail.ASPX?LID=790486 (accessed Aug 2007).

Nuclear Weapon Archive website: http://nuclearweaponarchive.org/Usa/Tests/Dominic.html (accessed Aug 2007).

Professional pilots' rumour network website, 'Did you fly the Vulcan??' with contributions from various authors: http://www.pprune.org/forums/showthread.php?t=111797 (accessed Aug 2007).
Rockets in Europe website: http://fuseurop.univ-perp.fr/bwater_e.htm (accessed Aug. 2007).
Schake, Kurt Wayne, 'Strategic frontier: American bomber bases overseas 1950–60', dissertation for the Norwegian University of Science and Technology, Jan 1998: http://handle.dtic.mil/100.2/ADA353633 (accessed Jul 2008).
Sublette, Carey, *Nuclear weapons frequently asked questions*, §4.5: http://nuclearweaponarchive.org/Nwfaq/Nfaq4-5.html (accessed Aug 2007).
Subterranea Britannica website: http://www.subbrit.org.uk/sb-sites/sites/r/rugby_radio/ indexr69.shtml and http://www.subbrit.org.uk/sb-sites/sites/c/criggion_radio/ (accessed Aug 2007).
Upavon parish council website: http://www.upavonpc.co.uk (accessed July 2007).
US 59th Ordnance Brigade's website: http://www.usarmygermany.com/units/Ordnance/USAREUR_59thOrdBde%201.htm#IUKCorps (accessed Aug 2007).

Unpublished conference presentations

Roy Dommett, 'Ballistic missile defence', lecture to the guided flight group of the Royal Aeronautical Society, 28 Apr 1994.
Guy Finch, 'The air staff and the deterrent 1943–63', presentation to the British Rocketry Oral History Project conference at Charterhouse, April 2006.
Matthew Grant, presentation to the British Rocketry Oral History Project conference at Charterhouse, April 2004.
SqnLdr Michael Hely, at the RAF historical society seminar at Hendon, 11 Apr 2001 (see also printed record of the meeting in *Journal of the RAF Historical Society* 26).
Don McIntyre, 'Project Crystal: lithium-6 for H-bombs', presentation to the British Rocketry Oral History Project conference at Charterhouse, April 2007.
Richard Maguire, 'Cancelling Blue Streak', presentation to the British Rocketry Oral History Project conference at Charterhouse, April 2006.
Kate Pyne, 'Warheads and rockets: UK nuclear warheads for almost anything with a point at one end and a flame at the other', presentation to the British Rocketry Oral History Project conference at Charterhouse, April 2003.
Robin Woolven, 'UK involvement in the Cuban missile crisis', presentation to the British Rocketry Oral History Project conference at Charterhouse, March 2008.

Index

Aberporth, 106, 131
ABM (anti-ballistic missile) research, 79, 81, 82, 93, 111, 126, 128–9, 150, 152, 153, 223–4, 239, 251–2
  see also penetration
Acheson, Dean, former US Secretary of State, 69, 71, 156, 173
Acorn, warhead design, 120
AC Spark Plug, US defence company, 99
Aden, 71, 72, 73, 146, 161, 190
Adenauer, Konrad, West German Chancellor, 7, 159, 160, 170, 183
ADM (atomic demolition munition), 90, 132–3, 196, 223
Admiralty, 6, 10, 13, 19, 25, 43, 49–50, 57–8, 60, 67, 76, 100, 114–15, 122, 125, 128, 136–8, 140, 148, 169, 170, 187–8, 192, 197, 218–21, 222, 228, 233, 236, 248, 295
  functions, 16–17
  see also Royal Navy and individual requirements, aircraft and weapons
Aerojet, US company, 134, 135, 136
Africa, 73, 161, 244
Air Council, 18, 81, 97, 98, 99, 114, 115, 149, 213, 214, 276
aircraft carriers, 16, 17, 72, 73, 83, 92, 100, 114, 115, 123, 133, 134, 138, 161–4, 214, 216, 221, 226, 254
air defence, Soviet, 64, 105, 137, 146, 206
air defence, UK, 125–7, 249
Air Ministry, 6, 13, 16, 17, 41–2, 45–50, 66, 72, 75–6, 81, 90, 97, 105, 106–8, 115, 120, 122, 124, 125–8, 131, 136, 137–9, 148, 149, 163, 166, 169, 185, 186, 205–6, 208, 210–12, 215, 216, 218–22, 225, 226, 231, 236, 243, 247, 248, 249, 251, 252, 266, 294, 295
  functions, 18–19, 79
  see also RAF and individual OR requirements, aircraft and weapons
Akrotiri, RAF, 98, 99, 215
Albright, David, 84
Aldermaston, *see* AWRE
Amery, Julian, Conservative minister, 10, 98, 107, 148, 150, 166
Ampthill, 85
Anderson, George, US admiral, 157
'anglicisation' of warheads, 35, 78, 89–90, 120–1, 126, 199, 200, 242
Anglo-American relations, 25–6, 27–36, 64–71, 145–6, 169–73, 175–82, 240–7
Ann Arbor, 146, 171
Anthorn, 233
Antler, nuclear test series, 113
appeasement, 21, 155
Ark Royal, HMS, 100, 164, 216
Armageddon, 59, 175
arms control, 9, 26, 36–40, 91, 150–5, 175, 244, 253
  see also nuclear testing
Armstrong Siddeley, aerospace company, 106
army, British, 16, 17, 20, 56, 59, 61, 80, 81, 82, 86, 102, 126, 127, 128, 132, 161, 162, 164, 196, 215, 217, 240, 242, 256
  see also War Office
Army Council, 131, 149
artillery, nuclear, 56, 81, 88, 102, 132, 196, 200, 217, 223, 242, 256
Ashton, Nigel, 9
ASROC, US anti-submarine weapon, 221
ASW (anti-submarine warfare), 55, 57, 81, 123, 188, 216, 218–22
  see also depth bombs
Athens, 146, 156

315

316 Index

Atlantic Ocean, 54, 113, 216, 233–4, 255
Atlas, US ICBM, 41, 74, 109, 111
Atomic Energy Act, US, 33, 34, 37, 240
Atomic Energy for Mutual Defence Purposes, see UK/US atomic bilateral
Atomic Energy Research Establishment, Harwell, 37, 85, 257
Australia, 86, 87, 88, 91–5, 108, 110, 113, 126, 161, 203, 221, 224, 244
see also Woomera
Australian Royal Commission into British nuclear testing, 91
Avro, aerospace company, 41, 97, 106, 107, 140, 227
Avro 730, supersonic bomber project, 19, 138
AW681, transport aircraft project, 222
AWRE Aldermaston (now AWE), 2, 6, 36, 40, 51, 78, 80, 84, 85, 103, 113–15, 120–2, 125, 126, 133, 141, 166, 194, 195–9, 219, 220, 223, 240, 241, 242, 246, 247, 257, 299
  functions and subordination, 20–1, 85
  and warhead work programme, 85–90, 199–202, 236–9

B-52, US bomber, 116–18
B-58, US bomber, 116
B-70, US bomber project, 41, 75, 116, 169, 172
BAC (British Aircraft Corporation), 131, 138, 140, 162, 227, 247
Baghdad Pact, see CENTO
Bali-Hai, 175, 288
Ball, Desmond, 48, 167
Ball, George, US State Department official, 171
Ballhaus, William, US missile guidance engineer, 75
Bangkok, 166
Bangor, 85
BAOR (British Army of the Rhine), 56, 130, 32, 217, 223, 242

Barents Sea, 115, 136
Barrow-in-Furness, 232
battlefield, and nuclear weapons, 18, 56, 60, 62, 64, 72, 129, 133, 140, 153, 217, 223, 239, 241, 242, 246
see also central front, tactical nuclear weapons and individual weapons
Bawtry, RAF, 205
Bay of Bengal, 176
Begg, Adm Sir Varyl, 157, 187
Berlin, 38, 54, 151, 155, 156, 177, 245
Bermuda, 153
beryllium, 90, 136, 228
Bevin, Ernest, Labour politician, 51
Bikini, 151
bilateral, see UK/US atomic bilateral
Birch Grove, 154
Birkenhead, 232
Birmingham, 60–1
Black Knight, research rocket, 93, 108, 111, 224, 226, 227
Blackpool, 53, 149
Bloodhound, SAM, 82, 93, 94, 125–8, 140, 227, 245
  see also Red Duster
Blue Danube, atomic bomb, 40, 78, 81, 92, 104, 112–14, 132, 195, 196, 256
Blue Peacock, ADM project, 132
Blue Steel, powered bomb, 43, 44, 76, 80, 81, 82, 93, 98, 110, 116, 119, 138, 140, 158, 162, 165, 169, 187, 194, 196, 204, 207, 210, 214, 220, 225, 226, 22, 244, 247, 248, 256, 294
  detailed development and service entry, 105–8, 212–13
Blue Steel Mk.2, long-range powered bomb project, 42, 44, 80, 82, 107, 247
Blue Streak, MRBM, 1, 3, 12, 14, 15, 26, 62, 65, 68, 73, 76, 78, 79, 81, 88, 93, 94, 97, 99, 100, 105, 117, 127, 129, 135, 136, 141, 146, 158, 190, 211, 222, 239, 240, 241, 245, 246, 247, 248, 250, 253, 266, 276, 277, 300
  cancellation, 48–50, 51, 52, 251

technical development, 108–12
political history pre-cancellation, 42–8
Blue Water, surface-to-surface missile, 81, 82, 93, 124, 126, 138, 140, 162, 194, 196, 197, 215, 227, 241, 245, 246
technical development, 130–2, 222–3
BMEWS (Ballistic Missile Early-Warning System), 34, 97, 129, 224
BNDSG (British Nuclear Deterrent Study Group), 14, 43–50, 65, 75–7, 107, 129, 137, 146, 164–5, 223
Board of Admiralty, 16, 18, 58, 128, 136, 149, 216, 295
Bomber Command, RAF, 36, 95–100, 101, 102, 105, 141, 165, 173, 174, 194, 203–10, 213, 215, 226, 233, 256, 275
bonkers, 110, 277
Bonn, 160
boosting, warhead design technique, 86–8, 240
Borneo, 190
Boscombe Down, 103
Botti, Timothy, 263
Bowie, Robert, US State Department official, 69
Boyd-Carpenter, John, Conservative minister, 238
Boyle, MRAF Sir Dermot, 19, 30, 43, 49, 50, 60, 94, 252, 254, 255, 260, 262, 266
BQ267, sub-kiloton warhead project, 82, 133, 196
see also Davy Crockett
Breighton, RAF, 214
Bremen, 254
Bristol, aerospace company, 125, 128, 131, 139, 140, 224, 227, 284
Broadhurst, Air Marshal Sir Harry, 95
broken-backed warfare, 55, 57, 157
Brook, Sir Norman, Cabinet Secretary, 10, 30, 60, 147, 165, 204, 214, 255, 286

Brooke, Henry, Conservative minister, 166
Brookes, Andrew, 205, 206, 207
Brown, Harold, US defence official, 168, 171
Brown Bunny, ADM project, 132
Bruce, David, US ambassador, 152, 173, 174
Bruggen, RAF, 98
Brundrett, Sir Frederick, defence scientist, 14, 34, 42, 43, 48, 50, 84, 86, 87, 88, 103, 119
Buccaneer, Royal Navy strike aircraft, 17, 100, 138, 216, 219, 226, 227
Bundy, McGeorge, US official, 182, 245
Burgee, test device, 87
Burghfield, ROF, 85, 112, 199, 214
Burke, Arleigh, US admiral, 17, 65, 67, 134, 135, 136, 137, 243
Burke, Edmund, 186
Burma, 17, 214
Burrows, Andrew, *see* Norris
Butler, 'Rab', Conservative minister, 39, 150, 175, 180, 181
Butterworth, 94
Buzzard, RAdm Sir Anthony, 63

C-131, US transport aircraft, 118
CA (Controller Aircraft), 20, 103, 104, 112, 125, 212, 213, 216
cabinet, 12–13, 37, 39, 51, 53, 67–8, 79, 83, 102, 146, 147, 149, 150, 152, 158, 164, 177, 180–2, 184, 185, 225, 232
Caccia, Sir Harold, diplomat, 33, 65, 151
Calder Hall, 35, 83, 198
Cammell Laird, shipbuilder, 232
Campaign for Democratic Socialism, 52
Camp David, 38, 65
Canada, 34, 254
Canberra, light bomber aircraft, 19, 78, 94, 98, 99, 102, 113, 114, 115, 123, 137, 138, 185, 214, 215, 219, 254, 256, 275
Capenhurst, 79, 83, 84, 195, 197–9, 237, 238, 257, 272

318 *Index*

Cardiff, ROF, 85
Carlisle, 60–1
Carrington, Peter, 6th Baron, Conservative minister, 49, 148, 157, 181, 188, 230, 231
Carron, Bill, trades unionist, 53
Carry On Up The Khyber, 255
Caspian Sea, 205
Castlereagh, Lord, nineteenth-century Foreign Secretary, 7
Centaur, HMS, 100, 216
CENTO (Central Treaty Organisation), 53, 71, 81, 162, 215
central front, NATO, strategy and tactics for, 3, 55, 58, 60, 64, 129, 137, 155, 156, 159, 241
Chapelcross, 83, 198
Checkpoint Charlie, 156
Chequers, 30, 73, 83, 154, 162, 166
Chevaline, 1970s/1980s Polaris improvement project, 230, 231
Chiefs of Staff, 6, 11, 12, 29, 37, 43, 48, 49, 58, 60, 63, 72, 83, 94, 102, 113, 116, 132, 157, 159, 161, 163, 164, 166, 174, 208, 266, 286
   function, 15–16, 102, 148–9
Chilver, Richard, MoD official, 46, 63, 110
China, 37, 71, 72, 214, 248
Chorley, ROF, 84, 85
Christmas Island, UK nuclear test site, 86, 97, 151, 152, 153, 228
Churchill, Sir Winston, 9, 10, 11, 86, 149, 254
cities, *see* damage criteria
civil defence, 5, 53
civil reactors, *see* nuclear power
Clark, Ian, 37, 39, 49, 204
Claude V Ricketts, USS, 186
Clay, Gen Lucius, US Army, 156
Clemenceau, French aircraft carrier, 216
Cleo, warhead design, 219
CND (Campaign for Nuclear Disarmament), 51–3, 68, 175
Coastal Command, RAF, 220, 221
Cockburn, Robert, 20
Cockcroft, Sir John, 37

Coker, John, 198
Collins, Canon John, 51
Coltishall, 178
Comet, transport aircraft, 50, 178
command and control, 2, 25, 35, 61, 68, 80, 102–3, 155, 195, 204–5
   see also Murphy-Dean agreement
Committee of 100, 51
Congo, 177
Congress, US, 33, 75, 133, 154, 168, 172, 173, 252
Coningsby, RAF, 98, 204, 275
Conservative party, 1, 7, 10, 32, 38, 145, 164, 181, 189, 190, 192, 193, 242
Constant, Hayne, 76, 77
Convair, US aerospace company, 109
conventional (non-nuclear) forces, 3, 4, 9, 11, 16, 25, 27, 29, 32, 44, 49, 53, 55, 57–9, 62, 63, 72, 73, 123, 135, 146, 155–7, 162, 164, 180–1, 190, 191, 208, 242
Cook, Sir William, 21, 86
Cormorant, nuclear test, 202
Cornwall, 205
Corporal, US surface-to-surface missile, 80, 82, 102, 130, 131, 217, 23, 242, 256, 282
   technical development, 129
cost of UK nuclear weapons, 3, 8–9, 59, 67, 105, 107, 110, 163–4, 166, 167–8, 181, 184–5, 198, 211, 216, 219, 226, 248–50, 290
Cottesmore, RAF, 97, 203, 211, 214
Couchman, Adm Sir Walter, 49, 50, 66
Coulport, naval armament depot, 233
County-class destroyers, 126, 128
Cowley, LtGen Sir John, 59
Criggion, 233
Crosland, Anthony, 52
Cross, Air Marshal Sir Kenneth, 95, 96, 174, 204, 205, 212, 213
Crossbow committee, 11, 254
Crusade, re-entry experiments, 224
Cuban missile crisis, 154, 157, 173–5, 176, 205, 244

CVA-01, aircraft carrier project, 216
Cyprus, 73, 78, 98, 99, 115, 190, 215, 242

damage criteria for strategic deterrence, 43, 60, 101, 165, 248, 265, 286
  see also nuclear targets
Davy Crockett, nuclear mortar, 82, 123, 132, 133, 196, 282
Dayton, Ohio, 116, 117
Dazzle, re-entry experiments, 224
Dean, Sir Maurice, 50, 100, 289
Dean, Sir Patrick, see Murphy-Dean agreement
Decca, radio navigation system, 234
decoys, 79, 111, 112, 121, 128, 129, 211, 223, 228, 230, 246, 251
  see also penetration
Defence and Oversea Policy Committee, 149
Defence Board, 42, 58, 60, 62
  functions, 13–14
Defence Committee, Australian cabinet, 94
Defence Committee, British cabinet, 14, 27, 28, 29, 31, 42, 43, 48, 66, 67, 71, 72, 73, 83, 88, 89, 91, 97, 127, 131, 138, 160, 161, 162, 165, 166, 195, 197, 203, 206, 212, 214, 218, 223, 225, 226, 231, 232, 238, 243, 291
  functions, 13, 149
Defence Council, 149
Defence Research Committee, 149
Defense Department, US, 48, 49, 68, 74, 84, 117, 145, 147, 167, 168, 170, 171, 186, 243, 246
de Gaulle, Charles, French President, 7, 157–60, 170, 173, 183, 183, 192, 244, 252
de Havilland, aerospace company, 106, 108, 109, 227, 247
Denis Ferranti, engineering company, 85
depth bombs, nuclear 72, 82, 123, 218–22, 295
  see also ASW
Devonport, 232

de Zulueta, Philip, 40, 60, 287
Dickson, MRAF Sir William, 15, 19, 58
Dieppe, 254
Direct Action Committee, 51
dispersal of nuclear forces, 56, 80, 96, 97, 103, 104, 114, 126, 174, 204, 208, 209, 213, 248
Dobrynin, Anatoliy Fedorovich, Russian diplomat, 154, 174
Dolphin, John, 278
Dommett, Roy, 111, 129, 224
Dortmund, 130
Dougherty, Gen Russell, USAF, 207
Douglas, US aircraft company, 99, 116, 211
Douglas-Home, see Home
Dounreay, 257
Dowding, Air Marshal Sir Hugh, 19
Dreadnought, HMS, 35, 137
DRP(AES) committee, 16, 88, 90, 105, 112, 119, 123, 124, 132, 225
  functions, 14
DRPC (Defence Research Policy Committee), 43, 124, 129, 131, 133, 140, 206, 213, 237
  functions, 14, 79, 149
Dr Strangelove, 5, 255
dual custody of US nuclear weapons, 3, 82, 82, 95, 11, 103, 132, 196, 221, 223, 242, 244
  see also Project E
Dulles, John Foster, US Secretary of State, 32
Dunkirk, 177
Durlacher, Admiral Sir Laurence, 76
Düsseldorf, 254

Eagle, HMS, 100
East Anglia, 47, 79
East Germany, 155, 186
east of Suez, 73, 100, 146–7, 160–4, 216, 241, 243, 254
ECM (electronic counter-measures), 97, 98, 109, 133, 195, 206, 107, 226, 242, 248
Edgerton, David, 19, 86, 250
Edmonds, Anthony, see Geelhoed
Eglin Air Force Base, Florida, 118, 211

320 Index

Elliott Bros, defence electronics company, 106, 124
Emu Field, UK nuclear test site, 92
English Electric, aerospace company, 108, 109, 126, 127, 128, 131, 138, 140
Eniwetok, 151
Enterprise, USS, 216
ET317, UK Polaris warhead project, 196
Ethan Allen, USS, 228
Eton, 10
ExComm (Executive Committee), 173–4
external neutron initiation, 92, 210
see also internal neutron initiation

F-104, US fighter-bomber aircraft, 185
F-111, US strike aircraft, 94, 185
Falmouth, 232
far east, 72, 73, 102, 115, 116, 161, 164, 166, 195, 208, 214, 215, 216, 245, 254
Farnborough, *see* RAE
Faslane, 232, 235
FBM (Fleet Ballistic Missile) programme, 134, 135, 228
see also Polaris
Feltwell, RAF, 99
Ferranti, defence electronics company, 109, 125, 140
see also Denis Ferranti (not a part of the main Ferranti group)
Festing, Gen Sir Francis, 17, 18, 58, 72
Fieldhouse, Richard, *see* Norris
Fife, US warhead design, 120
Fighter Command, RAF, 19, 95, 96, 126
Filbert, warhead design, 120
Finch, Guy, 19
Finningley, RAF, 97, 274
fissile material, 2, 4, 8, 13, 36, 79, 83–5, 87, 88, 92, 104, 105, 113, 166, 194, 195, 198–9, 201, 214, 217, 226, 229, 238, 246, 250, 257
economy in, extravagance in, shortage of, 43, 78, 80, 87, 119, 125, 126

UK/US barter arrangements, 35, 37, 85
see also plutonium, uranium
Fletcher, James, 74
flexible response strategy, 55, 62, 155–7, 167
Foreign Office, 21, 76, 160, 178, 184, 185, 246
Forrestal, USS, 216
France, 5, 30, 35, 37, 55, 63, 93, 132, 145, 147, 155, 157–60, 182, 183, 184, 192, 209, 216, 245, 253, 255
Fraser, Hugh, Conservative minister, 148, 213, 231
Frigate Bird, US nuclear test, 228
Fryer, GCapt Geoffrey, 75, 167, 168, 171, 211, 212
Future Policy Committee, 30, 31, 59, 71, 165, 243
Fylingdales, RAF, 34, 129

Gaither report, 62, 27
Gaitskell, Hugh, Labour opposition leader, 52, 145, 147, 189, 190
GAM-87, *see* Skybolt
Gardiner, Sir George, 20
Gareloch, 66, 232
Gates, Thomas, US Defense Secretary, 32, 66, 67, 69, 74, 147, 158
Gaydon, RAF, 97
Geelhoed, Bruce, and Anthony Edmonds, 68
Geilenkirchen, RAF, 98, 256
General Electric, US industrial company, 99, 135
General Motors, US industrial company, 99
Geneva, 37, 38, 39, 40, 89, 150, 151, 153, 154, 190
Genie, US air-to-air rocket weapon, 80, 82, 126, 127, 281
George Washington, USS, 135, 231
Germany, 11, 60, 61, 133, 205, 252, 254
see also East and West Germany
Glasgow, 68, 85
GM462, warhead project, 131, 196
see also Blue Water
Gowing, Margaret, 2

Grandy, Air Marshal Sir John, 213
Granite-type, thermonuclear warhead design, 87, 89, 104, 106, 113
Grapple-M, projected UK nuclear test series, 88
Grapple-N, projected UK nuclear test series, 89
Grapple-O, projected UK nuclear test series, 89
Grapple-Z, UK nuclear test series, 38, 87, 88, 240
great prize, 38
Greeks and the Romans, 32
Green Grass, warhead, 89, 92, 104, 105, 106, 109, 201
Gretton, VAdm Sir Peter, 18
Grimsby, 125

Hailsham, Quintin Hogg, 2nd Viscount, Conservative minister, 20, 154, 166, 197
Hainan, 214
Handley Page, aerospace company, 97, 139, 247
Hansen, Chuck, 228
Harriman, Averell, US ambassador, 154
Harris, MRAF Sir Arthur, 19
Hartley, AVM Christopher, 178, 179, 180, 182, 206, 289
Harwell, *see* Atomic Energy Research Establishment
Hawker-Siddeley, aerospace company, 227, 247
Haworth, Leland, US atomic energy commissioner, 200
H-bomb, *see* hydrogen bomb
Head, Anthony, Conservative politician, 32
Healey, Denis, Labour politician, 191
Heathcoat-Amory, Derick, Conservative minister, 11, 13, 29, 46
Hecla, HMS, 234
Hennessy, Peter, 147
Henry, Cdr Michael RN, 234
Hercules Powder Co., US company, 228
Hermes, HMS, 100, 116, 216, 278

Herter, Christian, US Secretary of State, 32, 69
Heuser, Beatrice, 159
High Wycombe, 205
Hiroshima, 253
Hitch, Charles, US Defense Department official, 168, 186
Hockaday, Arthur, MoD official, 178
Holy Loch, 1, 26, 63, 64–9, 76, 147, 173, 232, 235, 240, 241, 244
Home, Alec, 14th Earl (later Sir Alec Douglas-Home), Conservative Prime Minister, 2, 10, 39, 152, 154, 165, 175, 176, 182, 184, 185, 186, 202, 208, 237, 244
   nuclear policy, 149–50, 192
Honest John, US surface-to-surface rocket, 82, 102, 132, 217, 223, 242, 256, 282
Hong Kong, 73, 190
Honington, RAF, 97, 114, 203, 211, 214
Hood, Samuel, 6th Viscount, 178
Hound Dog, US cruise missile, 168, 176, 179, 289
House of Commons, *see* parliament
House of Lords, *see* parliament
House of Representatives, *see* Congress
Howard, Michael, 148
HP.117, aircraft design, 139
HR169, Polaris penetration study, 231
HTP (high-test peroxide), 106, 107, 108, 213
Hudleston, Air Marshal Sir Edmund, 43, 165, 166
Hudswell Clarke, engineering company, 85
Hull, Gen Sir Richard, 18, 148
Hulme, Alan, Australian Minister of Supply, 94
Hunting, engineering company, 85, 124
hybrid SSN/missile submarine, 170, 231, 232
hydrogen bomb, 1, 2, 9, 21, 36–7, 51, 78, 86, 87, 88, 135, 202, 240
   see also Granite-type, primary, secondary

IANF (Inter-Allied Nuclear Force), 184, 185, 208
ICBM (inter-continental ballistic missile), 41, 62, 74, 167, 204
Ikara, Australian anti-submarine weapon, 93, 216, 218, 219, 220, 221
implosion, 87, 90, 92, 113, 194, 200, 201, 211, 240, 252
independent UK deterrence, 2, 3, 7, 18, 25, 28–30, 32, 42–6, 49–50, 53, 58, 59, 70, 72, 76, 114, 145, 146, 150, 159, 161, 165, 171, 172, 176, 177, 180–2, 185, 187–92, 195, 230, 243–6
India, 36, 177
Indian Ocean, 214
Indigo Hammer, warhead project, 81, 82, 89, 92, 126, 130
interdependence, 25, 28, 33–5, 129, 189, 244, 246
internal neutron initiation, 92, 114
see also external neutron initiation
Invergordon, 232
Iraq, 72, 289
IRBM (intermediate-range ballistic missile), 42, 62, 63, 99, 134, 204, 277
Ismay, Hastings, 1st Baron, 148, 149
Italy, 62, 255

J-21, US warhead design, 120
Jackson, Senator Henry, 33
Jacob, Sir Ian, 148, 149
James, T C G, 73, 266
James Bond, 175
Javelin, fighter aircraft, 113
Jellicoe, George, 2nd Earl, 10, 192
Jenkins, Roy, Labour politician, 52
JIGSAW (Joint Inter-service Group for the Study of All-out War), 60, 61
J Langham Thompson, electronics company, 124
Joint Chiefs of Staff, US, 39, 37, 39, 62, 65, 69, 150, 174
John, Adm Sir Caspar, 17, 67, 72, 148, 157, 188
Johnson, Lyndon B, US President, 150, 156

Joint Global War Committee, 59
Joint Intelligence Committee, 57, 165
Jones, Aubrey, Conservative minister, 11
Jones, Peter, 90
JOWOG (Joint Working Group), 90, 91, 224
JPS (Joint Planning Staff), 15, 71, 126, 157, 161
JRSWG (Joint Re-entry Systems Working Group), 236
Jupiter, US IRBM, 62, 134

Kaufmann, William, 168
Kearfott, US defence company, 109
Kelvin and Hughes, electronics company, 85
Kendrew, John, MoD official, 60
Kennedy, John F, US President, 6, 7, 9, 26, 32, 48, 62, 74, 76, 147, 155, 156, 158, 159, 160, 164, 166, 167, 168, 174, 179, 182, 183, 186, 188, 200, 209, 244, 245, 246, 252, 289
and nuclear testing, 150–5
policy on British nuclear weapons, 69–70, 145, 176–7
relationship with Macmillan, 70–1, 145
and Skybolt crisis/Nassau, 169–73, 175–7
Kent, Ronald, Air Ministry official, 75
kerosene, 99, 106, 108
Key West, 71
Khrushchev, Nikita Sergeevich, Soviet leader, 33, 38, 39, 40, 45, 150, 154, 155, 174, 183, 289
Killian, James, US scientist, 33, 40
Kissinger, Henry, US academic and politician, 253
Kistiakowsky, George, US scientist, 39, 74
Kittens, minor trials, 91–2
Kuwait, 73, 176

Laarbruch, RAF, 98
Labour party, 1, 12, 26, 28, 52, 53, 68, 145, 147, 156, 160, 186, 189, 190, 191, 192, 232, 241, 243

LABS (low-altitude bombing system), 98, 113, 24, 215, 219, 220
Lambe, Adm Sir Charles, 17, 49, 58, 66, 71, 72
Latvia, 207
Leeds, 85
Le Fanu, Adm Sir Mike, 137, 228
LeMay, Gen Curtis E USAF, 4, 19, 40, 41, 75, 95, 135, 167, 169, 172, 243, 252, 293
Lemnitzer, Gen Lyman US Army, 209, 210, 293
Leningrad, 60, 61, 101, 165
Levin, Nyman, AWRE Director, 21, 86, 122, 133
Liddell-Hart, Basil, 17
Lighthill, James, RAE Director, 77, 171, 179, 182, 290
Lighthouse, projected UK nuclear test series, 88
Lightning, interceptor aircraft, 126, 127, 128
limited war, 16, 26, 30, 54, 58, 59, 71, 72, 123, 128, 161, 162, 188, 231
see also central front, tactical nuclear weapons
Lincolnshire, 5, 47, 97, 98, 125
Linköping, 207
lithium, 84, 85, 90
Lithuania, 207
Live Oak, 156
Livermore, US nuclear-weapons laboratory, 38, 84, 119, 120
Lloyd, Selwyn, Conservative minister, 7, 11, 147
Lloyd-George, David, first world war Prime Minister, 7
Loch Alsh, 232
Loch Linnhe, 67, 68
Lockheed, US aerospace company, 134, 135, 136, 228
Loran-C, radio navigation system, 233, 234
Los Alamos, US nuclear-weapons laboratory, 86, 120, 121, 200
Los Angeles, 94
LOX (liquid oxygen), 99, 108
Luton, 131

M115, artillery gun, 132
McCone, John, USAEC chairman, 32
McElroy, Neil, US Defense Secretary, 32, 42
Mackay, James, Admiralty official, 57, 58, 137, 188, 189, 230
Mackenzie, VAdm Sir Hugh, 233
Macleod, Iain, Conservative politician, 147
Macmillan, Harold, Conservative Prime Minister, 6, 7, 10, 11, 13, 43, 50, 51, 59, 60, 86, 91, 94, 147, 148, 149, 155, 158, 159, 165, 173, 174, 175, 200, 214, 222, 248, 250, 275, 289, 294
and arms control, 36–40, 89, 150–5, 244, 253
defence and nuclear-weapons policies, 8–9, 25, 27–32, 43, 73, 83, 146, 160–4, 242–3, 253, 255
and Skybolt crisis, 169–73, 175–82, 187, 188, 190
and United States, 8, 25–6, 32–6, 64–71, 145, 241, 243–6
McNamara, Robert S, US Defense Secretary, 48, 70, 74, 75, 146, 155, 156, 164, 167, 168, 183, 204, 209, 214, 217, 228, 246, 252
and Skybolt crisis, 167–73, 177, 179, 188
Makins, Sir Roger, UK ambassador, Treasury official and UKAEA chairman, 20, 151, 152, 199, 200, 201
Malaya, 17, 73, 94, 161, 244, 294
Malvern, 223, 224
Mansergh, VAdm Sir Aubrey, 187
Maralinga, UK nuclear test site, 91, 92, 97, 203
Marconi, electronics company, 108, 109, 128
Marham, RAF, 97, 98, 99, 114, 203, 208, 210, 215, 293
Marquand, David, 51
Marshall Islands, 151
massive retaliation strategy, 3, 4, 27, 31, 53, 54, 57, 59, 146, 155, 156, 157, 241

324 *Index*

Maudling, Reginald, Conservative minister, 150, 162, 164, 181
May, Ernest and Philip Zelikow, 174
MC 14/2, NATO strategy document, 54, 55, 71, 155
MC 70, NATO strategy document, 132, 180
Mediterranean, 161, 233, 234
Menaul, AVM Stewart 'Paddy', 186, 283
Menden, 132
Mendès-France, Pierre, French Prime Minister, 158
Menzies, Sir Robert, Australian Prime Minister, 91, 94
Merchant, Livingston, US diplomat, 183, 184
Messmer, Pierre, French politician, 158, 159
Micky Finn, RAF exercise, 97, 204
middle east, 17, 19, 161, 244, 255
Ministry of Aviation, 11, 13, 20, 50, 59, 76, 79, 80, 81, 107, 124, 126, 127, 128, 131, 133, 140, 169, 211, 224, 225, 226, 227, 228, 229, 230, 236, 247, 249
  functions, 20, 148–9
Ministry of Defence, 3, 11, 19, 46, 52, 59, 63, 76, 77, 84, 121, 124, 147, 164, 169, 185, 198, 236, 237, 247, 257
  functions, 13–16, 148–9
Ministry of Supply, 13, 16, 20, 79, 80, 81, 85, 103, 112, 113, 115
minor trials, 87, 91–3, 203
Minuteman, US ICBM, 41, 74, 167, 168, 169, 229
Mirage IV, French bomber aircraft, 182
MIRV (multiple independently-targeted re-entry vehicles), 152, 167, 230
missile guidance, 20, 74–5, 78, 99, 106, 108–9, 116–18, 125–7, 130, 131, 133–5, 140, 158, 170–1, 211–12, 222, 228, 235
MIT (Massachusetts Institute of Technology), 134, 135

Mitchell, Sir Steuart, defence scientist, 20, 111, 140, 223
Mk.5, US atomic bomb, 114, 256
Mk.7, US atomic bomb, 98, 215, 256, 275
Mk.28, US H-bomb and warhead, 88, 89, 99, 100, 115, 119, 122, 215, 256, 275
  see also Peter, Python, Red Snow
Mk.43, US H-bomb, 215, 256
Mk.44, US kiloton nuclear warhead, 88, 126
  see also Tony, Tsetse
Mk.44, US torpedo, 221
Mk.47, US Polaris warhead, 87, 88, 119, 120, 123, 135, 139
  see also Steven
Mk.49, US thermonuclear warhead, 99, 119, 120
Mk.56, US strategic missile warhead, 120
Mk.57, US kiloton nuclear warhead, 218, 238, 295
Mk.58, US Polaris warhead, 228, 236, 237, 238
Mk.59, US Skybolt warhead, 120, 121
MLF (NATO Multi-Lateral Force), 5, 69–71, 145, 146, 160, 169, 182–6, 187, 192, 196, 208, 242, 290
Montgomery of Alamein, Viscount, 184
Morgan, Sir Morien, defence scientist, 20
Morton, Peter, 93, 109
Moscow, 38, 101, 119, 145, 154, 155, 165, 167, 183, 192, 248
Mottershead, Frank, MoD official, 63, 64, 71, 156, 217, 241
Mountbatten of Burma, AdmFlt Earl, 1, 3, 11, 15, 16–17, 18, 19, 25, 29, 43, 49, 57, 58, 60, 65, 66, 72, 73, 83, 100, 134, 135, 136, 137, 138, 146, 148, 161, 163, 184, 209, 216, 242, 243, 245, 251, 254, 255, 268, 269
Mount Palomar, California, 118, 211
Murphy, Robert, *see* Murphy-Dean agreement

Murphy-Dean agreement, 36, 68, 241
mutual deterrence, 16, 59, 60, 69
   see also nuclear sufficiency

N113, *see* Scimitar
NA.39, *see* Buccaneer
Nagasaki, 253
NASA (National Aeronautics and Space Administration), 74
Nassau, 7, 146, 150, 159, 163, 164, 170, 171, 175–82, 184, 186, 187, 188, 189, 190, 191, 208, 209, 225, 228, 229, 230, 231, 232, 238, 248, 289
NATO (North Atlantic Treaty Organisation), 1, 2, 3, 5, 14, 25, 26, 27, 33, 42, 51, 52, 53–7, 59, 60, 69–71, 73, 81, 82, 95, 102, 123, 129, 131, 132, 145, 146, 147, 155–7, 158, 159, 160, 163, 164, 173, 176, 180, 181, 182–6, 189, 191, 192, 195, 196, 208, 209, 215, 216, 217, 232, 233, 241, 243, 244, 253
NATO MRBM force, 62–8, 82, 158, 160, 183
   see also central front, limited war, MLF
Nautilus, USS, 220
Naval Review, 187
Nehru, Jawaharlal, Indian Prime Minister, 36, 176
Nevada, US nuclear test site, 152, 194, 200, 201, 202, 203, 219, 237
Nienburg, 132
Nike Hercules, US SAM, 94
Nitze, Paul, US Defense Department official, 209
Nobska conference, 134
Normandy campaign (1944), 56, 254, 268
Norris, Stan, Andrew Burrows and Richard Fieldhouse, 238, 256
Norstad, Gen Lauris USAF, 55, 56, 57, 62, 63, 69, 173, 174
North American, US aerospace company, 99, 109
North Coates, RAF, 125

North Pickenham, RAF, 51
Northrop, US aerospace company, 117
Nortronics, US electronics company, 75, 117
Norway, 206
Novaya Zemlya, 205
NRDC (Nuclear Requirements for Defence Committee), 14, 195, 197, 198, 199, 202, 238
nuclear equipoise, *see* nuclear sufficiency
nuclear power and reactors, 5, 9, 35, 83, 84, 202
nuclear propulsion and reactors, 5, 25, 35, 84, 139, 159, 246
   see also SSN
Nuclear Strike Coordinating Committee, 102
nuclear sufficiency, 18, 25, 29, 30, 31, 49, 57–9, 64
   see also mutual deterrence
nuclear targets and targeting, 16, 25, 28, 35, 36, 45, 53, 56, 57, 60–2, 64, 65, 71, 77, 78, 79, 80, 98, 100, 101–2, 106, 113, 119–21, 122, 128, 130–1, 133, 137–8, 156, 158, 162, 165–6, 167–8, 171–2, 185, 204, 205, 207, 208, 209, 214–15, 218, 220, 222, 235–6, 254
   see also damage criteria
nuclear testing, British, 84, 88, 89, 93, 152, 194, 199–201, 229, 253
   see also Christmas Island, Emu Field, Maralinga, minor trials and individual test series
nuclear testing, international negotiations to limit, 13, 36–40, 89, 94, 145–6, 150–5, 183, 192, 202, 203
   see also arms control, nuclear test moratorium
nuclear test moratorium, 36, 37, 39, 51, 78, 88, 91, 118, 120, 153, 155, 240
Nuclear Test Policy Committee, 14
Nuclear Weapons Safety Committee, 103

326 Index

OAW (Chiefs of Staff working party on Operational Use of Atomic Weapons), 16
operational research, 60, 61
OR (operational requirements), Air Ministry,
OR.343, 122, 138
OR.356, 216, 219, 295
OR.357, 219, 295
OR.1001, 81
OR.1127, 81, 115, 196
OR.1132, 81, 196
OR.1136, 81, 110, 196
OR.1139, 81, 108
OR.1141, 81, 110
OR.1142, 81, 110
OR.1149, 82
OR.1153, 82
OR.1155, 82
OR.1156, 82
OR.1157, 82
OR.1159, 80, 82, 105, 107, 110
OR.1160, 82
OR.1161, 82, 90
OR.1166, 82
OR.1167, 82
OR.1168, 226
OR.1171, 82, 111, 196
OR.1172, 82, 196
OR.1176, 82, 122–5, 196, 218, 280
OR.1177, 82, 122–5, 138, 196, 218
OR.1178, 82
OR.1179, 82, 120, 196
OR.1182, 76, 77, 82, 140, 226, 251, 252, 253, 284
OR.1187, 82, 196
OR.1195, 196
Ordnance Board, 103
organisation of defence, 8–9, 12–21, 147–9
Ormsby-Gore, David, British ambassador, 168, 169, 173, 174, 188, 287
ORPs (operational readiness platforms), 96
Ottawa, 184, 208

Pacific Ocean, 36, 86, 113, 136, 151, 254
Paderborn, 132
Palmer, Sidney, naval constructor, 137
Pandora, *see* OR.1182
Paris, 39, 159, 185, 233
parliament, UK, 2, 9, 10, 20, 26, 36, 39, 48, 51, 68, 75, 148, 149, 152, 153, 159, 175, 184, 186, 190, 198
  role in nuclear policy-making, 12, 250
Patricroft, ROF, 85
Pearl Harbor, 40
penetration, penetration aids (for bombers), 41, 137, 139, 205, 206, 248
penetration, penetration aids (for missiles), 43, 79, 111, 21, 152, 189, 211, 228, 229, 230, 231, 236, 237, 247, 251, 252, 300
  see also ABM, decoys
Penley, Bill, defence scientist, and ABM, 223, 224, 251
Penney, Sir William, AWRE Director, 21, 37, 86, 87, 89, 152, 202, 238, 252, 255
Pentagon, *see* Defense Department
pentomic army division, 55
Pershing, US surface-to-surface missile, 185
Persian Gulf, 136
Peter, thermonuclear primary, 122
Pierre, Andrew, 189, 192, 250
Pike, MRAF Sir Thomas, 19, 50, 76, 139, 148, 174, 212, 213, 215, 231, 254, 255, 266, 281
Pixie, warhead design, 89, 126
Playfair, Sir Edward, MoD official, 15, 76, 77
Plowden, Sir Edwin, 20, 35, 252
plutonium, 35, 83–5, 86, 87, 90, 113, 119, 126, 198, 202, 237, 238, 257
Poland, 60
Polaris, US submarine-launched ballistic missile, 5, 26, 79, 87, 88, 109, 110, 111, 119, 124, 129, 139,

145–7, 158, 168, 173, 186–7, 188–9, 191, 192, 194, 195, 196, 216, 222, 224–7, 241, 244–6, 248, 252, 298
Admiralty and Royal Navy views, 11, 16, 17, 49, 66–7, 76, 136–7, 170, 187–8
as alternative to Blue Streak, 43–5, 49
as alternative to Skybolt, 65–8, 73–7, 139, 164–5, 169–71, 176–82
and NATO MRBM force/MLF, 62–3, 69–70, 182–6
Sales Agreement, 146, 185, 188, 189, 230, 246
technical development, versions and warheads, 134–6, 188, 202–3, 214, 227–38
and US base at Holy Loch, 64–8
US political history, 40, 74, 133–5, 168
Porton, 217
Powell, Sir Richard, MoD official, 15, 43
Power, Adm Sir Manley, 136
Power, Gen Thomas USAF, 12, 41, 94, 167, 243
Pravda, 154
Presidential Science Advisory Committee, US, 74
primary, thermonuclear, 88, 92, 93, 113, 119, 120, 121, 122, 126, 200–1, 211, 219, 237, 239, 280
Profumo, John, Conservative minister, 148, 149
Project E, 80, 81, 98, 100, 104, 114, 115, 126, 130, 210, 215, 216, 221, 243, 278, 293
see also dual custody
Project N, 100, 221
proliferation of nuclear weapons, 37, 94, 172, 183, 190, 244
Proteus, USS, 68
PT176, kiloton warhead project for WE177, 124, 196
Pugwash, 154
'purple pamphlet', army doctrine publication, 56

Pyne, Kate, 262, 274, 297
Python, US thermonuclear primary, 122

QRA (quick-reaction alert), 97, 173, 174, 204, 215, 248

R-1 effect, 88, 125
RAE Farnborough, 20, 77, 106, 108, 114, 115, 122, 128, 140, 171, 217, 218, 226, 227, 231
RAF (Royal Air Force), 3, 15, 16, 17, 18–19, 20, 25, 27, 42, 47, 50, 51, 57, 72, 75, 78, 80–2, 95–104, 112–17, 120, 122, 125, 127, 130, 131, 137, 138, 170, 172, 173, 186, 194–7, 203–16, 217, 219–21, 225, 240, 243, 245, 248, 254, 256
see also Air Ministry and individual OR requirements, aircraft and weapons
Rats, minor trials, 87, 91–2
RE179, Skybolt warhead project, 125, 196, 211, 217
readiness and readiness levels, 2, 44, 78, 80, 92, 95–7, 99, 102, 104, 115, 141, 174, 204, 208, 209, 212–14, 233, 235
Red Beard, tactical nuclear bomb, 78, 81, 82, 83, 92, 94, 98–9, 100, 122, 124–6, 132, 137, 138, 141, 166, 195, 196, 201, 207, 214, 215, 216, 218, 220, 238, 252, 256, 275, 278, 295
technical development and deployment, 113–16, 122, 217, 220
Red Beard replacement, *see* WE177
Red Duster, SAM project, 125–7
see also Bloodhound
Redmayne, Martin, Conservative politician, 147, 181
Red Snow, anglicised Mk.28 thermonuclear warhead, 82, 89, 92, 99, 105, 106, 107, 108, 110, 111, 119, 120, 124, 196, 200, 210, 212, 214, 217, 237, 238, 244, 273
Red Top, air-to-air missile project, 126

328 *Index*

re-entry, re-entry vehicles, 78, 90, 99, 108, 110–11, 117–21, 128, 129, 135–6, 152, 158, 195, 224, 228–30, 234, 236, 246
  see also ABM, decoys, MIRV, penetration
Reggane, French nuclear test site, 158
Regulus, US submarine-launched cruise missile, 133
Renown, HMS, 232
Resolution, HMS, 232, 234
Ricketts, Claude V, US admiral, 184
Rickover, Hyman, US Navy nuclear propulsion chief, 35, 159, 183
RO106, kiloton warhead capsule project, 81, 82, 83, 126, 195, 196, 201, 218, 222, 223
  see also Tony
Rocketdyne, US rocket propulsion company, 99
ROF (Royal Ordnance Factories), *see* Burghfield, Chorley, Patricroft
Rolls-Royce, aero engine company, 35, 108, 109
Rosyth, 232
Royal Air Force, *see* RAF
Royal Navy, 11, 14, 16, 17, 20, 49, 57, 66, 80, 81, 100, 102, 113–16, 123, 125–6, 136–8, 157, 163, 185, 187–8, 195, 197, 216–18, 221, 222, 231, 233, 234, 235, 242
  see also Admiralty and individual ships, aircraft and weapons
Royal Radar Establishment, 223
Rubel, John, US Defense Department official, 11, 179, 252
Rugby, 233
rum, 185
RUSI (Royal United Service Institution), 48, 59
Rusk, Dean, US Secretary of State, 150, 170, 171
Russell, Bertrand, 3rd Earl, 51, 175
Russell, Richard B, US senator, 75, 169
Russia, *see* Soviet Union

SA-2, Soviet SAM, 206
SA-3, Soviet SAM, 206, 227

SAC (Strategic Air Command), 19, 36, 40, 41, 48, 64, 70, 95, 101, 102, 156, 172, 173, 205, 208, 243, 245, 254
SACEUR (Supreme Allied Commander Europe), 36, 55, 63–5, 70, 102, 173, 183, 275, 293
  commitment of UK nuclear forces to, 36, 98–9, 114, 138, 173, 195, 203, 208–10, 215, 226, 243
SACLANT (Supreme Allied Commander Atlantic), 57, 157, 208
safety of UK nuclear weapons, 80, 87, 90, 92, 93, 103, 104, 113–16, 119, 120, 122, 152, 199–202, 220–1, 236, 237
Sainte-Assise, 233
SAM (surface-to-air missiles), 81, 82, 88, 98, 125, 127, 196, 204, 206, 222, 245
  see also individual projects and weapons
Sandys, Duncan, Conservative minister, 4, 9, 10, 11, 12, 13, 16, 19, 26, 27, 29, 31, 32, 37, 41, 42, 43, 46, 48, 50, 52, 53, 56, 58, 83, 98, 108, 110, 127, 138, 146, 160, 161, 241, 242, 248, 254, 265
  and 1957 defence white paper, 3, 9, 19, 26–7, 29, 53, 160–1, 242
Saunders-Roe, aerospace company, 108
Scampton, RAF, 97, 203, 210, 212, 213, 293
Scandinavia, 205
Scarborough, 52
Schlesinger, James, US politician, 75
Schwartz, Stephen, 249
Scimitar, Royal Navy strike aircraft, 100, 113, 138
Scotland, 26, 65–8, 83, 118, 205
Scott, Len, *see* Twigge
Scott, Sir Robert, MoD official, 15, 77, 148, 151, 163, 164, 165, 178, 179, 186, 187
Seaborg, Glenn, US scientist and USAEC chairman, 150, 152, 202

Seaslug, Royal Navy SAM, 81, 82, 93, 124–6, 128, 194, 196, 197, 222
SEATO (South East Asia Treaty Organisation), 53, 71, 72, 73, 81, 94, 162, 195, 214, 215, 216
Sea Vixen, Royal Navy fighter/ground attack aircraft, 100, 219
secondary, thermonuclear, 84, 119, 201, 237, 280
Second World War, 1, 11, 15, 18–19, 21, 34, 56, 71, 86, 100, 102, 159, 165, 250, 253–5
Selkirk, George Douglas-Hamilton, 10th Earl, 10, 11, 29, 42, 43, 49, 58, 260, 265
Sellafield, 257
Senate, *see* Congress
Sennelager, 132
Sergeant, US surface-to-surface missile, 131, 245
Shackleton, maritime patrol aircraft, 222
SHAPE (Supreme HQ Allied Powers Europe), 208
SHAPEX, 269
shield forces, 30, 55, 56, 57, 62, 157
Shuckburgh, Sir Evelyn, British diplomat, 208
Simeon, Cdr Michael RN, 137
Simpson, John, 84
Singapore, 71, 72, 73, 98, 146, 161, 176, 195, 214, 242, 254, 294
SINS (ship's inertial navigation system), 233, 234
SIOP (single integrated operational plan), US, 102, 155, 156, 167, 204, 235
Skaggerak, 207
Skybolt, US air-launched ballistic missile, 1, 3, 5, 34, 70, 71, 79, 80, 82, 83, 84, 107–8, 123–5, 129, 133, 138–40, 161–4, 186, 188, 189, 194–6, 204, 206, 222, 224, 226, 227, 229, 231, 237, 238, 240, 241, 243, 245, 247, 248, 251, 269, 290
   Air Ministry and RAF views, 47–8
   as alternative to Blue Streak, 26, 47–50

   as alternative to Polaris, 65–8, 73, 75–7, 141, 159, 164–6
   technical development and warheads, 90, 111, 116–21, 168, 199–202, 210–12, 217, 219
UK/US technical and financial agreement, 120–1
UK/US 'Skybolt crisis', 169–73, 175–82
   and US base at Holy Loch, 63–8
   US political history, 70, 74–5, 117, 166–9
Soviet Union, 33, 40, 71, 77, 140, 148, 159, 167, 168, 177, 183, 229, 242, 244, 252, 254, 300
   and UK defence policy 27–31, 191, 248
   and UK and NATO strategy, 41–5, 47–8, 53–5, 57, 58, 60–5, 70, 72, 95–8, 101–2, 120, 156–7, 164–5, 195, 204–5, 251
   and technical capabilities of UK weapons, 111, 113, 117, 119, 126–7, 132, 139, 146, 195, 204, 205–7, 221, 223, 227, 248
   and arms control, 36–40, 150–5
Spadeadam, 110
Spearpoint, BAOR exercise, 217
Sperry, electronics company, 108, 109
Spinardi, Graham, 247
SPO (Special Projects Office), US Navy, 134, 135, 137, 228, 233, 234
Sputnik, 33, 41, 62, 227, 240
SS-3, Soviet surface-to-surface missile, 251
SS-4, Soviet surface-to-surface missile, 251
SSN (nuclear hunter-killer submarine), 17, 66, 100, 134, 137, 159, 169, 170, 188, 191, 220, 221, 231, 232
Stage 1 UK air defence, 88, 125
Stage 1½ UK air defence, 88, 125
Stassen, Harold, US politician, 36
State Department, US, 36, 49, 65, 68, 69, 70, 71, 145, 153, 170, 182, 183, 189

Steven, anglicised Mk.47 warhead project, 119
Stevenage, 131
strategic bombing, 15, 18, 19, 254
Strategic Scientific Policy Committee, Air Ministry, 46, 139
Strath, Sir William, MoS official, 20, 50
Stratton, Gen Sir William, 58
Strauss, Lewis, USAEC chairman, 32, 34, 252
Sublette, Carey, 87
SUBROC, US anti-submarine weapon, 221
Suez crisis (1956), 8, 17, 32 177, 180, 190, 244, 251
summit meetings, 6, 38, 39, 65, 79, 150, 170, 175, 246
Super Octopus, British warhead design technique, 194, 195, 200, 201, 219, 252
Sverdlov-class cruisers, 100, 113
Sweden, 16, 207–8, 293

tactical nuclear weapons, 3, 16, 55, 62, 63, 72, 113, 124, 129, 131, 153, 156, 162, 166, 194, 195, 220, 242, 246, 249
  see also battlefield, central front, limited war and individual weapons
Talgarno, 79, 93
Tedder, MRAF Arthur, 1st Baron, 19
Teesside, 8
Teller, Edward, US nuclear scientist, 38, 119, 134, 252
Templer, FM Sir Gerald, 11, 17, 18, 29, 57, 58
Tengah, RAF, 98, 214, 215
The Man in the White Suit, 255
thermonuclear weapons, *see* hydrogen bomb
The War Game, 5
Thor, US IRBM, 3, 33, 36, 42, 43, 62, 80, 82, 111, 134, 173, 174, 175, 195, 204, 256, 275
  technical detail and RAF service, 99–101, 103, 174, 194, 214

Thorneycroft, Peter, Conservative minister, 10, 11, 60, 83, 124, 147, 148, 150, 157, 158, 162–4, 166, 169, 170, 172, 177, 179–82, 184–8, 195, 207–9, 212, 216, 223, 225, 226, 231, 248
Thunderbird, SAM, 127
Tims, minor trials, 87, 91–2, 203
Titan, US ICBM, 41
Tony, anglicised Tsetse/Mk.44 kiloton warhead, 52, 81, 82, 83, 120–2, 126, 130–1, 133, 195, 196, 199, 201, 218, 222–3, 292
Tortoise, warhead implosion system, 113
trades unions, 52, 53, 160, 198, 267
Trafalgar Square, 51, 52
Transit, US satellite navigation system, 234
Treasury, 21, 46, 131, 138, 166, 187, 198, 219, 238, 250
Trenchard, MRAF Hugh, 1st Viscount, 18
tribal forts, 138
tritium, 84, 85, 87, 88, 90, 240
Tsetse, US kiloton warhead, 121, 126, 201, 292
TSR.2, strike/reconnaissance aircraft, 17, 19, 76, 78, 94, 107, 122–4, 127, 133, 137–40, 162, 164, 166, 169, 185, 195, 197, 215, 216, 218, 219, 225–7, 246, 247, 254, 283
TTCP (Tri-national Technical Cooperation Programme), 34, 224
Turkey, 62, 205, 206
Twigge, Stephen and Len Scott, 205
Twining, Gen Nathan USAF, 19, 37
two-stage nuclear weapons, *see* hydrogen bomb
Type 82 destroyer, 221

U-2, US reconnaissance aircraft, 39, 174
U-235, *see* uranium, highly enriched

Index 331

UKAEA (UK Atomic Energy Authority), 20, 35, 85, 86, 151, 166, 198, 199, 257
UK/US atomic bilateral (UK-US Agreement for Cooperation on the Uses of Atomic Energy for Mutual Defence Purposes, 1958 and 1959), 1, 25, 35, 37, 43, 64, 85, 87, 89, 91, 95, 104, 115, 122, 145, 199, 224, 240
Ulysses, warhead design, 124
Una, warhead design, 122, 124, 131, 280
United Nations, 151, 191
United States, 1–9, 11, 12, 14, 15, 17, 19, 21, 25–40, 42, 44, 45, 47, 48, 55–8, 60, 62–71, 74–8, 80–91, 93–5, 98–105, 107, 109–12, 114–24, 126, 127, 129–38, 145, 146, 148, 150–60, 165–8, 170–7, 179–92, 195, 196, 198–202, 204, 205, 207, 208, 211, 214, 216, 218, 220–5, 227–34, 236–49, 251–7, 290
    see also Anglo-American relations, UK/US atomic bilateral, individual US persons, departments, armed services, ships, aircraft and weapons
Upavon, 47
Upwood, RAF, 98, 275
uranium, 90, 92
uranium, highly enriched (U-235), 83–5, 86, 87, 104, 113, 119, 197, 199, 237, 257, 272
USAEC (US Atomic Energy Commission), 32, 35, 37, 150, 200, 202, 252
USAF (US Air Force), 4, 19, 40–1, 46, 47, 55, 75, 102, 116–19, 126, 133, 135, 172, 245
US Army, 55, 134
US Army Air Force, 102
US Navy, 26, 40, 62, 66, 100, 110, 133, 136, 221, 222, 245
USSR, see Soviet Union

V-1, German cruise missile, 133
V-2, German ballistic missile, 133
Valiant, medium bomber aircraft, 33, 41, 97–9, 102, 114–15, 137–8, 173–4, 203, 208, 210, 214–15, 226, 232, 256, 293
Vandenberg Air Force Base, California, 99
van Rolleghem, LtGen Florent, Belgian air force, 210
V-bombers, 3, 26, 41–9, 53, 70, 75–6, 78, 79, 81, 88, 92, 94, 96–8, 100–6, 112–17, 123, 126, 127, 137, 141, 146, 161–3, 170, 174, 179–81, 184, 185, 189, 194, 195, 203–12, 214, 215, 219, 225–7, 242, 243, 248, 249, 256, 294
    see also Bomber Command, Valiant, Victor, Vulcan
VC-10, transport aircraft, 50, 73, 76, 139, 162, 286
Vere-Harvey, Sir Arthur, 291
Vickers, aerospace company, 41, 76, 97, 131, 138, 139, 232
Victor, medium bomber aircraft, 41, 97, 106, 116, 117, 139, 203, 204, 207, 213, 214, 219, 247
Victorious, HMS, 100, 114, 138, 216, 278
Vienna, 150
Violet Club, interim megaton weapon, 78, 81, 103–5, 113, 256, 276
Violet Friend, ABM project study, 128
Violet Mist, ADM, 81, 132, 133
Vixens, minor trials, 91, 92, 203
VLF (very low frequency radio), 233
von Neumann, John, US mathematician, 40
Vulcan, medium bomber aircraft, 41, 96, 97, 105, 116–19, 139, 179, 203, 204, 207, 211–13, 215, 219

W130, see OR.1182
W140, see OR.1182
Waddington, RAF, 96, 97, 114, 203, 211, 274
Walker, John, 253
Walsh, Jim, 94
Ward, George, Conservative minister, 10, 47, 58, 126, 127

War Office, 10, 13, 16, 25, 72, 103, 124, 129, 130–2, 140, 148, 162, 223, 252
  functions, 17–18
  see also army
Washington, 21, 33, 35, 39, 42, 47, 49, 63, 65, 68, 75, 145, 147, 151, 153, 154, 158, 167, 168, 170, 172, 174, 185, 187, 208, 211, 222, 243, 245, 246, 269
Wasp, light anti-submarine helicopter, 221
Watkinson, Harold, Conservative minister, 12, 15 46, 48–50, 57, 60, 63–8, 73, 75, 76, 127, 135, 138, 147, 148, 152, 158–62, 164–6, 172, 197, 198, 211, 214, 246, 248, 269, 286, 291
WE177, improved kiloton bomb, 82, 85, 194–7, 199, 203, 214, 215, 221, 222, 226, 227, 238, 241, 249, 251, 252, 296
  technical development, 122–5, 217–20
Weapons Development Committee, 149, 237, 299
weapons of mass destruction, 253, 254
Weapons Systems Evaluation Group, US, 74
Wee Gwen, warhead design, 133, 282
West Germany, 5, 37, 51, 55, 60, 67, 98, 130, 132, 145, 157–60, 182, 183, 184, 185, 186, 190, 191, 215, 242, 243, 245, 252, 256, 290
Westinghouse, US engineering company, 35
Westminster, *see* parliament
White, Gen Thomas USAF, 19, 116, 279
Whitehall, 2, 6, 16, 17, 21, 25, 29, 30, 47, 57, 58, 60, 79, 124, 127, 132, 138, 148, 159, 167, 169, 175, 185, 198, 199, 204, 212, 217, 233, 237, 242, 243, 245, 247–50, 252, 253

Wiesner, Jerome, US Defense Department official, 153, 171, 252
Wildenrath, RAF, 98, 256
Wilhelmshaven, 254
Wilson, Charles, US Defense Secretary, 32, 41
Wilson, Harold, Labour Prime Minister, 1, 15, 186, 190–3, 241, 244
Windscale, 83, 84
Winfrith, 257
Wittering, RAF, 97, 112, 203, 204, 213, 214
Woodford, 106
Woomera, 91, 93, 94, 106, 108, 110, 111, 131, 213
Wright, Adm Jerauld USN, 57
WS 138A, *see* Skybolt
Wynn, Humphrey, 275

X-12, *see* OR.1182

Yellow Anvil, artillery shell warhead project, 81, 89, 132
Yellow Sun, megaton bomb, 78, 81, 103–6, 110, 113, 194, 196, 204, 207, 210, 212, 214, 244, 256, 276, 293
York, Herbert, US Defense Department official, 74, 84, 252, 264
Young, Ken, 172

ZA297, high-yield warhead project for WE177, 196
Zagros mountains, 71
Zelikow, *see* May
Ziegler, Philip, 148
Zog, King of Albania, 10
Zuckerman, Sir Solly, MoD chief scientist, 3, 4, 15, 17, 18, 21, 46, 48, 56, 60, 62, 72, 74–7, 83, 101, 111, 135, 139, 140, 148, 149, 151–4, 166, 170–2, 179, 182, 184, 186–8, 210, 211, 217, 220, 229, 231, 237–9, 241, 242, 246, 248, 251, 255, 268, 269, 290